ADV

BREAKING THE

SPANISH
BARRIER

ADVANCED

John Conner
Cathy Folts

Student Edition

BREAKING THE BARRIER, INC.
THE LANGUAGE SERIES WITH ALL THE RULES YOU NEED TO KNOW
THE FASTEST PATH TO TRUE LANGUAGE FLUENCY

For Lisa, Jamie, Hannah, Alexandra, Sarah,
Alexis and Fritz

ACKNOWLEDGMENTS

Thanks to Cindy Beams who was there at the beginning of this amazing adventure. Thanks also to Andy Anderson for his many suggestions, Guillermo Barnetche for his stunning artwork, Conrad Kent for his help throughout the years, Professor Donald Lenfest of Ohio Wesleyan University for his editing, Ann Talbot for her masterful layout, María Vallier for her proofreading, and to our students, whose numerous ideas improved the text tremendously. A special thanks to Miguel Romá for his superb editing and to Barbara Peterson, contributing editor, for her wonderful suggestions.

AN INVITATION

We invite you to join many of our readers who, over the years, have shared their suggestions for improvements as well as their personal knowledge of the Hispanic world. In doing so, they have become our partners. We are grateful for their invaluable contributions as the evolution of **Breaking the Barrier** *belongs, in part, to them.*

BREAKING THE BARRIER, INC.
63 Shirley Road
Groton, MA 01450
Phone: 978-448-0594
Fax: 978-448-1237
E-mail: info@tobreak.com
www.tobreak.com

ISBN: 0-9903122-6-7

S3SE0719

PREFACE

BREAKING THE **S**PANISH **B**ARRIER is a core text, workbook and handy reference all-in-one. It can stand alone, or complement the multitude of Spanish language resources currently available.

We believe the fastest path to fluency is built upon a rock-solid understanding of grammar. **B**REAKING THE **S**PANISH **B**ARRIER provides the essential roadmap for this journey.

In each of the following twelve lessons, you will find country maps, vocabulary, a review of key grammatical concepts, explanations of new material, many practice exercises, as well as a review test. Sentences throughout the book highlight current people, places and events from the Spanish-speaking world. You will find the tone of these pages informal and conversational — a one-on-one session between teacher and student.

WE LOOK FORWARD TO ACCOMPANYING YOU
AS YOU **B**REAK THE **S**PANISH **B**ARRIER.

¡BUENA SUERTE!

JOHN **C**ONNER
Author and Series Editor

* Accompanying audio files, recorded by native speakers from around the world, are available on www.tobreak.com.

ᘒᘒ TABLE OF CONTENTS ᘒᘒ

MÉXICO

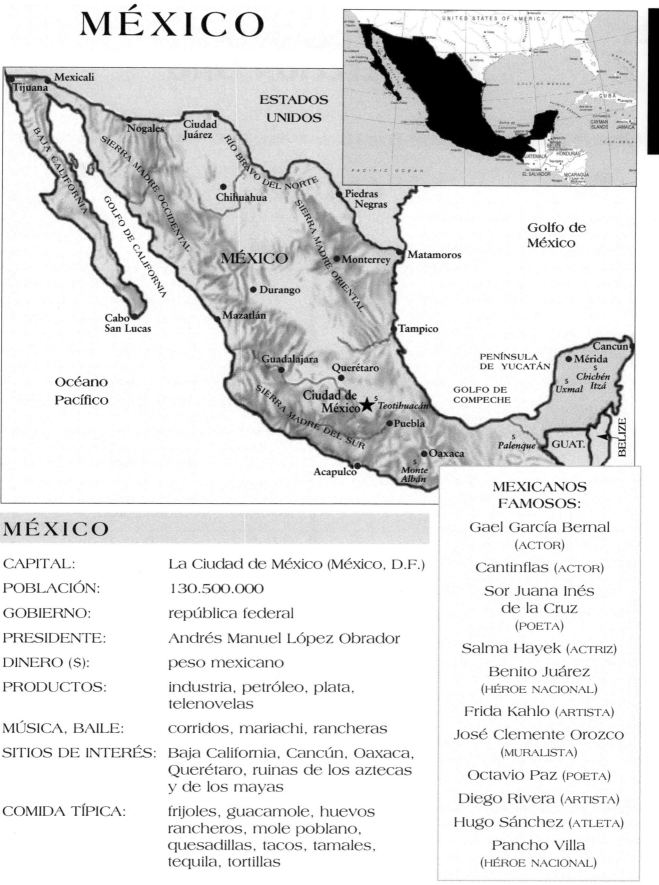

MÉXICO

CAPITAL: La Ciudad de México (México, D.F.)

POBLACIÓN: 130.500.000

GOBIERNO: república federal

PRESIDENTE: Andrés Manuel López Obrador

DINERO ($):   peso mexicano

PRODUCTOS: industria, petróleo, plata, telenovelas

MÚSICA, BAILE: corridos, mariachi, rancheras

SITIOS DE INTERÉS: Baja California, Cancún, Oaxaca, Querétaro, ruinas de los aztecas y de los mayas

COMIDA TÍPICA: frijoles, guacamole, huevos rancheros, mole poblano, quesadillas, tacos, tamales, tequila, tortillas

MEXICANOS FAMOSOS:

Gael García Bernal (ACTOR)

Cantinflas (ACTOR)

Sor Juana Inés de la Cruz (POETA)

Salma Hayek (ACTRIZ)

Benito Juárez (HÉROE NACIONAL)

Frida Kahlo (ARTISTA)

José Clemente Orozco (MURALISTA)

Octavio Paz (POETA)

Diego Rivera (ARTISTA)

Hugo Sánchez (ATLETA)

Pancho Villa (HÉROE NACIONAL)

Practice this vocabulary with our mobile app! Visit tobreak.com/app for more details.

VOCABULARIO LECCIÓN UNO

ADJETIVOS

actual	current, present day	*calvo/a*	bald
afilado/a	sharp (e.g., knife)	*capaz*	capable
agotado/a	exhausted	*cariñoso/a*	affectionate
agradecido/a	grateful	*caro/a*	expensive
agudo/a	sharp, astute	*cauteloso/a*	cautious, careful, wary
agrio/a (amargo/a)	sour (bitter)	*celoso/a*	jealous
amoroso/a	loving	*cercano/a*	nearby, neighboring
ansioso/a	anxious, eager	*chico/a*	little, small
aplicado/a	applied, dedicated, industrious	*ciego/a*	blind
		confuso/a	confused, confusing
ardiente	burning, passionate	*corpulento/a*	stout, heavy-set, burly
asado/a	roasted	*corriente*	current, present
atado/a	tied	*cortés*	courteous, polite
atento/a	attentive	*cotidiano/a*	daily, everyday
atrevido/a	bold, daring	*cristiano/a*	Christian
barato/a	cheap	*cuadrado/a*	square
blando/a	soft	*culpable*	guilty
borracho/a	drunk	*débil*	weak
bravo/a	brave, fierce, angry	*derecho/a*	right
bullicioso/a	noisy, rowdy, boisterous	*dichoso/a*	lucky, happy, fortunate
		diestro/a	right-handed

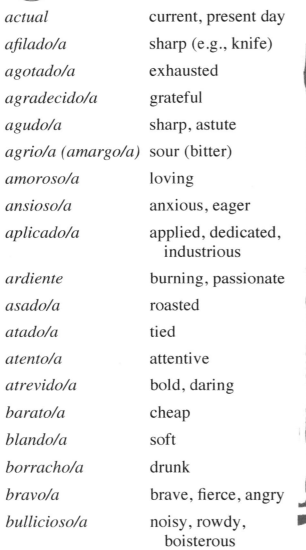

This symbol lets you know where you can practice along using the recorded audio.

LECCIÓN UNO

KEY GRAMMAR CONCEPTS

A) EL PRESENTE DEL INDICATIVO → *The present indicative*

B) EL PRETÉRITO → *The preterite*

C) LOS INTERROGATIVOS → *Interrogatives*

D) LAS CONJUNCIONES → *Conjunctions*

E) LOS PRONOMBRES PERSONALES → *Subject pronouns*

A) EL PRESENTE DEL INDICATIVO

The **present tense** is used to describe actions that are currently happening, to note current conditions or traits, to describe customary events, and, at times, to tell what will happen in the not-too-distant future.

EXAMPLES: *Inés **habla** con Raúl en la biblioteca.*
Inés is talking with Raúl in the library.

***Hace** mucho sol en Guadalajara.*
It's very sunny in Guadalajara.

*En mi colegio siempre **jugamos** al fútbol por la tarde.*
In my school, we always play soccer in the afternoon.

*Mañana **salgo** para Oaxaca.*
Tomorrow I'm leaving for Oaxaca.

1) REGULAR VERBS

HABLAR		COMER		VIVIR	
hablo	hablamos	como	comemos	vivo	vivimos
hablas	habláis	comes	coméis	vives	vivís
habla	hablan	come	comen	vive	viven

Helpful Tip: There is an accent on the *"vosotros/vosotras"* form only.

2) STEM-CHANGING VERBS (A.K.A. "BOOT" VERBS)

These verbs have a **stem change** in four of the six conjugations. As you can see, the conjugations that change stem appear to form a boot.

There are three categories of these verbs:

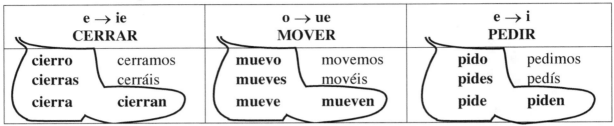

e → ie CERRAR		o → ue MOVER		e → i PEDIR	
cierro	cerramos	**muevo**	movemos	**pido**	pedimos
cierras	cerráis	**mueves**	movéis	**pides**	pedís
cierra	**cierran**	**mueve**	**mueven**	**pide**	**piden**

Here is a list of the most common verbs in each category. If you don't know some of these words, check the dictionary in the back of the book:

e → ie		o → ue		e → i	
advertir	mentir	almorzar	mover	competir	reír
cerrar	negar	colgar	oler*	conseguir	reñir
comenzar	nevar	contar	poder	corregir	repetir
convertir	pensar	costar	probar	despedir	seguir
defender	perder	devolver	recordar	elegir	servir
divertir	preferir	doler	resolver	freír	sonreír
empezar	querer	dormir	rogar	impedir	teñir
encender	recomendar	encontrar	sonar	medir	vestir
entender	referir	jugar (u→ue)	soñar	pedir	
enterrar	regar	llover	torcer		
herir	sentar	morir	volver		
hervir	sentir	mostrar			
invertir	sugerir				

*oler: **huelo, hueles, huele,**
olemos, oléis, **huelen**

3) SPELLING-CHANGERS

Some verbs undergo **spelling changes** in order to preserve the sound of a particular letter found in the infinitive. For example, the *"yo"* form of the present tense of *"escoger"* is *"escojo."* It is not *escogo! This change occurs because the letter "g" before an "i" or "e" sounds one way, but is pronounced differently before "a," "o," or "u."

cer → zo TORCER*		cer/cir → zco CONOCER		ger/gir → jo DIRIGIR	
tuerzo	torcemos	**conozco**	conocemos	**dirijo**	dirigimos
tuerces	torcéis	conoces	conocéis	diriges	dirigís
tuerce	tuercen	conoce	conocen	dirige	dirigen

Note: This verb is also a "boot" verb!

Verbs in these categories:

cer → zo	cer/cir → zco		ger/gir → jo	
convencer	apetecer	ofrecer	coger	exigir
ejercer	conducir	parecer	dirigir	fingir
torcer (ue)	conocer	permanecer	elegir	proteger
vencer	introducir	producir	escoger	recoger
	merecer	traducir		

guir → go SEGUIR*		uir → uyo, uyes, uye, uyen CONSTRUIR	
sigo	seguimos	**construyo**	construimos
sigues	seguís	**construyes**	construís
sigue	siguen	**construye**	**construyen**

*****Note:** This verb is also a "boot" verb!

Verbs in these categories:

guir → go	uir → uyo, uyes, uye, uyen	
conseguir (i)	concluir	distribuir
distinguir	construir	huir
seguir (i)	contribuir	incluir
	destruir	

4) IRREGULAR VERBS

These verbs are simply strange. They have unexpected spelling changes.

It is necessary to memorize these forms carefully; practice will make perfect!

CABER		CAER		DAR		DECIR	
quepo	cabemos	**caigo**	caemos	**doy**	damos	**digo**	decimos
cabes	cabéis	caes	caéis	das	dais	dices	decís
cabe	caben	cae	caen	da	dan	dice	dicen
ESTAR		**HACER**		**IR**		**OÍR**	
estoy	estamos	**hago**	hacemos	**voy**	**vamos**	**oigo**	oímos
estás	estáis	haces	hacéis	**vas**	**vais**	**oyes**	oís
está	están	hace	hacen	**va**	**van**	**oye**	**oyen**
PONER		**SABER**		**SALIR**		**SER**	
pongo	ponemos	**sé**	sabemos	**salgo**	salimos	**soy**	**somos**
pones	ponéis	sabes	sabéis	sales	salís	**eres**	**sois**
pone	ponen	sabe	saben	sale	salen	**es**	**son**
TENER		**VALER**		**VENIR**		**VER**	
tengo	tenemos	**valgo**	valemos	**vengo**	venimos	**veo**	vemos
tienes	tenéis	vales	valéis	vienes	venís	ves	veis
tiene	tienen	vale	valen	viene	vienen	ve	ven

PRACTICE EXERCISES

1. **Write the correct present indicative form of each infinitive:**

   a. Nosotros _____ que hablar español durante la clase. (tener)

   b. Tú siempre _____ hacer muchas cosas tontas en el dormitorio. (querer)

   c. Normalmente nado mientras María y tú _____ un castillo de arena. (construir)

   d. Adamari López no _____ oír nada porque hay mucho ruido aquí. (poder)

   e. Vosotros _____ muchas hamburguesas cada semana. (comer)

   f. No _____ nada; no soy un estudiante aplicado. (saber)

   g. Ellos _____ italiano perfectamente porque son de Roma. (comprender)

   h. Brandon Ríos _____ frecuentemente al gimnasio para levantar pesas. (ir)

   i. "Es obvio que yo no _____ a nadie", comentó el abogado, muy frustrado. (convencer)

   j. Cuando estoy en el supermercado, _____ mis productos favoritos. (escoger)

   k. Estoy muy triste porque no _____ en esta silla tan estrecha. (caber)

l. Yo normalmente _____ la verdad, pero tú no la

_____ nunca. (decir/decir)

m. ¿Por qué siempre _____ esos chicos cuando llega la policía? (huir)

2. Conjugate these verbs fully in the present indicative:

estar	destruir	vencer
_____	_____	_____
_____	_____	_____
_____	_____	_____

3. The following paragraph contains six errors. Underline each error and write the correct word above it:

Cuando estudio en la biblioteca, pono mis libros encima de la mesa. Mis amigos no queren estudiar conmigo porque no me gusta hablar con ellos. Yo les digo: "Silencio, por favor. Vosotros no aprendeis nada cuando habláis. Conoco al bibliotecario. Voy a hablar con él si no me escucháis". Naturalmente, mis amigos se enojan conmigo, pero no me importa. Yo sabo prepararme para los exámenes. Mis profesores me respietan y mis padres me aman.

B) El pretérito

The **preterite tense** is used to describe completed actions in the past. These actions are traditionally single events finished in the past (not a habit). Think of a movie director filming a scene; after the director yells "ACTION," the camera rolls, the actors act, the camera films, and then the director yells "CUT" or "THAT'S A TAKE." A preterite event is what was filmed (e.g., the actress **kissed** the actor, the horse **won** the race, the child **broke** the new toy). The preterite emphasizes the conclusion or ending point of an event or narrative.

✳ **Examples:** *Ellos **ganaron** la lotería ayer.*
They won the lottery yesterday.

*El boxeador **rompió** la ventana con el puño.*
The boxer broke the window with his fist.

Whenever you tell how long something was done, you convey an ending point; therefore, use the preterite.

✳ **Example:** *Yo **hablé** con mi mamá por media hora anoche.*
I spoke with my mom for half an hour last night.

The preterite may also signal the beginning of a past event.

✳ **Example:** ***Empezó** a llover a las seis y media.*
It began to rain at six-thirty.

1) Regular verbs

HABLAR		COMER		VIVIR	
hablé	hablamos	comí	comimos	viví	vivimos
hablaste	hablasteis	comiste	comisteis	viviste	vivisteis
habló	hablaron	comió	comieron	vivió	vivieron

Helpful Tips: **1)** There are accents on the *"yo"* and the *"Ud."/"él"/"ella"* forms only.
2) The *"vosotros"* form simply adds *"-is"* to the *"tú"* form of the preterite.

2) STEM-CHANGING VERBS (A.K.A. "BOOT" VERBS)

-AR and -ER "boot" verbs do not have any stem changes in the preterite.

The vowels are completely regular:

CERRAR		MOVER	
cerré	cerramos	moví	movimos
cerraste	cerrasteis	moviste	movisteis
cerró	cerraron	movió	movieron

-IR "boot" verbs, however, do change in the preterite. They have a vowel change in the 3rd person singular and plural: **o → u** or **e → i**.

The stem change occurs at the bottom of the boot — does it look more like a slipper now?

DORMIR		PEDIR	
dormí	dormimos	pedí	pedimos
dormiste	dormisteis	pediste	pedisteis
durmió	durmieron	pidió	pidieron
MORIR		**REÍR**	
morí	morimos	reí	reímos
moriste	moristeis	reíste	reísteis
murió	murieron	rió	rieron

¡CUIDADO! There are "extra" accent marks with the verb *"reír"* (as well as with *"sonreír"*).

3) SPELLING-CHANGERS

These verbs also change one or more of their letters in certain conjugations. The purpose of some of these changes is to preserve some consonant sound found in the infinitive.

The spelling changes are found in the 1st person of some verbs and in the 3rd person in others:

car → qué BUSCAR		gar → gué PAGAR		zar → cé ALZAR	
busqué	buscamos	**pagué**	pagamos	**alcé**	alzamos
buscaste	buscasteis	pagaste	pagasteis	alzaste	alzasteis
buscó	buscaron	pagó	pagaron	alzó	alzaron

Helpful Tip: The *"yo"* form of the preterite of *"buscar"* is *"busqué."* It is not *buscé! The reason is that the letter "c" before an "i" or "e" sounds one way, but is pronounced a different way before "a," "o," or "u."

Verbs in these categories:

car → qué		gar → gué		zar → cé	
aparcar	practicar	ahogar	jugar	alcanzar	empezar
atacar	roncar	apagar	llegar	almorzar	lanzar
buscar	sacar	cargar	negar	alzar	rezar
explicar	tocar	colgar	pagar	comenzar	
		entregar	regar		
			rogar		

eer → eyó, eyeron **LEER**		oír → oyó, oyeron **OÍR**		uir → uyó, uyeron **HUIR**	
leí	leímos	oí	oímos	huí	huimos
leíste	leísteis	oíste	oísteis	huiste	huisteis
leyó	**leyeron**	**oyó**	**oyeron**	**huyó**	**huyeron**

Verbs in these categories:

eer → eyó, eyeron	oír → oyó, oyeron	uir → uyó, uyeron
creer	oír	construir
leer		destruir
		huir

4) IRREGULAR VERBS

These verbs are also strange. They have unexpected changes.

It is necessary to memorize these forms:

ANDAR		CABER		CONDUCIR		DAR	
anduve	anduvimos	cupe	cupimos	conduje	condujimos	di	dimos
anduviste	anduvisteis	cupiste	cupisteis	condujiste	condujisteis	diste	disteis
anduvo	anduvieron	cupo	cupieron	condujo	condujeron	dio	dieron

DECIR		ESTAR		HACER		IR	
dije	dijimos	estuve	estuvimos	hice	hicimos	fui	fuimos
dijiste	dijisteis	estuviste	estuvisteis	hiciste	hicisteis	fuiste	fuisteis
dijo	dijeron	estuvo	estuvieron	hizo	hicieron	fue	fueron

PODER		PONER		PRODUCIR		QUERER	
pude	pudimos	puse	pusimos	produje	produjimos	quise	quisimos
pudiste	pudisteis	pusiste	pusisteis	produjiste	produjisteis	quisiste	quisisteis
pudo	pudieron	puso	pusieron	produjo	produjeron	quiso	quisieron

SABER		SER		TENER		TRADUCIR	
supe	supimos	fui	fuimos	tuve	tuvimos	traduje	tradujimos
supiste	supisteis	fuiste	fuisteis	tuviste	tuvisteis	tradujiste	tradujisteis
supo	supieron	fue	fueron	tuvo	tuvieron	tradujo	tradujeron

TRAER		VENIR		VER	
traje	trajimos	vine	vinimos	vi	vimos
trajiste	trajisteis	viniste	vinisteis	viste	visteis
trajo	trajeron	vino	vinieron	vio	vieron

Helpful Tips: **1)** There are no accent marks in any of these forms!
2) The verbs *"ir"* and *"ser"* have the same forms in the preterite. Only through context can you tell what verb is being used.
3) When there is a "j" in a 3rd person singular or plural ending, the "i" drops out (e.g. *dijo/dijeron, trajo/trajeron*).

 # PRACTICE EXERCISES ▶

1. Write the correct preterite form of each infinitive:

a. Ayer nosotros _____ los ejercicios en la pizarra. (escribir)

b. El pobre borracho no _____ abrir la puerta de su casa. (poder)

c. Vosotros _____ a Acapulco el año pasado. (ir)

d. Yo _____ mi coche de Chiapas a Monterrey. (conducir)

e. Ellos _____ los dos primeros capítulos. (leer)

f. Mi bisabuela sólo _____ cinco horas anoche. (dormir)

g. Mi sobrino me _____ una subscripción para la revista *People en español*. (vender)

h. Ella y yo _____ las frases del latín al español. (traducir)

i. Nadie _____ después de escuchar el chiste verde. (reír)

j. Los coches de Enrique Iglesias no _____ en el garaje pequeño. (caber)

2. Conjugate these three verbs fully in the preterite:

volver	decir	apagar

_____ _____ _____ _____ _____ _____

_____ _____ _____ _____ _____ _____

_____ _____ _____ _____ _____ _____

3. The following paragraph contains seven incorrect verbs. Underline each error and write the correct word above it:

Un verano fui a la playa con mi familia. Pasemos dos semanas en una casa bella. Durante el viaje mi mamá condució nuestro coche nuevo y mi padre, muy envidioso, la siguió en el viejo. Mi abuela no pudio acompañarnos ese año porque estaba enferma. Cuando llegé a casa, fui a un mercado bullicioso y me compré baterías nuevas para la cámara. Sacé muchas fotos de mi familia. Después, mis padres se acuestaron y se dormieron en seguida. Yo fui a una discoteca cercana.

C) LOS INTERROGATIVOS

Interrogatives are words that ask questions. In Spanish they always carry a written accent mark in a direct question or in a statement where there is an indirect question.

EXAMPLES: *¿Por qué estudias español?*
Why do you study Spanish?

¿Quién es el presidente de México?
Who is the president of Mexico?

No sé dónde vives. *
I don't know where you live.

*Note: In this sentence, there is an indirect question expressed: *¿Dónde vives?*

If there is no question, direct or indirect, these words are not "true" interrogatives and, therefore, don't have accents.

EXAMPLES: *El restaurante donde sirven papas fritas ricas es Five Guys.*
The restaurant where they serve tasty french fries is Five Guys.

No he visto The Wizard of Oz *porque tengo miedo de la bruja mala.* *
I haven't seen *The Wizard of Oz* because I'm afraid of the evil witch.

¡CUIDADO! *Remember, *"porque"* here means "because"; it is one word and has no accent.

The most common interrogatives are:

¿Cómo?	→	How?
¿Cuál?/¿Cuáles?	→	Which?/Which ones?/What?
¿Cuándo?	→	When?
¿Cuánto?/¿Cuánta?	→	How much?
¿Cuántos?/¿Cuántas?	→	How many?
¿Dónde?/¿Adónde?/¿De dónde?	→	Where?/To where?/From where?
¿Para qué?	→	Why?/For what purpose?
¿Por qué?	→	Why?/For what reason?
¿Qué?	→	What?/Which?
¿Quién?/¿Quiénes?	→	Who?

Helpful Tip: Most of these interrogatives are straightforward. What often confuses English speakers is the difference between *"Qué/Cuál"* when they precede *"ser."* This construction is confusing because both could mean "What?" or "Which?". The following chart will help highlight their differences.

¿Qué?	OR	¿Cuál/Cuáles?
(asks for a definition, explanation or classification before *"ser"*)		(asks for a selection or choice from a group before *"ser"*)
¿Qué es el ajedrez? (What is the definition of chess?) *El ajedrez es un juego.* *¿Qué son, demócratas o republicanos?* (What are they — Democrats or Republicans?) *Son demócratas.*		*¿Cuál es la capital de Tennessee?* (Of all the cities in Tennessee, which is the capital?) *La capital de Tennessee es Nashville.* *¿Cuál es la tarea para el lunes?* (What's Monday's homework [out of all homework that could be assigned]?) *Hay una prueba de vocabulario.*
Right before a noun, *"qué"* is usually used and asks for a selection: *¿Qué libro es tu favorito?* (What is your favorite book?)		*"Cuál/Cuáles"* is used before the preposition *"de"*: *¿Cuál de los chicos es más alto?* (Which of the kids is taller?)

 # PRACTICE EXERCISES

1. **Complete the following sentences with an interrogative:**

   a. ¿_____ compras helado en Tijuana?

   b. ¿_____ estudias italiano? –Porque quiero hablar con mi abuela italiana.

   c. ¿_____ tiempo hace hoy? –Hace mucho frío.

   d. Nunca sé _____ personas van a llegar a mi clase, 15 ó 16.

   e. La actual presidenta del club normalmente me pregunta _____ hay reuniones.

   f. ¿_____ se llamaba el líder del grupo musical *Miami Sound Machine*? –Gloria Estefan.

   g. ¿_____ número es tu favorito, el 7 o el 13?

   h. María nunca me explicó _____ llegar al aeropuerto más cercano.

   i. ¿_____ son los meses del verano? –Junio, julio y agosto.

   j. ¿_____ son tus abuelos, demócratas o republicanos?

2. The following dialogue contains five interrogative errors. Underline each error and write the correct word above it:

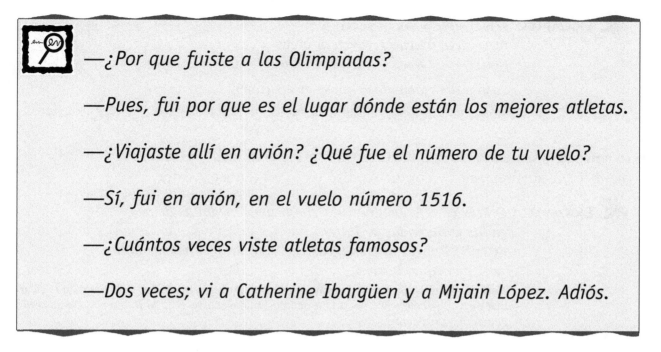

—¿Por que fuiste a las Olimpiadas?

—Pues, fui por que es el lugar dónde están los mejores atletas.

—¿Viajaste allí en avión? ¿Qué fue el número de tu vuelo?

—Sí, fui en avión, en el vuelo número 1516.

—¿Cuántos veces viste atletas famosos?

—Dos veces; vi a Catherine Ibargüen y a Mijain López. Adiós.

D) LAS CONJUNCIONES

Conjunctions are words that join sentences or parts of sentences. In English they are words such as "and," "or," "either," "nor," "neither."

The words in Spanish are:

Conjunctions
$y \ (e) \rightarrow$ and
$o \ (u) \rightarrow$ or, either
$ni \rightarrow$ nor, neither

Let's look at some special cases that arise with some of these conjunctions:

◆ **When the conjunction *"y"*** precedes a word beginning with the letter *"i"* or the letters *"hi"* (but not *"hie,"* because there the *"i"* is pronounced like the consonant *"y"* in the combination *"ie"*), the *"y"* changes to *"e."*

EXAMPLES: *Manny Machado y Carlos Correa* = Manny Machado and Carlos Correa
BUT: *Ferdinand e Imelda* = Ferdinand and Imelda

aguja y tela = needle and cloth
BUT: *aguja e hilo* = needle and thread
Note: *nieve y hielo* = snow and ice

◆ **When the conjunction *"o"*** precedes a word beginning with the letter *"o"* or the letters *"ho,"* the *"o"* changes to *"u."*

 **EXAMPLES:** *seis o siete* = six or seven
 BUT: *siete **u** ocho* = seven or eight
 Note: *6 ó 7* = 6 or 7 (An accent is added to *"o"* between numerals.)

 casa o apartamento = house or apartment
 BUT: *casa **u** hotel* = house or hotel

◆ **In a negative sentence,** the conjunction *"ni"* or the conjunctions *"ni . . . ni"* (neither . . . nor) replace *"o"* or the words *"o . . . o"* (either . . . or).

 **EXAMPLE:** *O México o Argentina va a ganar unas medallas de oro en las Olimpiadas de Paris.*
 BUT: ***Ni** Bolivia **ni** Honduras van a ganar muchas medallas de oro en Paris.*

 Note: A Spanish speaker will normally use a <u>plural</u> verb after *"ni . . . ni"* unless it is clear that the two people could not do the action simultaneously. e.g., *Ni Rubio ni Sanders **será** el próximo presidente.*

 # PRACTICE EXERCISES ▶

1. Pick one of the following conjunctions for each of the sentences below *(o, u, y, e, ni)*:

a. Veinte _____ ochenta son cien.

b. Ni Pitbull _____ Daddy Yankee van a la playa.*
 *Note: The verb *"van"* here is plural; in English we would use a singular verb.

c. La sangría tiene fruta _____ hielo.

d. Ni María _____ Emilio van a la conferencia.

e. O Big Bird _____ Mr. Snuffleupagus es el animal más grande de la Plaza Sésamo.

f. Siete _____ ocho son quince.

g. Los pobres soldados agotados no tienen ni agua _____ comida.

h. Me gustan mucho los cursos que combinan literatura _____ historia.

i. ¿Quién te invitó a la fiesta, Ramón _____ Óscar?

2. The following paragraph contains five conjunction errors. Underline each error and write the correct word above it:

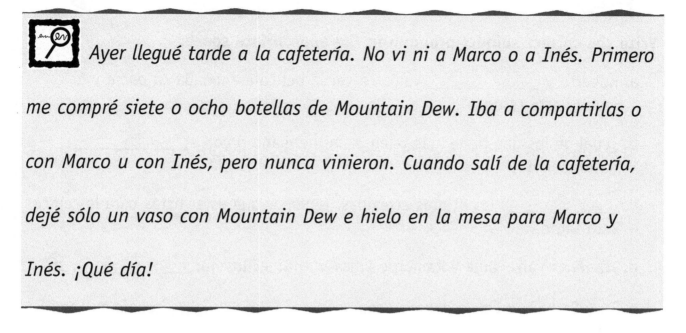

Ayer llegué tarde a la cafetería. No vi ni a Marco o a Inés. Primero me compré siete o ocho botellas de Mountain Dew. Iba a compartirlas o con Marco u con Inés, pero nunca vinieron. Cuando salí de la cafetería, dejé sólo un vaso con Mountain Dew e hielo en la mesa para Marco y Inés. ¡Qué día!

E) Los pronombres personales

Pronouns are words that take the place of nouns. There are many categories of pronouns. This lesson will review **subject pronouns.** In English you use either a noun or a subject pronoun with all verbs; in Spanish, subject pronouns are unnecessary unless used for emphasis or clarity.

Examples: *¿Vas al concierto? –**Yo** no voy, pero **ella** va.*
Are you going to the concert? –I'm not going, but she is.

*¿Quiénes van a comer la torta? –**Ellos.***
Who is going to eat the cake? –They are.

Here is the list of subject pronouns in Spanish:

yo	*nosotros/nosotras*
tú	*vosotros/vosotras* (in Spain only)
él/ella/Ud.	*ellos/ellas/Uds.*

They correspond to these pronouns in English:

I	we
you (familiar/informal)	you all (familiar/informal)
he/she/you (polite/formal)	they/you all

Write the correct subject pronoun in the appropriate space:

a. Roberto y _____ vamos a ver la película animada *La dama y la muerte* esta tarde.

b. ¿Cuál de los dos tiene más talento, mi hermano o yo? –¡_____, naturalmente!

c. _____, las atletas atrevidas, tenemos que estar listas para las cinco esta tarde.

d. ¿Quiénes van, Paula y Ramón o Luisa y Ana? –Ellos no; _____, sí.

e. Tú y Catherine vais a ganar el campeonato; _____ tenéis mucho talento.

ORAL PRACTICE
PREGUNTAS EN GRUPOS DE DOS

These two sets of questions use grammatical structures and vocabulary from this lesson. Working with a partner, alternate asking and answering each question. When you get to the bottom of each list, start over at the top, switching roles. As a variation, write out the answers in complete sentences.

A) ¿Tienes un deseo **ardiente** de estudiar español?

¿Te sientes un poco **confuso/a** cuando estás en esta clase?

¿Eres fuerte o **débil**?

¿Por qué es importante ser **cortés** con tus amigos?

¿Cuál es más **caro**, un coche nuevo o un edificio nuevo?

¿Qué cosa no tiene una persona **calva**?

¿Qué problemas existen para una persona **ciega**?

B) ¿**Conduces** tu propio coche?

¿**Hiciste** mucha tarea para hoy?

¿**Cuál** es la capital de México?

¿**Qué** nombre te gusta más, Teófilo u Óscar?

¿**Sabes** pilotar un avión?

¿**Oíste** el último discurso del presidente?

¿Quién **va** a ganar la Serie Mundial de béisbol este año?

 **PRUEBA DE REPASO**

A) EL PRESENTE DEL INDICATIVO

1. Fill in the blanks with the correct present indicative form:

a. Cada noche Scrooge _____ su dinero. (contar)

b. Mi perrito _____ debajo de la silla verde. (dormir)

c. El padre _____ una casa de muñecas para su hija.
(construir)

d. ¿_____ (vosotros) suficiente dinero para salir esta
noche? (Tener)

e. El ladrón calvo escapa de la cárcel y _____ de la policía.
(huir)

f. ¿A qué hora _____ el programa *Dancing with the Stars?* (empezar)

g. La profesora _____ los exámenes en su oficina. (corregir)

h. Nos gusta cuando _____ mucho y no tenemos que ir a la
escuela. (nevar)

i. ¿(Tú) _____ estudiar por la noche o por la mañana?
(preferir)

2. Conjugate these verbs in the present indicative:

torcer   escoger   oír

_____ _____ _____ _____ _____ _____

_____ _____ _____ _____ _____ _____

_____ _____ _____ _____ _____ _____

3. The following paragraph contains six incorrect verbs. Underline each incorrect verb and then write the correct form above it:

Estoy loco por Liliana, aunque no la conoco personalmente.

Ella esta en mi clase de español y es una alumna muy aplicada. Yo no

entendo nada del español; nunca recordo el vocabulario y ¡los verbos

irregulares son imposibles! Todo esto no me importa, porque durante

toda la clase yo sueno con Liliana. Me gustaría salir con ella, pero no

sabo si Liliana quiere ser mi novia. En clase, cuando trabajamos en

grupos de dos, ella no me hace caso.

B) EL PRETÉRITO

1. Fill in the blanks with the correct preterite form of each infinitive:

a. El profesor de historia nos _____ una prueba difícil ayer. (dar)

b. El taxista _____ rápidamente al aeropuerto. (conducir)

c. Sólo _____ cuatro personas en ese ascensor tan pequeño. (caber)

d. Yo _____ mis gafas por todas partes, pero no las encontré. (buscar)

e. Nosotros _____ *The House on Mango Street*, la novela de Sandra Cisneros, en dos días. (leer)

f. Tú _____ el primero en entregarle el ensayo a la maestra. (ser)

g. Cuando estaba en el hospital, mis amigos me _____ unas flores preciosas. (traer)

h. Vosotros sólo _____ en Querétaro cinco días. (estar)

i. El cartero miedoso no _____ entregar el correo porque el perro lo amenazaba. (poder)

j. Los chicos _____ que salir a las seis de la tarde para ver la película de Cantinflas. (tener)

2. Conjugate these verbs in the preterite:

mover	tocar	producir
_____ _____	_____ _____	_____ _____
_____ _____	_____ _____	_____ _____
_____ _____	_____ _____	_____ _____

3. The following paragraph contains seven incorrect verbs. Underline each incorrect verb and write the correct form above it:

Ayer, en la clase de español, tuvimos que escribir diálogos cortos. Desgraciadamente, yo no tení que trabajar con Liliana. ¡Qué mala suerte! Ella elegí trabajar con Antonio. Antonio es el mejor jugador de fútbol de la escuela. También habla muy bien el español porque vivó un par de años en Argentina. A mí no me cae bien Antonio; no es un chico cortés. Durante toda la clase, Liliana y Antonio se reyeron mucho. Yo tuve que trabajar con Lorena, la chica más aburrida de la clase. Nuestro

diálogo fui un desastre, con muchos problemas de gramática y con poco

vocabulario nuevo. Yo me poní triste porque no podí conversar

con Liliana.

C) LOS INTERROGATIVOS

1. Write the appropriate interrogative in the spaces below:

a. ¿_____ fue el primer presidente de los Estados Unidos?

b. ¿_____ es tu número de teléfono?

c. ¿_____ empieza el año académico?

d. ¿_____ se dice *"zebra"* en español?

e. Le pregunté al meteorólogo: ¿_____ va a hacer buen tiempo?

f. ¿_____ partidos de tenis hay esta semana? —Dos.

g. No recuerdo _____ he dejado el cuchillo afilado.

h. ¿_____ de estas bebidas te gusta más: Pepsi o Coke?

i. ¿_____ es el *"gazpacho"*?

j. No entiendo _____ siempre esperas hasta el último momento para hacer la tarea.

k. No recuerdo _____ día vi al hombre ciego en el parque.

2. The following dialogue contains five errors related to interrogatives. Find and correct them:

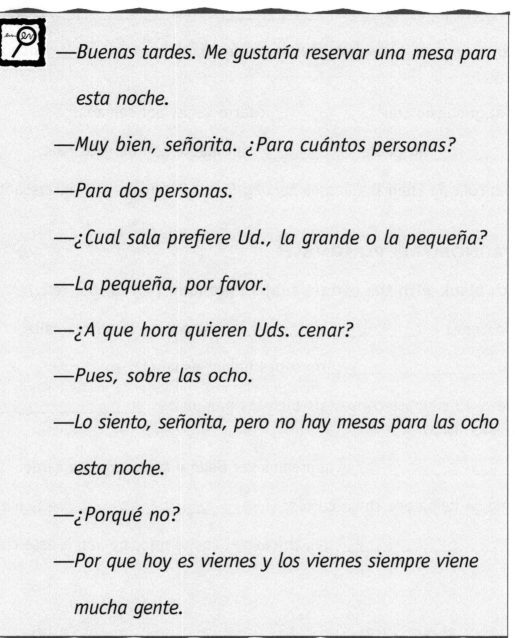

—Buenas tardes. Me gustaría reservar una mesa para esta noche.

—Muy bien, señorita. ¿Para cuántos personas?

—Para dos personas.

—¿Cual sala prefiere Ud., la grande o la pequeña?

—La pequeña, por favor.

—¿A que hora quieren Uds. cenar?

—Pues, sobre las ocho.

—Lo siento, señorita, pero no hay mesas para las ocho esta noche.

—¿Porqué no?

—Por que hoy es viernes y los viernes siempre viene mucha gente.

D) LAS CONJUNCIONES

Fill in the blanks with the appropriate conjunction (o, u, y, e, ni):

a. Hoy hay un torneo de golf entre padres _____ hijos.

b. _____ *The Good Wife* ni *Downton Abbey* van a volver a la tele.

c. Vamos a ir de compras o a Michael Kors _____ a Zara.

d. Los vegetarianos no comen _____ carne _____ pescado.

e. ¿Cuánto pagaste por ese cuaderno cuadrado, siete _____ ocho dólares?

f. Voy al gimnasio tres _____ cuatro veces por semana.

g. _____ mi padre _____ mi madre son de este país.

h. La película de Ellen DeGeneres *Finding Dory* es cómica ____ interesante.

E) LOS PRONOMBRES PERSONALES

Fill in each blank with the correct subject pronoun *(yo, tú, Ud., etc.)*:

a. Mario López y _____ vivimos en la misma calle.

b. ¿_____ no sabes hablar español?

c. Javier y tú siempre contestáis bien las preguntas; _____ sois muy listos.

d. _____ queremos ver *Bella y la Bestia* esta tarde.

e. ¿Cómo se llama ese chico cortés? –_____ se llama Jaime.

f. _____, las chicas del coche rojo, no van a este colegio.

ESPAÑA

Océano Atlántico

FRANCIA

La Coruña
Santiago de Compostela
Bilbao
LA CORDILLERA CANTÁBRICA
LOS PIRINEOS
Valladolid
Salamanca
Zaragoza
Barcelona
Segovia
Madrid
RÍO TAJO
Toledo
ESPAÑA
Valencia
GOLFO DE VALENCIA
Córdoba
SIERRA MORENA
Alicante
Mar Mediterráneo
PORTUGAL
GOLFO DE CÁDIZ
Sevilla
ANDALUCÍA
Cádiz
Málaga
Granada
SIERRA NEVADA

ESPAÑOLES FAMOSOS:

Pedro Almodóvar
(DIRECTOR DE CINE)

Antonio Banderas
(ACTOR)

Emilia Pardo Bazán
(ESCRITORA)

Montserrat Caballé
(CANTANTE DE ÓPERA)

Pablo Casals
(MÚSICO)

Miguel de Cervantes
(AUTOR DE DON QUIJOTE)

Penélope Cruz
(ACTRIZ)

Salvador Dalí
(ARTISTA)

Plácido Domingo
(CANTANTE)

Generalísimo
Francisco Franco
(DICTADOR)

Pau Gasol
(JUGADOR DE BALONCESTO)

Antoni Gaudí
(ARQUITECTO)

Francisco Goya
(ARTISTA)

El Greco (ARTISTA)

Miguel Induráin
(CICLISTA)

Ana María Matute
(ESCRITORA)

Rafael Nadal
(TENISTA)

Pablo Picasso (ARTISTA)

Andrés Segovia
(MÚSICO)

Miguel de Unamuno
(ESCRITOR Y FILÓSOFO)

Diego Velázquez
(PINTOR)

ESPAÑA

CAPITAL:	Madrid
POBLACIÓN:	46.700.000
GOBIERNO:	monarquía parlamentaria
JEFE DEL ESTADO:	El rey don Felipe VI
PRESIDENTE DEL GOBIERNO:	Pedro Sánchez
DINERO ($):	euro
PRODUCTOS:	aceite de oliva, naranjas, vino
MÚSICA, BAILE:	flamenco, sevillanas
SITIOS DE INTERÉS:	Acueducto (Segovia), La Alhambra (Granada), La Mezquita (Córdoba), Museo del Prado (Madrid), Museo Guggenheim (Bilbao), Parque Güell (Barcelona)
COMIDA TÍPICA:	cochinillo, cordero, gazpacho, paella, sangría, tapas, tortilla española, vino

VOCABULARIO LECCIÓN DOS

ADJETIVOS

difunto/a	dead, deceased	*harto/a*	fed up, full
discreto/a	discreet	*herido/a*	wounded
distinto/a	different, distinct	*hondo/a*	deep
dorado/a	golden	*humilde*	humble
dulce	sweet	*ilustre*	illustrious
duro/a	hard	*impreso/a*	printed
engañado/a	tricked, deceived	*infeliz*	unhappy
entero/a	whole, entire	*inferior*	inferior, lower
envidioso/a	envious, jealous	*ingenuo/a*	naive
espeso/a	thick, dense	*inmortal*	immortal
estrecho/a	narrow	*íntimo/a*	intimate, close
feroz	fierce, ferocious	*inútil*	useless
fiel	faithful	*izquierdo/a*	left
fijo/a	fixed, firm	*jubilado/a*	retired
fino/a	fine, delicate	*judío/a*	Jewish
flaco/a	thin, skinny	*justo/a*	just, fair, appropriate
formidable	wonderful, terrific		
franco/a	frank	*largo/a*	long
genial	smart, original, exceptional	*lejano/a*	distant
		lento/a	slow
grave	serious	*leve*	slight, light
guapo/a	good-looking		

LECCIÓN DOS

KEY GRAMMAR
CONCEPTS

A) EL IMPERFECTO → *The imperfect*

B) EL PRETÉRITO Y EL IMPERFECTO → *The preterite and the imperfect*

C) EL PROGRESIVO → *The progressive*

D) LOS MANDATOS INFORMALES → *Familiar commands*

E) LAS PREPOSICIONES → *Prepositions*

A) EL IMPERFECTO

The **imperfect** is another past tense. It is used to describe actions that weren't completed, to make descriptions, to tell time, and to describe habits.

EXAMPLES: *Leíamos* El País *cuando nuestros vecinos, los Sastre, vinieron a vernos.*
> We were reading *El País* when our neighbors, the Sastres, came to see us.

El árbitro **era** *un hombre bajo, calvo y corpulento.*
> The referee was a short, bald, and burly man.

Eran *las cinco y media cuando Sarita se levantó.*
> It was five-thirty when Sarita got up.

Cuando yo **era** *joven,* **bebía** *Seven-Up con mi abuelo.*
> When I was young, I used to drink Seven-Up with my grandfather.

HOW IS THE IMPERFECT TENSE FORMED?

1) REGULAR VERBS

With the exception of only three verbs, all verbs in the imperfect are regular. There are no "boot" verbs; there are no special spelling-changers. For this reason, the imperfect is often a favorite tense of Spanish students.

Here are the imperfect conjugations for almost every verb!

HABLAR		VOLVER		PEDIR	
hablaba	hablábamos	volvía	volvíamos	pedía	pedíamos
hablabas	hablabais	volvías	volvíais	pedías	pedíais
hablaba	hablaban	volvía	volvían	pedía	pedían

Helpful Tips: **1)** The 1st person singular and 3rd person singular have the same form in the imperfect. Context will indicate the subject.
2) -**AR** verbs have an accent only on the *"nosotros/nosotras"* form.
3) The -**ER** and -**IR** verbs have accents on every form.

2) IRREGULAR VERBS

There are only three irregular verbs in the imperfect. They are *"ir," "ser,"* and *"ver."*

Here are their conjugations:

IR		SER		VER	
iba	íbamos	era	éramos	veía	veíamos
ibas	ibais	eras	erais	veías	veíais
iba	iban	era	eran	veía	veían

 # PRACTICE EXERCISES ▶

1. Change these verbs into the correct form of the imperfect:

Examples: sé → **sabía**   hablaste → **hablabas**

a. dirijo   → _____   **f.** vuelves → _____

b. compran → _____   **g.** sigo   → _____

c. supisteis → _____   **h.** vamos → _____

d. pueden → _____   **i.** fue   → _____

e. rompió → _____   **j.** dijiste → _____

2. Use the correct form of the imperfect in these sentences:

a. _____ la una y media de la mañana cuando terminó el concierto de David Bisbal. (Ser)

b. El mantel largo no _____ azul marino; por eso no lo compré. (parecer)

c. Mi perro _____ cada vez que yo _____ a casa. (ladrar/volver)

d. Mi tía _____ mucho más alta que mi tío. (ser)

e. Todos los viernes mis padres _____ a un restaurante cercano; mis hermanos y yo nos quedábamos en casa. (ir)

f. Pedro Almodóvar _____ un libro cuando su hermano Agustín entró en la casa. (leer)

3. In this paragraph, there are five errors. Identify them and correct them:

Nunca queraba ir a la escuela cuando era joven. Normalmente me quedé en la cama mientras mi despertador sonó. Un día mi madre comenzaba a llamarme a las siete de la mañana. No le hice caso. Pero cuando ella me echaba el vaso de agua fría en la cabeza, grité como un loco.

Understanding the difference between the **preterite** and the **imperfect** is a sign of a good Spanish speaker. Students often take a while to get the hang of this concept. Keep in mind that the speaker of a sentence has a good deal of freedom in choosing a tense. Oftentimes, sentences can make perfect sense using either the preterite or the imperfect; it all depends on the meaning you want to convey.

The English sentence "Mary bought flowers for me" can be expressed in different ways in Spanish — both in the preterite and in the imperfect. Let's look.

EXAMPLES: *María me* **compró** *flores.*
> Mary bought flowers for me. (Only once or just a few times. Not a habit.)

María me **compraba** *flores.*
> Mary bought flowers for me. (It was a habit. She <u>used to</u> buy me flowers.)

The following chart helps to highlight the differences between the preterite and the imperfect. When in doubt, decide if the action is complete; could it be filmed by a director with a clear ending? If so, use preterite. If not, go with imperfect.

Preterite	Imperfect
◆ Single, complete event	◆ Incomplete, ongoing event
◆ The beginning or ending point of an action	◆ Description
◆ When you tell how long an action lasted	◆ Telling time in the past
	◆ Habitual actions

Some verbs have different meanings in the preterite and imperfect.

Pretérito		Imperfecto	
conocí →	I met	*conocía* →	I used to know/I knew
supe →	I learned, I found out	*sabía* →	I used to know/I knew
quise →	I tried	*quería* →	I wanted to/liked
no quise →	I refused to	*no quería* →	I didn't want to/like
hubo →	there occurred*	*había* →	there was, there were*
pude →	I managed to	*podía* →	I had the ability to
no pude →	I failed to	*no podía* →	I couldn't

*i.e., an event: *Hubo una fiesta; hubo muchos accidentes* — "hubo" (the preterite of "haber") is always singular here!

*i.e., an object; a concept: *Había un perro flaco en la calle; había tres preguntas en el examen; había mucha confusión* — "había" is always singular here!

PRACTICE EXERCISE

The following two paragraphs are typical of the classics that have been written by Spanish teachers to help you learn to distinguish between the preterite and imperfect.

Conjugate each infinitive with either the preterite or the imperfect — the one that you believe best captures the spirit of the narrative:

a. Yo _____ (nacer) el veintinueve de agosto. Me

_____ (gustar) mucho ese día cuando _____ (ser)

joven. Mis padres siempre me _____ (comprar) regalos interesantes:

un año _____ (recibir) una tortuga; otro año me

_____ (dar) una mesa pequeña. Siempre les _____

(decir): "Muchas gracias". Una vez mi tío me _____

(sorprender). Se _____ (vestir) de payaso y no lo

_____ (reconocer). Cuando por fin _____ (saber)

que _____ (ser) mi tío, yo _____ (ponerse)

muy contento.

b. _____ (Ser) las dos de la tarde cuando el examen

_____ (comenzar). Los alumnos _____ (tomar) los

lápices y _____ (escuchar) atentamente las preguntas orales.

Después de quince minutos, _____ (ocurrir) algo muy extraño. Un

pájaro herido _____ (entrar) por la ventana. _____

(Volar) de un lado para otro. Nadie _____ (poder) concentrarse.

Por fin todos nosotros _____ (tener) que salir de la clase. ¡Qué

mala suerte!

C) EL PROGRESIVO

The **progressive** is a tense that gives extra emphasis to an act that is actually <u>in progress</u> — an event that is occurring at the exact moment that the speaker is describing. Often the words *ahora, ahora mismo,* or *en este (ese)* momento are found in sentences with this tense.

EXAMPLES: *Está lloviendo ahora mismo.*
It is raining right now.

Penélope Cruz estaba durmiendo cuando llegué.
Penélope Cruz was sleeping when I arrived.

The following sentence illustrates well the usefulness of the progressive:

Toco el piano a menudo, pero no estoy tocándolo en este momento.
I often play the piano, but I am not playing it right now.

HOW IS THE PROGRESSIVE TENSE FORMED?

This tense is a combination of a form of the verb *"estar," "seguir,"* or *"continuar"* (in the present or the imperfect tense) followed by a present participle.

PRESENT	estoy	estamos	sigo	seguimos	continúo	continuamos	
	estás	estáis	sigues	seguís	continúas	continuáis	**hablando**
	está	están	sigue	siguen	continúa	continúan	**+ comiendo**
IMPERFECT	estaba	estábamos	seguía	seguíamos	continuaba	continuábamos	**viviendo**
	estabas	estabais	seguías	seguíais	continuabas	continuabais	
	estaba	estaban	seguía	seguían	continuaba	continuaban	

HOW IS THE PRESENT PARTICIPLE FORMED?

1 **The forms for most verbs are regular.**

> *hablar* → *hablando* (speaking)
> *comer* → *comiendo* (eating)
> *vivir* → *viviendo* (living)

2 -IR "boot" verbs have a special vowel change, the same vowel change that occurs in the 3rd person of the preterite.

dormir → durmiendo	reír → riendo
morir → muriendo	sentir → sintiendo
pedir → pidiendo	servir → sirviendo

Note: There is also one **-ER** verb that follows this rule: *poder → pudiendo.*

3 In present participles, "i" → "y" between two vowels and with the infinitive *"ir."*

caer → cayendo	leer → leyendo
creer → creyendo	oír → oyendo
ir → yendo	traer → trayendo

4 Verbs that end in *"-ñir"* lose the "i" after "ñ" in the present participle. These words might be new to you.

gruñir → gruñendo (growling)
reñir → riñendo (scolding)
teñir → tiñendo (dyeing)

How else is the present participle used?

The present participle can be used as an adverb of manner, telling how something was done.

 **EXAMPLES:** *Aprendí la gramática estudiando los ejercicios.*
        I learned grammar (by) studying the exercises.

        Nos conocimos jugando al tenis.
        We met each other playing tennis.

The present participle, however, <u>cannot</u> be used as a noun as we often do with the "-ing" form in English.

 **EXAMPLES:** *Hablar español es divertido.* = Speaking Spanish is fun.
        (You may <u>not</u> say: *Hablando español es divertido.)

        Se prohíbe fumar. = Smoking is prohibited.
        (You may <u>not</u> say: *Fumando se prohíbe.)

Object pronouns can either be <u>attached</u> to the present participle or put <u>before</u> the form of *"estar."* If you attach the pronoun, be certain to add an accent mark as in the example below.

 EXAMPLE: *Estoy cepillándome los dientes con Crest.*
(Me estoy cepillando los dientes con Crest.)
I'm brushing my teeth with Crest.

> **Helpful Tip:** The present participle often refers back to the subject, particularly with verbs of perception *(oír, recordar, ver, etc.)*, explaining how something was done. For example, *"Te vi llegando"* may be interpreted: "I saw you as **I** was arriving." If **you** were arriving, however, the sentence could read: *"Te vi llegar."* I saw you as **you** were arriving. This use of the infinitive is mentioned later in *Lección Siete*.

¡CUIDADO! The progressive may <u>not</u> be used as a substitute for the future as we do in English.

 EXAMPLE: *Llegan mañana* = They are arriving tomorrow.
(You should <u>not</u> say: *Están llegando mañana.*)

 PRACTICE EXERCISES

1. Change these verbs into the corresponding form of the progressive:

Examples: hablas → **estás hablando**   comían → **estaban comiendo**

a. mueren → _____

b. íbamos → _____

c. pides → _____

d. leéis → _____

e. comprende → _____

f. repetían → _____

g. estudiabas → _____

h. comía → _____

2. Use a form of the progressive that best fits the context of these sentences:

a. Ana _____ *Don Quijote* cuando entré en la casa. (leer)

b. En este momento _____ fuertemente. (nevar)

c. Tom Brady _____ ayer después de ganar el campeonato de fútbol americano otra vez. (celebrar)

d. Anoche nosotros todavía _____ a la medianoche. (estudiar)

e. Mis amigos dicen que _____ de sed. (morirse)

3. Use the present participle or the infinitive as needed:

a. _____ se aprende mucho. (Estudiar)

b. _____ en la casa, tropecé y me rompí el dedo gordo del pie. (Entrar)

c. _____ en la biblioteca no es bueno porque puede molestar a los lectores. (Hablar)

4. There are five errors in this paragraph. Identify and correct them:

La semana pasada yo estabas hablendo por teléfono con Rosa cuando alguien llamó a la puerta. Una mujer, muy agitada, estaba danda fuertes golpes a la puerta y gritando. Dijo que estaba yenda al banco cuando vio un accidente muy grave. Colgué el teléfono porque quería ayudarla. Estaba respiriendo rápidamente cuando abrí la puerta. La señora gritó una vez más y se fue.

D) LOS MANDATOS INFORMALES

Commands ask someone to do or not to do something. In Spanish, commands have different forms depending on the person(s) to whom they are directed. Familiar commands have different forms in the affirmative and in the negative. An object pronoun must be attached to the end of any affirmative command, but must come before a negative command.

Affirmative (+)	Negative (−)
EXAMPLES: *¡**Habla**, Marta!*	*¡No **hables**, Marta!*
*¡**Escríbeme** una carta, José!*	*¡No me **escribas** una carta, José!*
*¡**Vended** (vosotros) el coche!*	*¡No **vendáis** el coche!*
*¡**Salid** ahora mismo!*	*¡No **salgáis** ahora mismo!*

Here are the command forms for *"tú"* and *"vosotros"*:

1) "TÚ" AFFIRMATIVE COMMANDS (+)

For regular, affirmative, singular, familiar commands, simply take the 3rd person singular form of the present indicative:

HABLAR	COMER	VIVIR
¡Habla (tú)!	¡Come (tú)!	¡Vive (tú)!

CERRAR	VOLVER	MENTIR
¡Cierra (tú)!	¡Vuelve (tú)!	¡Miente (tú)!

Here are the irregular, affirmative *"tú"* commands:

(+)

decir	→	*di*	(tú)	*¡Di la verdad!*
hacer	→	*haz*	(tú)	*¡Haz la tarea!*
ir	→	*ve**	(tú)	*¡Ve a la clase!*
poner	→	*pon*	(tú)	*¡Pon la Coca-Cola en la nevera!*
salir	→	*sal*	(tú)	*¡Sal de aquí!*
ser	→	*sé*	(tú)	*¡Sé bueno!*
tener	→	*ten*	(tú)	*¡Ten paciencia!*
venir	→	*ven*	(tú)	*¡Ven acá!*

***Note:** "Ir" and "ver" have the same affirmative "tú" command. Context will make the meaning clear.

2) "TÚ" NEGATIVE COMMANDS (−)

The negative form of familiar, singular commands uses the 2nd person singular subjunctive form (explained in greater detail in *Lección Cuatro*). For most verbs, simply take the *"yo"* form of the present indicative, remove the final *"o,"* and then add *"es"* for **-AR** verbs and *"as"* for **-ER** and **-IR** verbs.

-AR	-ER	-IR
¡No hables (tú)! ¡No cierres (tú)!	¡No comas (tú)! ¡No vuelvas (tú)!	¡No vivas (tú)! ¡No mientas (tú)!

Here are the negative *"tú"* forms of the verbs that are irregular in the affirmative:

(−)

decir	→	*no digas*	*(tú)*	*¡No digas tonterías!*
hacer	→	*no hagas*	*(tú)*	*¡No hagas tanto ruido!*
ir	→	*no vayas*	*(tú)*	*¡No vayas al cine sin mí!*
poner	→	*no pongas*	*(tú)*	*¡No pongas los pies en la mesa!*
salir	→	*no salgas*	*(tú)*	*¡No salgas con ellos!*
ser	→	*no seas*	*(tú)*	*¡No seas bruto!*
tener	→	*no tengas*	*(tú)*	*¡No tengas miedo!*
venir	→	*no vengas*	*(tú)*	*¡No vengas todavía!*

3) "VOSOTROS/VOSOTRAS" AFFIRMATIVE COMMANDS (+)

Simply remove the *"r"* of the infinitive and add a *"d."* If the verb is reflexive, however, remove the *"r"* of the infinitive and add *"os"*; add an accent to the *"i"* in a reflexive **-IR** verb.

HABLAR	COMER	VIVIR
¡Hablad!	¡Comed!	¡Vivid!

SENTARSE	VOLVERSE	VESTIRSE
¡Sentaos!	¡Volveos!	¡Vestíos!

¡CUIDADO! The only verb that is an exception is *"irse."* The affirmative *"vosotros/vosotras"* command is: *"¡Idos!"*

IRSE
¡Idos!

4) "VOSOTROS/VOSOTRAS" NEGATIVE COMMANDS (−)

This form uses the 2nd person plural of the subjunctive, also explained in greater detail in *Lección Cuatro*. The endings are *"éis"* for **-AR** verbs and *"áis"* for **-ER** and **-IR** verbs.

¡No habléis!	*¡No comáis!*	*¡No viváis!*
¡No os sentéis!	*¡No os volváis!*	*¡No os vistáis!*
¡No os levantéis!	*¡No os caigáis!*	*¡No os durmáis!*

Helpful Tips: **1)** There are no stem-changers in the subjunctive in the *"vosotros/vosotras"* forms for **-AR** and **-ER** verbs.

2) **-IR** verbs have a special stem change (e → i and o → u) in the *"vosotros/vosotras"* form.

3) The spelling-changers change spelling in every person of the subjunctive, including *"vosotros/vosotras."*

---

5) CHART OF REPRESENTATIVE FAMILIAR COMMANDS

Seeing the forms together may help you remember them.

	tú (+)	*tú (−)*	*vosotros (+)*	*vosotros (−)*
HABLAR	*¡Habla!*	*¡No hables!*	*¡Hablad!*	*¡No habléis!*
COMER	*¡Come!*	*¡No comas!*	*¡Comed!*	*¡No comáis!*
VIVIR	*¡Vive!*	*¡No vivas!*	*¡Vivid!*	*¡No viváis!*
CERRAR	*¡Cierra!*	*¡No cierres!*	*¡Cerrad!*	*¡No cerréis!*
VOLVERSE	*¡Vuélvete!*	*¡No te vuelvas!*	*¡Volveos!*	*¡No os volváis!*
DORMIR	*¡Duerme!*	*¡No duermas!*	*¡Dormid!*	*¡No durmáis!*
LEVANTARSE	*¡Levántate!*	*¡No te levantes!*	*¡Levantaos!*	*¡No os levantéis!*
DIRIGIR	*¡Dirige!*	*¡No dirijas!*	*¡Dirigid!*	*¡No dirijáis!*
TENER	*¡Ten!*	*¡No tengas!*	*¡Tened!*	*¡No tengáis!*
IRSE	*¡Vete!*	*¡No te vayas!*	*¡Idos!*	*¡No os vayáis!*

PRACTICE EXERCISES

1. Write the appropriate command form only on the lines provided:

	tú (+)	tú (-)	vosotras (+)	vosotros (-)
a. ¡Recordar!	_____			_____
b. ¡Vender!			_____	
c. ¡Decir!	_____			
d. ¡Fingir!		_____		_____

¡CUIDADO! (You must preserve the sound of the infinitive!)

	tú (+)	tú (-)	vosotras (+)	vosotros (-)
e. ¡Sentarse!	_____			
f. ¡Reírse!			_____	_____
g. ¡Exprimir!		_____		_____
h. ¡Venir!	_____			
i. ¡Traducir!		_____	_____	

¡CUIDADO! (Don't forget that this verb is a spelling-changer!)

	tú (+)	tú (-)	vosotras (+)	vosotros (-)
j. ¡Volverse!	_____			

2. In the following speech there are seven errors in the command forms. Identify and fix them:

Estoy muy contento, amigos, de hablar con vosotros hoy. Sentados todos y no preocupéisse de nada ahora. Soy vuestro líder, vuestra inspiración. Tiened fe en mí y juntos vamos a resolver todos los problemas del mundo. Estad seguros de que estoy aquí para ayudaros. Pero, antes de continuar, por favor poneed veinte dólares en el sombrero hondo que mi asistente, Ramón, ahorita os va a ofrecer. (¡Chis! Ramón, rápido. Tiene cuidado y acuérdase de dejar el sombrero en la oficina.) A propósito, queridos amigos, acepto Visa y MasterCard. Simplemente escribed el número en el papel y no os olvidéis de escribir la fecha de vencimiento.

E) LAS PREPOSICIONES

1) DO YOU REMEMBER THE MOST COMMON PREPOSITIONS IN SPANISH?

Common Prepositions

a	→	at, to		
alrededor de	→	around		
ante	→	before (e.g., *ante el juez*)		
antes de	→	before		
bajo	→	below (figurative)		
con	→	with		
contra	→	against		
de	→	of, from		
debajo de	→	below (physical)		
delante de	→	in front of		
desde	→	since, from		
después de	→	after		

detrás de	→	behind
en	→	in, on
encima de	→	on top of
entre	→	between, among
hacia	→	towards
hasta	→	until
para	→	by, for, in order to
por	→	by, for, through
según	→	according to
sin	→	without
sobre	→	about, over, on top of
tras	→	behind, after

2) WHEN A VERB DIRECTLY FOLLOWS A PREPOSITION, THE VERB MUST BE AN INFINITIVE.

Because we use the "-ing" form as a noun in English, this rule is a hard one to remember.

EXAMPLES: *Estoy cansada de **estudiar**.*
I am tired of studying.

Note: It is wrong to say: *"Estoy cansada de estudiando."* Remember that, in Spanish, *"estudiando"* can only be used as a verb or an adverb.

*Antes de **despedirnos** anoche, mi novio y yo nos dimos un beso.*
Before saying goodbye last night, my boyfriend and I kissed.

*Sin **pensar**, hablé.*
Without thinking, I spoke.

3) PRONOUNS AFTER PREPOSITIONS

a) After a preposition, the following pronouns are usually found:

mí	*nosotros, nosotras*
ti	*vosotros, vosotras*
él, ella, Ud.	*ellos, ellas, Uds.*
ello (neuter form)	

Note: There is an accent on *"mí"* to distinguish it from the possessive *"mi."*

 **EXAMPLES:** *Carlos siempre piensa en **mí**.*
Carlos always thinks about me.

*Compré la guayabera para **él**.*
I bought the guayabera (shirt) for him.

*No vengas a la fiesta sin **ellos**.*
Don't come to the party without them.

*¿Tienes miedo de volar? –Yo nunca pienso en **ello**.*
Are you scared of flying? –I never think about it.

¡CUIDADO! After the preposition *"con,"* you will see these special forms:

> *conmigo*
> *contigo*

Note: The other forms are normal: *con él, con nosotros, con ellas, etc.*

 EXAMPLES: *Ellos siempre van **conmigo** a los conciertos de Luis Miguel.*
They always go with me to Luis Miguel concerts.

*Necesito hablar **contigo** ahora.*
I need to speak with you now.

*No voy **con él**, sino con Myrka Dellanos.*
I'm not going with him, but rather with Myrka Dellanos.

¡CUIDADO! Use subject pronouns instead of prepositional pronouns after *"entre"* and *"según."*

EXAMPLES: ***Entre tú** y **yo** hay mucha tensión.*
Between you and me there is a lot of tension.

***Según tú**, no soy discreto.*
According to you, I am not discreet.

b) **If the object of the preposition refers back to the subject**, you will need to use a pronoun from the following list.

These are the reflexive forms used after a preposition:

mí	*nosotros, nosotras*
ti	*vosotros, vosotras*
sí	*sí*

¡CUIDADO! The only exceptions, once again, come after the preposition *"con"*: ***conmigo, contigo, consigo,** con nosotros/nosotras, con vosotros/vosotras, **consigo**.*

EXAMPLES: *Los estudiantes siempre tienen las mochilas **consigo**.*
  The students always have their backpacks along (with themselves).

*Compraste el aceite de oliva para **ti mismo**.*
  You bought the olive oil for yourself.

*Luz Elena González lo hizo para **sí misma**.*
  Luz Elena González did it for herself.

*"Ganamos el campeonato para **nosotros mismos**", dijo el futbolista Xavi Hernández.*
  "We won the championship for ourselves," said the soccer player Xavi Hernández.

*Hacen chocolates por **sí mismos**.*
  They make chocolates by themselves.

Note: The words *"mismo/misma/mismos/mismas"* will often follow the reflexive pronoun for emphasis.

PRACTICE EXERCISES

1. **Write the appropriate preposition, pronoun, possessive adjective, or verb form in the space provided:**

   a. Estoy harto de _____ la música de Daddy Yankee. (listening)

   b. _____ paraguas es muy viejo. (My)

   c. Estoy pensando en _____, amor mío. (you)

   d. Shakira a veces compra regalos inútiles para _____.
   (herself — emphasized)

   e. Estas flores finas son para _____. (you all — familiar)

   f. Tus ilustres amigos quieren ir _____ mañana. (with you)

   g. Los pájaros a veces cantan para _____. (us)

   h. Después de _____ el proyecto sobre Che Guevara, vamos a alquilar el vídeo *Diarios de motocicleta*. (finishing)

i. Los profesores siempre les dan demasiada tarea a _____.
(them)

j. Hay muchas personas infelices que sólo piensan en _____.
(themselves — emphasized)

k. Entre _____ y _____, no me gusta esa corbata
estrecha que lleva Ramón. (you/me)

l. No podemos esquiar mañana. ¿Qué opinas de _____? (it)

2. There are six errors in the following poem; identify and correct them:

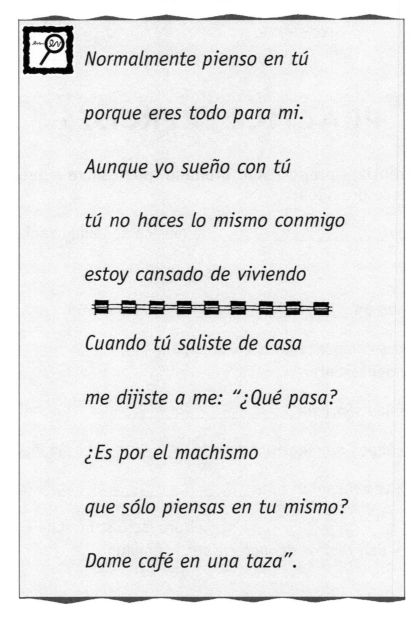

Normalmente pienso en tú

porque eres todo para mi.

Aunque yo sueño con tú

tú no haces lo mismo conmigo

estoy cansado de viviendo

Cuando tú saliste de casa

me dijiste a me: "¿Qué pasa?

¿Es por el machismo

que sólo piensas en tu mismo?

Dame café en una taza".

These two sets of questions use grammatical structures and vocabulary from this lesson. Working with a partner, alternate asking and answering each question. When you get to the bottom of each list, start over at the top, switching roles. As a variation, write out the answers in complete sentences.

A) ¿Adónde vas **después** de las clases?

Según tú, ¿qué equipo profesional de béisbol es el mejor?

Para ti, ¿cuál es el mejor helado?

¿Están tus zapatos **debajo de** tu cama?

¿Estás hablando **conmigo** ahora?

¿Qué mes va **antes de** marzo?

¿Te gusta hacer la tarea **por** ti mismo/misma?

B) ¿**Estás hablando** en inglés o en español ahora?

¿Llegaste a clase **cantando** o **bailando** hoy?

¿**Gritar** en la biblioteca es una buena o una mala idea?

¿Qué **hacían** tus amigos cuando **te acostaste** anoche?

¿Qué clase de libros **leías** cuando **eras** joven?

¿**Estás pidiéndoles** a tus padres más dinero ahora que antes?

¿**Estás pensando** en hacerte profesor de español?

"El poeta de la Gran Vía"

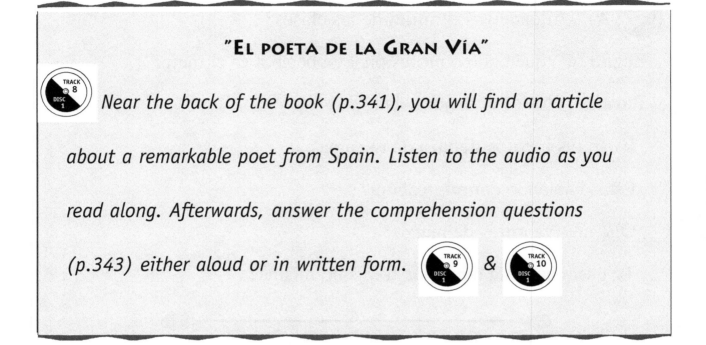

Near the back of the book (p.341), you will find an article about a remarkable poet from Spain. Listen to the audio as you read along. Afterwards, answer the comprehension questions (p.343) either aloud or in written form.

 # PRUEBA DE REPASO

A) EL IMPERFECTO

1. Change these verbs to the corresponding form of the imperfect tense:

a. van → _____   **d.** pido → _____

b. conducimos → _____   **e.** lee → _____

c. queréis → _____   **f.** bailas → _____

2. Use the correct form of the imperfect tense in the following sentences:

a. Me parecía que _____ a llover; por eso no fui a la playa hoy. (ir)

b. Carlos Santana y yo pedimos una pizza grande porque _____ mucha hambre. (tener)

c. Cuando yo _____ joven, visitaba a mi abuela cada domingo. (ser)

d. A mi perrito le _____ roer las zapatillas viejas de mi padre. (gustar)

e. _____ las diez de la mañana cuando Michael Pineda llegó al estadio. (ser)

f. Todos _____ muy nerviosos cuando comenzó el examen. (estar)

3. There are six errors in the following paragraph. Underline and correct them:

Una noche, yo estaba dormiendo cuando, de repente, sonó el teléfono. Pensé que estaba soñando, porque normalmente nadie llamabas a esas horas de la noche. Como el teléfono seguía sonaba, yo supía que esto no era un sueño. Ni mi madre o mi padre estaban en casa. El teléfono continuando sonando. Me levanté y lo contesté. No había nadie, sólo silencio.

B) EL PRETÉRITO Y EL IMPERFECTO

Complete this paragraph by conjugating each infinitive in either the preterite or the imperfect tense. Choose the tense that you believe best captures the feeling of the narrative:

El año pasado, mi familia y yo _____ (pasar) unos días en Washington, D.C. Nosotros _____ (ir) a los museos y también _____ (visitar) la Casa Blanca. El día que fuimos a la Casa Blanca, recuerdo bien que nosotros _____ (levantarse) muy temprano. Primero _____ (comer) un desayuno ligero y luego _____ (salir) en autobús. Aunque todavía _____ (ser) temprano, _____ (hacer) mucho calor porque _____ (ser) verano. Cuando _____ (llegar) a la Casa Blanca, nos sorprendió la cantidad de gente que ya _____ (haber) allí. Nosotros _____ (tener) que hacer cola por casi una hora.

C) EL PROGRESIVO

1. Change these verbs into the corresponding form of the progressive:

a. pagas   → _____

b. duermen → _____

c. lee   → _____

d. servís → _____

e. digo   → _____

f. comía → _____

2. Use the present participle or the infinitive as needed:

a. Nos enamoramos _____ el español juntos. (practicar)

b. _____ es emocionante y educativo. (Viajar)

c. _____ un examen sin estudiar es peligroso. (Tomar)

d. Me puse enfermo _____ tantas patatas fritas. (comer)

D) LOS MANDATOS INFORMALES

1. Change the following sentences to affirmative commands. Choose the appropriate command form based on the subject of each sentence:

a. Tú comes muy rápido. _____

b. Vosotros os sentáis aquí. _____

c. Tú te levantas temprano. _____

d. Tú te pones la gorra de béisbol. _____

e. Vosotros me esperáis en el parque. _____

2. Now change the affirmative commands from the previous exercise to negative commands:

a. _____

b. _____

c. _____

d. _____

e. _____

E) Las preposiciones

1. Write the appropriate preposition, pronoun or verb form in the space provided:

a. Los adolescentes están hartos de _____ a los adultos. (listening)

b. "Este anillo es para _____, Thalía", dijo Tommy Mottola. (you)

c. Es importante lavarse las manos _____ comer. (before)

d. Me encantaría cenar _____ esta noche. (with you, familiar)

e. Preparamos esta tarta para _____. (ourselves, feminine)

f. ¿Quieres dar un paseo en el coche _____? (with me)

g. Después de _____ la película *Apollo 11,* fuimos a tomar un café. (seeing)

h. ¿Te vas al parque con _____? (him)

i. "Ellos no pueden ganar el campeonato sin _____", pensó Albert Pujols. (me)

j. Esa chica sólo se preocupa por _____. (herself, emphasized)

2. There are eight errors of various kinds in the lyrics of this love song. Underline and correct them:

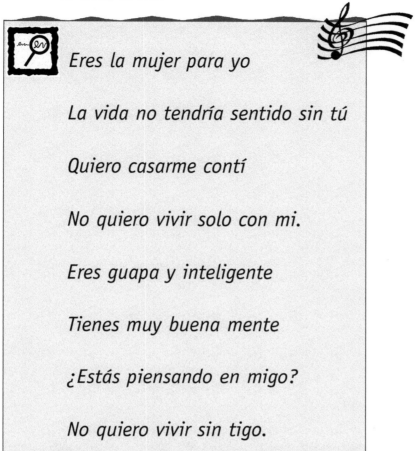

Eres la mujer para yo

La vida no tendría sentido sin tú

Quiero casarme contí

No quiero vivir solo con mi.

Eres guapa y inteligente

Tienes muy buena mente

¿Estás piensando en migo?

No quiero vivir sin tigo.

3. Complete this paragraph by providing the correct form of each verb. ¡CUIDADO! You will have to choose among a present participle, the preterite or the imperfect.

Una vez dentro de la Casa Blanca, nosotros _____ (hacer)

muchas cosas. Un guía flaco nos _____ (enseñar) algunas

salas y oficinas del presidente. ¡_____ (Ser) impresionantes!

Nosotros _____ (pasar) una hora entera _____

(mirar) las fotos, los muebles y los documentos históricos. Durante toda la visita,

el guía seguía _____ (hablar) de la Casa y de los distintos

presidentes que habían vivido allí. Cuando nosotros por fin _____

(salir), ya _____ (ser) la hora de comer.

COLOMBIA

COLOMBIA

CAPITAL:	Bogotá
POBLACIÓN:	47.700.000
GOBIERNO:	república
PRESIDENTE:	Iván Duque Márquez
DINERO ($):	peso colombiano
PRODUCTOS:	azúcar, café, fruta, petróleo
MÚSICA, BAILE:	cumbia, influencia afro-caribeña, salsa
SITIOS DE INTERÉS:	el bosque de lluvia, Cali, Cartagena, Ciudad Perdida, Medellín, San Andrés, Villa de Leiva
COMIDA TÍPICA:	ajiaco, arroz con pollo, canasta de coco, guayaba, mazamorra, sancocho, tamales

COLOMBIANOS FAMOSOS:

Fernando Botero
(ARTISTA)

Gabriel García Márquez
(ESCRITOR)

Cecilia Herrera
(ARTISTA)

Juanes
(CANTANTE)

Juan Pablo Montoya
(ATLETA)

Mariana Pajón
(ATLETA)

Shakira
(CANTANTE)

José Asunción Silva
(POETA)

Camilo Villegas
(ARTISTA)

VOCABULARIO LECCIÓN TRES

ADJETIVOS

libre	free, available	*mudo/a*	mute, dumb
ligero/a	light, nimble	*necio/a*	stupid, foolish
liso/a	smooth, flat	*nublado/a*	cloudy
listo/a	ready, clever, smart	*o(b)scuro/a*	dark, obscure
luminoso/a	bright, brilliant	*obstinado/a (terco/a)*	stubborn, obstinate
lleno/a	full	*occidental*	western
maduro/a	mature, ripe	*opuesto/a*	opposite
maleducado/a	rude	*ordinario/a*	ordinary, common
malcriado/a	ill-bred, spoiled, bad-mannered	*orgulloso/a*	proud
maldito/a	accursed, damned	*oriental*	eastern
manchado/a	stained	*otoñal*	autumnal
maravilloso/a	wonderful, marvelous	*peinado/a*	combed
		pelirrojo/a	red-headed
mediano/a	medium, average	*penoso/a*	painful
melancólico/a	gloomy, melancholy	*perezoso/a*	lazy
		pesado/a	heavy, annoying
mezclado/a	mixed	*pícaro/a*	roguish, rascally
mimado/a	spoiled	*pintoresco/a*	picturesque
modesto/a	modest	*postizo/a*	false, fake
mojado/a	wet	*precioso/a*	precious, cute
moreno/a	brunette, brown, dark-haired, dark-skinned		

LECCIÓN TRES

KEY GRAMMAR CONCEPTS

A) EL PRESENTE PERFECTO → *The present perfect*

B) EL PLUSCUAMPERFECTO → *The pluperfect*

C) EL FUTURO Y EL FUTURO PERFECTO → *The future and future perfect*

D) EL CONDICIONAL Y EL CONDICIONAL PERFECTO → *The conditional and conditional perfect*

E) LOS PARTICIPIOS PASADOS COMO ADJETIVOS → *Past participles as adjectives*

A) EL PRESENTE PERFECTO

The **present perfect** is a very common tense in Spanish, and especially so in Spain. It is used to describe actions begun in the past that, from the speaker's perspective, have finished recently or have continued until now. Actions in the present perfect are connected in some way to the present; their effects are still with you.

EXAMPLES: *"**He desayunado** con Gerard Piqué", dijo Shakira.*
"I have eaten breakfast today with Gerard Piqué," said Shakira.

***Se han mejorado** este año.*
They have improved this year.

*El cantante colombiano Juanes **ha contestado** el teléfono.*
The Colombian singer Juanes has answered the telephone.

*Los chicos me **han llamado** hoy.*
The boys have called me today.

Contrast with preterite:

Santa Claus vino el año pasado.
Santa Claus came last year.

*Santa Claus **ha venido** este año.*
Santa Claus has come this year.

HOW IS THE PRESENT PERFECT TENSE FORMED?

This tense is a compound formed with the present tense of *"haber"* (the auxiliary verb meaning "to have") and the past participle of a verb.

The present tense of *"haber"* is:

he	hemos
has	habéis
ha	han

Past participles of regular verbs are formed by taking off the last two letters of the infinitive and adding *"-ado"* to **-AR** verbs and *"-ido"* to **-ER** and **-IR** verbs.

Past participles of regular verbs:

HABLAR	COMER	VIVIR
habl**ado**	com**ido**	viv**ido**

The present perfect tense, then, of these verbs is:

he hablado	hemos hablado	he comido	hemos comido	he vivido	hemos vivido
has hablado	habéis hablado	has comido	habéis comido	has vivido	habéis vivido
ha hablado	han hablado	ha comido	han comido	ha vivido	han vivido

Object pronouns will precede *he-has-ha-hemos-habéis-han*.

❋ **EXAMPLE:**   *Los chicos **me** han hablado hoy.*
        The boys have talked to me today.

        *¿Por qué no **te** has sentado todavía?*
        Why haven't you sat down yet?

There are a number of verbs with irregular past participles in Spanish. Some students find the following trick helpful in remembering the most common verbs with irregular forms: Think of an imaginary person named **Reverend Mac**, who has a **Ph.D.**

The most common irregular past participles:

Roto	→	*(Romper)*
Escrito	→	*(Escribir)*
Vuelto	→	*(Volver)*
Visto	→	*(Ver)*
Muerto	→	*(Morir)*
Abierto	→	*(Abrir)*
Cubierto	→	*(Cubrir)*
Puesto	→	*(Poner)*
Hecho	→	*(Hacer)*
Dicho	→	*(Decir)*
Descubierto	→	*(Descubrir)*

Note: Three verbs have two past participles:

1) *freír* (to fry) *(freído, frito)* Use either past participle in perfect tenses *(Hemos **frito** los huevos; Hemos **freído** los huevos)*, but use "*frito*" exclusively as an adjective *(Me gustan los huevos **fritos**)*.

2) *imprimir* (to print) *(imprimido, impreso)* Use either past participle in perfect tenses *(He **imprimido** el documento; He **impreso** el documento)*, but use "*impreso*" exclusively as an adjective *(Tengo toda la tarea **impresa** y lista para entregar)*.

3) *proveer* (to provide) *(proveído, provisto)* Here you can use either form, both in perfect tenses *(Hemos **proveído** los números; Hemos **provisto** los números)*, and as adjectives *(Las mantas **proveídas** en el hotel son de lana; Las mantas **provistas** en el hotel son se lana)*.

There are also some past participles that have an accent mark:

caer → *caído*	*oír* → *oído*
creer → *creído*	*reír* → *reído*
leer → *leído*	*traer* → *traído*

 Do you see what these six infinitives have in common?

No matter what the subject is, the past participle in all perfect tenses will end with the letter "o." This past participle is part of the verb and will <u>not</u> agree with the subject.

✶ **EXAMPLE:** *Dolores ha **comido** la torta.*

Note: "Dolores ha comida la torta" is wrong!

Helpful Tip: All perfect tenses would be loved by Santa Claus. They all start with the letter "h" and end with the letter "o."

i.e., <u>**H**</u>e comid<u>**o**</u>, <u>**H**</u>as estudiad<u>**o**</u>, <u>**H**</u>an escrit<u>**o**</u> → **¡Ho-Ho-Ho!**

1. **Write the appropriate form of the present perfect in the space provided:**

   a. Nosotros _____ demasiado este año. (trabajar)

   b. Tú _____ el lápiz. (romper)

   c. Uds. nunca _____ la Estatua de la Libertad. (ver)

   d. El golfista Camilo Villegas _____ unos trofeos impresionantes este año. (recibir)

   e. Los atletas cubanos _____ muchas medallas de oro. (ganar)

   f. Yo _____ en la silla pequeña. (sentarse)

   g. Vosotros _____ muchas mentiras en la escuela. (decir)

   h. Nosotros no _____ terminar el proyecto pesado. (querer)

   i. Isabel Allende _____ muchos libros buenos recientemente. (escribir)

   j. Mis padres siempre _____ en hablar conmigo sobre mi futuro. (insistir)

2. **The following paragraph contains six errors; identify and correct them:**

   Hoy ha seído un día muy difícil para mí. Primero, mi madre me ha

   hablada por teléfono. Ella nunca está contenta con lo que hago.

   Segundo, se me ha olvidados escribirles una carta a mis abuelos. Luego,

   me he peleado con mi hermano menor, Carlos. Siempre me molesta y hoy

me a insultado mucho. También, mi perro ha rompido mi lámpara

favorita. Además, mi novio todavía no ha volvido de su viaje y no voy a

poder ir al cine esta noche. ¡Qué día! Voy a volver a la cama.

B) EL PLUSCUAMPERFECTO

The **pluperfect** is used to describe an action that occurred in the past <u>before</u> a specific point in time or <u>before</u> another action had begun.

EXAMPLES: *Ayer, antes de las tres, yo **había hablado** con Michelle Bachelet, expresidenta de Chile.*
Before three o'clock yesterday, I had spoken with Michelle Bachelet, the former president of Chile.

***Habíamos terminado** de comer antes de ver la Copa Mundial en la tele.*
We had finished eating before watching World Cup soccer on television.

On a time line, the first pluperfect sentence would look like this:

<————————x——————————x——————————x————————>

| *Yo había hablado* | *a las tres* | *presente* |
| *con Michelle Bachelet* | *ayer* | |

Here are some more pluperfect sentences:

EXAMPLES: *¿**Habías estudiado** español antes de asistir al colegio?*
Had you studied Spanish before attending high school?

***Habíamos terminado** la tarea antes de las seis.*
We had finished the homework before six.

*Yo ya **había aprendido** a bailar el tango mucho antes de conocerte.*
I had already learned to dance the tango long before meeting you.

HOW IS THE PLUPERFECT TENSE FORMED?

This tense is also a compound one, formed with the imperfect tense of *"haber"* (the auxiliary verb meaning "to have") and the past participle of a verb.

Imperfect of *"haber"*		+	Past participle
había	*habíamos*		*hablado*
habías	*habíais*		*comido*
había	*habían*		*vivido*

The pluperfect, then, is a combination of these forms of *"haber"* with a past participle: *había hablado, habías hablado, etc.*

Helpful Tip: The word *"ya"* meaning "already" is often found in a pluperfect (or present perfect) sentence. (***Ya** había ido de compras antes del mediodía.* I had already gone shopping before noon.)

 PRACTICE EXERCISES

1. Write a form of the pluperfect in the space provided:

a. Marisela _____ a su novio cariñoso muchas veces antes de despedirse de él. (besar)

b. Jorge pensaba que _____ una nueva estrella luminosa. (descubrir)

c. Antes de llegar el profesor, las chicas me _____ algo de interés. (contar)

d. Antes de entrar en la universidad, nosotros nunca _____ nada ilegal. (hacer)

e. Cuando volví a casa, mi abuela ya me _____ una torta de chocolate. (preparar)

f. ¿ _____ (tú) ya los exámenes antes de la reunión? (corregir)

g. Uds. _____ el coche en el estacionamiento cuando, de repente, empezó a llover. (dejar)

h. Cuando me ofrecieron los dulces, yo ya _____ los dientes. (cepillarse)

i. A la edad de quince años, el cantante Juanes ya _____ a bailar bien. (aprender)

2. The following paragraph contains six errors; identify and correct them:

Ya conocía a algunos chicos de este pueblo antes de mudarme aquí. José me habían llamado dos veces por teléfono y Ramón me había veído en la playa el verano pasado. Los dos me parecían bastante guapos aunque no eran muy divertidos. Había oido que eran miembros del mismo equipo de béisbol. Los dos habían queridos tener una cita conmigo, pero nunca me habían interesado sus peticiones. José nunca había salidos con chicas antes y Ramón abía salido con una chica diferente cada fin de semana. Naturalmente, nunca más voy a salir con ellos.

This section will consider:

1) The future tense

2) The future of conjecture

3) The future perfect

1) The future tense

The **future** is used to describe actions that will occur subsequent to the present time.

There are three ways to talk about an action in the future.

1 **The present indicative**

Often an adverb of time will tell when the action will occur.

> **Examples:** *Jeremy Lin y Ricky Rubio **llegan mañana**.*
> Jeremy Lin and Ricky Rubio are arriving tomorrow.
>
> *Esos chicos necios **vienen más tarde**.*
> Those foolish kids are coming later.

2 **The immediate future**

This construction is used frequently to describe an action in the future. The immediate future normally refers to an event that, in the speaker's mind, will occur relatively soon. You simply conjugate the present tense of *"ir"* and add the preposition *"a"* and an infinitive.

> | *voy* | *vamos* | | | |
> |-------|---------|---|---|---|
> | *vas* | *vais* | **+** | **"a"** **+** | **infinitive** |
> | *va* | *van* | | | |

> **Examples:** *Sofía Vergara **va a llamarme** esta tarde.*
> Sofía Vergara is going to call me this afternoon.
>
> *Gloria Estefan **va a dar** un concierto este fin de semana.*
> Gloria Estefan is going to give a concert this weekend.
>
> *Mis padres, que son muy tercos, no **van a comprarme** el traje que quiero.*
> My very stubborn parents are not going to buy me the suit that I want.

3 The true future

The true future describes events that may be somewhat further away in time in the speaker's mind.

EXAMPLES: *Los seres humanos **vivirán** en la Luna para el año 2050.*
Humans will live on the Moon by the year 2050.

*Nos **graduaremos** en dos años.*
We will graduate in two years.

*Mis padres nunca me **permitirán** conducir su coche nuevo.*
My parents will never let me drive their new car.

*El astrólogo Walter Mercado **ganará** mucho dinero.*
The astrologist Walter Mercado will earn a lot of money.

HOW IS THE FUTURE TENSE FORMED?

1 Regular verbs

HABLAR		COMER		VIVIR	
hablaré	hablaremos	comeré	comeremos	viviré	viviremos
hablarás	hablaréis	comerás	comeréis	vivirás	viviréis
hablará	hablarán	comerá	comerán	vivirá	vivirán

Note: As you can see, **-AR**, **-ER**, and **-IR** verbs all have the same endings. These endings are added to the infinitive. All conjugations have accent marks, with the exception of the *"nosotros/nosotras"* form.

Look at these verb endings in isolation:

é	emos
ás	éis
á	án

Do they remind you of any form that you have already learned? Think of the present tense of the verb *"haber"*:

h*e*	h*emos*
h*as*	hab*éis*
h*a*	h*an*

Helpful Tip: If you ever forget the future endings, try to remember the present tense of *"haber"*!

2 Irregular verbs

Some verbs have irregular forms in the future. Fortunately, the endings for these verbs are exactly the same as the endings of regular verbs. The only changes happen in the stem of the verb.

Here are the forms for irregular verbs in the future:

HACER		SABER		SALIR	
haré	haremos	sabré	sabremos	saldré	saldremos
harás	haréis	sabrás	sabréis	saldrás	saldréis
hará	harán	sabrá	sabrán	saldrá	saldrán

Once you have learned the *"yo"* forms of the irregular futures, you can figure out all of the other forms because the endings are always the same. The irregular stem is constant in all forms. Here are the ones that you should know.

The irregular verbs fall into these three categories:

1. **Verbs with special stems**
   decir → *diré, etc. . . .*
   hacer → *haré*

2. **Verbs that lose the infinitive ending vowel (e)**
   caber → *cabré*
   haber → *habré*
   poder → *podré*
   querer → *querré*
   saber → *sabré*

3. **Verbs in which the infinitive ending vowel ("e" or "i") is replaced by "d"**
   poner → *pondré*
   salir → *saldré*
   tener → *tendré*
   valer → *valdré*
   venir → *vendré*

2) THE FUTURE OF CONJECTURE

When a verb tense doesn't match real time, it takes on a special meaning. When the <u>future</u> tense refers to the <u>present</u>, it expresses conjecture or wondering.

EXAMPLES: *¿Qué hora será?*
   I wonder what time it is.

   Plácido Domingo estará en casa ahora escuchando su álbum, Songs.
   Plácido Domingo probably is at home now listening to his album, *Songs*.

   ¿Quién será?
   I wonder who it is? (Who could that be?)

   Tendrás hambre ahora.
   You must be hungry now.

3) THE FUTURE PERFECT

The **future perfect** describes an event that will take place prior to another event, or before a time in the future.

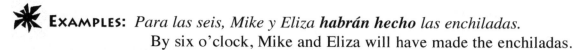 **EXAMPLES:** *Para las seis, Mike y Eliza **habrán hecho** las enchiladas.*
By six o'clock, Mike and Eliza will have made the enchiladas.

*Antes de las siete **nos habremos cepillado** los dientes.*
Before seven we will have brushed our teeth.

*Los chicos lo **habrán entendido** todo.*
The kids will have understood it all.

HOW IS THIS COMPOUND TENSE FORMED?

It's simple. Use the future tense of "haber" with a past participle:

Future of *"haber"*	+	Past participle
habré habremos		**hablado**
habrás habréis		**comido**
habrá habrán		**vivido**

 # PRACTICE EXERCISES ▶

1. Fill in the spaces with one of the ways to express the future:

a. En el año 2024 las Olimpiadas _____ lugar en Paris. (tener)

b. Luego, nosotros _____ la película *Avengers: Endgame*. (ver)

c. Tú _____ la maldita tarea para las seis. (terminar)

d. Alguien está llamando a la puerta. ¿Quién _____? (ser)

e. Los chicos perezosos me _____ el libro en tres años. (devolver)

f. Yo _____ una torta de almendra para su fiesta de cumpleaños. (hacer)

g. Vosotros _____ a las cinco de la tarde. (salir)

h. Mi madre me _____ para el primer día de mi campamento. (escribir)

i. ¿No me _____ uno de tus secretos íntimos? (contar)

j. No estoy seguro, pero probablemente ellos _____ tiempo libre. (tener)

2. Conjugate the following verbs in the appropriate tense:

    decir (futuro)   **comprender** (futuro perfecto)   **hacer** (futuro inmediato)

_____   _____   _____

_____   _____   _____

_____   _____   _____

_____   _____   _____

_____   _____   _____

_____   _____   _____

3. The following narrative contains six errors. Identify them and correct them:

Voy llamar a mi amiga Marisa. Estoy seguro de que habrá llegada a casa. Sé que irá a salir un poco después de las dos porque tiene una entrevista importantísima. Esta tarde va a hablar con el representante de una universidad. Me ha dicho que en el futuro ella asistiré a la Universidad Nacional de Colombia. Dice también que un día nosotras seramos actrices famosas. Un momento. Están llamando a la puerta. ¿Quién serán?

D) EL CONDICIONAL Y EL CONDICIONAL PERFECTO

This section will consider:

1) THE CONDITIONAL TENSE

2) THE CONDITIONAL OF CONJECTURE

3) THE CONDITIONAL PERFECT

1) THE CONDITIONAL TENSE

a) The conditional is used to explain what would happen in a **hypothetical situation**.

> **EXAMPLES:** *Iría al teatro para ver* Harry Potter and the Cursed Child *si tuviera un boleto.*
> I would go to the theater to see *Harry Potter and the Cursed Child* if I had a ticket.
>
> ***Comeríamos** los aguacates si estuvieran maduros.*
> We would eat the avocados if they were ripe.
>
> **Note:** In these examples, the imperfect subjunctive is used after the word *"si."* This construction will be covered in *Lección Seis*.

b) The conditional is also commonly used **to describe an action subsequent to another past action or to a time in the past**. In the same way that the present and the future are linked *(Dices que lloverá),* so, too, are the past and the conditional *(Dijiste que llovería);* the conditional has been called "the future of the past."

> **EXAMPLES:** *Anoche Ramona me dijo que **llegaría** a las tres hoy.*
> Last night Ramona told me that she would arrive at three today.
>
> *Mis amigos me informaron que **comprarían** la tienda de campaña más tarde.*
> My friends informed me that they would buy the tent later.

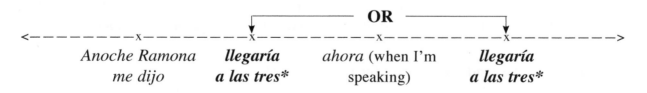

Note: On this time line, you can see the first example shown. Last night, Ramona told me that she would be arriving in the future (at three o'clock today). *Three o'clock, of course, can be either before or after the moment when I'm speaking.

c) The conditional is used, finally, **to make a softened or polite request**, such as in a restaurant or on the telephone.

❋ EXAMPLES: *Me **gustaría** hablar con el hombre de los dientes postizos, por favor.*
   I'd like to speak with the man with false teeth, please.

   ***Deberías** estudiar más si quieres tener buenas notas.*
   You should study more if you want to have good grades.

   *¿**Podría** Ud. decirme cuándo sale el próximo avión para Bogotá?*
   Could you (Would you be able) tell me when the next plane leaves for Bogotá?

HOW IS THE CONDITIONAL TENSE FORMED?

1 Regular verbs

HABLAR		COMER		VIVIR	
hablaría	hablaríamos	comería	comeríamos	viviría	viviríamos
hablarías	hablaríais	comerías	comeríais	vivirías	viviríais
hablaría	hablarían	comería	comerían	viviría	vivirían

Helpful Tips: **1)** As you can see, **-AR**, **-ER**, and **-IR** verbs all have the same endings. All forms have accent marks.
2) The endings are added to the **infinitive** of each verb. Where have you seen these endings before? The imperfect of **-ER** and **-IR** verbs!

2 Irregular verbs

The following verbs have irregular stems in the conditional. These are the same verbs that are irregular in the future tense. Fortunately, the endings of regular and irregular conditional verbs are the same. The only changes are in the stem of the verb.

Here are the conditional forms for irregular verbs:

HACER		SABER		SALIR	
haría	haríamos	sabría	sabríamos	saldría	saldríamos
harías	haríais	sabrías	sabríais	saldrías	saldríais
haría	harían	sabría	sabrían	saldría	saldrían

Once you have learned the *"yo"* forms of the irregular conditionals, you can figure out all of the other conjugations. The irregularity stays constant in all forms, just as in the future tense.

The irregular verbs fall into three categories:

1. Verbs with special stems

    decir → *diría, etc. . . .*

    hacer → *haría*

2. Verbs that lose the infinitive ending vowel (e)

    caber → *cabría*

    haber → *habría*

    poder → *podría*

    querer → *querría*

    saber → *sabría*

3. Verbs in which the infinitive ending vowel ("e" or "i") is replaced by "d"

    poner → *pondría*

    salir → *saldría*

    tener → *tendría*

    valer → *valdría*

    venir → *vendría*

Note: These verbs are grouped in the same three categories as in the future tense.

2) THE CONDITIONAL OF CONJECTURE

The **conditional tense** is also used to express conjecture or wonder about past events. You use the conditional tense to describe an action that <u>may have happened</u> in the past. The "clash" of tenses (using the conditional, when the preterite or imperfect would be expected) creates what is called the conditional of conjecture.

✳ **EXAMPLES:** *¿Qué hora **sería**?*

    I wonder what time it was. (What time was it probably?)

    *¿Dónde estaba la chica pelirroja ayer?—**Estaría** en casa.*

    Where was the red-headed girl yesterday?—She was probably at home.

3) THE CONDITIONAL PERFECT

The **conditional perfect** describes an event that would have taken place if something else had happened.

✳ **EXAMPLES:** ***Habríamos entendido** la gramática si hubiéramos estudiado un poco más.*

    We would have understood the grammar if we had studied a little more.

    ***Habría comido** las galletas si hubiera comprado leche.*

    I would have eaten the cookies if I had bought milk.

Note: In these examples, another compound tense called the pluperfect subjunctive is used after the word *"si."* This tense will be covered fully in *Lección Seis*.

It's easy. Use the conditional tense of "haber" with a past participle:

Conditional of *"haber"*		+	Past participle
habría	*habríamos*		*hablado*
habrías	*habríais*		*comido*
habría	*habrían*		*vivido*

PRACTICE EXERCISES

1. **Choose between the conditional and conditional perfect tenses:**

   a. El poeta melancólico anunció que nunca más _____ sonetos tristes. (escribir)

   b. Si hubiera llegado antes, yo _____ mi nuevo álbum de Calle 13. (escuchar)

   c. No estoy seguro, pero _____ las ocho cuando llegaron a la fiesta. (ser)

   d. Yo _____ a tu casita cerca de la playa si lloviera hoy. (ir)

   e. Los pájaros _____ si no se hubieran asustado tanto. (cantar)

   f. Los oficiales anunciaron que Megan Rapinoe, una de las mejores futbolistas del mundo, _____ hablar con la prensa más tarde. (poder)

   g. Le dije a mi madre que _____ los dientes antes de acostarme. (cepillarse)

   h. Me _____ aprender más sobre la vida de Simón Bolívar. (gustar)

   i. Mi compañero de cuarto dijo que él _____ la mesa más tarde. (poner)

   j. _____ decirle a María que la amo, pero no me atrevo. (Querer)

2. Conjugate the following verbs in the appropriate tense:

tener (condicional)   **ir** (condicional perfecto)   **satisfacer*** (condicional)

_____   _____   _____

_____   _____   _____

_____   _____   _____

_____   _____   _____

_____   _____   _____

_____   _____   _____

*Note: This verb, meaning "to satisfy," conjugates in all tenses like "*hacer*."

3. The following paragraph contains five errors; identify and correct them:

Cuando era niño, mi padre me dijo que un día me llevaria a ver un desfile en Chicago. Una mañana nublada y oscura de verano, mi papá me informó que poderíamos ir. Fuimos al centro de Chicago en tren. Como era tan joven, no tuve que pagar. ¡Qué bueno!, porque habería costado mucho. Cuando llegamos, le dije a un señor: "Por favor, quería ir al baño". El señor dijo: "No hay baños". Mi padre exclamó: "¡Caramba!". Lloré y le dije que me gustarría volver a casa.

E) LOS PARTICIPIOS PASADOS COMO ADJETIVOS

Earlier in this lesson we learned that past participles are used with *"haber"* to form perfect tenses: the present perfect, pluperfect, future perfect, and conditional perfect. Past participles in these tenses are part of the verb, and always end with the letter *"o."*

Past participles are also commonly used as **adjectives**, modifying nouns. These past participles will always agree with the nouns they modify; as a consequence, they will end with *"o," "a," "os,"* or *"as."*

EXAMPLES: *La biblioteca está **abierta**.*
The library is open.

*Los libros **cerrados** no enseñan nada.*
Closed books don't teach anything.

*El chico **cubierto** de chocolate es mi hijo, Jamie.*
The boy covered with chocolate is my son, Jamie.

*Las lenguas **habladas** me parecen más prácticas.*
Spoken languages seem more practical to me.

Past participles function grammatically as adjectives when used with:

◆ *"ser"* to form the passive voice (see *Lección Seis*)
◆ *"estar"* to describe a completed action or resultant state

EXAMPLES: *La carrera fue **ganada** por el atleta de los zapatos dorados.*
The race was won by the athlete with the golden shoes.

*El contestador automático está **roto**.*
The answering machine is broken.

PRACTICE EXERCISES

1. Write the proper form of the past participle in the following sentences:

a. Un lápiz _____ no sirve para nada. (romper)

b. Hemos _____ una isla pintoresca. (descubrir)

¡CUIDADO! Remember "Ho-Ho-Ho!"

c. ¿Están Uds. listos? La comida ya está _____. (hacer)

d. En boca _____ no entran moscas. (cerrar)

e. Mis almacenes favoritos, Macy's y Bloomingdale's, están _____ los domingos. (abrir)

f. Gracias a Dios, los animales _____ no habían sufrido mucho. (morir)

g. La mesa, _____ con un mantel nuevo, estaba muy linda. (cubrir)

h. Las cartas preciosas, _____ por los chicos, están en la mesa. (escribir)

i. Isabel y Marcos, otra vez habéis _____ demasiado tarde. (volver)

j. Las nuevas luces ya están _____ en la calle. (poner)

2. Identify the four errors in this beautiful poem and correct them:

La cama hecho

es bonita.

Los tacos quemado

son feos.

He escrita mucha poesía,

aunque no tengo talento.

Ahora este poema está hacida.

These two sets of questions use grammatical structures and vocabulary from this lesson. Working with a partner, alternate asking and answering each question. When you get to the bottom of each list, start over at the top, switching roles. As a variation, write out the answers in complete sentences.

A) ¿Cuál de tus clases es la más **pesada**?

¿Eres una persona **modesta**?

¿Tienes muchas ideas **luminosas**?

¿Te has sentido alguna vez **libre** como el viento?

¿Qué país **occidental** crees que tiene más petróleo, Estados Unidos o Venezuela?

¿De qué estás muy **orgulloso/a**?

¿Qué haces en un día **ordinario**?

B) ¿Dónde **vivirás** en el año 2040?

¿A qué hora **saldrás** de tu casa mañana?

¿Qué te **darán** tus amigos para tu cumpleaños este año?

Después de clase, ¿me **dirás** un secreto?

¿**Habrá** gente viviendo en la Luna en el año 2060?

¿**Podrás** ir conmigo a la tienda este fin de semana para comprar ese álbum increíble de Shakira?

No has comido nada hoy. Pues, **tendrás** hambre, ¿verdad?

A) EL PRESENTE PERFECTO

1. Change these verbs into the correct form of the present perfect tense:

   a. escribes → _____

   b. hacen → _____

   c. vemos → _____

   d. come → _____

   e. creo → _____

2. Complete these sentences using the appropriate form of the present perfect tense:

   a. Nosotros _____ dos horas para llegar aquí. (conducir)

   b. ¿_____ (tú) el secreto de la eterna juventud?
   (Descubrir)

   c. Yo _____ la mesa; ya es hora de comer. (poner)

   d. Hoy mi hijo _____ cuarenta dólares lavando coches.
   (ganar)

   e. ¡Perdonad, no he oído nada! ¿Qué me _____? (decir)

   f. Mis primos _____ a visitarnos esta mañana. (venir)

   g. Javier _____ muchísimo esta noche; le encanta esta
   nueva música tejana. (bailar)

   h. Los vecinos todavía no _____ de Europa. (volver)

3. The following letter contains eight errors. Underline and correct them:

Querida Nuria:

¿Cómo estás? Hace mucho tiempo que no tengo noticias tuyas. Yo tampoco te he escribido este mes. Es que he estada muy ocupada, estudiendo inglés por las mañanas e trabajando en un restaurante por las tardes. Todavía no he conocida a mucha gente aquí en Palo Alto. Ayer me llamó Jaime desde Santiago. ¡Me encantó hablar con el! Dice que ha leido una novela de Gabriel García Márquez. ¿La has leído tú? No he tenido tiempo de leer ni novelas o periódicos. Llámame pronto. ¡Me vuelvo loca!

Un abrazo,

Chita

B) EL PLUSCUAMPERFECTO

1. **Complete these sentences with the correct form of the pluperfect tense:**

   a. Cuando llegué a casa, mi familia ya _____. (cenar)

   b. Aunque los estudiantes _____ el imperfecto antes, todavía no lo comprendían bien. (estudiar)

   c. Eran las cinco de la tarde y el sol ya se _____. (poner)

   d. Antes de ir a Aruba, María Teresa nunca _____ fuera de su país. (estar)

   e. Yo creía que ellas _____ la verdad, pero no toda la verdad. (decir)

   f. ¿Vosotros ya _____ al supermercado antes de venir aquí? (ir)

   g. A la edad de diez años, yo no _____ jamás la nieve. (ver)

   h. Para el año 1966, Gabriel García Márquez todavía no _____ su obra maestra, *Cien años de soledad*. (completar)

2. **Translate the following sentences:**

   a. I had never studied a foreign language before attending high school.

   _____

   _____

   b. When the first class ended, we had already learned the days of the week.

   _____

   _____

   c. They told me that they had always been lucky in Reno.

   _____

C) El futuro y el futuro perfecto

1. Complete these sentences using either the future or future perfect tense:

a. El teléfono nunca suena a estas horas. ¿Quién _____? (ser)

b. Mi hermano menor _____ la cena esta noche. (preparar)

c. Para el final de este semestre, esta clase _____ todos los verbos irregulares. (aprender)

d. ¿_____ los invitados llegar a nuestra casa sin mapa? (Saber)

e. ¿Tú me _____ cuando estés en Cartagena? (escribir)

f. ¿Vosotros _____ tiempo este fin de semana para ver la película de Almodóvar, *Julieta?* (tener)

g. El vuelo _____ para París dentro de unos minutos. (salir)

h. Mañana hará mucho calor. Los niños _____ ir a la piscina. (querer)

2. The following paragraph has eight errors. Underline and correct them:

Este fin de semana voy a visitar a mis abuelos en Vermont. Mi hermana y mí pasaramos dos días allí en las montañas. A nuestros nos gusta mucho pasar tiempo en casa de los abuelos por qué siempre hay mucho que hacer. Dicen que el viernes por la noche nevaré en las montañas. Si nieva, vamos a esquiamos el sábado. El sábado por la noche habrá otra nevada. Para el domingo, habrá nevar mucho y ¡habramos esquiado dos días enteros!

D) EL CONDICIONAL Y EL CONDICIONAL PERFECTO

1. **Choose between the conditional and conditional perfect tenses in the following sentences:**

   a. Mis padres dijeron que me _____ un iPhone nuevo. (comprar)

   b. La maestra dijo que no nos _____ tarea para las vacaciones. (dar)

   c. Le prometí a mi madre que _____ la habitación este sábado. (limpiar)

   d. ¡Nosotros nunca _____ aprender todas estas palabras para mañana! (poder)

   e. ¿Te _____ ir al concierto de Maluma? (gustar)

   f. Si vosotros hubierais estudiado más, no _____ estas notas tan malas. (sacar)*

   *Note: The pluperfect subjunctive is used here after *"si,"* which means you usually use the conditional perfect, but the pluperfect subjunctive is possible, too!

   g. Anoche llamaron a la puerta a las once y media. Me pregunto quién

   _____. (ser)

2. **Translate the following sentences using the conditional:**

   a. Could you (familiar) please pass me the salad?

   _____

   b. Ernest might have been at home yesterday.

   _____

   c. I'd like to travel to Cartagena.

   _____

E) Los participios pasados como adjetivos

1. Write the correct form of the past participle in the following sentences:

a. El hombre _____ de rojo es el malo de la película. (vestir)

b. En puerta _____ no entran ladrones. (cerrar)

c. La mesa está _____ para cuatro personas. (poner)

d. Las luces están _____ y parece que no hay nadie en casa. (apagar)

e. Antes los supermercados no estaban _____ los domingos. (abrir)

f. Los estudiantes _____ cerca de las ventanas tienen frío. (sentar)

g. No podemos ver el programa porque el televisor está _____ (romper)

h. La novela todavía no está _____ al inglés. (traducir)

i. Estas papas _____ están muy sabrosas. (freír)

2. There are ten errors of various kinds in the lyrics to this love song. Underline and correct them:

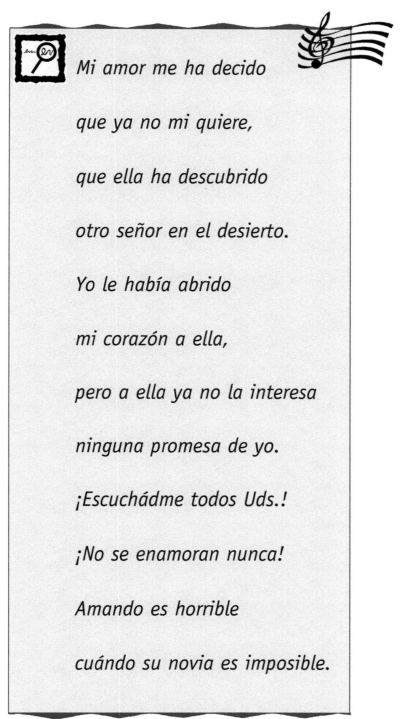

Mi amor me ha decido

que ya no mi quiere,

que ella ha descubrido

otro señor en el desierto.

Yo le había abrido

mi corazón a ella,

pero a ella ya no la interesa

ninguna promesa de yo.

¡Escuchádme todos Uds.!

¡No se enamoran nunca!

Amando es horrible

cuándo su novia es imposible.

ARGENTINA

ARGENTINA

CAPITAL:	Buenos Aires
POBLACIÓN:	44.500.000
GOBIERNO:	república federal representativa
PRESIDENTE:	Mauricio Macri
DINERO ($):	peso argentino
PRODUCTOS:	agricultura, carne, petróleo
MÚSICA, BAILE:	milonga, tango, zamba
SITIOS DE INTERÉS:	Los Andes, la Casa Rosada, las Cataratas del Iguazú, La Pampa, Patagonia
COMIDA TÍPICA:	arroz con pollo, churrasco, empanadas, locro, mate, parrillada

ARGENTINOS FAMOSOS:

Jorge Mario Bergoglio
(PAPA FRANCISCO)

Jorge Luis Borges
(ESCRITOR)

Julio Cortázar
(ESCRITOR)

Raquel Forner
(ARTISTA)

Manu Ginóbili
(ATLETA)

Diego Maradona
(FUTBOLISTA)

Lionel Messi
(FUTBOLISTA)

Juan y Evita Perón
(POLÍTICOS)

Manuel Puig
(ESCRITOR)

Gabriela Sabatini
(TENISTA)

VOCABULARIO LECCIÓN CUATRO

ADJETIVOS

preciso/a	necessary, precise, clear	*seco/a*	dry
profundo/a	deep	*seguro/a*	sure, secure
propio/a	own, proper	*semanal*	weekly
protegido/a	protected	*semejante*	similar
pulido/a	polished	*sencillo/a*	simple
quebrado/a	broken	*separado/a*	separate
querido/a	dear	*serio/a*	serious
raro/a	rare, strange	*siguiente*	following, next
real	real, royal	*simpático/a*	nice, pleasant
reciente	recent	*soberbio/a*	proud, haughty
redondo/a	round	*solo/a*	alone, lonely
remoto/a	remote	*sordo/a*	deaf
risueño/a	smiling, cheerful	*soso/a*	lacking salt, bland
rizado/a	curly		
rubio/a	blond(e)	*suave*	soft, smooth
ruidoso/a	noisy	*suelto/a*	loose
sabio/a	wise, learned	*superior*	superior, upper
sagrado/a	sacred	*tonto/a*	foolish, silly
salado/a	salty	*tranquilo/a*	calm, peaceful
salvo/a	safe	*verdadero/a*	true, real
sano/a	healthy	*vulgar*	common, ordinary
satisfecho/a	satisfied	*zurdo/a*	left-handed

LECCIÓN CUATRO

KEY GRAMMAR CONCEPTS	**A)** **EL PRESENTE DEL SUBJUNTIVO** (LOS MANDATOS DIRECTOS, LOS MANDATOS INDIRECTOS, CÓMO SE CONJUGAN) → *The present subjunctive (its use with direct commands, indirect commands, how to conjugate)*
	B) **LOS PRONOMBRES COMPLEMENTOS** (REFLEXIVOS, INDIRECTOS, DIRECTOS, DOS PRONOMBRES) → *Object pronouns (reflexive, indirect, direct, double object pronouns)*
	C) **LOS ACONTECIMIENTOS INESPERADOS** → *Unintentional events*
	D) **LAS COMPARACIONES IGUALES Y DESIGUALES** → *Equal and unequal comparisons*

A) EL PRESENTE DEL SUBJUNTIVO

The **subjunctive mood** is used a great deal in Spanish. While the subjunctive is used occasionally in English, most of us are not really aware of it (e.g., God **bless** you; They insist we **be** here early; I require that he **study** his algebra). This lesson will consider the use of the subjunctive with direct and indirect commands.

1) FORMS FOR ALL FORMAL AND ALL NEGATIVE FAMILIAR COMMANDS —
The present subjunctive is used with:

◆ all formal commands *"Ud./Uds."* (+/–)
◆ "we" commands (e.g., Let's eat!), *"nosotros/nosotras"* (+/–)
◆ all negative familiar commands: *"tú"* (–) and *"vosotros/vosotras"* (–)

✳ EXAMPLES:

*¡**Estudie** Ud. las siguientes fórmulas!*
Study the following formulas!

*¡**Caminen** Uds. más despacio!*
Walk more slowly!

*¡**Escríbannos** Uds. inmediatamente!*
Write to us immediately!

*¡**Durmámonos** temprano esta noche!*
Let's go to sleep early tonight!

*¡No **coma** Ud. las espinacas!*
Don't eat the spinach!

*¡No se lo **des** a nadie!*
Don't give it to anyone!

*¡No **hagamos** la tarea!*
Let's not do the homework!

*¡No se **vistan** ahora!*
Don't get dressed now!

¡Démoselo a Jessica Alba!
  Let's give it to Jessica Alba!

*¡No **se lo demos** a él!*
  Let's not give it to him!

¡Escribamos los ejercicios aquí!
  Let's write the exercises here!

*¡No **te sientes** en la silla redonda!*
  Don't sit down in the round chair!

¡Vámonos ahorita!
  Let's go now!

*¡No **salgáis** sin pedir permiso!*
  Don't go out without asking permission!

The final *"s"* of the first person plural, affirmative command drops off:
◆ when adding *"nos"* — e.g., *durmám<u>onos</u>*
◆ when adding a double object pronoun beginning with *"se"* — e.g., *démo<u>selo</u>*

The double *"n"* in *"Escríbannos Uds."* is necessary to distinguish this command from *"Escríbanos Ud."* Unexpectedly, the command "Let's Go!" is translated *"¡Vámonos!"* or *"¡Vamos!"* The subjunctive form *"vayamos"* is not used here.

You might find it helpful to see a few verbs conjugated in all the command forms:

	HABLAR	COMER	VIVIR	DORMIRSE	DAR	TENER
tú (+)	¡Habla!	¡Come!	¡Vive!	¡Duérmete!	¡Da!	¡Ten!
tú (–)	¡No hables!	¡No comas!	¡No vivas!	¡No te duermas!	¡No des!	¡No tengas!
Ud. (+)	¡Hable!	¡Coma!	¡Viva!	¡Duérmase!	¡Dé!	¡Tenga!
Ud. (–)	¡No hable!	¡No coma!	¡No viva!	¡No se duerma!	¡No dé!	¡No tenga!
nosotros (+)	¡Hablemos!	¡Comamos!	¡Vivamos!	¡Durmámonos!	¡Demos!	¡Tengamos!
nosotros (–)	¡No hablemos!	¡No comamos!	¡No vivamos!	¡No nos durmamos!	¡No demos!	¡No tengamos!
vosotros (+)	¡Hablad!	¡Comed!	¡Vivid!	¡Dormíos!	¡Dad!	¡Tened!
vosotros (–)	¡No habléis!	¡No comáis!	¡No viváis!	¡No os durmáis!	¡No deis!	¡No tengáis!
Uds.. (+)	¡Hablen!	¡Coman!	¡Vivan!	¡Duérmanse!	¡Den!	¡Tengan!
Uds. (–)	¡No hablen!	¡No coman!	¡No vivan!	¡No se duerman!	¡No den!	¡No tengan!

2) THE PRESENT SUBJUNCTIVE IS USED TO EXPRESS INDIRECT COMMANDS

Because one never knows for sure if a person will follow a command, Spanish uses the subjunctive mood to help express this uncertainty. An indirect command is a sentence that generally has a <u>main clause</u> that expresses a command and a <u>dependent clause</u> that tells what someone else should do. The subjunctive is found in the dependent clause, after the word *"que."*

✳ **EXAMPLES:** *Mi entrenador quiere que yo **corra** cinco millas hoy.*
  My coach wants me to run five miles today. (Will I run? Maybe.)

*Nuestra escuela es demasiado seria. Nos piden que **llevemos** ropa formal cada día.*
  Our school is too serious. They ask that we wear formal clothes each day. (Will we wear them? Maybe.)

*Nuestros padres exigen que mi hermano y yo **hagamos** la cama por la mañana.*

Our parents demand that my brother and I make our beds in the morning. (We may or may not make them.)

*"Te digo que **te vayas** en seguida", le dijo el boxeador Abner Mares a Jesús Cuellar.*

"I'm telling you to leave immediately," (Are you going to leave? I hope so, but I don't know) said the boxer Abner Mares to Jesús Cuellar.

As you can see in these examples, there is always a change of subject between the main clause and the dependent clause. If there is no change of subject, use the infinitive.

EXAMPLES: *Mi entrenador quiere **correr**.*
My coach wants to run.

*Mis padres insisten en **hacer** la cama cada día.*
My parents insist on making the (their) bed every day.

Here is a list of common verbs that usually call for the subjunctive:

Main clause — 1ˢᵗ subject		Relative pronoun	Dependent clause with new subject
aconsejar (to advise)	*permitir* (to permit)		
decir* (i) (to tell)	*preferir (ie)* (to prefer)		
desear (to desire)	*prohibir* (to prohibit)		**Verb in the subjunctive**
escribir* (to write)	*querer (ie)* (to want)	**+ que +**	
esperar (to hope, expect)	*recomendar (ie)* (to recommend)		
exigir (to demand)	*rogar (ue)* (to beg, to implore)		
insistir en (to insist on)	*sugerir (ie)* (to suggest)		
mandar (to order)	*suplicar* (to beg, to implore)		
pedir (i) (to ask)			

¡CUIDADO! *These two verbs — *decir* and *escribir* — may require the subjunctive, but they also can use the indicative. It all depends on whether you are giving a command or simply relaying information:

EXAMPLES: *María me dice que llueve hoy.*
Mary tells me that it is raining today.

Note: There is no command; she gives me information only, so the subjunctive is not necessary.

*María me dice que **practique** el tenis.*
Mary tells me to practice tennis.

Note: There <u>is</u> a command here, so the subjunctive must be used.

3) FIVE CATEGORIES OF VERBS

There are the same five categories of verbs in the subjunctive mood as in the indicative: regular, stem-changers, irregular, spelling-changers, and super-irregulars. Here are the forms:

1 Regular verbs

HABLAR		COMER		VIVIR	
hable	hablemos	coma	comamos	viva	vivamos
hables	habléis	comas	comáis	vivas	viváis
hable	hablen	coma	coman	viva	vivan

Note: As you can see, these verbs have the "opposite" set of endings added to the stem of the *"yo"* form. **-AR** verbs end in: *"e, es, e, emos, éis, en,"* while **-ER** and **-IR** verbs end in: *"a, as, a, amos, áis, an."*

2 Stem-changers

-AR		-ER		-IR	
SENTAR		**PERDER**		**MORIR**	
siente	sentemos	pierda	perdamos	muera	muramos
sientes	sentéis	pierdas	perdáis	mueras	muráis
siente	sienten	pierda	pierdan	muera	mueran
VOLAR		**VOLVER**		**ALSO: pedir:** pida, pidas, pida, pidamos, pidáis, pidan **reír:** ría, rías, ría, riamos, riáis, rían	
vuele	volemos	vuelva	volvamos		
vueles	voléis	vuelvas	volváis		
vuele	vuelen	vuelva	vuelvan		

Note: All **-AR**, **-ER**, and **-IR** boot verbs have stem changes in the normal BOOT formation. **-IR** verbs also have an extra change in the *"nosotros/nosotras"* and *"vosotros/vosotras"* forms. This special **-IR** vowel change is the same one used in the 3rd person singular and plural of these verbs in the preterite (e.g., *durmió → durmamos/durmáis*, *murió → muramos/muráis*, *sirvió → sirvamos/sirváis*, *sintió → sintamos/sintáis*).

3 Irregular verbs

CABER		CAER		DECIR	
quepa	quepamos	caiga	caigamos	diga	digamos
quepas	quepáis	caigas	caigáis	digas	digáis
quepa	quepan	caiga	caigan	diga	digan
HACER		**OÍR**		**PONER**	
haga	hagamos	oiga	oigamos	ponga	pongamos
hagas	hagáis	oigas	oigáis	pongas	pongáis
haga	hagan	oiga	oigan	ponga	pongan
SALIR		**TENER**		**VALER**	
salga	salgamos	tenga	tengamos	valga	valgamos
salgas	salgáis	tengas	tengáis	valgas	valgáis
salga	salgan	tenga	tengan	valga	valgan

VENIR		VER	
venga	vengamos	vea	veamos
vengas	vengáis	veas	veáis
venga	vengan	vea	vean

Note: You may recall that all of these verbs are irregular in the *"yo"* form of the present. Thus, all of these subjunctive forms, built on the 1st person, carry the same change.

4 Spelling-changers

Many of the following verbs change spelling to help preserve some sound found in the infinitive.

CAR → QUE		CER → ZA		CER/CIR → ZCA	
aparcar	roncar	cocer (ue)	torcer (ue)	apetecer	ofrecer
buscar	sacar	convencer	vencer	conducir	parecer
explicar	tocar	ejercer		conocer	permanecer
				introducir	producir
				merecer	traducir
				obedecer	
buscar		**torcer**		**conocer**	
busque	busquemos	tuerza	torzamos	conozca	conozcamos
busques	busquéis	tuerzas	torzáis	conozcas	conozcáis
busque	busquen	tuerza	tuerzan	conozca	conozcan

GAR → GUE		GER → JA	GIR → JA
ahogar	llegar	coger	dirigir
apagar	negar (ie)	escoger	elegir
cargar	pagar	proteger	exigir
colgar (ue)	regar (ie)	recoger	fingir
entregar	rogar (ue)		
jugar (ue)			
pagar		**escoger**	**dirigir**
pague	paguemos	escoja escojamos	dirija dirijamos
pagues	paguéis	escojas escojáis	dirijas dirijáis
pague	paguen	escoja escojan	dirija dirijan

GUIR → GA	UIR → UYA		ZAR → CE	
conseguir (i)	concluir	distribuir	alcanzar	empezar (ie)
distinguir	construir	huir	almorzar (ue)	lanzar
seguir (i)	contribuir	incluir	alzar	rezar
	destruir	sustituir	comenzar (ie)	
	disminuir			
seguir	**huir**		**empezar**	
siga sigamos	huya	huyamos	empiece	empecemos
sigas sigáis	huyas	huyáis	empieces	empecéis
siga sigan	huya	huyan	empiece	empiecen

Note: A number of verbs above including *"torcer," "colgar," "seguir,"* and *"empezar"* are both stem-changers and spelling-changers.

5 Super-irregulars

These verbs are completely irregular and must be memorized.

DAR		ESTAR		HABER	
dé	demos	esté	estemos	haya	hayamos
des	deis	estés	estéis	hayas	hayáis
dé	den	esté	estén	haya	hayan
IR		**SABER**		**SER**	
vaya	vayamos	sepa	sepamos	sea	seamos
vayas	vayáis	sepas	sepáis	seas	seáis
vaya	vayan	sepa	sepan	sea	sean

PRACTICE EXERCISES

1. **Conjugate the verbs into the appropriate tense and mood. Most sentences will take the subjunctive; however, some may need the indicative or an infinitive.**

   a. Espero que el futbolista Iker Casillas me _____ pronto. (pagar)

   b. Insistes en que nosotros no _____. (dormirse)

   c. ¡Te digo que _____ ahora mismo! (callarse)

   d. Necesitamos _____ las manos antes de comer. (lavarse)

   e. Sé que _____ a nevar mucho este invierno. (ir)

   f. Espero que no _____ más guerras en el mundo.* (haber)

   ¡CUIDADO! *Be careful here; this verb will be in the singular! e.g., *Hay un coche; hay dos coches.* "Haber" is a strange verb!

   g. Mi madre quiere que yo _____ a todos los vecinos del barrio. (conocer)

   h. Prohíbo que ellos _____ solos en la calle. (jugar)

i. Mis padres me escriben que les _____ lo más pronto posible. (llamar)

j. Alejandra le ruega a su hermana Hannah que _____ el volumen de la música. (subir)

2. Conjugate these verbs fully in the present subjunctive:

	pedir		construir
_____	_____	_____	_____
_____	_____	_____	_____
_____	_____	_____	_____

	ser		dormirse
_____	_____	_____	_____
_____	_____	_____	_____
_____	_____	_____	_____

3. Write the correct "Ud." or "Uds." affirmative command form of the following verbs:

a. hablar (Ud.) → _____   **f.** negar (Uds.) → _____

b. comer (Uds.) → _____   **g.** buscar (Ud.) → _____

c. volverse (Uds.) → _____   **h.** protegerse (Uds.) → _____

d. ser (Ud.) → _____   **i.** explicar (Ud.) → _____

e. decir (Uds.) → _____   **j.** traducir (Uds.) → _____

4. The following letter contains six verbal errors. Identify them and fix them:

Querido Elvis:

¿Cómo estás? Quiero que te sientas ahora mismo, solo, en tu silla favorita para leer bien esta carta. Insisto en que no hay ninguna distracción. Apaga el radio, mi amor. Deseo informarte que no puedo ir contigo al concierto este fin de semana. Mi mamá me prohíbe que salgo con una estrella tan famosa de rock and roll. Estoy muy triste y deprimida. No quiero seguir viviendo. Pero tengo un plan. Pronto me voy a escapar de esta cárcel. Te ruego que me esperas. He hablado con mi profesora. Le dije: "Señora Rodríguez, ayúdeme; háblame, por favor". Pero sólo se rió de mí. Como ves, no hay solución. Espero que puedes comprender mi problema.

Con besos cariñosos,

Silvia

B) LOS PRONOMBRES COMPLEMENTOS

Object pronouns can replace nouns in a sentence.

Here is a list of object pronouns in Spanish:

Reflexive		Indirect		Direct	
me	*nos*	*me*	*nos*	*me*	*nos*
te	*os*	*te*	*os*	*te*	*os*
se	*se*	*le*	*les*	*lo, la**	*los, las**

*Note: In Spain, the object pronouns *"le"* and *"les"* are also used as <u>masculine</u> direct object pronouns when referring to people.

SEVEN INTERESTING FACTS ABOUT OBJECT PRONOUNS:

1) PLACEMENT BEFORE CONJUGATED VERBS
Object pronouns generally come <u>before</u> conjugated verbs.

EXAMPLES: *José **se** lava la cara antes de cenar.*
José washes his face before eating supper.

*Mis nietos **me** mandan regalos fabulosos para mi cumpleaños.*
My grandchildren send me great presents for my birthday.

*¿Has visto la última tira cómica de **Peanuts**? –Sí, **la** he visto.*
Have you seen the last **Peanuts** comic strip? –Yes, I have seen it.

*"Normalmente **les** digo la verdad a todos mis verdaderos amigos", dijo Juan Martín del Potro.*
"I usually tell the truth to all my true friends," said Juan Martín del Potro.

2) PLACEMENT AFTER CERTAIN VERB FORMS
There are three cases when object pronouns may <u>follow</u> verbs:

1 Affirmative commands
You <u>must</u> attach object pronouns to direct, affirmative commands. It may be necessary to add an accent mark to preserve the stress of the original word.

EXAMPLES:

¡Cómelo!	Eat it!
¡Estúdienlas!	Study them!
¡Dámelo!	Give it to me!
¡Hazme un favor!	Do me a favor!
¡Apagadle la luz!	Turn off the light for her (or him)!

Note: The object pronouns <u>precede</u> the negative command: *¡No **lo** comas! ¡No **las** estudien! ¡No **me lo** des! ¡No **me** hagas un favor! ¡No **le** apaguéis la luz!*

2 Infinitives

The object pronoun(s) may be attached to the infinitive <u>or</u> placed directly before the conjugated verb that precedes the infinitive. (If you add one object pronoun to the infinitive, no accent is needed; if you add two object pronouns, you will have to add an accent mark.)

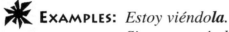 **EXAMPLES:**

*Voy a llamar**te**.*	***Te** voy a llamar.*
*Quería invitar**los** a mi casa.*	***Los** quería invitar a mi casa.*
*Tengo que escribir**les**.*	***Les** tengo que escribir.*
*Voy a regalár**telo**.*	***Te lo** voy a regalar.*

3 Present participles

The object pronoun(s) may be attached to the present participle or placed before the conjugated verb that precedes it. You will always have to add an accent mark when you attach one or more object pronouns to a present participle.

EXAMPLES:

*Estoy viéndo**la**.*	***La** estoy viendo.*
*Sigo comprándo**lo**.*	***Lo** sigo comprando.*
*Estamos dándo**telos** ahora.*	***Te los** estamos dando ahora.*

3) MORE THAN ONE OBJECT PRONOUN IN A SENTENCE

If there is more than one object pronoun in a sentence, the order is:

$$1^{st} \rightarrow \textbf{R}eflexive$$
$$2^{nd} \rightarrow \textbf{I}ndirect$$
$$3^{rd} \rightarrow \textbf{D}irect$$

You may find it helpful to memorize the word: **"RID"** (**R**eflexive, **I**ndirect, **D**irect).

EXAMPLES:

*¿La empanada? **Te la** estoy sirviendo.*
The empanada? I'm serving it to you.

*¿Las nuevas canciones de Bruno Mars? ¡Cómpra**melas**!*
The new songs of Bruno Mars? Buy them for me!

*¿La cara? Siempre **me la** lavo antes de acostarme.*
My face? I always wash it before going to bed.

*¿El dinero? Van a enviár**noslo**.*
The money? They are going to send it to us.

¡CUIDADO! These object pronouns are always placed together; they cannot be split up! As you can see in the above sentences, both object pronouns are placed either before or after the verb.

4) A SPECIAL CASE — THE USE OF "SE"

There is a special case in which the 3rd person indirect object pronoun *"le"* or *"les"* is replaced by the word *"se."* This change occurs when *"le"* or *"les"* is followed by the direct object pronoun *"lo," "la," "los,"* or *"las."*

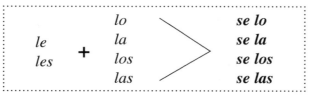

		lo	se lo
le		la	se la
les	+	los	se los
		las	se las

EXAMPLES: *¿Las llaves sueltas? **Se las** di a Shalim.* (In this sentence, the word *"le"* was replaced by *"se."*)
The loose keys? I gave them to Shalim.

*¿Los libros? **Se los** vendí a mis amigos.* (In this sentence, the word *"les"* was replaced by *"se."*)
The books? I sold them to my friends.

WHY WAS THIS RULE INVENTED?

This rule avoids putting two short words side-by-side that begin with "l," e.g., "le lo" or "les las." It's easier to distinguish these words when the first word is changed to *"se."*

5) AN OPTIONAL PREPOSITIONAL PHRASE FOR CLARITY

Because the obligatory *"le"* or *"les"* may be ambiguous *(to him, to her, to you, to them, to you all)*, an optional prepositional phrase may be used to clarify the meaning.

EXAMPLES: *Sebastián siempre **les** da un anillo **a sus novias**.*
Sebastián always gives a ring to his girlfriends.

*Eva Longoria normalmente **les** dice la verdad **a sus amigas**.*
Eva Longoria normally tells the truth to her friends.

Helpful Tip: In the first sentence *"les"* and *"a sus novias"* refer to the same persons. It is good for you to get in the habit of using this redundant indirect object pronoun, particularly with verbs of communication (e.g., *decir, escribir*). *"Le"* or *"les"* announces that there is an indirect object, and the prepositional phrase clarifies it.

---

6) ADDING STRESSED PRONOUNS

To give extra emphasis to, or to clarify, unstressed pronouns, simply add the following stressed pronouns to the sentence:

a mí	*a nosotros/nosotras*
a ti	*a vosotros/vosotras*
a él	*a ellos*
a ella	*a ellas*
a Ud.	*a Uds.*

The reflexive pronoun *"se"* is emphasized by adding *"a sí"*: *Clara se habla a sí misma; los chicos se visten a sí mismos.* Clara talks to herself; the kids dress themselves.

✳ **EXAMPLES:** *A mí me gustaría jugar al golf como Elena Ochoa y Sergio García.*
I'd like to play golf like Elena Ochoa and Sergio García.

Les ofrecemos a Uds. un trabajo semejante.
We are offering you all a similar job.

La chica se considera a sí misma una estrella.
The girl considers herself a star.

7) WHEN "NOS" IS ADDED TO AN AFFIRMATIVE NOSOTROS COMMAND

Remember that when the reflexive object pronoun *"nos"* is added to an affirmative *"nosotros/nosotras"* command, the final *"s"* drops off this first person plural form.

✳ **EXAMPLES:** *¡Lavémonos las manos!*
Let's wash our hands!

¡Durmámonos a las once!
Let's go to sleep at eleven!

An *"s"* also disappears when the object pronouns *"se lo/la/los/las"* are added to an affirmative *"nosotros/nosotras"* command.

✳ **EXAMPLES:** *¿El reloj? ¡Comprémoselo a ella!*
The watch? Let's buy it for her!

¿La pelota? ¡Démosela a él!
The ball? Let's give it to him!

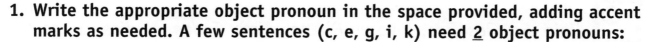

1. **Write the appropriate object pronoun in the space provided, adding accent marks as needed. A few sentences (c, e, g, i, k) need 2 object pronouns:**

   a. _____ pido que te calles.

   b. _____ estábamos buscando antes de la clase. (you, formal)

   c. ¿Las peras? ¡Compra_____ ahora, por favor! (them for me) (2)

   d. He comprado muchos boletos para el concierto de Willie Colón y Rubén

   Blades; _____ he metido en el bolsillo de mi chaqueta.

   e. ¿Las fotos raras? Juan _____ dio a Eduardo, su amigo rubio. (2)

   f. Mañana _____ escribiré una carta a mi amiga Shakira.

   g. ¿La revista semanal? Vamos a dar_____ a su mamá. (2)

   h. ¿Los ensayos? _____ voy a echar a la basura.

   i. ¿Los libros? ¡No _____ prestes a la chica del pelo rizado! (2)

   j. Paulina Rubio seguía llamando_____ todas las tardes. (you, familiar)

   k. ¿Las flores? ¡Compremos_____! (for her) (2)

2. In the following story, there are eight errors, mostly pronouns. Find and correct them:

Hola. Soy Josefina. Vivo en Buenos Aires. Todos los días voy con mis amigas a la piscina. Ayer llamé a Lorena antes de irme. La dije que había me levantado tarde y que necesitaba un poco más de tiempo. Lorena mi dijo que ella también estaba cansada, pero quería acompañarme. Cuando le vi, se mostré mi mochila. Le la di a ella porque pesaba mucho. Lorena empezó a andar más despacio. Se dije: "Apúrate. Tenemos prisa. ¡No sienteste! Nunca podremos participar en las Olimpiadas si no trabajamos un poco".

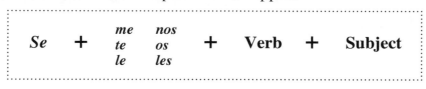

C) Los acontecimientos inesperados

The Spanish language makes use of a special construction with the pronoun *"se"* to refer to accidents or events that we didn't expect would happen.

Se	+	me te le	nos os les	+	Verb	+	Subject

The following verbs are among those commonly used in this construction: *acabar, caer, morir, olvidar, perder,* and *romper.*

¿◆? Do you notice that, in these Spanish sentences, the true subject of the verb often <u>follows</u> that verb?

EXAMPLES:

A *Julia **se le acabó** la comida.*	Julia ran out of food.
*¡**Se te cayeron** los pantalones!*	Your pants fell down!
***Se me murió** el canario.*	My canary died.
***Se les olvidó** el libro.*	They forgot the book.
***Se les olvidaron** los nombres.*	They forgot the names.
***Se me perdió** la maleta.*	I lost the suitcase.
***Se le rompió** la muñeca.*	He broke his wrist.
***Se me rompieron** las tazas.*	I broke the cups.

¿◆? Did you notice that the verb agrees with the subject (pants, wrist, cups, etc.) that followed in each sentence?

As you can see, the word *"se"* is followed by an indirect object pronoun (*me, te, le, nos, os, les*). The resulting construction almost makes it seem as though one had become the innocent victim of one of these events.

EXAMPLES: *Se me olvidó el nombre.*
I forgot the name.
(Literally: The name forgot itself to me . . . i.e., it's not my fault! In English, we take a little more responsibility for these actions, at least grammatically.)

¿Se te rompieron los anteojos?
Did you break your glasses?
(Did the glasses break themselves "on" you? You're the victim!)

PRACTICE EXERCISES

1. **Translate the following sentences, using the "se" construction for unintended events:**

   a. They forgot my name.

   _____

   b. They ran out of time.

   _____

   c. I have dropped my iPad and iPhone.

   _____

   d. My girlfriend always forgets my birthday.

   _____

   e. We lost our watch.

   _____

   f. Marco Rubio broke his cellphone.

   _____

2. **An English speaker wrote the following composition, not having learned the more idiomatic "se" construction for unintended events. Rewrite it, making four changes/additions:**

   Anoche perdí la billetera. Llevaba dentro todo mi dinero.

   Después olvidé hablar con la policía. Otro problema fue que mi

   hermano rompió todos los teléfonos de la casa. ¡Qué desastre!

D) LAS COMPARACIONES IGUALES Y DESIGUALES

There are two types of **comparative sentences**: those that express equality, and those that express inequality.

1) EQUAL COMPARISONS

The words in these comparisons may be nouns, adjectives, adverbs, or verbs.

a) Nouns

These sentences use the adjectives *"tanto,"* *"tanta,"* *"tantos,"* or *"tantas"* before a noun, and they use *"como"* after the noun.

EXAMPLES: *Tengo **tantos** discos compactos de* Los Tigres del Norte ***como** tú.*
> I have as many *Los Tigres del Norte* CDs as you.

*Hemos comprado **tantas** flores **como** ella.*
> We have bought as many flowers as she has.

*Juan Luis tiene **tanta** paciencia **como** un santo.*
> Juan Luis has as much patience as a saint.

*La familia real no necesita **tanto** dinero **como** nosotros.*
> The royal family doesn't need as much money as we do.

b) Adjectives/Adverbs

These sentences use the adverb *"tan"* before adjectives and adverbs, and they use *"como"* after them.

EXAMPLES: *Soy **tan** simpático **como** ella.*
> I am as nice as she is.

La película Jason Bourne *es **tan** emocionante **como*** The Bourne Identity.
> The movie *Jason Bourne* is as exciting as *The Bourne Identity.*

*Nosotros no podemos esquiar **tan** rápido **como** Bode Miller y Lindsey Vonn.*
> We can't ski as fast as Bode Miller and Lindsey Vonn.

c) Verbs

These sentences use the expression *"tanto como."* The second verb in the comparison is understood but often not expressed.

EXAMPLES: *Bailamos **tanto como** ellos (bailan).*
We dance as much as they do.

*Exijo **tanto como** ella (exige).*
I demand as much as she does.

*He dormido **tanto como** tú (has dormido).*
I have slept as much as you have.

2) UNEQUAL COMPARISONS

The key words for all unequal comparisons are: *"más"* or *"menos"* and *"que."* These words are generally used when comparing nouns, adjectives, adverbs, and verbs.

a) Nouns

EXAMPLES: *Tengo **más** raquetas de tenis **que** Rafael Nadal.*
I have more tennis racquets than Rafael Nadal.

*Invierto **menos** dinero **que** mi cuñada.*
I invest less money than my sister-in-law.

*Preparo **menos** comida salada **que** mi hermano.*
I prepare less salty food than my brother.

b) Adjectives/Adverbs

EXAMPLES: *Yo patino **más** rápido **que** Rudy Galindo.*
I skate faster than Rudy Galindo.

*Martina es **menos** trabajadora **que** su hermana.*
Martina is less hard-working than her sister.

*Leo **más** despacio **que** mis amigos.*
I read more slowly than my friends.

*Mis pensamientos son **menos** profundos **que** los tuyos.*
My thoughts are less profound than yours.

*Esta sopa está **más** sosa **que** esa otra.*
This soup is more bland than that other one.

c) Verbs

> ✳ **EXAMPLES:** *Estudio **más que** tú.*
> I study more than you.
>
> *Estudio **menos que** tú.*
> I study less than you.

Here are some irregular comparative forms that you should memorize:

worse →	*peor* (not *más malo)		younger →	*menor* (not *más menor)
better →	*mejor* (not *más bueno)		older →	*mayor* (not *más mayor)

Helpful Tip: *"Peor"* and *"mejor"* usually precede a noun; *"menor"* and *"mayor"* follow the noun.

> ✳ **EXAMPLES:** *Mi **mejor** amigo, Nick, me contó su **peor** chiste.*
> My best friend, Nick, told me his worst joke.
>
> *Mi hermano **menor**, Jim, se graduó de Ohio Wesleyan University y mi hermano **mayor**, Marcos, se graduó de Cornell.*
> My younger brother, Jim, graduated from OWU, and my older brother, Mark, graduated from Cornell.

d) Unequal comparisons containing numbers

When a <u>number</u> follows an unequal comparison in an affirmative sentence that compares the quantity of the <u>same</u> item, *"que"* is replaced by *"de."*

> ✳ **EXAMPLES:** *Tengo **más de** cuatro libros aquí.*
> I have more than four books here (i.e., I have five books or six books).
>
> *Hay **menos de** tres semanas de vacaciones.*
> There are fewer than three weeks of vacation (i.e., There are two weeks or one week of vacation).

If the comparison is of <u>different</u> things, however, *"que"* is used.

For example: *"Tengo más **que** dos guitarras"* means that I have more than (just) two guitars, i.e., I have two guitars and a clarinet. *"Tengo más **de** dos guitarras"* would suggest a <u>range</u> of numbers of the same item — three, four, five, twenty guitars!

In a negative sentence, either *"de"* or *"que"* could be used. *"De"* suggests a <u>range</u> of numbers (try to remember the word "de-range"), while *"que"* specifies an <u>exact</u> number.

✳ **EXAMPLES:** *No tengo más **de** cuatro libros.*
   I have no more than four books. (Four is the maximum — I may
   have one or two or three or four.)

   *No tengo más **que** cuatro libros.*
   I have only four books. (That's it; that's all I have — no more —
   but I do have exactly four of them and nothing else.)

e) Unequal comparisons with a new verb following *"que"*
If the second part of an unequal comparison has a new verb, one of the following will be used: *"del que," "de los que," "de la que," "de las que,"* or the neuter *"de lo que"* if there is no antecedent (noun to which it could refer).

✳ **EXAMPLES:** *Ella gasta más dinero **del que** gana.**
   She spends more money than she earns.

   *Note: The reason for this construction is that *"que"* means only "that" (not "than")
   between clauses. (The incorrect sentence: *"Gasta más dinero que gana" could only
   mean: "She spends more money <u>that</u> she earns.")

   *Pido más pizza **de la que** preparan.*
   I'm asking for more pizza than they are making.

   *Hemos visto más películas este año **de las que** hicieron en el año 1933.*
   We are seeing more movies this year than were made in 1933.

In the above examples, the same noun was the object of each verb: *gasta dinero, gana dinero; pido pizza, preparan pizza; hemos visto películas, hicieron películas.* However, if the verbs don't have the same noun as an object, or if adjectives or adverbs are being compared, use *"de lo que."*

✳ **EXAMPLES:** *Escribo más despacio **de lo que** pienso.*
   I write more slowly than I think.

   *Eran mucho más guapos **de lo que** esperaba.*
   They were much better looking than I expected.

   *Estudié menos **de lo que** te imaginas.*
   I studied less than you can imagine.

PRACTICE EXERCISES

1. **Choose one of the following word or words that you feel best complete these sentences** *(tanto, tanta, tantos, tantas, tanto como, que, de, tan, como, más, menos, del que, de los que, de la que, de las que, de lo que)*:

a. Hacemos _____ ejercicios sencillos como ellos.

b. El famoso Marcos ha ganado _____ premios que su hermano.

c. "Tengo hambre. Me gustaría pedir _____ frijoles", dijo Cristián de la Fuente.

d. Tenemos más _____ siete estudiantes costarricenses en la clase; hay once.

e. Hay _____ personas en Vermont que en Massachusetts.

f. Hay _____ días en agosto como en enero.

g. Antonio Banderas ha hecho más películas _____ Gael García Bernal.

h. Selena escribió canciones más bonitas _____ uno se puede imaginar.

i. Corremos _____ nuestros amigos.

j. Los fuegos artificiales eran más emocionantes _____ pensaba.

k. Vimos más abejas en nuestro picnic _____ matamos.

l. Mi suegra, aunque es vieja, tiene más energía _____ yo.

m. No van a llegar más _____ siete personas; eso es bueno, porque sólo tenemos siete camas.

2. The following dream contains six errors. Identify them and correct them:

Anoche soñé con los equipos de baloncesto de nuestro colegio.

Creo que nuestros equipos tienen mucho más talento como otros equipos.

Por desgracia, normalmente perdemos tan partidos que ellos. Un año el

equipo de los chicos sufrió tan derrotas como días hay en la temporada;

otro año las chicas ganaron tantos partidos que los chicos: ninguno. En

mi sueño, dos estudiantes nuevos llegaron a mi colegio: un chico, tan

alto que una jirafa y una chica más fuerte como un león. ¡Ganamos todos

los partidos y éramos los campeones! Por desgracia, me desperté.

These two sets of questions use grammatical structures and vocabulary from this lesson. Working with a partner, alternate asking and answering each question. When you get to the bottom of each list, start over at the top, switching roles. As a variation, write out the answers in complete sentences.

A) ¿Tienes **tantos** libros **como** tus amigos?

¿Bebes **tanto** café **como** tus padres?

¿Eres **tan** alto/a **como** tu hermano/a?

¿Hablas **tan** rápido **como** tu profesor?

¿Estudias **tanto como** yo?

¿Tienes **tanta** paciencia **como** tu mejor amigo?

¿Es tu profesor de español **tan** popular **como** tu profesor de matemáticas?

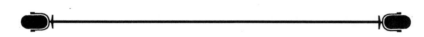

B) ¿Tienes **más** ropa de moda **que** tus amigos?

¿Eres **más** alto/a **que** una jirafa?

¿Hablas **menos** rápido **que** tu profesor?

¿Estudias **más que** yo?

¿Gastas **más** dinero **del que** ganas?

¿Tienes **más de** cinco libros en tu mochila?

¿Es esta clase **más** interesante **de lo que** esperabas?

 # Prueba De Repaso

A) El presente del subjuntivo

1. Choose among the infinitive, subjunctive or present indicative to best complete these sentences:

a. Estoy seguro de que la matrícula de esta universidad _____ cada año. (aumentar)

b. Mis padres me piden que _____ antes de la medianoche. (volver)

c. Esperan _____ la deforestación de los bosques de lluvia. (eliminar)

d. La madre, risueña, le dice al niño que _____ las espinacas ahora mismo. (comerse)

e. Nuestro profesor de español está loco: ¡quiere que nosotros

_____ conjugar todos los verbos irregulares! (saber)

f. El chico celoso insiste en que su novia no _____ con otros chicos. (salir)

g. Todos los ciudadanos de ese pueblo remoto piensan que el alcalde

_____ un señor sabio. (ser)

h. Te ruego que no _____ de mí. (reírse)

i. Miguel Bosé quiere que Shakira _____ otra canción con él; la última, *Si tú no vuelves,* fue un gran éxito. (hacer)

2. Conjugate these verbs in the present subjunctive:

estar	dirigir	morir
_____ _____	_____ _____	_____
_____ _____	_____ _____	_____
_____ _____	_____ _____	_____

3. The following letter contains seven errors. Underline and correct them:

Querido Antonio:

Yo comprendo que quieres aprender inglés, pero no te permito que haces esos intercambios de idioma con esa chica norteamericana. Créeme, es tonta y ingenua. Ella insiste en aprenda español porque quiere salga con tú. Prefiero que no tienes más citas con ella. ¡Escúchasme bien!

Un beso cariñoso,

Liliana

B) LOS PRONOMBRES COMPLEMENTOS

1. Complete these sentences with the appropriate object pronoun(s):

a. Siempre _____ cuento mis problemas a mis gatos.

b. ¿El secreto? No _____ diré a nadie. (2)

c. ¡No grites! _____ oigo perfectamente.

d. El teléfono sonaba, pero yo no _____ contesté.

e. ¿Dónde están mis gafas? No _____ encuentro en ningún sitio.

f. Juan es muy vanidoso. Le gusta mirar _____ en el espejo.

g. ¿_____ contasteis las noticias a vuestros parientes?

h. ¿Quién le dio una mala nota a Miguel? –La profesora de inglés _____ dio. (2)

2. Change the following sentences to formal, direct affirmative commands:

a. Uds. tienen buena suerte. _____

b. Ud. me escucha bien.   _____

c. Uds. pagan la cuenta.   _____

3. Now change your affirmative commands to negative commands:

a. _____

b. _____

c. _____

C) LOS ACONTECIMIENTOS INESPERADOS

1. Translate the following sentences using the *"se"* construction for unintended events:

a. We forgot the sharp knives.

_____

b. Mark's pants fell down.

_____

c. I always lose my Spanish homework.

_____

2. Antonio's North American friend, Susan, hasn't yet learned the "se" construction for unintended events. She also has problems with the correct placement of object pronouns. If you look closely, you will also find that Susan has not totally grasped how to give commands properly in Spanish. In the following paragraph that Susan wrote for her Spanish class, there are seven errors. Underline and correct them:

Conocí a mi nuevo amigo, quien le llama Antonio, el mes pasado.

Antonio habla muy bien el español porque aprendió lo en Sudamérica.

Sé que su padre es de allí, pero olvidé en qué país nació. Antonio

me siempre habla en español, por eso yo estoy lo aprendiendo bien.

Cuando yo lo hablo en inglés, mi amigo me dice: "¡Dicemelo en español!"

D) LAS COMPARACIONES IGUALES Y DESIGUALES

1. **Choose the words that best complete the following comparisons** *(tanto, tanta, tantos, tantas, tanto como, que, tan, como, más, menos, de, del que, de los que, de la que, de las que, de lo que)*:

a. Ryan Gosling es más guapo _____ Chris Pine.

b. Beyoncé no canta mejor _____ Rihanna.

c. La película *A Christmas Carol* es tan interesante _____ el libro.

d. El programa *Walking Dead* no es más popular _____ *Game of Thrones*.

e. Compramos más helado _____ comimos.

f. Esta clase sabe tanto _____ la clase avanzada.

g. ¿Tiene Benicio del Toro más talento _____ Omar Chaparro?

h. En *MTV* salen _____ anuncios como vídeos.

i. Belinda es tan guapa _____ Thalía.

j. Mi ensayo era más profundo _____ el profesor esperaba.

k. Hay más _____ diez días de vacaciones este año . . . hay catorce.

2. The following dialogue contains eight errors. Underline and correct them:

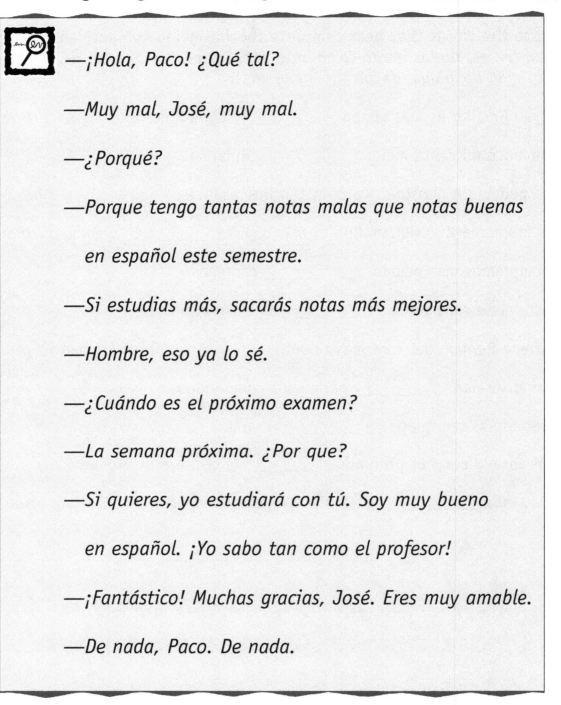

—¡Hola, Paco! ¿Qué tal?

—Muy mal, José, muy mal.

—¿Porqué?

—Porque tengo tantas notas malas que notas buenas en español este semestre.

—Si estudias más, sacarás notas más mejores.

—Hombre, eso ya lo sé.

—¿Cuándo es el próximo examen?

—La semana próxima. ¿Por que?

—Si quieres, yo estudiará con tú. Soy muy bueno en español. ¡Yo sabo tan como el profesor!

—¡Fantástico! Muchas gracias, José. Eres muy amable.

—De nada, Paco. De nada.

ESTADOS UNIDOS

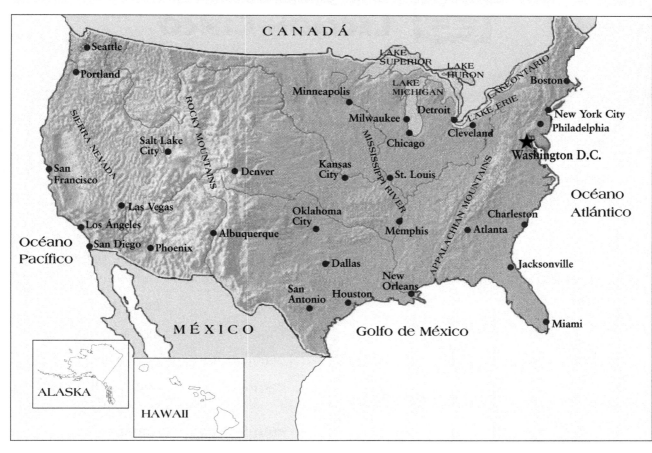

ESTADOS UNIDOS

CAPITAL:	Washington, D.C.
POBLACIÓN:	326.100.000
GOBIERNO:	república constitucional
PRESIDENTE:	Donald Trump
DINERO ($):	dólar
PRODUCTOS:	agricultura, tecnología
MÚSICA, BAILE:	"bluegrass," country, jazz, rap, "square dance"
SITIOS DE INTERÉS:	las Cataratas del Niágara, el Gran Cañón del Colorado, Yosemite
COMIDA TÍPICA:	carne, hamburguesas, maíz, panqueques, pavo asado, perros calientes, pizza, tarta de manzana

ESTADOUNIDENSES FAMOSOS:

César Chávez
(ACTIVISTA)

Rosa Gumataotao Ríos
(TESORERA)

Scott Gómez
(ATLETA)

Ellen Ochoa
(ASTRONAUTA)

Bill Richardson
(POLÍTICO)

Marco Rubio
(POLÍTICO)

Loretta y Silvia Sánchez
(POLÍTICAS)

Sonia Sotomayor
(JUEZ DEL TRIBUNAL SUPREMO)

VOCABULARIO LECCIÓN CINCO

SUSTANTIVOS

el	almacén	department store
	(los grandes almacenes)	
el/la	amante	lover
el	anillo	ring
el	arándano *(rojo)*	blueberry, cranberry
la	autopista *(autovía)*	highway, freeway
la	autoridad	authority
el	banco	bench, pew, bank
la	bandeja	tray
la	bandera	flag
el	barrio	neighborhood, section, quarter
la	bata	bathrobe
la	beca	scholarship
la	boda	wedding
la	campaña	campaign
el	cansancio	tiredness, fatigue
el	cariño	affection
la	confianza	confidence, trust (in)
el	consejo	advice
el	correo	mail

el	derecho	right, privilege
la	despedida	farewell, parting
el	detalle	detail
el	dibujo	sketch, painting, drawing
el	dolor	pain, grief
la	edad	age
el/la	empleado/a	employee
la	entrada	admission, ticket, entrance
el	entrenamiento	training
la	entrevista	interview
la	frontera	border, frontier
el	gusto	taste, flavor
la	herramienta	tool
la	jaula	cage
la	matrícula	tuition
el	negocio	business
la	niñez	childhood
el	repaso	review
el	sueldo	salary

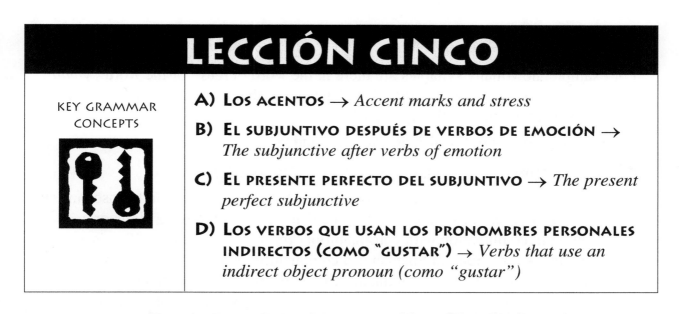

LECCIÓN CINCO

KEY GRAMMAR CONCEPTS

A) LOS ACENTOS → *Accent marks and stress*

B) EL SUBJUNTIVO DESPUÉS DE VERBOS DE EMOCIÓN → *The subjunctive after verbs of emotion*

C) EL PRESENTE PERFECTO DEL SUBJUNTIVO → *The present perfect subjunctive*

D) LOS VERBOS QUE USAN LOS PRONOMBRES PERSONALES INDIRECTOS (COMO "GUSTAR") → *Verbs that use an indirect object pronoun (como "gustar")*

 A) LOS ACENTOS

The ability to write and pronounce new words accurately depends, in part, on understanding the rules of accentuation. This section will explain the mysteries of **accent marks.** Once you understand the basic concepts, they become remarkably easy!

There are two categories of words in Spanish: those that have no written accent mark, and those that do have them.

1 Words without an accent mark

How do you know which syllable in a word receives emphasis or stress? For example, when you look at the word *"perro,"* should you say *"**pe**-rro"* or *"pe-**rro**"*? When you see *"hotel,"* should you say *"**ho**-tel"* or *"ho-**tel**"*? The answers are easy: *"**pe**-rro"* and *"ho-**tel**."* But, how can you tell?

◆ If a word ends in a vowel or with the letters "n" or "s," the natural stress of that word is on the <u>next to last</u> syllable.

◆ If a word, however, ends with a consonant (other than "n" or "s"), the stress is naturally on the <u>last</u> syllable.

The stressed syllable in each of the following words is highlighted:

✳ **EXAMPLES:**   ven-***ta***-na   fe-no-me-***nal***
                    re-***loj***   ciu-***dad***
                    com-pren-***de***-mos   tor-***tu***-ga
                    plan-ta   ***le***-o
                    co-***mer***   ***gran***-de
                    ha-blan   ju-***gue***-te
                    ex-tra-or-di-***na***-rio   em-pu-***jar***

Do You Remember What Makes Up a Syllable?

For example, how many syllables are there in the word *"crees"* or the word *"viuda"*? Answer: 2 — *"cre-es"* and *"viu-da."* Understanding that there are strong vowels and weak vowels in Spanish will help explain.

◆ The strong vowels in Spanish are "a," "e," and "o."

◆ The weak vowels are "u" and "i" ("You and I are weak!").

◆ A syllable can be defined by a single vowel or by a single vowel and consonant(s): *"u-no"* or *"tris-te."* A syllable can also be defined by a diphthong alone or a diphthong in combination with consonant(s): *"au-to"* or *"vein-te."* What is a diphthong? A diphthong in Spanish is a combination of a strong vowel and an <u>unaccented</u> weak vowel (e.g., ai, ia, au, ua, ei, ie, eu, ue, oi, io, ou, uo) **or** a combination of weak vowels (e.g., iu, ui). Two <u>strong</u> vowels together form two syllables (e.g., *le-o, ca-os*).

2 Words with an accent mark

Whenever the Spanish language breaks the normal rules of stress described above, there will be a written accent mark on the syllable that is emphasized. A written accent mark always takes precedence! An accent mark can turn a weak vowel into a strong one, thereby breaking a diphthong into two separate syllables (e.g., *rí-o*). This fact is true even if the letter "h" separates a strong and weak vowel (e.g., *pro-hí-be, re-hí-zo*).

❋ **Examples:**
re-**lám**-pa-go	ru-**bí**-es	so-**fá**
co-**mió**	na-**ción**	di-**jé**-ra-mos
dí-a	ha-**blá**-ba-mos	

Sometimes accent marks are used for reasons that have nothing to do with pronunciation.

◆**Accent marks can distinguish one word from another**. For example, the word *"té"* means "tea," but the word *"te"* is the object pronoun meaning "you," "to you," or "yourself." Both of these words are pronounced the same way; the written accent, however, makes the meaning of each word different.

No Accent	Accent
de (of, from)	*dé* (the 1st and 3rd person subjunctive form of *"dar"*)
esta (this, an adjective)	*está* (3rd person of *"estar"*) *ésta* (this one, a pronoun)
este (this, an adjective)	*esté* (subjunctive form) *éste* (this one; a pronoun)
mas (but)	*más* (more)
mi (my)	*mí* (me . . . form used after a preposition)
se (reflexive pronoun)	*sé* (I know)
si (if)	*sí* (yes)
solo (alone)	**sólo* (only)
tu (your)	*tú* (you)

*The accent on this word is beginning to become optional in modern Spanish, unless there is a chance of ambiguity (e.g., *vendré sólo (solo) hoy.*)

◆ **All interrogatives have an accent**, whether in a direct question or in a statement with an implied question.

> **EXAMPLES:** *¿**Por qué** no tienes más confianza?*
> Why don't you have more confidence?
>
> *No sé **dónde** vives.*
> I don't know where you live.

◆ **Exclamatives also carry an accent mark.**

> **EXAMPLES:** *¡**Cuánto** has crecido!*
> You've grown so much!
>
> *¡**Qué** ricas están las enchiladas!*
> The enchiladas are delicious!

PRACTICE EXERCISES

1. Divide the following words into syllables, underlining the syllable that should be stressed. Afterwards, write in parentheses the number of syllables that the word contains.

Examples: pizarra → **pi-za-rra (3)**   adiós → **a-diós (2)**

a. tijeras → _____

b. río → _____

c. Córdoba → _____

d. estudiantes → _____

e. árboles → _____

f. refrigerador → _____

g. cuarenta → _____

h. prohíbo → _____

i. crear → _____

j. pretexto → _____

k. buena → _____

l. frío → _____

m. fingen → _____

n. fenomenal → _____

o. veintidós → _____

p. cree → _____

q. ti → _____

r. corpulento → _____

s. ruidoso → _____

t. mecánico → _____

B) EL SUBJUNTIVO DESPUÉS DE VERBOS DE EMOCIÓN

We saw in *Lección Cuatro* that the subjunctive is used to form all formal and all negative commands as well as to express an indirect command. This lesson looks at the second broad category of subjunctive use: **after verbs of emotion**.

EXAMPLES: *Me alegro de que Lucero y Luis Miguel **canten** esta noche.*
I'm glad that Lucero and Luis Miguel are singing tonight.

*Tenemos miedo de que el niño **rompa** el cristal.*
We're scared that the boy will break the windowpane.

*Me frustra que Ricky y Mercedes no **puedan** asistir al concierto de Don Omar.*
It frustrates me that Ricky and Mercedes can't attend the Don Omar concert.

As you can see, all of these sentences contain the following three ingredients:

Indicative verb of emotion (in main clause)	**+**	***que***	**+**	**Subjunctive verb** (in the dependent clause)

The following are among the most common verbs or expressions that signal emotion:

Deseo	*Me fascina*	*Me irrita*	*Ojalá*
Espero	*Me fastidia*	*Me molesta*	*Siento*
Me alegro de	*Me frustra*	*Me preocupa*	*Temo*
Me encanta	*Me gusta*	*Me sorprende*	*Tengo miedo de*
Me entristece	*Me importa*		

EXAMPLES: ***Se alegran** de que **estés** aquí.*
They're glad that you're here.

*No **me alegro** de que **estés** aquí.*
I'm not glad that you're here.

Note: It doesn't matter if the sentence is affirmative or negative!

***Temo** que no **haya** más entradas.*
I fear that there are no more tickets.

***Me preocupa** que mi perro todavía no **haya vuelto** a casa.*
It worries me that my dog still hasn't come home.

***Sentimos** que no todos los estudiantes **puedan** bailar la macarena.*
We regret that not all the students can dance the macarena.

*No **me sorprende** que nos **den** un premio.*
  I'm not surprised that they are giving us a prize.

*Me **frustra** que no **podamos** ver MTV por la noche.*
  It frustrates me that we can't watch MTV at night.

*¡**Ojalá** que no **llueva** esta tarde!*
  I hope that (if only) it doesn't rain this afternoon!

The fact that there is a dependent clause in these sentences, introduced by *"que,"* generally signals a change of subject. If there is not a change of subject, you would normally use an infinitive.

EXAMPLES: *"Me alegro de **cantar** esta noche", comentó Justin Timberlake.*
  "I'm glad to sing tonight," commented Justin Timberlake.

*Tenemos miedo de **salir** esta noche.*
  We're afraid to go out tonight.

WHAT IS THE THEORY BEHIND THIS USE OF THE SUBJUNCTIVE?

It was easy to see in *Lección Cuatro* why the subjunctive was used after indirect commands: you never really knew for sure if an order would be followed. That uncertainty called for the subjunctive, a grammatical mood that expresses uncertainty, haziness, or doubt.

In most of the examples presented above, however, there is no uncertainty at all about the event! For example, *"Me alegro de que estés aquí"* expresses a reality that is absolutely certain: I am happy that you are, in fact, here. Why, then, does one use the subjunctive?

It's almost as if the subjectivity or emotion expressed in the main clause gushes out into the dependent clause, changing the indicative mood into the subjunctive mood. These verbs have been weakened or made more tentative, or even "contaminated," by the emotion or opinion in the main clause. The verbs in the dependent clause, then, wear the emotion of the main clause on their sleeves. With a little practice, this use of the subjunctive will become second nature to you.

PRACTICE EXERCISES

1. **Write the proper form of the verb in the spaces provided. Many sentences will need the subjunctive; however, the indicative or an infinitive may be required in some instances.**

   a. Tememos que los empleados no _____ trabajar los domingos. (querer)

   b. Te alegras de que yo _____ todos los detalles. (saber)

   c. Me frustra que nosotros no _____ ver el partido del Real Madrid esta noche. (poder)

   d. Sé que el chico malcriado no _____ su cuarto. (limpiar)

   e. No nos sorprende que el hombre calvo _____ más pelo. (desear)

   f. José siente que sus amigos no _____ en la primera fila. (sentarse)

   g. A Roque le sorprende que nadie lo _____ a la boda. (invitar)

   h. Nos alegramos de _____ tus consejos ahora. (escuchar)

   i. Es evidente que las chicas no _____ la confianza anoche durante el partido. (perder)

   j. ¡Ojalá que alguien _____ mi dibujo! (escoger)

2. Identify and correct the seven errors in the following paragraph:

Me alegro mucho de que Santa Claus va a venir a mi casa esta noche. Todo el año he sido un chico muy bueno. ¡Cuanto he trabajado! Temo que Santa no sabe lo que he hecho este año. Estoy seguro de que me dé algo muy grande, caro e impresionante. Siento que mis amigos no son muy buenos. ¡Ojala que no reciben ni carbón ni piedras en las medias colgadas en la chimenea!

C) EL PRESENTE PERFECTO DEL SUBJUNTIVO

The **present perfect subjunctive** is found in a dependent clause, often after a verb of emotion. Just like the present perfect, this tense describes events begun in the past that, from the speaker's perspective, have occurred recently or are in some way connected to the present.

EXAMPLES: *Espero que mi madre me **haya comprado** el tercer libro de* Los juegos del hambre, Mockingjay.
I hope that my mother has bought me the third *Hunger Games* book, *Mockingjay*.

*Me alegro de que Uds. me **hayan prestado** las herramientas.*
I'm glad that you (all) have lent me the tools.

*¡Ojalá que el viejo todavía no **se haya muerto**!*
I hope that the old man hasn't died yet!

Helpful Tip: The present perfect subjunctive, like the present subjunctive, will only be found in a dependent clause after *"que."*

Contrast with present subjunctive:

*Espero que mi madre me **compre** algo.*
I hope that my mother buys (will buy) me something.

*Me alegro de que Uds. me **presten** lo que necesito.*
I'm happy that you (all) lend me what I need.

HOW IS THE PRESENT PERFECT SUBJUNCTIVE FORMED?

This tense has a compound construction formed by the present subjunctive of *"haber"* (the auxiliary verb meaning "to have") and the past participle of a verb *(Lección Tres)*.

The present subjunctive of *"haber"* is:

haya	*hayamos*
hayas	*hayáis*
haya	*hayan*

Helpful Tip: Sometimes students can remember these conjugations by linking the sound of *"haya"* with that made by karate experts preparing to split a pile of wood with their bare hands. Before impact, these martial arts enthusiasts seem to yell something that sounds like: **";HA—YA!".**

The present perfect subjunctive, then, looks like this:

HABLAR		COMER		VIVIR	
haya hablado	hayamos hablado	haya comido	hayamos comido	haya vivido	hayamos vivido
hayas hablado	hayáis hablado	hayas comido	hayáis comido	hayas vivido	hayáis vivido
haya hablado	hayan hablado	haya comido	hayan comido	haya vivido	hayan vivido

 PRACTICE EXERCISES

1. **Use the appropriate form of the present perfect or the present perfect subjunctive in the following sentences:**

   a. Me alegro mucho de que Helena y Román _____ a nuestro barrio. (volver)

   b. Los dependientes temen que yo no _____ por las camisetas que tengo en mi bolsa. (pagar)

   c. Sabemos que Selena Gómez _____ una nueva canción. (grabar)

   d. Tú todavía no _____ todo el correo. (leer)

   e. Esperamos que Enrique _____ el anillo. (comprar)

f. No nos alegramos de que los niños _____ los dibujos. (perder)

g. A la madre de Eduardo le frustra que su hijo no _____ mucha confianza en sí mismo. (tener)

h. Estoy seguro de que el hombre del bigote rizado _____ en la sala. (entrar)

i. Siento que Joaquín Rodrigo, compositor del *Concierto de Aranjuez,*

_____. (morirse)

2. There are seven errors in the following postcard; find them and fix them:

9 de diciembre

Querida María Elena:

Siento mucho que tú no me has contestado.

¿Qué pasa? ¿No me hayas oido? Hoy te llamé

varias veces. Me frustra que no me hayas decido

nada. ¿Eres mi amiga o no? Me alegro de que

has tenido tanto éxito y de que siempre has

triunfado. Pero, ¿por qué no piensas en mí,

Ramona, tu vieja amiga? ¡Ojalá que no te hayas

olvidada de mí! Por favor, llámame pronto.

Un abrazo,

Ramona

_____
_____
_____

There are a number of verbs in Spanish that usually take an indirect object pronoun. In most of these sentences, the subject <u>follows</u> the verb, making this construction a little different.

EXAMPLES: *Me gustan las hamburguesas y las papas fritas.*
I like hamburgers and french fries.

A ellos *les encanta la música cubana.*
They love Cuban music. (Cuban music delights them.)

Nos fascinan los pájaros de esa jaula.
We are fascinated by the birds in that cage. (The birds in that cage fascinate us.)

HOW ARE THESE SENTENCES CONSTRUCTED?

The indirect object pronoun usually comes first, followed by the verb and the subject. The verbs are most often in the 3rd person, either singular or plural.

Indirect Object Pronoun	+ Verb +	Subject
me nos		
te os		
le les		

Here are the most common verbs of this category:

encantar	*gustar*	*parecer*
faltar	*hacer falta*	*preocupar*
fascinar	*interesar*	*quedar*
fastidiar	*irritar*	*sorprender*
frustrar	*molestar*	

EXAMPLES: *Nos sorprende que ellos hayan comprado tanto jugo de arándano.*
We're surprised that they have bought so much cranberry juice.

Sólo me quedan dos minutos.
I only have two minutes left.

Al niño mimado le falta carácter.
The spoiled kid lacks character.

If the word *"que"* follows one of these verbs, as in the example above *(sorprende)*, that verb will always be singular. As you can see below, if one or more infinitives follow one of these verbs, the verb also remains singular.

 EXAMPLES: *Nos parece fantástico ver los vídeos de Taylor Swift.*
We think that it's great (It seems great to us) to watch the videos of Taylor Swift.

Me gusta bailar, pintar y cantar.
I like to dance, paint and sing.

Occasionally some of these verbs are conjugated in the 1st or 2nd person.

 EXAMPLES: *Me gustas.*
I like you. (Literally: You are pleasing to me.)

¿Te gusto?
Do you like me? (Literally: Am I pleasing to you?)

"Me gustas cuando callas porque estás como ausente". (Pablo Neruda)
"I like you when you are quiet because it's as though you weren't here."

PRACTICE EXERCISES

1. Write the appropriate object pronoun or verb form in the following sentences:

a. A mí _____ fascina que sepas patear el balón.

b. A Serena Williams le _____ jugar al tenis cuando era niño. (gustar)

c. Me _____ descansar y relajarme y dormir. (encantar)

d. A los clientes _____ sorprende que los dueños de la tienda no tengan mucho dinero.

e. Me _____ que no hay muchos hoteles baratos en San Diego. (parecer)

f. Nos _____ que haya tantas cosas que hacer en Fort Worth. (gustar)

g. A ti _____ irrita tener que escuchar los consejos de tanta gente.

h. ¿Qué os _____ los trajes de baño nuevos? (parecer)

i. Sólo me _____ diez dólares cuando salí de Las Vegas. (quedar)

j. En el futuro estoy segura de que a ellos nunca les _____ nada. (faltar)

2. Find the five errors in the following story:

Cuando tenía nueve años, me gustaba mucho los juguetes. A veces me fastidiaba mis padres porque no me compraban lo que quería. Un día le pregunté a mi mamá: "¿Te pareces bien si compro más tarjetas de Pokémon?" Mi madre me contestó: "Me parezco una mala idea. Me frustran trabajar y ahorrar tanto cuando sólo quieres comprar cosas necias". Como se puede ver, mi niñez no fue muy feliz.

These two sets of questions use grammatical structures and vocabulary from this lesson. Working with a partner, alternate asking and answering each question. When you get to the bottom of each list, start over at the top, switching roles. As a variation, write out the answers in complete sentences.

A) ¿Te gustaría tener tu propio **negocio**?

¿Necesita un carpintero muchas **herramientas**?

¿En qué deporte es esencial hacer mucho **entrenamiento**?

¿Te gustan los **detalles** de la gramática del español?

¿Prefieres el **correo** electrónico o el correo tradicional?

¿Tienes **confianza** en ti mismo/a cuando hablas español?

¿Usas una **bandeja** cuando comes en una cafetería?

B) ¿**Te encanta** el frío de diciembre?

¿Cuántos minutos de clase **nos quedan**?

¿**Te sorprende** que haga frío hoy?

¿**Te irritan** los mosquitos en verano?

¿**Te gustan** las telenovelas que ponen hoy en día?

¿**Te gusta** bailar y cantar enfrente de tus amigos?

¿Qué **te parecen** los vídeos de Taylor Swift?

El Día de las Velitas

At the back of the book (p.344), you will find an article about a special tradition in Colombia in early December. Listen to the audio as you read along. Afterwards, answer the comprehension questions (p.345) either aloud or in written form. &

A) LOS ACENTOS

Divide up the following words into syllables and circle the syllable that should be stressed:

a. cortina _____

b. conducir _____

c. tarjeta _____

d. periódico _____

e. zapatos _____

f. río _____

g. café _____

h. mantel _____

i. toalla _____

j. confianza _____

B) EL SUBJUNTIVO DESPUÉS DE VERBOS DE EMOCIÓN

1. Complete these sentences using the present subjunctive, the present indicative or an infinitive:

a. Los pasajeros tienen miedo de que _____ un elefante en el avión. (haber)

b. A la madre le molesta que sus hijos _____ por teléfono de sol a sol. (hablar)

c. "Sabemos que los primeros días de entrenamiento _____ a ser muy difíciles", dijo el capitán del equipo de fútbol americano de Episcopal High School. (ir)

d. ¡Ojalá que nuestros padres nos _____ ver la tele esta noche! (dejar)

e. Al cocinero le _____ preparar y servir comidas sabrosas. (encantar)

f. Sentimos mucho que Christina Aguilera no _____ a la tele este año con el programa *The Voice*. (volver)

g. No me sorprende que Kate del Castillo no _____ casada ahora. (estar)

h. No me gusta _____ durante los fines de semana. (estudiar)

i. Es evidente que Rafael Amaya _____ mucho éxito. (tener)

j. Los republicanos temen que los demócratas _____ las próximas elecciones. (ganar)

2. **The following letter contains seven errors, most of which relate to the subjunctive. Underline and correct them:**

Querida Manuela:

¡Me alegro mucho de que vienes a visitarme! Me sorprendió recibir tu carta; no sabía que ibas a estudiar en la Universidad de Michigan este año. Me encanta que estarás tan cerca de me, pero al mismo tiempo me frustra que tienes tanto trabajo y que no podrás salir mucho conmigo durante el año académico.

Bueno, me tengo que ir. Siento que esta carta es tan corta, pero son las once y media de la noche y todavía no he empezado la tarea para mañana. ¡Ojalá que la termino pronto!

Un abrazo,

Silvia

C) EL PRESENTE PERFECTO DEL SUBJUNTIVO

1. **Use the appropriate form of the present perfect indicative or present perfect subjunctive in the following sentences:**

   a. Tememos que _____ un accidente grave en la carretera. (ocurrir)

   b. Me molesta que vosotros _____ a los grandes almacenes. (ir)

   c. Al cartero le sorprende que el perro no lo _____. (morder)

   d. Mis abuelos están seguros de que dos marcianos _____ en el patio trasero de su casa. (aterrizar)

   e. Yo sé que Cristian _____ una beca para estudiar enología, el arte de producir vino, en Buenos Aires. (conseguir)

   f. No nos sorprende que los sueldos de los empleados no _____ mucho este año. (subir)

   g. "Espero que el repaso de hoy _____ útil", dijo el profesor. (ser)

   h. A Justin le molesta mucho que Selena no le _____ salir con otras chicas. (permitir)

2. There are seven errors in the following poem. Underline and correct them:

Esta mañana el sol ha salido,

los pájaros han cantando

e el correo haya llegado.

Esta mañana ho tomado

un café con leche

y pan tostado.

Me alegro de que esta mañana

es sábado

y de que nadie ha tenido que ir

al trabajo.

Pienso que el mundo,

como mí,

es feliz.

D) LOS VERBOS QUE USAN LOS PRONOMBRES PERSONALES INDIRECTOS

1. **Write the appropriate verb form or object pronoun in the following sentences:**

   a. A nosotros _____ gustan mucho las canciones de Ken-Y y Nicky Jam.

   b. ¿A ti _____ parece que Shakira tiene una buena voz?

   c. ¿Os _____ hacer cola y esperar tanto? (molestar)

   d. No podemos preparar este plato porque nos _____ los ingredientes adecuados. (faltar)

   e. A mis padres no les _____ dinero después de pagar la matrícula de esta universidad. (quedar)

   f. A mucha gente _____ encantan los colores otoñales de esta región.

   g. Me _____ las películas de Alfonso Cuarón. (fascinar)

   h. Cuando éramos jóvenes, nos _____ las largas vacaciones de verano. (gustar)

   i. A los alumnos de esta clase _____ irrita hablar únicamente en español.

   j. Si quieres ser dueño de tu propio negocio, _____ harán falta muchas ganas de trabajar.

2. Translate the following sentences:

a. Do they like to read and write?

_____

b. It worries me that she always returns home exhausted.

_____

c. It surprises her that these children are so lazy.

_____

d. We have no money left.

_____

PERÚ

PERÚ

CAPITAL:	Lima
POBLACIÓN:	32.200.000
GOBIERNO:	república presidencialista
PRESIDENTE:	Martin Vizcarra
DINERO ($):	nuevo sol
PRODUCTOS:	algodón, azúcar, metales, pescado
MÚSICA, BAILE:	"El cóndor pasa", huaylas, marinera norteña, zampoña
SITIOS DE INTERÉS:	Arequipa, Cuzco, lago Titicaca, Machu Picchu (templo de los incas), Parque Nacional del Manu
COMIDA TÍPICA:	ceviche, mazamorra morada, papas a la huancaína, pisco

PERUANOS FAMOSOS:

Eva Ayllón
(CANTANTE)

Chabuca Granda
(CANTAUTORA)

Javier Pérez
de Cuéllar
(DIPLOMÁTICO)

César Vallejo
(POETA)

Mario Vargas Llosa
(ESCRITOR)

Practice this vocabulary with our mobile app! Visit tobreak.com/app for more details.

 # VOCABULARIO LECCIÓN SEIS

TRACK 7 DISC 2

TRACK 8 DISC 2

SUSTANTIVOS

el **billete**	ticket (for bus, train, etc.)		*el* **martillo**	hammer
el **corazón**	heart		*el* **milagro**	miracle
la **cosecha**	crop		*la* **misa**	mass (church)
el **cumpleaños***	birthday		*el* **misterio**	mystery
el **destino**	destiny, fate, destination		*la* **natación**	swimming
			el **paraguas***	umbrella
la **deuda**	debt		*la* **pastilla**	pill
la **escalera**	ladder, stair		*la* **pelea**	fight
el **estómago**	stomach		*la* **percha**	hanger
la **falta**	lack, absence		*el* **porvenir**	future
la **felicidad**	happiness		*la* **prensa**	press (media)
el **final**	final, end		*la* **prueba**	proof, quiz, test
el **gerente**	manager		*el* **pulmón**	lung
el **gesto**	gesture		*la* **queja**	complaint
la **gota**	drop (of liquid)		*el* **rascacielos***	skyscraper
la **imagen**	image		*el* **sacacorchos***	corkscrew
el **informe**	report		*el* **sacapuntas***	pencil sharpener
la **juventud**	youth		*la* **salida**	exit
la **lengua**	tongue, language		*la* **seguridad**	security, certainty
la **leyenda**	legend		*la* **soledad**	solitude, loneliness
la **locura**	madness, insanity, folly		*el* **testigo**	witness
			las **tijeras**	scissors
la **madrugada**	dawn		*la* **uña,** *la* **uña del pie**	fingernail, toenail
la **maleta**	suitcase		*el* **veneno**	poison
			la **zanahoria**	carrot

*All of these words are compounds, formed from the 3rd person of a verb and the plural of a noun (*cumplir años–cumpleaños; parar aguas–paraguas; rascar cielos–rascacielos*, etc.).

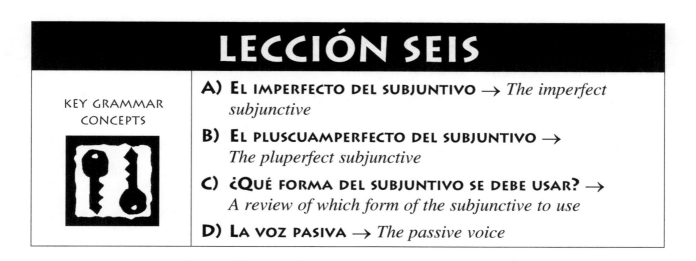

LECCIÓN SEIS

KEY GRAMMAR CONCEPTS

A) EL IMPERFECTO DEL SUBJUNTIVO → *The imperfect subjunctive*

B) EL PLUSCUAMPERFECTO DEL SUBJUNTIVO → *The pluperfect subjunctive*

C) ¿QUÉ FORMA DEL SUBJUNTIVO SE DEBE USAR? → *A review of which form of the subjunctive to use*

D) LA VOZ PASIVA → *The passive voice*

A) EL IMPERFECTO DEL SUBJUNTIVO

We have learned that the subjunctive is used with commands *(Lección Cuatro)* and after verbs of emotion *(Lección Cinco)*. All examples of the subjunctive thus far have referred to action in the present or in the future.

What form do we use, however, when the verb in the main clause is in a **past** tense, or when the action in the dependent clause is in the **past**?

The **imperfect subjunctive** and the pluperfect subjunctive are the two tenses used. The imperfect subjunctive is found in dependent clauses (after *"que"*) usually describing action in the past. The main clause will be either in a past indicative tense (preterite, imperfect, pluperfect, conditional), or possibly in a present or future tense.

This lesson will look only at the past subjunctive tenses used after a **command** or verb of **emotion**.

EXAMPLES: *Mi abuela quería que yo la **visitara** cada domingo.*
My grandma wanted me to visit her every Sunday.

*¡Ojalá que el equipo de Cristiano Ronaldo **ganara** el partido ayer!*
I hope that Cristiano Ronaldo's team won the game yesterday!

*Me alegro de que Ricky Rubio **jugara** tan bien durante su octava temporada en la NBA.*
I'm glad that Ricky Rubio played so well during his eighth season in the NBA.

*¿Sentiste que Elián González **volviera** a Cuba?*
Were you sorry that Elián González returned to Cuba?

*Me gustaría que Uds. **compraran** otros discos de Eva Ayllón.*
I would like you all to buy other Eva Ayllón records.

¡CUIDADO! Remember, if there is no change of subject (and no *"que"*), there will be no subjunctive. e.g., *Me gustaría **comprar** otros discos compactos de Eva Ayllón.* I'd like to buy other Eva Ayllón CDs.

HOW IS THE IMPERFECT SUBJUNCTIVE FORMED?

Here is a simple formula that works for all verbs:

1 Take the 3ʳᵈ person plural of the preterite.
(e.g.,"*hablar*" → "*hablaron*")

2 Take off the *"on"* at the end of the word. (*"hablar__"*)

3 Add the following letters:

yo — "a"	*nosotros, nosotras — "amos"**
tú — "as"	*vosotros, vosotras — "ais"*
Ud., él, ella — "a"	*Uds., ellos, ellas — "an"*

***Note:** The *"nosotros/nosotras"* form will always need an accent on the antepenultimate syllable
— i.e., the third syllable from the end!

Here are the imperfect subjunctive forms of three common verbs:

HABLAR		COMER		VIVIR	
hablara	habláramos	comiera	comiéramos	viviera	viviéramos
hablaras	hablarais	comieras	comierais	vivieras	vivierais
hablara	hablaran	comiera	comieran	viviera	vivieran

¡CUIDADO! The *"nosotros/nosotras"* form is the <u>only</u> one that ever has an accent in the imperfect subjunctive.

Helpful Tip: What is great about the imperfect subjunctive is that the above formula works for all verbs. If you know the preterite form of a verb, you can easily conjugate the imperfect subjunctive. If you've forgotten the preterite forms, review *Lección Uno*.

Here are a few more examples of the imperfect subjunctive:

DAR		DECIR		DESTRUIR	
diera	diéramos	dijera	dijéramos	destruyera	destruyéramos
dieras	dierais	dijeras	dijerais	destruyeras	destruyerais
diera	dieran	dijera	dijeran	destruyera	destruyeran

IR/SER		PEDIR		TENER	
fuera	fuéramos	pidiera	pidiéramos	tuviera	tuviéramos
fueras	fuerais	pidieras	pidierais	tuvieras	tuvierais
fuera	fueran	pidiera	pidieran	tuviera	tuvieran

Note: There is another way to form the imperfect subjunctive. Although the following conjugations are not as common, you will likely hear and see these forms at some point. This other imperfect subjunctive formula starts the same way:

> **1)** Take the 3rd person plural of the preterite.
> **2)** Now take off *"ron."*
> **3)** Finally, add *"se, ses, se, semos, seis, sen."*

The imperfect subjunctive of *"hablar"* would be: *"hablase, hablases, hablase, hablásemos, hablaseis, hablasen."*

✳ **EXAMPLES:** *Nuestros padres nos dijeron que **asistiéramos** (asistiésemos) a una universidad de Wisconsin.*
   Our parents told us that we had to attend a university in Wisconsin.

   *Mis amigas te rogaron que les **dieras** (dieses) el informe.*
   My friends begged you to give them the report.

   *Espero que Uds. no le **dijeran** (dijesen) nada a nadie ayer.*
   I hope that you all didn't tell anyone anything yesterday.

   *"**Me alegro** de que el otro candidato no **destruyera** (destruyese) mi reputación", dijo Rafael Correa, expresidente de Ecuador.*
   "I am glad that the other candidate didn't destroy my reputation," said Rafael Correa, the former president of Ecuador.

 # PRACTICE EXERCISES ▶

1. Write the proper form of the imperfect subjunctive:

a. estar (nosotros)

_____

b. comprender (vosotras)

_____

c. ser (ellos)

_____

d. morir (él)

_____

e. caber (yo)

_____

f. decir (yo)

_____

g. volver (nosotros)

_____

h. entregar (tú)

_____

i. hacer (Uds.)

_____

j. leer (ella)

_____

2. Write the correct form of the verb in the following sentences. Most sentences will use the imperfect subjunctive. However, some sentences may require a form of the indicative or an infinitive:

a. ¡Ojalá que los Wildcats de Northwestern _____ el partido de baloncesto ayer! Es mi equipo favorito. (ganar)

b. Mi padre me prohibió que _____ por teléfono con el boxeador, Canelo Álvarez. (hablar)

c. Los plomeros no querían que mi hijo los _____ mientras trabajaban en la cocina. (ayudar)

d. Mis amigas insistían en _____ el nuevo episodio de *Bailando por un sueño*. (grabar)

¡CUIDADO! (Don't forget that you need a *"que"* if you plan to use the subjunctive!)

e. Sabemos que _____ mucha contaminación en este río durante los años cincuenta. (haber)

f. Ayer, después de un partido terrible, nos alegramos de que el entrenador aún _____ seguir trabajando con nosotros. (querer)

g. Mi abuelo siempre me pedía que no _____ en su mecedora (rocking chair). (sentarse)

h. Me molestó mucho que mis amigos me _____ su escalera vieja. (vender)

i. Me irritó que ellos no _____ a entregarme el informe. (ir)

j. Esperaba que tú no me _____ ayuda con las maletas. (pedir)

3. Find the five errors in the following confession and correct them:

 Es verdad, robé el banco, pero nunca quise que mis amigos me ayudaron. Yo simplemente quería entrara en el banco discretamente para robar unos millones de euros. Sentí mucho que mis amigos, esos imbéciles, llegaron a la puerta del banco con sus ridículas máscaras. Sabía que nunca tendríamos éxito. Cuando la policía llegó, me molestó mucho que mis amigos dicieran que yo tenía la culpa. Ahora estoy aquí solito en la cárcel. No sé qué vaya a hacer.

B) EL PLUSCUAMPERFECTO DEL SUBJUNTIVO

The **pluperfect subjunctive** is simply a compound form of the imperfect subjunctive. This form is like the pluperfect indicative tense in that it refers to an action that occurred prior to another action, or prior to a specific point in time in the past. Like the imperfect subjunctive, the pluperfect subjunctive is found after verbs of emotion. In later lessons, we will also see this form used commonly in certain "if clauses" and in sentences expressing doubt or uncertainty.

EXAMPLES: *Esperabas que el pelotero Yasiel Puig **hubiera llegado** al estadio antes de las siete.*
    You were hoping that the ballplayer Yasiel Puig had arrived at the stadium before seven o'clock.

*Me alegré de que ya **hubieras escuchado** el disco navideño de Christina Aguilera.*
    I was glad that you had already listened to Christina Aguilera's Christmas album.

*Siento que nosotros no **hubiéramos puesto** la mesa antes de tu llegada.*
I regret that we hadn't set the table before your arrival.

*¡Ojalá que yo te **hubiera llamado** ayer!*
If only I had called you yesterday!

¡CUIDADO! Remember that an object pronoun, such as "*te*," will always come <u>before</u> the conjugated form of "*haber*" in all perfect tenses.

HOW IS THE PLUPERFECT SUBJUNCTIVE FORMED?

The formula for this tense is simple:

Imperfect subjunctive of *"haber"*	+	Past participle
hubiera hubiéramos		**hablado**
hubieras hubierais		**comido**
hubiera hubieran		**vivido**

Helpful Tip: It may be a good idea to review the irregular past participles from *Lección Tres*. Again, any object pronoun must go before the form of *"haber."*
Example: *Me sorprendió que tú no **me** hubieras **dicho** la verdad.*

Here are more sentences with the pluperfect subjunctive:

EXAMPLES: *A mis amigos les molestaba que la profesora nunca les **hubiera dado** una buena nota.*
It bothered my friends that the teacher had never given them a high grade.

*Me alegré de que los insectos no **hubieran destruido** toda la cosecha.*
I was happy that the insects hadn't destroyed the entire crop.

*Nos sorprendió que el paciente no **se hubiera muerto**.*
It surprised us that the patient hadn't died.

*Habríamos preferido que ellos no **hubieran revelado** el secreto.*
We would have preferred that they hadn't revealed the secret.

*Al fotógrafo cubano Albert Korda le irritaba que nunca le **hubieran dado** suficiente crédito por su famosa foto del Che Guevara.*
It bothered the Cuban photographer Albert Korda that he had never been given enough credit for his famous photograph of Che Guevara.

PRACTICE EXERCISES

1. **Write the proper form of the pluperfect subjunctive:**

   a. ir (vosotras)

   _____

   b. romper (nosotros)

   _____

   c. estar (ellos)

   _____

   d. morir (él)

   _____

   e. producir (yo)

   _____

   f. componer (yo)

   _____

   g. volver (nosotras)

   _____

   h. entregar (tú)

   _____

   i. saber (Uds.)

   _____

   j. crear (ellas)

   _____

2. **Use either the pluperfect subjunctive or pluperfect indicative in the following sentences:**

   a. Me alegré de que Uds. _____ la noticia sobre el príncipe Felipe de Borbón antes que yo. (leer)

   b. Esperábamos que tú no _____ el regalo antes de tu cumpleaños. (abrir)

   c. Sentí mucho que los animales _____ antes de llegar al zoológico. (enfermarse)

   d. Era cierto que nadie _____ mis quejas. (escuchar)

e. Mis amigos estaban contentos de que la película de Bérénice Bejo,

A Knight's Tale, todavía no _____ cuando llegaron. (comenzar)

f. A Charlie le encantó que la niñera le _____ la leyenda misteriosa. (contar)

g. Temían que el perro _____ el veneno que guardaban en el garaje. (comerse)

3. Find the three errors in the following song:

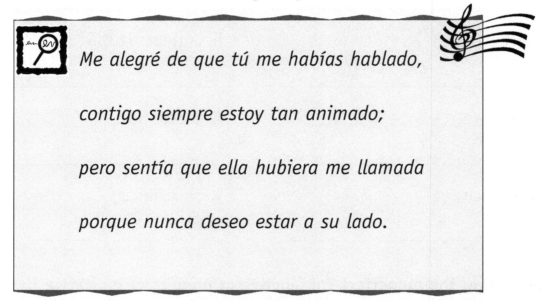

Me alegré de que tú me habías hablado,

contigo siempre estoy tan animado;

pero sentía que ella hubiera me llamada

porque nunca deseo estar a su lado.

The following chart, outlining a sequence of tenses, will help you when deciding between the present and past subjunctive.

If the sentence calls for the subjunctive, and if the verb in the main clause is in the:	then choose:
PRESENT **present** **present perfect** **future** **future perfect** **command form**	**a present or past subjunctive** ■ present subjunctive ■ present perfect subjunctive ■ imperfect subjunctive ■ pluperfect subjunctive

✳ **EXAMPLES:**

*Me alegro de que **te vayas**.*	I'm glad that you are going.
*Me alegro de que **te hayas ido**.*	I'm glad that you have gone.
*Me alegro de que **te fueras** ayer.*	I'm glad that you went away yesterday.
*Me alegro de que **te hubieras ido** ayer.*	I'm glad that you had gone away yesterday.

However, if the sentence calls for the subjunctive, and if the verb in the main clause is in the:	then you must use:
PAST **preterite** **imperfect** **pluperfect** **conditional** **conditional perfect**	**a past subjunctive** ■ imperfect subjunctive ■ pluperfect subjunctive

✳ **EXAMPLES:**

*Me alegré de que **te fueras**.*	I was glad that you went away.
*Me alegré de que **te hubieras ido**.*	I was glad that you had gone away.

PRACTICE EXERCISES

1. Write the appropriate form of each verb in the space provided:

a. Siempre insistía en que mis hijos me _____ a misa. (acompañar)

b. Temo que Javier no _____ con sus deberes antes del otoño. (cumplir)

c. Me gustaría que ellos no _____ tan rápido por la autopista. (conducir)

d. Tom Brady estaba muy feliz de que los Patriots_____ el Super Bowl en 2019. (ganar)

e. Nos alegramos de que Uds. _____ las maletas anoche. (hacer)

f. Tenía miedo de que nadie nos _____. (oír)

g. Los carpinteros nos pidieron que _____ unos martillos. (traer)

h. Mis nietos habían esperado que tú _____ ir al concierto de Beyoncé también. (poder)

i. ¡Ojalá que ella _____ esos melocotones tan ricos! (comprar)

j. Dile a la enfermera que _____ enseguida para darme una pastilla. (venir)

2. Fix the five errors that you find in the postcard below:

 Queridos Daniel y Tomás:

Gracias por su carta. Me alegro de que Uds.

están en Salamanca. ¡Ojalá que ya han visto la

Plaza Mayor! Elisa y yo comimos allí hace

muchos años. Les recomiendo que buscan una

*tienda de discos que se llama **Longplay**. Mis*

amigos trabajan allí. Cuando yo vivía en

Salamanca, compraba muchos discos. El dueño,

Eugenio, era mi vecino. Siempre insistía en que

nosotros lo visitemos en la tienda. Espero que

*Uds. van a **Longplay** antes de salir para Cuéllar.*

Un abrazo,

Juan

GET GRAMMAR

D) La voz pasiva

While the active voice has a subject that <u>acts upon</u> an object (e.g., *María golpeó la silla*), the **passive voice** has the subject <u>acted upon</u> *(La silla fue golpeada por María)*. To change a sentence from the active voice to the passive voice, the direct object of the active sentence becomes the new subject. The old subject of the active sentence becomes what is called "the agent."

EXAMPLES: *Los chicos **son capturados por** la policía.*
The kids are captured by the police.

*El actor Sergio Mayer y la actriz Issabela Camil **fueron casados por** un cura.*
The actor Sergio Mayer and the actress Issabela Camil were married by a priest.

*Nuevos planetas **serán descubiertos por** los astronautas.*
New planets will be discovered by the astronauts.

*Esas novelas **han sido escritas por** varios autores ecuatorianos.*
Those novels have been written by several Ecuadorian authors.

How is the passive voice formed?

The true passive is made up of the following components:

New subject (direct object of active sentence)	+	**Form of "ser"**	+	**Past participle** (agrees with new subject)	+	*Por**	+	**Agent** (old subject of active sentence)

"Por" is sometimes replaced by *"de"* when the action is emotional: *El dictador es odiado **de** todos.*

Let's convert a few sentences:

Active sentence: *Los hermanos compraron los relojes.*
Passive sentence: *Los relojes **fueron comprados por** los hermanos.*

Active sentence: *Los chicos aman a la nueva niñera.*
Passive sentence: *La nueva niñera **es amada por** (de) los chicos.*

Active sentence: *Inventaré una máquina increíble.*
Passive sentence: *Una máquina increíble **será inventada por** mí.*

REMINDERS:

◆ The past participle will agree in gender and number with the subject of *"ser."*

◆ Use prepositional pronouns after *"por"* and *"de"*: *mí, ti, Ud., él, ella, nosotros/nosotras, vosotros/vosotras, Uds., ellos, ellas.*

◆ *"Ser"* can be conjugated in any tense; use the same tense as you would use with the active voice.

◆ It is not always essential to include *"por"* and the agent (e.g., *El hotel fue pintado el verano pasado*).

◆ The passive construction tends to be used more frequently in writing than in speaking. Other passive constructions, including those that use *"se"* *(Lección Nueve)*, seem more common in speech.

 PRACTICE EXERCISES

1. Change the following active sentences into the passive voice:

a. El cocinero hace muchas tortas de chocolate.

_____

b. Escribiste un ensayo magnífico.

_____

c. Los guerrilleros no respetaban a su líder, "El Grandote".

_____

d. Preparamos muchas composiciones el año pasado.

_____

e. Eloísa y Roberto contaban el cuento frecuentemente.

_____

f. Haremos un castillo grande en la arena.

_____

2. Now change these passive sentences back to the active voice:

a. La carne del tigre muerto fue comida por los buitres.

_____

b. La receta de enchiladas te ha sido devuelta por mí.

_____

c. Muchos vasos habían sido rotos en la cafetería por Marisela.

_____

d. Las puertas habrán sido abiertas por mí.

_____

3. Fix the four errors that you find in the following conversation:

—¿Quién ha hecho esta torta tan bonita?

—La torta fue hecho por yo.

—Muchas gracias. Pero no tienes ni un centavo.

¿Quién compró los ingredientes?

—Los ingredientes fueron comprado por mi

amigo Cristóbal.

—Tu amigo es amado de todos, ¿no?

—Al contrario. Es odiada de todos.

These two sets of questions use grammatical structures and vocabulary from this lesson. Working with a partner, alternate asking and answering each question. When you get to the bottom of each list, start over at the top, switching roles. As a variation, write out the answers in complete sentences.

A) ¿Qué cosas puedes cortar con unas **tijeras**?

¿Hay algo **misterioso** en nuestro libro de español?

¿Conoces "La **leyenda** de Sleepy Hollow"?

¿Tienen los políticos miedo de la **prensa**?

¿Usas muchos **gestos** cuando hablas?

¿A qué edad termina la **juventud**?

¿Te gustan las **pruebas** de matemáticas?

B) ¿Te alegraste de que **hubiera nevado** mucho antes del año nuevo?

¿Sentiste que los Cubs no **ganaran** la Serie Mundial de béisbol el año pasado?

¿Pedías a tus amigos que te **dieran** muchos regalos para la Navidad?

¿Temías que un ladrón **entrara** anoche en tu casa?

¿Te molestaba que tus amigos no **hubieran estudiado** mucho antes del examen final?

¿Te prohibían tus padres que **hablaras** mucho por teléfono cuando eras joven?

¿Sentiste que tu profesor no te **hubiera hablado** antes de clase hoy?

PRUEBA DE REPASO

A) EL IMPERFECTO DEL SUBJUNTIVO

1. Change these verbs to the corresponding form of the imperfect subjunctive:

a. vas   → _____   **f.** vuelve   → _____

b. digo   → _____   **g.** tenemos → _____

c. piden   → _____   **h.** doy   → _____

d. probáis   → _____   **i.** conducen → _____

e. construimos → _____   **j.** ves   → _____

2. Complete these sentences with an appropriate form of the verb in parentheses. You will have to choose among the following: present subjunctive, imperfect subjunctive, present indicative or an infinitive.

a. Espero que Pablo Montero _____ el paquete que le mandamos la semana pasada desde Boca Grande. (recibir)

b. Ojalá que esta tarde no _____ una pelea durante el partido de fútbol. (haber)

c. Nos sorprendió que las imágenes de la guerra nunca _____ en la prensa el año pasado. (salir)

d. Teníamos miedo de que el informe que entregamos ayer no _____ lo que el gerente esperaba. (ser)

e. A Julia le frustraba que Carlos no _____ decirle que estaba enfermo. (querer)

f. Es cierto que *NCIS: Los Ángeles* _____ tanto éxito como
The Bachelor. (tener)

g. Anoche mi hermana me pidió que le _____ diez dólares. (dar)

h. Me encanta _____ durante el verano. (nadar)

3. There are five errors in the following letter. Underline and correct them:

Querido Manolo:

¿Cómo estás? Me sorprende que no me has escrito desde hace tanto tiempo. ¡Ojalá que estés bien y que pronto me mandarás una carta! Mi vida sigue ser interesante: salgo cada noche y no vuelvo hasta la madrugada. Anoche mis padres me pidieron que llegaba a casa más temprano, pero no les hice caso. No me gusta escuchando sus quejas. Ahora me tengo que ir.

Un abrazo,

Pepe

B) EL PLUSCUAMPERFECTO DEL SUBJUNTIVO

1. Change these verbs to the corresponding form of the pluperfect subjunctive:

a. murieron

_____

b. destruimos

_____

c. ve

_____

d. pido

_____

e. escucháis

_____

f. lees

_____

2. Complete these sentences with the appropriate form of the pluperfect indicative, the pluperfect subjunctive or an infinitive:

a. Las autoridades esperaban que el testigo les _____ toda la verdad. (decir)

b. A la gente del barrio le fastidiaba que un zorro _____ a dos gatos de la viuda García. (matar)

c. Era cierto que la policía _____ la autopista principal por asuntos de seguridad. (cerrar)

d. ¡Yo no quería _____ las uñas con tijeras! (cortarse)

e. Nos encantó que los amantes _____ el Día de San Valentín. (conocerse)

f. Me daba miedo que vosotros _____ que yo había matado a la vecina con el veneno. (descubrir)

g. Los empleados sentían mucho que su viejo gerente _____. (morirse)

h. Te dije que yo ya _____ las zanahorias en la ensalada. (poner)

3. There are eight errors in the following advertisement. Underline and correct them:

¿Sufre Ud. de soledad? ¿Le falta a Ud. amigos u amigas? Pues,

¡no espera más! Venga a nuestra bonita isla y pase unos días con

nosotros. Ud. conoceré a gente simpática, cariñosa y increíblemente

guapa. Si le gustan la locura y el misterio, si quiere bailar hasta la

madrugada, nuestra isla va a le encantar. Hace la maleta ahora mismo,

saque todo su dinero del banco y ¡venga a visitar nuestros!

C) ¿QUÉ FORMA DEL SUBJUNTIVO SE DEBE USAR?

1. Complete the following sentences with an appropriate form of the verb. Most answers will be subjunctive, but one sentence uses the indicative.

a. Nos molestaba que la gente del barrio siempre _____ mucho ruido por la noche. (hacer)

b. El gerente tiene miedo de que la deuda de la empresa _____ demasiado grande. (ser)

c. Cuando llegué a la escuela, me sorprendió que _____ una pelea entre dos chicos del barrio. (ocurrir)

d. A ti te gustaría que tus padres _____. (desaparecerse)

e. Creo que estudiar el subjuntivo _____ útil. (ser)

f. La madre de Liliana le dijo que no _____ con ese jugador de fútbol. (salir)

g. Nosotros sentimos mucho que vosotros no _____ bien antes de hacer el examen final la semana pasada. (dormir)

h. El veterinario insistía en que el perrito herido _____ una noche más en la clínica. (quedarse)

2. Underline and correct the five errors in this country-western song:

Se me perdí el dinero

Se me olvidó el perro

Mi coche no funciona

Mi casa está desordenado

Me gustaría que vuelvas

No quiero vivir más

Sin tú a mi lado

¡Qué triste he estado!

Siento que te fueras

Espero que vuelves

D) La voz pasiva

Rewrite the following sentences using the passive voice:

a. La maestra nos lee una leyenda muy rara.

_____

_____

b. Un ángel maravilloso le contará el porvenir a la gente del pueblo.

_____

_____

c. Al día siguiente un doctor humilde curó a los ciegos, a los mudos y a los sordos.

_____

_____

d. Nadie ha buscado una prueba del gran misterio.

_____

_____

ECUADOR &VENEZUELA

ECUADOR

CAPITAL:	Quito
POBLACIÓN:	16.600.000
GOBIERNO:	república
PRESIDENTE:	Lenín Moreno
DINERO ($):	dólar (EEUU), sucre
PRODUCTOS:	bananas, gambas, madera, petróleo
MÚSICA, BAILE:	cachullape, salsa, sanjuanes
SITIOS DE INTERÉS:	Chimborazo, Islas Galápagos
COMIDA TÍPICA:	caldo de patas, ceviche, llapingachos (cheese and potato cakes), locro, patacones

VENEZUELA

CAPITAL:	Caracas
POBLACIÓN:	32.300.000
GOBIERNO:	república federal presidencialista
PRESIDENTE:	Nicolás Maduro
DINERO ($):	bolívar fuerte
PRODUCTOS:	arroz, café, petróleo
MÚSICA, BAILE:	boleros, joropo, salsa
SITIOS DE INTERÉS:	Gran Sabana, Llanos, Mérida, Parque Central (Caracas), Río Orinoco, Salto del Ángel (highest waterfall in world), San Juan
COMIDA TÍPICA:	arepas, cachapas, empanadas, hallaca, merengada, pabellón criollo, sancocho

ECUATORIANOS FAMOSOS:

Eugenio Espejo
(ESCRITOR, MÉDICO)

Oswaldo Guayasamín
(PINTOR)

Jefferson Pérez
(ATLETA)

VENEZOLANOS FAMOSOS:

Baruj Benacerraf (CIENTÍFICO)

Simón Bolívar
(GENERAL,
"EL LIBERTADOR")

Miguel Cabrera (BEISBOLISTA)

Hugo Chávez (POLÍTICO)

GUSTAVO DUDAMEL
(MÚSICO)

Rómulo Gallegos (ESCRITOR)

Mercedes Pardo (ARTISTA)

Teresa de la Parra (ESCRITORA)

163

VOCABULARIO
LECCIÓN SIETE

SUSTANTIVOS

la actitud	attitude	
el ala *(f.)*	wing	
el alba *(f.)*	dawn	
el algodón	cotton	
la armonía	harmony	
la campana	bell	
el dibujo	sketch, painting, drawing	
la enseñanza	teaching	
la escoba	broom	
el éxito	success	
la herida	wound, injury	
el idioma	language	
las lentillas, *(los)* lentes de contacto	contact lenses	
la melodía	melody	
la pareja	pair, couple	
el pecado	sin	
la pintura	painting	
el plazo	period of time	
la política	politics	
la puesta del sol	sunset	
la raíz	root	
la red	net, network	
el resumen	summary	

el retrato	picture, portrait
el riesgo	risk
la risa	laugh, laughter
el rumbo	direction, course
la ruta	route
el saludo	greeting
el sentimiento	feeling, sentiment
la serie	series
el siglo	century
el sistema	system
el sonido	sound
el susurro	whisper
el talento	talent
la tarea	task, assignment, homework
el tejado	roof
la temporada	season (e.g., sports season)
la tienda de campaña, *la* carpa	tent
la tortuga	turtle
la trama	plot (of a story)
el trozo	bit, piece, selection
la vela	candle

LECCIÓN SIETE

KEY GRAMMAR CONCEPTS

A) EL SUBJUNTIVO DESPUÉS DE VERBOS Y EXPRESIONES DE DUDA → *The subjunctive after verbs and impersonal expressions that suggest doubt or uncertainty*

B) EL SUBJUNTIVO O EL INDICATIVO DESPUÉS DE OTRAS EXPRESIONES IMPERSONALES → *The subjunctive or indicative after other impersonal expressions*

C) EL SUBJUNTIVO DESPUÉS DE LOS ANTECEDENTES INDEFINIDOS O NEGATIVOS (FANTASMAS) → *The subjunctive in dependent clauses after indefinite or negative antecedents (GHOSTS)*

D) LOS USOS DEL INFINITIVO → *The uses of the infinitive*

A) EL SUBJUNTIVO DESPUÉS DE VERBOS Y EXPRESIONES DE DUDA

We saw in *Lección Cuatro* that the subjunctive is used with many direct command forms, as well as in sentences that express an indirect command. In *Lección Cinco,* the subjunctive appeared in dependent clauses after verbs of emotion. This lesson and the next will consider the third and final category of the subjunctive — UNREALITY. These lessons will show you events, actions, or thoughts that are somehow hazy, uncertain, possible but not definite, not real, contrary to fact, or unlikely. You will see constructions that do not offer the certainty, the bright sunshine, or the stamp of approval to use the indicative — the mood of reality.

VERBS AND IMPERSONAL EXPRESSIONS THAT EXPRESS DOUBT ━━━━━

If the main clause expresses doubt about the verb in the dependent clause, you must use the subjunctive. The subjunctive reflects the fact that the action or idea of the dependent clause may not take place or may never have taken place.

EXAMPLES: *Dudo que mis amigos Ricky Rubio y Manu Ginóbili **vengan** a la fiesta.*
I doubt that my friends Ricky Rubio and Manu Ginóbili are coming to the party.

*Nadie creía que Ricky Martin **hubiera decidido** volver a Broadway.*
No one believed that Ricky Martin had decided to return to Broadway.

*Negamos que tú nos **digas** la verdad.*
    We deny that you are telling us the truth.

*Dudabas que nuestra amiga, Adele, te **llamara**.*
    You doubted that our friend, Adele, called you.

*Es posible que nadie **haya hecho** la tarea hoy.*
    It's possible that no one has done the homework today.

WHICH VERBS AND IMPERSONAL EXPRESSIONS* EXPRESS DOUBT OR UNCERTAINTY IN SPANISH? WHAT IS THE FORMULA FOR THIS CONSTRUCTION?

The verbs listed below are in the present; they can, of course, be in any tense.

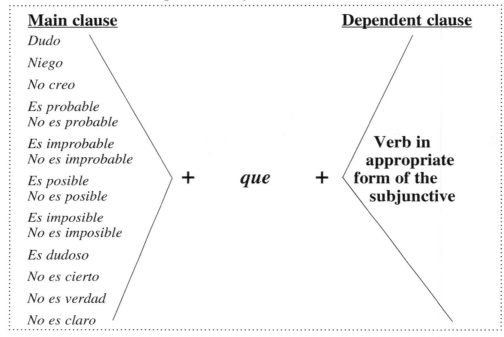

Main clause
Dudo
Niego
No creo
Es probable
No es probable
Es improbable
No es improbable
Es posible
No es posible
Es imposible
No es imposible
Es dudoso
No es cierto
No es verdad
No es claro

+   *que*   **+**

Dependent clause

Verb in appropriate form of the subjunctive

*Note: An impersonal expression usually begins with the 3rd person singular of "ser" and is followed by an adjective. For example, "Es dudoso" and "Era imposible" are impersonal expressions. The subject of these sentences is "it" — an impersonal subject, i.e., not related to a person.

All of these expressions warn the listener that what follows in the dependent clause may not be 100% true or certain. Some expressions convey this feeling in stronger terms than others. For example, *"No es verdad que hables francés"* is more categorical than *"Es posible que hables francés."* Both sentences, however, use the subjunctive.

EXAMPLES: *Dudo que los Marlins de Miami **ganen** otro campeonato este año.*
        I doubt that the Miami Marlins will win another championship this year.
    Note: The present subjunctive can be used for future actions, too.

*No era verdad que los osos **atacaran** a los campistas.*
It wasn't true that the bears attacked the campers.

*Ellos negaron que yo **hubiera pagado** la cuenta.*
They denied that I had paid the bill.

*Era poco probable que **encontráramos** un apartamento barato.*
It was unlikely that we would find a cheap apartment.

*No creo que la profesora me **devuelva** el examen mañana.*
I don't think that the teacher will return the test to me tomorrow.

WHAT HAPPENS TO SOME OF THESE EXPRESSIONS IF THEY BECAME AFFIRMATIVE OR NEGATIVE?

✳ **EXAMPLES:** *"**No creo** que Sergio García **juegue** hoy"*
takes the subjunctive.

*"**Creo** que Sergio García **juega** hoy,"*
however, uses the indicative.

*"**Niego** que Uds. **sean** de Chicago"*
takes the subjunctive.

*"**No niego** que Uds. **son** de Chicago,"*
however, uses the indicative.

*"**Dudo** que **esté nevando** ahora"*
takes the subjunctive.

*"**No dudo** que **está nevando** ahora,"*
however, uses the indicative.

When *"creer"* or *"no creer"* is used in a <u>question</u>, the tables usually turn a little.

✳ **EXAMPLES:** *¿Crees que Momma Mia **sea** una película buena?*
Do you think that *Momma Mia* is a good movie?

*¿No crees que The Sound of Music **es** una película extraordinaria?*
Don't you think that *The Sound of Music* is a great movie?

In the first sentence above, the speaker chooses the subjunctive to express uncertainty. In the second sentence, it's almost as though the speaker wants to put words in the listener's mouth. The speaker <u>clearly</u> thinks that the movie is great!

The general idea in this section is to use logic. Ask yourself:

◆ "Does the speaker want to **affirm** or **support** an idea?" → **Use indicative.**
◆ "Does the speaker want to **doubt**, **call into question**, or **deny** an idea?" → **Use subjunctive.**

¡CUIDADO! *"Tal vez"* and *"quizá(s)*" are two common expressions that express doubt and, therefore, require the subjunctive. What makes them unusual is that they don't need a *"que."*

EXAMPLES: ***Tal vez*** *Kate Ladecky, la nadadora,* ***venga*** *mañana.*
Perhaps Kate Ladecky, the swimmer, is coming tomorrow.

Quizá tengamos *más éxito en el futuro.*
Perhaps we'll have more success in the future.

 ## PRACTICE EXERCISES ▶

1. **Write the appropriate form of the verb in the space provided. Most sentences, but not all, will call for a form of the subjunctive:**

   a. Es posible que la información no _____ en la prensa. (salir)

   b. Negabas que yo _____ en peligro anoche. (estar)

   c. Creo que Burger King _____ bueno. (ser)

   d. No creo que Burger King _____ bueno. (ser)

   e. ¿Crees que Burger King _____ bueno? (ser)

   f. ¿No crees que Burger King _____ bueno? (ser)

   g. Dudas que _____ muchas tortugas en este lago. (haber)

   h. Es dudoso que nuestros amigos _____ la mesa ayer. (poner)

   i. No creía que mi cuñada _____ la lotería. (ganar)

   j. "Era imposible _____ el retrato durante la madrugada", dijo El Greco. (pintar)

   ¡CUIDADO! (There is no *"que"* here that introduces a new clause!)

   k. Es cierto que mis abuelos no _____ Internet mucho. (usar)

l. No es verdad que Cristóbal Colón _____ en España. (nacer)

m. Quizá nosotras no _____ llegar a la raíz del problema. (poder)

2. **Find and correct the five errors in this tale:**

> Cuando llegué al aeropuerto no creía que mis padres estaban allí. No creía que hayan llegado antes que yo. Cuando los vi, estaban en la sala de espera de jetBlue. Le dije a mi papá: "¡Es imposible que Uds. llegaron aquí en media hora! ¿Es posible que Uds. conducieron tan rápido? ¿Es probable que tu coche viejo fue a ochenta millas por hora? Papá, dime la verdad: ¿Qué pasó?".

It is easy to understand why the impersonal expressions at the beginning of this lesson called for the subjunctive. Expressions such as "It's possible" or "It's improbable" clearly raised some doubts about the verbs in the dependent clause. As a consequence, those verbs take the subjunctive.

What about other impersonal expressions?

Most impersonal expressions will, in fact, require the subjunctive after *"que."*

EXAMPLES: *No es bueno que Alejandro Fernández nunca me llame.*
It's not good that Alejandro Fernández never calls me.

Era necesario que nos limpiáramos las botas.
It was necessary that we clean our boots.

Es esencial que Uds. sepan preparar una enchilada de queso.
It's essential that you all know how to prepare a cheese enchilada.

Era fantástico que Diego Maradona nunca fingiera una lesión.
It was fantastic that Diego Maradona never faked an injury.

No será preciso que los guardas registren cada mochila.
It will not be necessary that the guards search each backpack.

Why do the previous sentences need the subjunctive?

The theory is that the speaker is expressing an opinion or making a value judgment about an idea in the dependent clause. At times, it looks like a command *(Es necesario que estudies)*; other times it's more akin to an emotion *(Es magnífico que bailes la macarena)*. The bottom line is that you are sharing your two cents about the verb in the dependent clause; that verb wears your opinion on its sleeve. It's tainted. It's in the subjunctive. Be sure to remember that if there is no *"que,"* there is no subjunctive. Use the infinitive.

EXAMPLES: *Es malo que algunos atletas tomen drogas.*
It's bad that some athletes take drugs.

Es malo tomar drogas.
It's bad to take drugs.
(There is no change of subject here, so the infinitive is used.)

Era importante que Uds. se levantaran temprano.
It was important that you all got up early.

Era importante levantarse temprano.
It was important to get up early.
(There is no change of subject here, so the infinitive is used.)

WHICH IMPERSONAL EXPRESSIONS DON'T USE THE SUBJUNCTIVE?

The only impersonal expressions that don't use the subjunctive in a dependent clause are the ones that express **certainty**.

Here's a list of the most common expressions of certainty:

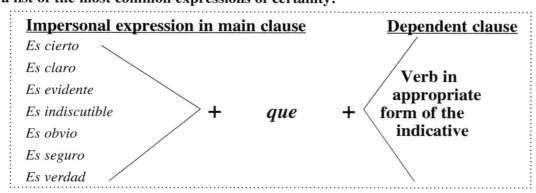

Impersonal expression in main clause	Dependent clause
Es cierto	
Es claro	
Es evidente	
Es indiscutible	**+** *que* **+** Verb in appropriate form of the indicative
Es obvio	
Es seguro	
Es verdad	

✴ **EXAMPLES:** *Es evidente que esos actores, Christian Meier y John Leguizamo, tienen talento.*
It's evident that those actors, Christian Meier and John Leguizamo, have talent.

Es verdad que uno y uno son dos.
It's true that one and one are two.

Era claro que mi hermano podía jugar al ajedrez mejor que yo.
It was clear that my brother could play chess better than I could.

Es cierto que eran las tres cuando Hillary Clinton entró por la puerta de la embajada.
It's certain that it was three o'clock when Hillary Clinton entered through the embassy door.

If the impersonal expressions listed above are made negative, they will need the subjunctive!

✴ **EXAMPLES:** *No era cierto que su lenguaje fuera políticamente correcto.*
It wasn't certain that your language was politically correct.

No es seguro que mis amigos hayan llegado.
It isn't certain that my friends have arrived.

No es verdad que haga frío hoy.
It's not true that it's cold today.

PRACTICE EXERCISES

1. Use the subjunctive, indicative, or infinitive:

a. Es bueno que ellos no _____ en la biblioteca. (gritar)

b. Era cierto que Benicio del Toro y Luis Fonsi _____ mi coche. (conducir)

c. Es extraño que no _____ muchos insectos cerca de la vela. (haber)

d. Era obvio que nadie _____ la campana. (tocar)

e. Será preciso _____ una carta lo más pronto posible. (enviar)

f. Mi suegra siempre dice: "Es bueno _____ los platos primero y descansar luego". (lavar)

g. No es necesario que Uds. _____ las capitales de Sudamérica. (saber)

h. Era interesante que nadie en la playa _____ traje de baño. (llevar)

i. Es verdad que Patrick Kane, Zdeno Chára, Scott Gómez y yo

_____ un paseo por el parque ayer. (dar)

j. Será esencial que todos _____ puntualmente y

_____ un lápiz y un cuaderno. (llegar, traer)

2. Find the five errors in this note left by a student for his teacher:

Estimado profesor Anderson:

Lo siento mucho. No fue bueno que yo recibí una nota de "20" en la prueba de vocabulario. Sé que es esencial que estudiamos mucho antes de tomar una prueba. Ud. siempre dice en clase: "Es preciso que todos trabajan más que una mula". Pero, la verdad es que prefiero hacer otras cosas. Es verdad que el español sea importante. Pero a mí me encantan las plantas. Prefiero hablar con mis rosas y geranios. Es bueno esté con ellas, también. Perdóneme.

Su estudiante favorito,

Aníbal

This section will discuss a use of the subjunctive that drives most students crazy. This occurs when the subject of a main clause is not definite or may not even exist. It's almost as if a **ghost** were the subject of the sentence! In the dependent clause, the subjunctive is needed. It usually takes a while to understand why. Once you get the hang of it, however, the concept isn't that hard. Let's start with a few examples.

EXAMPLES: *No hay nadie que* **hable** *árabe en esta clase.*
There is no one who speaks Arabic in this class.

Gloria y Emilio Estefan buscaban un apartamento que **tuviera** *tres habitaciones y Jacuzzi.*
Gloria and Emilio Estefan were looking for an apartment that had three bedrooms and a Jacuzzi.

¿Hay alguien que **desee** *acompañarme a la fiesta?*
Is there anyone who wishes to accompany me to the party?

No hay ningún elefante que **pueda** *volar.*
There is no elephant that can fly.

Cualquier* persona que **llegue** *tarde no podrá entrar.*
Anyone who arrives late will not be able to enter.

****Note:** It seems strange, but true, that the word *"cualquiera"* is shortened to *"cualquier"* both before masculine <u>and</u> feminine words (e.g., *cualquier libro, cualquier revista*)!

As you can see, the verb following *"que"* in all of these sentences is in some form of the subjunctive. It has to be subjunctive because the concept or the subject in the main clause is not definite. A negative antecedent may even deny or call into question the existence of whatever you are talking about. You can't take a picture of it. It's murky. It's something you were searching for (but haven't found). It doesn't exist. It didn't exist. It may not exist. As a consequence, the dependent clause is dependent on something like a **ghost**. The subjunctive is used, then, to express this ghost-like dependence.

What is so frustrating for students becomes evident when analyzing a sentence like the following one:

No hay nadie aquí que **toque** *el clarinete.*
There is no one here who plays the clarinet.

Students will invariably say that *"toque"* should be *"toca,"* using an argument like this: "But it's definite! No one here plays the clarinet. It's a fact. It's certain. It's true. Use the indicative. This is crazy. I don't get it!"

Don't despair! The reason the subjunctive is used in the previous sentence has to do with the **construction** of the sentence.

If we were to rewrite the sentence, it could look like this:

> *Nadie aquí **toca** el clarinete.*
> No one here plays the clarinet.

In this sentence, the indicative is used. There is **one** clause. The verb and subject agree, and everyone is happy to see the indicative.

However, the original sentence is constructed differently. In Spanish construction, if the **main** clause is indefinite or negative, the verb in the **dependent** clause has to be subjunctive. That dependent verb is depending on a subject that doesn't exist, is indefinite, or otherwise hazy. We couldn't show a snapshot of the subject to anyone. That fact will push the second verb into the subjunctive.

Helpful Tip: Remember, "ghost" in main clause, subjunctive in dependent clause!

Here is the formula for this type of construction:

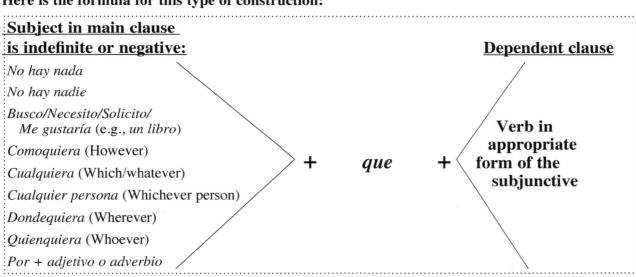

Subject in main clause is indefinite or negative:
- *No hay nada*
- *No hay nadie*
- *Busco/Necesito/Solicito/ Me gustaría* (e.g., *un libro*)
- *Comoquiera* (However)
- *Cualquiera* (Which/whatever)
- *Cualquier persona* (Whichever person)
- *Dondequiera* (Wherever)
- *Quienquiera* (Whoever)
- *Por + adjetivo o adverbio*

+ *que* **+** **Verb in appropriate form of the subjunctive** (Dependent clause)

The following sentences highlight the last six examples listed above.

EXAMPLES: ***Comoquiera** que **prepares** el pollo, no estará tan sabroso como el de mi abuelita.*
However you prepare the chicken, it will not be as tasty as my grandma's.

***Cualquiera** que **utilices** será magnífico.*
Whichever one you use will be great.

*Cualquier plan que **uses** será magnífico.*
Whatever plan that you use will be great.

*Dondequiera que Uds. **viajen**, aprenderán mucho.*
Wherever you all travel, you will learn a lot.

*Quienquiera que **enseñara** a este grupo de estudiantes tuvo mucha suerte.*
Whoever taught this group of students was very lucky.

*Por rica que **sea**, Cruella no podrá comprar los perritos.*
However rich she may be, Cruella will not be able to buy the puppies.

Remember, the main clause in this construction must be indefinite or non-existent. A change of one little word could tip the sentence from indefinite to definite, from subjunctive to indicative.

 EXAMPLES: *Busco una persona que **hable** francés e italiano.*
I'm looking for a person (any person — I have no one specific in mind) who speaks French and Italian.

Note: There is no personal "*a*" because "*una persona*" doesn't refer to a specific person.

*Busco a la persona que **habla** francés e italiano.*
I'm looking for the person (I have someone specific in mind — note the use of the <u>definite</u> article "*la*") who does, in fact, speak French and Italian.

*¿Conoces una persona que **pueda** ayudarnos?*
Do you know someone who can help us?

*Conozco a una persona que **puede** ayudarnos.*
I know a person who can help us.

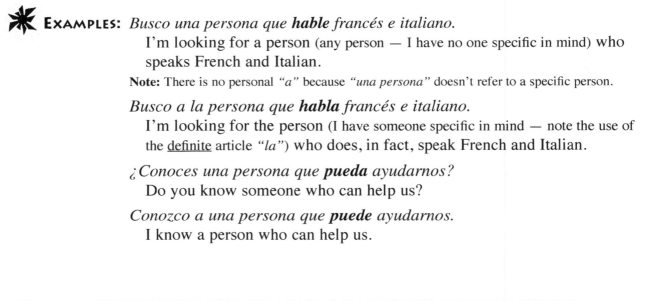

PRACTICE EXERCISES

1. Write the appropriate verb form in the spaces provided:

a. Busco un cliente que _____ muchísimo dinero. (tener)

b. Adondequiera que Uds. _____, les escribiré. (ir)

c. No hay ningún grupo que _____ como One Direction. (cantar)

d. Hay alguien aquí que _____ muy guapo. (ser)

  ¡CUIDADO! (This is <u>not</u> a question. The speaker is saying that there is, in fact, someone here who is good-looking.)

e. No había nadie que _____ lo que el profesor decía sobre la trama de la novela. (comprender)

f. Por humilde que _____, aceptará el premio. (ser)

g. Conozco a una persona que _____ una casa en Vermont. (tener)

h. Me gustaría conocer una persona que _____ a Woodstock en los 60. (ir)

i. No hay nada en el menú que nos _____. (apetecer)

j. Voy a comer un trozo de cualquier torta que tú _____. (pedir)

2. **You are writing a want-ad, looking for a roommate. Fill in the blanks with words that make sense:**

   a. Busco un/una compañero/compañera de cuarto que _____.

   b. Busco una persona que me _____ cada día.

   c. Necesito una persona que _____ la renta.

   d. Cualquier persona que _____ conmigo necesitará mucha paciencia.

   e. Por simpática que _____, es preciso que la persona tenga mucho dinero.

   f. Necesito una persona que _____ todos los días después de las siete.

   g. Quienquiera que _____, tendrá que respetar mis deseos.

   h. Tengo un perro que _____ mucho; por eso no quiero más animales en casa.

D) LOS USOS DEL INFINITIVO

Throughout this book, we have seen the **infinitive** used frequently. This section will review those uses and present a few new ones.

1 May follow another verb

The infinitive may follow another verb, serving as the object of that verb. We use this construction all the time.

> **EXAMPLES:** *Tony Romo y Victor Cruz no desean **hablar** ahora.*
> Tony Romo and Victor Cruz don't want to talk now.
>
> *Prefiero **sentarme** en un asiento de pasillo.*
> I prefer to sit in an aisle seat.

2 Used after prepositions

Don't forget, the infinitive is used after <u>all</u> prepositions. In English, we would use the "-ing" form of the verb — the gerund.

> **EXAMPLES:** *Estoy pensando en **comer** ahora.*
> I'm thinking about eating now.
>
> *Soñamos con **terminar** el dibujo para el fin de semana.*
> We dream about finishing the sketch by the weekend.
>
> *La periodista María Celeste Arrarás acaba de **entrevistar** a Julián Castro en San Antonio.*
> The journalist María Celeste Arrarás just interviewed Julián Castro in San Antonio.

3 Can function as a noun

a) The infinitive can serve as the subject of a sentence, sometimes along with the definite article. In English we would often use a gerund instead.

> **EXAMPLES:** *(El) **hablar** en la cafetería me aburre.*
> Talking in the cafeteria bores me.
>
> *Se prohíbe **fumar** en el tren.*
> Smoking is prohibited on the train.
>
> *Me gusta **correr** al lado del río.*
> I like running by the river.
>
> ***Ver** es **creer**.*
> Seeing is believing. (In proverbs, the definite articles drop out.)

b) The infinitive can also function as a noun, often after verbs of perception. In these sentences, the action of the infinitive is associated with the object.

> ✳ **EXAMPLES:** *Te vi llegar.*
>   I saw you arrive (I saw your arrival).
>
>   *Oímos los perros ladrar durante la noche.*
>   We heard the dogs barking during the night (We heard the barking of the dogs).

4 Used as a command

The infinitive is often used as a command, particularly on signs. On trains or giant billboards, you might see commands such as the ones below.

> ✳ **EXAMPLES:** *NO FUMAR*
>   NO SMOKING
>
>   *NO MASCAR CHICLE EN CLASE*
>   NO GUM-CHEWING IN CLASS

5 Used after *"que"*

The infinitive is used after *"que"* in a few set expressions (e.g.,*"tener que,"* *"hay que"*). Here are some examples where the infinitive, rather than a conjugated verb, follows *"que."*

> ✳ **EXAMPLES:** *Tengo que llamar a mi abuelo ahora.*
>   I have to call my grandfather now.
>
>   *Hay que hacer mucho esfuerzo para conseguir un buen empleo.*
>   One must look hard to find a good job.
>
>   *No nos queda mucho que limpiar.*
>   There is not much left for us to clean.

6 Can also take the place of the subjunctive

The infinitive can also take the place of the subjunctive in indirect commands with one of these verbs: *"dejar,"* *"hacer,"* *"mandar,"* *"permitir,"* and *"prohibir."* Only these verbs (not others!) allow you to use either the subjunctive or an infinitive.

> ✳ **EXAMPLES:** *Mi mamá me hace lavar el coche cada semana.*
>   **OR:** *Mi mamá hace que yo lave el coche cada semana.*
>   My mom makes me wash the car each week.
>
>   *El general nos mandó ayudarlo.*
>   **OR:** *El general nos mandó que lo ayudáramos.*
>   The general ordered us to help him.
>
>   *Te prohíbo estudiar.*
>   **OR:** *Te prohíbo que estudies.*
>   I prohibit you from studying.

Fix the seven errors related to infinitive use in the following narrative:

 Yo estaba esperando en la estación de tren. Vi lleganda a Jennie. Llegó de Maracay, después de viajando toda la noche. Le dije: "Bienvenida, Jennie. Viendo es creyendo; ¡estás aquí!". Tuvimos que esperando unos minutos allí. El guarda nos prohibió saliéramos inmediatamente. Comencé a fumar aunque un letrero decía: NO FUMANDO. No me gustó ese consejo; siempre hago lo que me da la gana.

These two sets of questions use grammatical structures and vocabulary from this lesson. Working with a partner, alternate asking and answering each question. When you get to the bottom of each list, start over at the top, switching roles. As a variation, write out the answers in complete sentences.

A) ¿Cuántas **alas** tiene un pájaro?

¿A qué hora comienza el **alba**?

¿Tienen tus padres **retratos** de todos sus hijos?

¿Qué **ruta** tomas cuando vuelves a tu casa?

¿Qué cantante tiene mucho **talento**?

¿Cuál es tu **temporada** de deportes favorita?

¿Tienen **raíces** fuertes los árboles altos?

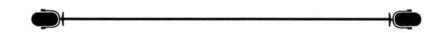

B) ¿Hay alguien que **hable** italiano en esta clase?

¿Existe un elefante que **pueda** volar?

¿Hay algún estudiante en esta clase que **sepa** bailar el cha-cha-chá?

¿Conoces a alguien que **fuera** a Perú el año pasado?

¿Buscas un novio/a que **sepa** cocinar platos colombianos muy ricos?

¿Hay un grupo musical ahora que **sea** tan bueno como los Beatles?

Por muy famosa que **sea** esa actriz, ¿es simpática?

PRUEBA DE REPASO

A) EL SUBJUNTIVO DESPUÉS DE VERBOS Y EXPRESIONES DE DUDA

1. **Complete these sentences with the appropriate form of the verb in parentheses:**

   a. Era dudoso que el sistema de seguridad _____ bien. (funcionar)

   b. No es verdad que el testigo _____ en el juicio ayer. (mentir)

   c. ¿Cree Ud. que este retrato _____ mucho dinero? (valer)

   ¡CUIDADO! (You are asking someone here for an opinion. You don't know what this person thinks!)

   d. No creo que _____ mucho para la salida del tren para Caracas. (faltar)

   e. Es cierto que esta camisa blanca _____ de algodón. (ser)

   f. ¿No creen Uds. que los alumnos de este colegio _____ de cansancio? (sufrir)

   ¡CUIDADO! (You are expressing your own opinion here. You definitely believe that these students are suffering!)

   g. No era probable que el pájaro _____ tres alas. (tener)

   h. ¿Puedes _____ el partido sin lentes de contacto? (ver)

2. There are six errors in this telephone dialogue. Underline and correct them:

—Staples Center. Dígame.

—Buenas tardes. Soy el señor Hernández. ¿Es posible reservemos entradas para el concierto de Shakira del sábado por la noche?

—No, señor Hernández. Lo siento, pero hay un problema: no hay entradas para el concierto de este sábado.

—¡No puede ser! No es posible que no hay boletos para este sábado. He invitado a todos mis alumnos a asistir al concierto de Shakira este fin de semana. Y ahora, ¿qué hago?

—Pues, Shakira canta esta noche también, y todavía quedan entradas. ¿Quiere Ud. compre entradas para esta noche?

—¡Claro que sí! Me alegro mucho de que Uds. pueden ayudarme.

—El único problema, Sr. Hernández, es que el sistema de sonido no funciona muy bien. Si Uds. van esta noche, es posible que no oyen la música.

—Eso no importa. Dudo que mis estudiantes escuchan la música. Creo que sólo quieren salir de la escuela y no pensar en la tarea. ¿Cuánto cuestan las entradas?

B) EL SUBJUNTIVO O EL INDICATIVO DESPUÉS DE OTRAS EXPRESIONES IMPERSONALES

1. **Complete these sentences with the appropriate form of the verb in parentheses:**

   a. Es verdad que el actor Demián Bichir _____ mucho talento. (tener)

   b. Era obvio que nadie _____ ir a Planet Hollywood otra vez. (querer)

   c. Era necesario _____ al gato del tejado. (bajar)

   d. No fue nada bueno que no _____ un repaso antes del examen. (haber)

   e. Será necesario que Uds. _____ un retrato en esta clase. (pintar)

   f. Es importante _____ que el cansancio puede terminar en enfermedad. (saber)

   g. Era claro que a los estudiantes les _____ el estilo de enseñanza de esa profesora. (encantar)

   h. "Es malo que la temporada de golf en Canadá _____ tan poco tiempo", dijo Camilo Villegas. (durar)

2. There are seven errors in the following speech. Underline and correct them:

Buenos días. Me gustaría hablar hoy de la importancia de las lenguas extranjeras. Es preciso que vosotros aprendéis un idioma extranjero. El habláis otra lengua es muy importante para tengáis éxito en la vida. Por eso, en nuestra escuela, os hacemos estudiáis un idioma. Nosotros sabemos que esto no sea fácil. Para aprender bien una lengua, es esencial tenéis mucha paciencia. Hay que hagáis mucho esfuerzo, estudiando y practicando cada día.

C) EL SUBJUNTIVO DESPUÉS DE LOS ANTECEDENTES INDEFINIDOS O NEGATIVOS (FANTASMAS)

1. Complete these sentences with the appropriate form of the verb in parentheses:

a. No hay nadie que _____ inglés en ese pueblo. (entender)

b. ¿Hay una chica simpática que no _____ novio en este colegio? (tener)

c. Por dondequiera que nosotros _____, conoceremos a gente muy interesante. (viajar)

d. ¿Conoces una persona que _____ bailar flamenco? (saber)

e. Por impaciente que _____, los cantantes Pitbull y Jennifer Lopez necesitan esperar unos minutos más. (ser)

f. No había nadie que _____ tanto talento como Pablo Picasso. (tener)

g. Buscaba un artista que _____ mi retrato. (pintar)

h. Cualquier ruta que vosotros _____ os llevará a Roma. (seguir)

i. Conozco una tienda donde sólo _____ camisas de algodón. (vender)

j. Me gustaría escribir una carta que _____ bien mis sentimientos. (expresar)

2. Underline and correct the five errors in this short poem:

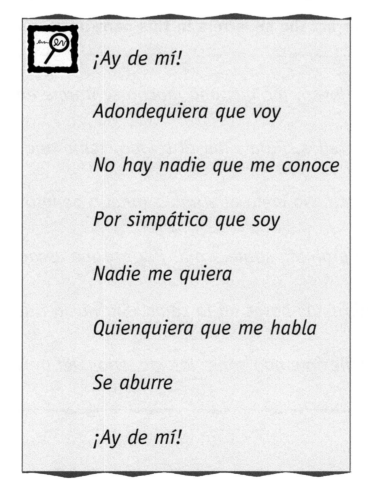

¡Ay de mí!

Adondequiera que voy

No hay nadie que me conoce

Por simpático que soy

Nadie me quiera

Quienquiera que me habla

Se aburre

¡Ay de mí!

D) Los usos del infinitivo

1. Translate the following sentences:

a. I forbid you to read the report now.

_____

b. We had to visit our grandparents every Sunday.

_____

c. Speaking English in this class is not a good idea.

_____

2. Underline and correct the six errors in this narrative:

Cuando era joven, me gustaba mucho sentarme en el tejado de la casa y mirar las estrellas. Para subir al tejado, tenía que salía por la ventana de mi cuarto. No creía que había ningún peligro en hago eso, pero mi madre me prohibía subiera allí. Por eso me escapaba de noche, después de estando unas horas en la cama. Sin hacía ruido, me sentaba en la oscuridad, reflexionando sobre los misterios del universo.

BOLIVIA & CHILE

BOLIVIA

CAPITALES:	La Paz (¡La capital más alta del mundo!), Sucre
POBLACIÓN:	11.100.000
GOBIERNO:	república
PRESIDENTE:	Evo Morales
DINERO ($):	boliviano
PRODUCTOS:	agricultura, artesanía, minerales
MÚSICA, BAILE:	auqui-auqui, cueca, tinku
SITIOS DE INTERÉS:	El lago Titicaca, Parque Nacional Madidi, Salar de Uyuni
COMIDA TÍPICA:	empanadas, humitas, marraqueta (pan), salsa picante

CHILE

CAPITAL:	Santiago
POBLACIÓN:	18.000.000
GOBIERNO:	república
PRESIDENTE:	Sebastián Piñera
DINERO ($):	peso chileno
PRODUCTOS:	agricultura, cobre, vino
MÚSICA, BAILE:	costillar, cueca, refalosa
SITIOS DE INTERÉS:	Los Andes, desierto de Atacama, Isla de Pascua, Tierra del Fuego, Valle de la Luna
COMIDA TÍPICA:	cazuela de ave, empanadas, parrillada de mariscos, pastel de chocho, sopaipillas, vino

BOLIVIANOS FAMOSOS:

Marina Núñez del Prado
(ESCULTORA)

Víctor Paz
(POLÍTICO)

Edmundo Paz Soldán
(ESCRITOR)

Javier Taborga
(ATLETA)

CHILENOS FAMOSOS:

Isabel Allende
(NOVELISTA)

Salvador Allende
(POLÍTICO)

Gabriela Mistral
(POETA)

Pablo Neruda
(POETA)

Bernardo O'Higgins
(HÉROE NACIONAL)

Practice this vocabulary with our mobile app! Visit tobreak.com/app for more details.

VOCABULARIO LECCIÓN OCHO

SUSTANTIVOS

el	*anuncio*	advertisement, announcement
la	*arena*	sand
la	*bolsa*	bag, purse
el	*bosque*	forest, woods
el	*buzón*	mailbox
el	*casco*	helmet
el	*castigo*	punishment
la	*computadora,* el *ordenador (Sp.)*	computer
el	*contestador automático*	answering machine
la	*contraseña*	password
el	*correo electrónico*	e-mail
la	*cuenta*	bill
el	*cuento*	story, tale
el	*defecto*	defect
la	*dependienta*	salesclerk
el	*dependiente*	salesclerk
la	*energía nuclear*	nuclear energy
el	*enojo*	anger
el	*equipaje*	luggage
la	*finca,* la *granja*	farm
el/la	*gobernador/a*	governor
el	*gobierno*	government
el	*horario*	schedule

la	*infancia*	childhood
la	*madera*	wood
la	*mancha*	stain
el	*montón*	heap, pile
la	*naturaleza*	nature
el	*nivel*	level
las	*noticias*	news
la	*ola*	wave
el	*opuesto*	opposite
el	*orgullo*	pride
la	*reina*	queen
el	*rey*	king
la	*sabiduría*	knowledge
el/la	*senador/a*	senator
el	*tamaño*	size
la	*tela*	cloth, material
la	*vejez*	old age
la	*venganza*	revenge, vengeance
la	*ventaja*	advantage
la	*vergüenza*	shame, embarrassment
la	*víctima*	victim
la	*violencia*	violence
el	*voto*	vote
el	*vuelo*	flight

LECCIÓN OCHO

KEY GRAMMAR
CONCEPTS

A) **EL USO OBLIGATORIO DEL SUBJUNTIVO DESPUÉS DE ALGUNAS EXPRESIONES ADVERBIALES (ESCAPA)** → *The mandatory use of the subjunctive after certain adverbial expressions*

B) **EL SUBJUNTIVO O EL INDICATIVO DESPUÉS DE OTRAS EXPRESIONES ADVERBIALES (CHAD-ATE)** → *The subjunctive or indicative after other adverbial expressions*

C) **LAS CLÁUSULAS CON "SI"** → *If clauses*

D) **EL USO DEL IMPERFECTO DEL SUBJUNTIVO PARA HACER PETICIONES CORTESES** → *The use of the imperfect subjunctive to make a polite request*

A) EL USO OBLIGATORIO DEL SUBJUNTIVO DESPUÉS DE ALGUNAS EXPRESIONES ADVERBIALES (ESCAPA)

In this lesson we will take one final look at the **subjunctive**. This first section introduces **adverbial expressions** that will be popular with all students of Spanish. The reason? When a verb follows any one of these expressions, you <u>must</u> use the subjunctive. There is no choice. It is automatic!

Some students will find it helpful to memorize the following list by remembering this word: ***ESCAPA***.

***E**n caso de que*	→	in case
***S**in que*	→	without
***C**on tal que*	→	provided that
***A** menos que*	→	unless
***P**ara que*	→	in order that
***A**ntes de que*	→	before

All of the *ESCAPA* expressions end in *"que."* The sentences that will be presented in this section would read quite differently without the *"que."* e.g., *¿El libro? Lo había comprado* **antes**. *Lo compré* **antes de** *volver a casa. Lo compré* **antes de que** *Uds. me lo recomendaran.*

✳ **EXAMPLES:** *Llévate la chaqueta **en caso de que haga** frío.*
　　　　　　　　Take your jacket in case it is cold.

　　　　　　　*Saliste **sin que** yo te **hablara**.*
　　　　　　　　You left without my speaking to you.

　　　　　　　*Recibirás una buena nota **con tal que no hables** inglés en la clase*
　　　　　　　de español.
　　　　　　　　You will receive a good grade provided that you don't speak English
　　　　　　　　in Spanish class.

　　　　　　　*Voy a salir ahora **a menos que quieras** hablar conmigo.*
　　　　　　　　I'm going to leave now unless you want to speak with me.

　　　　　　　*Jugaba mucho al tenis con mis hijos **para que pudieran** jugar mejor*
　　　　　　　que yo.
　　　　　　　　I used to play a lot of tennis with my kids so that they could play better
　　　　　　　　than I do.

　　　　　　　***Antes de que empiecen** las clases en septiembre, voy a volver a*
　　　　　　　mi restaurante favorito en La Paz.
　　　　　　　　Before classes start in September, I'm going to return to my
　　　　　　　　favorite restaurant in La Paz.

Helpful Tips: **1)** It is important to note that the action that follows each of these *ESCAPA* expressions has not happened yet, or is somehow uncertain. It is this condition of uncertainty or incompleteness that calls for the subjunctive.
2) An *ESCAPA* construction means <u>automatic</u> subjunctive. Your only question is whether you should use a present subjunctive (present or present perfect) or a past subjunctive (imperfect or pluperfect).

Let's rewrite all of the above sentences in a different time frame.

✳ **EXAMPLES:** ***En caso de que hiciera** frío ayer, espero que te pusieras la chaqueta.*
　　　　　　　　In case it was cold yesterday, I hope you put on your jacket.

　　　　　　　*Vas a salir **sin que** yo te **hable**.*
　　　　　　　　You are going to leave without my speaking to you.

　　　　　　　***Con tal que no hablaras** inglés en la clase de español, estoy seguro que*
　　　　　　　recibiste una buena nota.
　　　　　　　　Provided that you didn't speak English in Spanish class, I'm sure that
　　　　　　　　you received a good grade.

　　　　　　　*Dije que saldría **a menos que quisieras** hablar conmigo.*
　　　　　　　　I said that I would leave unless you wanted to speak with me.

　　　　　　　*Juego mucho al tenis con mis hijos **para que puedan** jugar mejor que yo.*
　　　　　　　　I play a lot of tennis with my kids so that they can play better than I do.

Antes de que empezaran las clases en septiembre, volví a
mi restaurante favorito en La Paz.
> Before classes started in September, I returned to my favorite
> restaurant in La Paz.

As you can see, the basic requirements of the subjunctive are met no matter what time frame is used.

Helpful Tip: If you see an *ESCAPA* phrase, use subjunctive.

 # PRACTICE EXERCISES ▶

1. Write the appropriate verb form in the spaces provided:

a. Los líderes militares estaban seguros de la victoria antes de que el

presidente _____ la reunión. (comenzar)

b. En caso de que tú no _____ los dientes, avísame. No
tendré ningún interés en besarte. (cepillarse)

c. No voy a revelar todos los secretos del cuento para que los lectores

_____ el interés. (mantener)

d. Colgué el teléfono sin que tú _____. (contestar)

e. Mi contestador automático llegó por correo antes de que yo

_____ una línea telefónica. (tener)

f. Nadie dijo la verdad para que el emperador no _____
cuenta de que no llevaba ropa. (darse)

g. Vas a hablar español muy bien con tal que lo _____
estudiando. (seguir)

h. "Siempre expreso mis opiniones para que todos _____ lo
que pienso", dijo el cantante español Alejandro Sanz. (saber)

i. Cambiaron las cerraduras de las puertas para que los maestros no

_____ en el cuarto prohibido. (entrar)

j. Cuando fue al buzón, Hannah tomó su impermeable en caso de que

_____. (llover)

2. Find and correct the five *ESCAPA* errors in this report:

Hemos hecho un análisis de esta institución. Es necesario cambiar algunas cosas para que avanzamos. Primero hay que construir más edificios en caso de que hay muchos clientes nuevos. Pero antes de que comenzamos con los planes, es necesario recordar nuestros ideales y tener fe en la sabiduría de los que fundaron la empresa. Nuestra fundadora dijo una vez: "A menos que hay cambio de vez en cuando, una institución no crecerá". Antes de que dijo eso, nuestra compañía era pequeña. Ahora somos la más grande de Chile. Amigos, ha llegado la hora. ¡Votemos!

B) EL SUBJUNTIVO O EL INDICATIVO DESPUÉS DE OTRAS EXPRESIONES ADVERBIALES (CHAD-ATE)

Now let's consider certain adverbial clauses that could call for either the indicative or the subjunctive. As you will see, the time frame or the speaker's opinion will dictate whether to use the subjunctive or the indicative.

This section will look at seven adverbial expressions. Some students find it helpful to memorize them in the following way: think of a friend named **CHAD** who **ATE** too much.

Cuando	→ when	**A**sí que	→ as soon as
Hasta que	→ until	**T**an pronto como	→ as soon as
Aunque	→ although	**E**n cuanto	→ as soon as
Después de que	→ after		

Let's start with some model sentences in which the subjunctive follows these expressions.

EXAMPLES: *Cuando llegue Santa Claus mañana, me traerá regalos.*
When Santa Claus arrives tomorrow, he will bring me presents.

Voy a esperar aquí hasta que vengan José Carreras y Plácido Domingo.
I'm going to wait here until José Carreras and Plácido Domingo come.

Aunque llueva mañana, vamos a jugar al tenis.
Even though it may rain tomorrow, we're going to play tennis.

Después de que Ricky Martin cante, voy a tratar de hablar con él.
After Ricky Martin sings, I'm going to try to speak with him.

En cuanto veas tu equipaje, cógelo.
As soon as you see your luggage, grab it.

Mi madre me dijo que me llamaría tan pronto como llegara la abuela.
My mom told me that she would call me as soon as Grandma arrived.

In all of these examples, the subjunctive is used. The reason is rather simple, and it is in keeping with the theory of the subjunctive as the mood of uncertainty, unreality, or haziness. All of the actions that follow the adverbial expressions above **haven't happened yet**. They are actions that <u>at the moment</u> are **not verifiable**. As a consequence, the subjunctive is used after the adverbial expression. Why subjunctive?

Let's analyze a few of these sentences in more detail:

Cuando llegue Santa Claus mañana, me traerá regalos.

In this sentence, Santa Claus is arriving tomorrow. His arrival is not verifiable yet. You couldn't take a picture of Santa Claus, for example, because he hasn't shown up. The subjunctive is used after *"cuando"* to express that his arrival hasn't happened yet; it is not reality. Let's look at another sentence:

Aunque llueva mañana, vamos a jugar al tenis.

In the first part of this sentence, the speaker is expressing the idea that it might rain tomorrow. The rain might be coming tomorrow — it's not certain, however. The subjunctive lets the speaker express this uncertainty.

Note: *"Aunque"* is a little different from these other adverbial expressions because it may also be used to reflect a person's opinion. (e.g., *Aunque María es atlética, no juega al baloncesto*; Even though Mary is athletic, she doesn't play basketball; *Aunque María sea atlética, no juega al baloncesto*; Even though Mary may be athletic, she doesn't play basketball.)

Mi madre me dijo que me llamaría tan pronto como llegara la abuela.

This sentence shows that it is possible to use a past subjunctive, too. The speaker's mother said that she would call as soon as Grandma arrived. Had she arrived yet? No. Because this arrival had not happened (you couldn't have taken a picture of it), the past subjunctive is used.

WHAT HAPPENS IF THE ACTION IN THE ABOVE SENTENCES HAS ALREADY HAPPENED?

In other words, if we were to rewrite these same sentences in a different time frame, would they still need the subjunctive? The answer is no! Let's look.

EXAMPLES: *Cuando llegó Santa Claus el año pasado, me trajo regalos.*
When Santa Claus arrived last year, he brought me presents.

Esperé aquí hasta que vinieron mis amigos.
I waited here until my friends came.

Jugamos al tenis ayer aunque llovía.
We played tennis yesterday even though it was raining.

Después de que Ricky Martin cantó, traté de hablar con él.
After Ricky Martin sang, I tried to speak with him.

En cuanto viste tu equipaje, lo cogiste.
As soon as you saw your luggage, you grabbed it.

Mi madre me dijo que me había llamado tan pronto como llegó la abuela.
My mom told me that she had called me as soon as Grandma arrived.

All of these examples used the indicative. The reason? All of these actions, in fact, took place. You could have filmed every action. Let's look at two of the above sentences.

> *En cuanto viste tu equipaje, lo cogiste.*

In this sentence, you saw the luggage and then grabbed it. It happened. You could have filmed it. Here's one last example:

> *Esperé aquí hasta que vinieron mis amigos.*

In this sentence, I waited until my friends came. They definitely came. This action occurred. It could have been documented. It could have been a Kodak moment!

ARE THERE ANY OTHER SCENARIOS POSSIBLE AFTER THESE ADVERBS?

Yes. If you want to describe habitual actions, you will use an indicative tense. Let's look at these same sentences expressed in that way.

EXAMPLES: *Cuando llega Santa Claus, siempre me trae regalos.*
When Santa Claus arrives, he always brings me presents.

Espero aquí hasta que vienen mis amigos.
I (normally) wait here until my friends come.

Jugamos al tenis en la primavera aunque llueve a menudo.
We play tennis in the spring even though it often rains.

Después de que Ricky Martin canta, normalmente trato de hablar con él.
After Ricky Martin sings, I usually try to speak with him.

En cuanto ves tu equipaje, siempre lo coges.
As soon as you see your luggage, you always grab it.

Mi madre me dijo que me llamaba tan pronto como llegaba la abuela.
My mom told me that she used to call me as soon as Grandma arrived.

What all of the above sentences have in common is that they describe events that happen over and over. Reality is being described. Santa Claus <u>does</u> arrive, and he <u>always</u> brings me presents; I <u>always</u> try to speak with Ricky Martin after he sings; as soon as you see your luggage, you <u>always</u> grab it.

We have seen, therefore, three different scenarios after the **CHAD-ATE** adverbs:

---

1 **When describing future actions (even in the past!), use subjunctive**
Cuando llegue Santa Claus, me traerá regalos.
José me dijo que me llamaría cuando llegara Santa Claus.

2 **When describing past, completed actions, use indicative**
Cuando llegó Santa Claus, me trajo regalos.

3 **When describing habitual occurrences, use indicative**
Cuando llega Santa Claus, siempre me trae regalos.

PRACTICE EXERCISES

1. Write the appropriate verb form in the spaces provided:

a. Después de que tú _____ estos ejercicios, voy a salir. (terminar)

b. Cuando Mark Teixeira, CC Sabathia, Derek Jeter y yo

_____ juntos, siempre nos divertimos. (*estar*)

c. Mi amiga me informó que iría a ver la película *Toy Story 4* cuando _____ el trabajo. (terminar)

d. En cuanto _____ el dependiente, podremos comprar la tela. (llegar)

e. Así que todos _____ a los raperos Wisin & Yandel, comenzaron a gritar: "¡Bravo!". (ver)

f. Normalmente comenzamos a desayunar tan pronto como

_____ a la cocina. (llegar)

g. Tendremos que esperar hasta que Wilmer Valderrama _____ con el periódico para leer las noticias. (venir)

h. Aunque Carlos _____ muy simpático, me robó la Coca-Cola. (parecer)

Note: This last sentence illustrates the possibilities after *"aunque."* When expressing an opinion with *"aunque,"* you can choose indicative or subjunctive. If you choose indicative here, you say that Carlos, in fact, seems (or seemed) nice. If you choose subjunctive, you say that Carlos may seem (or might have seemed) nice. You can go either way here.

i. Siempre lavo los platos después de que mi familia _____. (cenar)

j. "Cuando las olas _____ más pequeñas, iré a la playa con mi familia", dijo el tenista boliviano Javier Taborga. (ser)

2. Find and correct the six errors in this speech given in the 1980's:

Estimados ciudadanos:

Estamos comenzando una nueva era tecnológica. Cuando todos nosotros tenemos computadoras en casa, seremos felices. Cuando los discos compactos han reemplazado los discos de vinilo, habrá fiestas. En cuanto hay teléfonos celulares por todas partes, y tan pronto como todo el correo es electrónico, estaremos más contentos del que se imaginan. Hace muchos años, cuando se descubriera la electricidad, nunca se habría imaginado un mundo como el nuestro. ¡Qué suerte tenemos, amigos!

"**If clauses**" in Spanish contain the word *"si."* These clauses may introduce a condition and a promise ("If it rains, he will not come") or a hypothetical situation ("If she were taller, she would be happier"). There are two categories of "if clauses" in Spanish: those that use the indicative, and those that use the subjunctive.

1 **"If clauses" that use the indicative**

"If clauses" that use the indicative describe a situation from the perspective of a scientist. A situation is described as fact (condition), and then the consequence of that situation is stated (promise). Let's look at a few sentences.

THE PRESENT WITH THE FUTURE

EXAMPLES: *Si **llueve** mañana, no **podremos** jugar al béisbol.*
  If it rains tomorrow, we will not be able to play baseball.

  ***Iremos** a la finca si **tenemos** tiempo.*
  We'll go to the farm if we have time.

  Note: It doesn't matter if the *"si"* is in the first or second part of the sentence.

  *Si Catalina **viene**, **hablaré** con ella.*
  If Cathy comes, I'll speak with her.

  *No **compraremos** el sofá si **cuesta** demasiado.*
  We will not buy the sofa if it costs too much.

  *Si no **llega** el correo antes de las tres, **tendré** que irme.*
  If the mail doesn't get here before three, I'll have to leave.

What these sentences share is the use of the present indicative after *"si"* with a form of the future in the other clause. All these sentences have the same type of format:

> **If "X" happens, what will be the consequence?**

Another possible construction for these sentences uses the present tense in both parts of the sentence. These sentences may present habitual actions. The word *"si"* in these sentences has the feeling of "when." We'll consider the same sentences above expressed a little differently.

THE PRESENT WITH THE PRESENT

EXAMPLES: *Si **llueve**, no **jugamos** al béisbol.*
  If (When) it rains, we don't play baseball.

  ***Vamos** a la finca si **tenemos** tiempo.*
  We go to the farm if (when) we have time.

*Si Catalina **viene, hablo** con ella.*
    If (When) Catalina comes, I speak with her.

*No **debes comprar** un sofá si **cuesta** demasiado.*
    You shouldn't buy a sofa if (when) it costs too much.

*Si no **llega** el correo antes de las tres, **me voy.***
    If (When) the mail doesn't arrive before three, I (normally) leave.

As you can see, all of these sentences express habitual activities:

> **If "X" happens, then "Y" always happens.**

2 "If clauses" that use the subjunctive

In these sentences, a **hypothetical** situation is presented. The situation is explained in a way that makes it seem doubtful, unlikely to happen, or even contrary to fact. It is for this reason that the subjunctive is used along with the conditional. Which form? Either the imperfect subjunctive or the pluperfect subjunctive.

THE IMPERFECT SUBJUNCTIVE WITH THE CONDITIONAL

EXAMPLES: *Si **lloviera**, no **jugaríamos** al béisbol.*
    If it were to rain (which it probably won't), we would not play baseball.

***Iríamos** a la finca si **tuviéramos** tiempo.*
    We would go to the farm if we had time (which we don't).

*Si Catalina **viniera, hablaría** con ella.*
    If Catalina were to come, I would speak with her.

*No **compraríamos** un sofá si **costara** demasiado.*
    We wouldn't buy a sofa if it were to cost too much.

*Si no **llegara** el correo antes de las tres, **me iría.***
    If the mail were not to arrive before three, I would leave.

It's worth remembering that the present subjunctive or present perfect subjunctive is <u>never</u> used in an "if clause"! The sentences above and the ones that follow here may be read as <u>excuses</u> for not doing something now, or for not having done something in the past.

These same sentences can be rewritten using the pluperfect subjunctive along with the conditional perfect.

THE PLUPERFECT SUBJUNCTIVE AND CONDITIONAL PERFECT

✳ **EXAMPLES:** *Si **hubiera llovido**, no **habríamos jugado** al béisbol.*
If it had rained, we would not have played baseball.

***Habríamos ido** a la finca si **hubiéramos tenido** tiempo.*
We would have gone to the farm if we had had time.

*Si Catalina **hubiera venido**, **habría hablado** con ella.*
If Catalina had come, I would have spoken with her.

*No **habríamos comprado** un sofá si **hubiera costado** demasiado.*
We wouldn't have bought a sofa if it had cost too much.

*Si no **hubiera llegado** el correo antes de las tres, yo me **habría ido**.*
If the mail hadn't arrived before three, I would have left.

Note: It would also be possible to use two pluperfect subjunctives in any of the sentences above: *"Si hubiera llovido, no <u>hubiéramos jugado</u> al béisbol."*

The words *"como si,"* meaning "as if," will <u>always</u> require a past subjunctive. *"Como si"* introduces an idea that appears to be contrary to fact.

SENTENCES WITH "COMO SI"

✳ **EXAMPLES:** *Los chicos hablan **como si** lo **supieran** todo.*
The kids talk as if they knew everything.

*Gastan dinero **como si fueran** millonarios.*
They spend money as if they were millionaires.

*Conducías el coche **como si hubieras bebido** demasiado.*
You were driving the car as if you had drunk too much.

*Esos turistas se comportan **como si no tuvieran** interés en la historia del país.*
Those tourists are acting as if they weren't interested in the history of the country.

This chart will help you remember the various possibilities for "if clauses":

Present + Present	*Si recibo dinero, lo invierto.* (If I receive money, I invest it.)	(habit)
Present + Future	*Si recibo dinero, lo invertiré.* (If I receive money, I will invest it.)	(scientific analysis/ condition-promise)
Imperfect subjunctive + Conditional	*Si recibiera dinero, lo invertiría.* (If I were to receive money, I would invest it.)	(contrary to fact/excuse)
Pluperfect subjunctive + Conditional perfect (+ pluperfect subjunctive)	*Si hubiera recibido dinero,* *lo habría invertido (lo hubiera invertido).* (If I had received money, I would have invested it.)	(contrary to fact/excuse)
Past subjunctive after *"como si"*	*Se comportan como si tuvieran* *dinero. Se comportaban como* *si hubieran tenido dinero.* (They act as though they had money. They acted as if they had had money.)	(contrary to fact)

 PRACTICE EXERCISES

1. Write the appropriate verb form in the spaces provided:

a. Si yo _____ a mi casa, mi madre estaría muy contenta.
(volver)

b. Si nosotros _____ dinero, siempre lo apostamos en
Monte Carlo. (tener)

c. Si hubiéramos tomado el tren a las diez, _____ al museo
de Salvador Dalí a las once. (llegar)

d. Los jóvenes se besan en el parque como si _____
enamorados. (estar)

e. Habría ido al concierto de Jay-Z y Beyoncé si mis amigos me

_____. (invitar)

f. Si nieva luego, mis hijos _____ muy contentos. (estar)

g. Si mi abuelo me llama por teléfono, siempre _____ media hora con él. (hablar)

h. Si el reloj no se me _____, habría podido deciros qué hora era. (romper)

i. Si bailarais como Chita Rivera y Chayanne, _____ muy ricos y famosos. (ser)

j. Si mi amigo Carlos Ponce me insultara otra vez, no _____ a su fiesta. (asistir)

k. Si mi contestador automático funcionara mejor, Adriana Castro y Carolina Herrera me _____ más mensajes. (dejar)

2. Find and correct the five errors of mood and tense in this narrative:

¡Mi hermano es insoportable! Se comporta como si yo tenga más de un millón de pesos. Si él no sea mi hermano, nunca hablaría con él. Un día fuimos a un buen restaurante boliviano. Si él no me invitó, yo nunca habría ido con él. Cuando llegó la cuenta, no podía creerlo: ¡tuvimos que pagar un montón de dinero! Sentía como si me estaba volviendo loco. Desafortunadamente, la tuve que pagar. Si él me invite en el futuro, no iré.

D) EL USO DEL IMPERFECTO DEL SUBJUNTIVO PARA HACER PETICIONES CORTESES

Another use of the **imperfect subjunctive** is for making a polite request. It is an alternative to the conditional with the following verbs: *"deber," "poder"* and *"querer."*

EXAMPLES: *Debiéramos (Deberíamos) prender la computadora. ¿Recuerdas la contraseña?*
We should turn on the computer. Do you remember the password?

¿Pudiéramos (Podríamos) reunirnos para hablar de nuestros problemas?
Could we get together to talk about our problems?

Quisiera (Querría) hablar contigo esta noche acerca del extraordinario libro de García Márquez Crónica de una muerte anunciada.
I'd like to speak with you tonight about García Márquez's extraordinary book *Chronicle of a Death Foretold.*

PRACTICE EXERCISES

Translate the following three sentences using the imperfect subjunctive:

a. I'd like to dance with you tonight.

_____

b. Could you please call me before midnight?

_____

c. We ought to order the tomato salad.

_____

These two sets of questions use grammatical structures and vocabulary from this lesson. Working with a partner, alternate asking and answering each question. When you get to the bottom of each list, start over at the top, switching roles. As a variation, write out the answers in complete sentences.

A) ¿Te gusta dar paseos largos por el **bosque**?

¿Hay un **contestador automático** en tu casa?

¿Tuviste una **infancia** feliz?

¿Cómo se llama el **rey** de España?

¿Cuántos **senadores** por cada estado hay en el Congreso?

¿Crees que hablar varios idiomas es una **ventaja**?

¿Es el **voto** de los pobres tan importante como el de los ricos?

B) Si **nieva** en el invierno, ¿**esquías** mucho?

Si **nieva** mañana, ¿**esquiarás**?

Si **nevara** mañana, ¿**esquiarías**?

Si **hubiera nevado** ayer, ¿habrías **esquiado**?

¿Hablas a veces **como si** lo **supieras** todo?

Si **tienes** mucho tiempo libre esta noche, ¿me **llamarás**?

Si **tuvieras** mucho tiempo libre esta noche, ¿me **llamarías**?

"ALL THAT JAZZ" – UNA ENTREVISTA CON TUTI FERNÁNDEZ

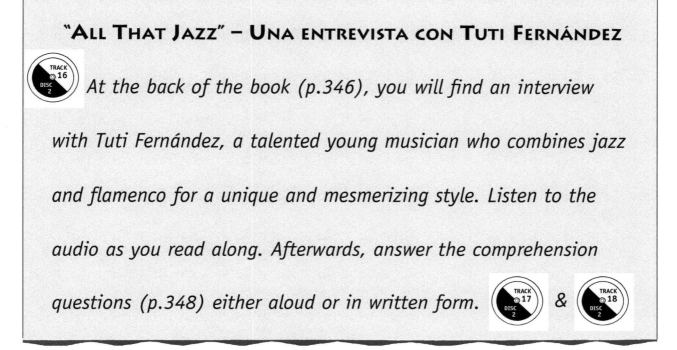

At the back of the book (p.346), you will find an interview with Tuti Fernández, a talented young musician who combines jazz and flamenco for a unique and mesmerizing style. Listen to the audio as you read along. Afterwards, answer the comprehension questions (p.348) either aloud or in written form.

PRUEBA DE REPASO

A) EL USO OBLIGATORIO DEL SUBJUNTIVO DESPUÉS DE ALGUNAS EXPRESIONES ADVERBIALES (ESCAPA)

1. **Complete these sentences with the appropriate form of the verb in parentheses:**

   a. La película de Carmen Maura y Lola Dueñas se cortó antes de que los amantes se

   _____. (besar)

   b. El gobernador declarará el estado de emergencia en caso de que

   _____ otro huracán este invierno. (haber)

   c. Te fuiste antes de que yo _____ charlar contigo. (poder)

   d. Con tal que _____ una beca, puedes pasar un año estudiando en Sucre, Bolivia. (conseguir)

   e. El gerente siempre estaba presente para que los empleados no

   _____ temprano de la oficina. (salir)

   f. Normalmente nos gusta bailar hasta la madrugada con la música de Paulina

   Rubio, a menos que _____ cansados. (estar)

   g. Es importante que Uds. terminen el examen antes de que

   _____ el timbre. (sonar)

   h. Te lo explico todo para que tú _____ mis sentimientos. (comprender)

B) El subjuntivo o el indicativo después de otras expresiones adverbiales (CHAD-ATE)

1. There are eight errors in the following letter. Underline and correct them:

Querida Margarita:

Cuando recibes esta carta, estaré en Santiago con nuestros queridos amigos chilenos. Siento que no puedes asistir a la boda de Paula y Ignacio; estoy segura de que a ellos también les gustara que estuvieras allí. Aunque no vas a la boda, sabrás todos los detalles, porque te voy a mandar un montón de fotos tan pronto como las tengo en mano. Nuestros amigos me dicen que van a llamarte el día de la boda, antes de que llegan todos los invitados. ¡Me encantaría hablara contigo desde Santiago también! Te escribiré otra carta en cuanto vuelvo a casa.

Un abrazo,

Gloria

2. Complete these sentences with the appropriate form of the verb in parentheses:

a. Iremos al concierto de Maluma después de _____ las entradas. (comprar)

b. Cuando los niños _____ a la playa, les gusta hacer castillos de arena. (ir)

c. En cuanto yo _____ los resultados del voto, os informaré por correo electrónico. (saber)

d. No estaremos contentas hasta que tú _____ estas tres películas de Benicio del Toro: *Traffic, Che y Avengers: Infinity War.* (ver)

e. En cuanto Uds. _____ a la frontera, tendrán que presentar los pasaportes. (llegar)

f. Cuando Jaime _____ la beca, sus padres le dieron una fiesta. (recibir)

g. Aunque _____ un montón de tarea, voy a ver *Despierta América* porque Alan Tacher y Karla Martínez son presentadores increíbles. (tener)

h. Cuando Pilar _____ a Santiago, conocerá a sus primos chilenos por primera vez. (viajar)

i. Tan pronto como mi madre _____ las noticias, me llamó por teléfono para contármelas. (oír)

j. Te dije que no te daría mi opinión hasta que tú me _____ todos los detalles. (contar)

3. There are seven errors in this advertisement. Underline and correct them:

¿Quiere Ud. aprender otra lengua? ¿Le gustaría hablar bien el español? En cuanto Ud. lee este anuncio, ¡llama a la ESCUELA CHAD, la mejor escuela de idiomas del planeta! Cuando Ud. ve nuestro horario de clases, verá que hay cursos para todos los niveles. Tan pronto como Ud. paga la matrícula, podrá tomar cursos de cualquiera lengua que le interesa. Aunque es una escuela barata (un curso de seis meses sólo

cuesta trescientos dólares), la ESCUELA CHAD es muy buena. En la ESCUELA

CHAD ofrecemos trescientas lenguas diferentes, pero le recomendamos que

elige el español, porque es el idioma más bello del mundo.

C) LAS CLÁUSULAS CON "SI"

1. Conjugate the infinitive into an appropriate form:

a. Si tengo tiempo, _____ a la playa. (ir)

b. Si yo sacara una buena nota en esta clase, _____ alegre. (estar)

c. Si tú me hubieras invitado al concierto, yo _____. (ir)

d. Si me levanto temprano, _____ en el jardín. (trabajar)

e. Mi amigo se comporta como si _____ mucho dinero. (tener)

f. Si tú _____ en Santa Cruz, habrías hablado español. (nacer)

2. Underline and correct the three errors in this short, but moving, love poem:

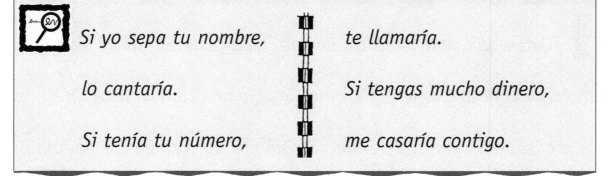

Si yo sepa tu nombre,   *te llamaría.*

lo cantaría.   *Si tengas mucho dinero,*

Si tenía tu número,   *me casaría contigo.*

3. Now write your own love poem, using three "if clauses":

(Answers will vary.)

_____

_____

_____

D) El uso del imperfecto del subjuntivo para hacer peticiones corteses

1. Translate these sentences using the imperfect subjunctive:

a. Could you please give me the suitcase? (Use the *Ud.* form.)

_____

b. I'd like to ask you (familiar) a favor.

_____

c. We should write the report soon.

_____

2. Underline and correct the eight errors in the following letter:

> *Ignacio:*
>
> *Gloria me ha informado que te vas a casar con Paula. ¡Idiota! ¡Tú me dijiste que querías casarte conmi! Si te cases con ella, estaré furiosa. En cuanto podría, voy a Santiago para que podemos hablar cara a cara. Es necesario que esperas hasta que yo llego allí. Aunque eres un idiota, te sigo queriendo mucho. ¡No te casas con Paula! Tan pronto como estamos juntos, ya no pensarás más en ella.*
>
> *Un beso,*
>
> *Margarita*

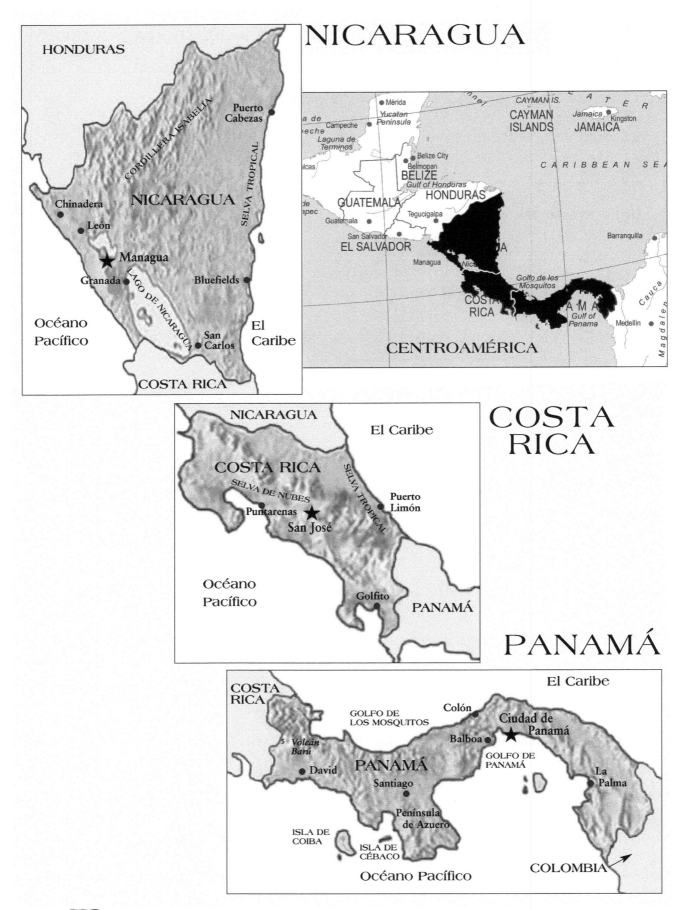

NICARAGUA

HONDURAS

CORDILLERA ISABELIA

NICARAGUA

SELVA TROPICAL

Puerto
Cabezas

Chinadera

León

★ Managua

Granada

LAGO DE NICARAGUA

Bluefields

Océano
Pacífico

San
Carlos

El
Caribe

COSTA RICA

Mérida

Yucatan
Peninsula

Campeche

a de
eche

Laguna de
Terminos

Belize City

BELIZE

Belmopan

Gulf of Honduras

CAYMAN IS.

CAYMAN
ISLANDS

ATER

Jamaica

JAMAICA

Kingston

CARIBBEAN SEA

GUATEMALA

HONDURAS

Tegucigalpa

Barranquilla

Guatemala

EL SALVADOR

San Salvador

Managua

Nica

UA

Golfo de los
Mosquitos

COSTA
RICA

AMA

Gulf of
Panama

Medellin

Cauca

Magdalen

CENTROAMÉRICA

COSTA RICA

NICARAGUA

El Caribe

COSTA RICA

SELVA TROPICAL

SELVA DE NUBES

Puntarenas

★ San José

Puerto
Limón

Océano
Pacífico

Golfito

PANAMÁ

PANAMÁ

COSTA
RICA

El Caribe

GOLFO DE
LOS MOSQUITOS

Colón

Ciudad de
Panamá ★

s Volcán
Barú

Balboa

GOLFO DE
PANAMÁ

David

PANAMÁ

Santiago

La
Palma

Península
de Azuero

ISLA DE
COIBA

ISLA DE
CÉBACO

COLOMBIA

Océano Pacífico

NICARAGUA, COSTA RICA & PANAMÁ

NICARAGUA

CAPITAL:	Managua
POBLACIÓN:	6.200.000
GOBIERNO:	república
PRESIDENTE:	José Daniel Ortega Saavedra
DINERO ($):	córdoba
PRODUCTOS:	algodón, café, fruta, petróleo, plátano
MÚSICA, BAILE:	bamba, rumba
SITIOS DE INTERÉS:	La Flor, las huellas de Acahualinc, El lago de Nicaragua
COMIDA TÍPICA:	baho, gallo pinto, nacatamales

NICARAGÜENSES FAMOSOS:

Violeta Barrios de Chamorro
(POLÍTICA)

Ernesto Cardenal
(POLÍTICO)

Rubén Darío
(POETA)

COSTA RICA

CAPITAL:	San José
POBLACIÓN:	4.900.000
GOBIERNO:	república democrática
PRESIDENTE:	Carlos Alvarado Quesada
DINERO ($):	colón costarricense
PRODUCTOS:	azúcar, bananas, café, melón, muebles, piña
MÚSICA, BAILE:	merengue, punto guanacasteco, salsa
SITIOS DE INTERÉS:	Monte Verde, Parques Nacionales Tortuguero y Corcovado, Volcán Arenal, Volcán Irazú
COMIDA TÍPICA:	casado, gallo pinto, gallos (filled tortillas), olla de carne, pan de yuca, sopa negra

COSTARRICENSES FAMOSOS:

Óscar Arias Sánchez
(POLÍTICO, GANADOR DE PREMIO NOBEL)

Franklin Chang
(ASTRONAUTA)

Editus
(CONJUNTO MUSICAL)

Claudia Poll
(ATLETA)

Silvia Poll
(ATLETA)

PANAMÁ

CAPITAL:	La Ciudad de Panamá
POBLACIÓN:	4.100.000
GOBIERNO:	democracia constitucional
PRESIDENTE:	Juan Carlos Varela
DINERO ($):	balboa, dólar americano
PRODUCTOS:	cacao, petróleo, piña, plátano
MÚSICA, BAILE:	afro-caribeña
SITIOS DE INTERÉS:	Archipiélago de San Blas, El canal de Panamá, Península Azuero, Volcán Barú
COMIDA TÍPICA:	arroz con coco, ceviche, chicha dulce, corvina, ropa vieja, sancocho de gallina, saos

PANAMEÑOS FAMOSOS:

Rubén Blades
(MÚSICO)

Roberto Durán
(BOXEADOR)

Mireya Moscoso
(POLÍTICA)

Mariano Rivera
(BEISBOLISTA)

VOCABULARIO LECCIÓN NUEVE

VERBOS

abandonar	to abandon	*borrar*	to erase
abrazar	to embrace, to hug	*brillar*	to shine
aburrirse	to become (get) bored	*brindar*	to toast (drink)
aconsejar	to advise	*calentar (ie)*	to heat
acostumbrarse a	to get used to	*castigar*	to punish
acusar	to accuse	*causar*	to cause
adquirir (ie)	to acquire	*colgar (ue)*	to hang (up)
agradecer	to thank, to be grateful for	*colocar*	to place, to arrange
		confiar en	to trust
ahorrar	to save	*confundir*	to confuse
alquilar	to rent	*conseguir (i)*	to get, to obtain
anochecer	to become night, to grow dark	*contar (ue) chismes*	to gossip
añadir	to add	*crecer*	to grow, to increase
aparecer	to appear	*deber*	to owe, ought to
apoyar	to support, to aid	*dejar*	to leave (behind), to allow
apretar (ie)	to tighten, to squeeze		
arreglar	to arrange, to fix	*deletrear*	to spell
asustar	to frighten, to scare	*derramar*	to spill
atraer	to attract	*desaparecer*	to disappear
atreverse a	to dare to	*desarrollar*	to develop
averiguar	to find out	*desayunar*	to have breakfast
avisar	to notify, to let know	*descansar*	to rest, to relax

LECCIÓN NUEVE

A) EL USO DE LAS CONSTRUCCIONES CON "SE" PARA EXPRESAR LA VOZ PASIVA O UN SUJETO IMPERSONAL

We saw in *Lección Seis* that the true passive voice is constructed in the following way: a new subject (the object of the old sentence), a form of *"ser,"* a past participle, the word *"por,"* and the agent (the subject of the active sentence). *"La pizza fue preparada por Margarita"* is an example of this type of sentence.

In this section, we will consider another way to express the passive voice. This construction uses the word *"se"* with a verb in the 3rd person singular or plural and is usually followed by the subject. This type of passive sentence is used a great deal in Spanish. It is seen more frequently than the true passive, particularly when the agent is of no interest to the speaker.

EXAMPLES: *Se venden cigarrillos en esa tienda.*
Cigarettes are sold in that store.

Se cultivaron unas flores exquisitas en esa finca.
Some exquisite flowers were grown on that farm.

En algunas partes norteñas de Alaska, se pueden vivir muchos meses sin ver el sol.
In some northern parts of Alaska, many months can be lived without seeing the sun.

Se alquilan coches baratos en Managua.
   Cheap cars are rented in Managua.

Se pierde mucho tiempo durante la juventud.
   A lot of time gets wasted during one's youth.

Se cierran las puertas de las tiendas a las seis.
   The doors of the stores are closed at six o'clock.

Se necesitan computadoras nuevas en mi oficina.
   New computers are needed in my office.

As you can see from these sentences, the verb agrees with the noun that follows it. All the nouns above, you may notice, are inanimate objects. The subject here is the noun that follows the verb. These nouns are the primary focus of the sentence: they are the stars. Grammatically, it's almost as if the verb were acting reflexively: the cigarettes sell themselves, the doors close themselves, etc.

HOW IS A PASSIVE SENTENCE USING "SE" PUT TOGETHER?

The formula is quite simple:

"Se"	**+**	**Verb**	**+**	**Subject**
		(in 3rd person singular or plural)		(the subject is an inanimate object)

WHAT HAPPENS, HOWEVER, IF THE NOUN THAT FOLLOWS IS A PERSON?

There are two scenarios:

1 **If the person is indefinite or unidentified**

If the person is indefinite or unidentified, the above formula works. You will notice that there is no personal *"a"* in any of the following sentences because the nouns are the grammatical subject and *"se"* is the passive marker. You will notice that the verb still agrees with the noun that follows it.

EXAMPLES: *Se busca una criada nueva en esa casa.*
   A new maid is being sought in that home.

Se desean profesores jóvenes que hablen español.
   Young teachers are wanted who speak Spanish.

No se necesita un cura como el suyo en nuestra iglesia.
   A priest like yours is not needed in our church.

Sólo se aceptan personas honestas.
   Only honest people are accepted.

2 If a specific person is referred to

If a <u>specific</u> person is referred to, however, a *"se"* passive construction is not technically possible in Spanish, although it is often translated that way into English. The direct object in these sentences is singled out with a personal *"a."* When that is the case, it is clear that the following noun cannot be the subject of the verb; because the subject is signaled by impersonal *"se,"* the verb always remains singular.

✳ EXAMPLES: *Se busca a la criada nueva porque ella robó los zafiros.*
One is looking for the new maid (the new maid is being looked for) because she robbed the sapphires.

Se mató a los revolucionarios.
One (someone) killed the revolutionaries. (The revolutionaries were killed.)

Se acuesta a los niños temprano.
One puts the kids to bed early. (The kids are put to bed early.)

Se necesita a las mujeres que cantaron en el festival el año pasado.
One needs the women who sang at the festival last year. (The women who sang at last year's festival are needed.)

Spanish also uses the impersonal *"se"* and a verb in the 3rd person **singular** form when no one in particular is the subject of the sentence. This construction simply describes the action because the subject is relatively anonymous or unimportant. In English, we use the words "one" or "you" or "a person" or "people" when we want to express the same idea.

✳ EXAMPLES: *Se habla español en la Ciudad de Panamá y en San José.*
One (A person) speaks Spanish in Panama City and in San José.

Se come bien en restaurantes panameños.
One eats well (You eat well) in Panamanian restaurants.

Se dice que el clima de Santa Fe es maravilloso.
It is said that the climate of Santa Fe is marvelous.

Se ve que muchos niños juegan en el parque.
One sees that many children are playing in the park.

As you can see, the structure of this type of sentence is straightforward:

"Se"	+	**Verb**	+	**Object**
		(in 3rd person singular)		(or adverb or prepositional phrase or subordinate clause)

Note: Some grammar theorists have approved the use of a singular verb even with the passive *"se"* followed by a plural subject. The resultant sentence "Se **vende** periódicos" is thus considered correct by some grammarians but an unthinkable error by others. Since the Spanish language has a strong tendency towards agreement, this sentence should almost always be written: *"Se **venden** periódicos."*

WHAT HAPPENS WHEN THERE IS A DIRECT OBJECT THAT REFERS TO SPECIFIC PEOPLE IN THESE TYPES OF SENTENCES?

Will the verb still be singular? Yes.

EXAMPLES: *Se **ayudó** a los hombres heridos.*
One helped the wounded men.

*Se **recibió** a los ministros con cortesía.*
One received the ministers courteously.

*Se **premiará** al mejor atleta.*
One will reward the best athlete.

Note: Because the personal *"a"* in these sentences introduces a **direct object**, the subject of these sentences remains impersonal. These sentences are not technically passive, although they are often translated that way in English: "The wounded men are helped," "The ministers are received courteously," and "The best athlete will be rewarded."

PRACTICE EXERCISES

1. Write the appropriate verb form in the spaces provided:

a. Se _____ muchos tipos de café en las tiendas de Juan Valdez. (vender)

b. No se _____ ni el japonés ni el ruso en este colegio. (estudiar)

¡CUIDADO! (Remember *"ni . . . ni"* uses a plural verb.)

c. Se _____ muchos dólares en 1929 cuando la Bolsa (Stock Market) bajó tanto. (perder)

d. Se _____ muchas ideas nuevas si esa empresa va a atraer más clientela. (necesitar)

e. La madre le dijo a la niñera: "En esta casa se _____ a los niños antes de acostarlos". (bañar)

f. Se _____ las puertas de la capilla a las ocho en punto. (cerrar)

g. Se _____ a la princesa Carolina con suma cordialidad en la fiesta la semana pasada. (recibir)

h. Se _____ al príncipe y a la princesa con suma cordialidad en la fiesta la semana pasada. (recibir)

i. Se _____ muchos artículos fascinantes en la revista *Vanity Fair*. (escribir)

j. No se _____ colocar muchos libros aquí. (poder)

2. Find and correct the six errors that appear in this account of the first day of tennis practice:

¡Qué día! No se pueden creer lo que pasó hoy. Los pobres estudiantes sufrieron mucho. Todas las pelotas se desapareció durante el verano y no se habían preparado las canchas. Los atletas le pedieron al jugador más joven que vuelva al gimnasio para preguntar qué pasó. Mientras tanto, el entrenador loco comenzó a hablar solamente en inglés. En nuestro colegio no se entiende bien esta lengua. En el verano se buscaron un entrenador que hablara español. Por desgracia, no se encontró a nadie. Por lo tanto, esta temporada de tenis va a ser muy interesante. No se saben qué va a ocurrir.

3. Write the appropriate verb form in the spaces provided:

a. Se _____ portugués en Río de Janeiro. (hablar)

b. Se _____ muy bien en el sur de este país. (vivir)

c. Se _____ que la pizza de Domino's es la mejor del mundo. (creer)

d. Se _____ hacer muchos ejercicios difíciles en el gimnasio. (poder)

e. Antes siempre se _____ al mejor cantante. (alabar)

f. Ayer se _____ a las niñas heridas. (auxiliar)

g. No se _____ decir tales cosas. (deber)

h. Se _____ que va a nevar mucho este invierno. (decir)

i. Se _____ a los bomberos guapos cada día en la plaza. (ver)

j. No se _____ mucho dinero durante la juventud. (ahorrar)

4. Translate the following sentences:

a. Many languages are spoken in this school.

_____

b. One never knows what the weather will be in the future.

_____

c. One eats very well in the cafeteria of our hospital.

_____

d. On the television program *La gorda y la flaca*, one can always find out what Diego Boneta and Marina de Tavira are doing.

_____

So far, we have seen two different ways to diminish the role of the subject: the true passive *(La pizza fue preparada por Margarita)* and the passive with *"se" (Se preparó la pizza)*. There is one other way (which we also use in English) to reduce the importance of the subject. Simply use the **indefinite third person plural** form.

Examples: *Construyeron esos edificios en 1990.*
Those buildings were built in 1990.
(They — indefinite — built those buildings in 1990.)

Hablan francés en Haití.
French is spoken in Haiti. (They speak French in Haiti.)

Dicen que va a granizar mañana.
They say that it is going to hail tomorrow.
(It is said that it is going to hail tomorrow.)

Preparan un desayuno delicioso en aquel restaurante.
They make a delicious breakfast in that restaurant.
(A delicious breakfast is prepared in that restaurant.)

*La **descubrieron** en un club tropical de Ipanema.*
She was discovered in a tropical club in Ipanema.
(They discovered her in a tropical club in Ipanema.)

As you can see, you may translate these sentences into English with either a passive construction or with the impersonal "they." The impersonal "they" refers to no one in particular.

Let's review the three ways to express the passive voice in Spanish:

1 **La pizza fue preparada (por Margarita).** (true passive)

2 **Se preparó la pizza.** (*"se"* construction to express passive)

3 **Prepararon la pizza.** (indefinite third person plural)

All three sentences could be translated: "The pizza was prepared." When there is a definite agent, only the first construction is possible. The true passive is used when the agent is expressed either with words — *La pizza fue preparada por Margarita* — or by implication — *La pizza fue preparada* (it is clear that <u>someone</u> completed the action, although that person may not be named).

PRACTICE EXERCISES

1. **Write the appropriate verb form in the spaces provided, using the third person plural passive construction:**

   a. _____ muchas canciones en Spotify. (Vender)

   b. No _____ filosofía en este colegio. (estudiar)

   c. En Wall Street _____ mucho dinero en 2008 cuando la Bolsa bajó tanto. (perder)

   d. En Calgary _____ muchos jugadores nuevos si los Flames quieren volver a ganar la Stanley Cup. (necesitar)

   e. En esa casa _____ a los niños antes de las nueve. (acostar)

   f. En San José _____ las puertas de los almacenes a las diez en punto. (abrir)

   g. _____ a mi cuñado con indiferencia cuando pasó el fin de semana en el norte de la ciudad. (Recibir)

   h. Anoche _____ a elegir un nuevo presidente de mi club de ajedrez. (ir)

   i. Normalmente _____ la puerta antes de comenzar con las ventanas. (colocar)

   j. _____ muchos discos de Ivy Queen y Tommy Torres en mi barrio. (Tocar)

2. Find and correct the five errors that appear in this eyewitness account of a robbery:

¡Qué noche! Robaron todas las casas anoche. Llevó televisores, cámaras y Playstation 4's. El barrio era un lugar de mucha plata: se construyó las casas con la ayuda de arquitectos famosos como Frank Lloyd Wright e I.M. Pei. Cuando la policía llegó, todos comenzaron a gritar y a llorar. Un señor asustado dijo: "Ha tomado mi tostador y mi microondas". Otro añadió: "Se decían que algo así nunca ocurriría en nuestro barrio". Un policía declaró: "Bueno, sólo se tomó las cosas de mucho valor, pero nadie murió". Todos comenzaron a arrojarle tomates.

One of the many challenges that confront non-native speakers of Spanish is having to choose between *"por"* and *"para."* Successful mastery of the following material demands memorization and practice. After a while, either *"por"* or *"para"* will sound right in
a given sentence. Occasionally either *"por"* or *"para"* can be used in the same sentence. The meanings of those sentences, however, will be different.

1) THE USES OF "POR"

◆ **in exchange for**

*Te doy cien dólares **por** tu bicicleta.*	I'll give you one hundred dollars for (in exchange for) your bicycle.
*Gracias **por** la invitación.*	Thanks for the invitation. (I give you thanks; you give me the invitation.)

◆ **duration of time**

*Laura vivió en Managua **por** tres años.*	Laura lived in Managua for three years.
*Ayer estudié **por** la mañana.*	Yesterday I studied in the morning.

◆ **rate**

*Conduje a 55 millas **por** hora.*	I drove 55 miles per hour.
*Sólo llegó el diez **por** ciento de los alumnos.*	Only ten percent of the students arrived.

◆ **movement through space**

*Pasé **por** la plaza dos veces hoy.*	I passed through the square twice today.
*Camino **por** la playa cada mañana.*	I walk along the beach each morning.
*¡Hay un incendio! ¡Tenemos que escapar **por** la ventana!*	There is a fire! We have to escape through the window!

◆ **agent marker for the true passive voice**

*La canción fue escrita **por** Juanes.*	The song was written by Juanes.
*El cronómetro que se usaba para calcular la longitud en el océano fue inventado **por** John Harrison.*	The chronometer that was used to calculate longitude in the ocean was invented by John Harrison.

- ◆ **motive, reason for doing something, on behalf of**

*Lo hice **por** amor.*	I did it for (because of) love.
*Me gradué de la universidad **por** mis padres.*	I graduated from college because of my parents.
*No jugué al tenis **por** la lluvia.*	I didn't play tennis because of the rain.

- ◆ **object of an errand**

*Fui a la tienda **por** pan.*	I went to the store for bread.
*El policía vino **por** el ladrón.*	The police officer came for the thief.

  Note: If these sentences were constructed differently, *"para"* would be used. e.g., *Fui a la tienda **para** comprar pan. El policía vino **para** llevar al ladrón.*

- ◆ **by means of**

*La carta llegó **por** avión.*	The letter arrived by plane.
*El señor Scudder siempre prefería viajar **por** tren.*	Mr. Scudder always preferred to travel by train.
*Llamé a Sara Ramírez **por** teléfono.*	I phoned Sara Ramírez.

- ◆ **taking the place of**

*Mi hermano está enfermo — no puede ir. Voy **por** él.*	My brother is sick — he can't go. I'll go for him (in his place).
*Mañana trabajo en la tienda **por** Juliana porque está en el hospital.*	Tomorrow I'm working in the store in Juliana's place because she's in the hospital.

- ◆ **before an infinitive meaning "because of" or "by"**

***Por** trabajar tanto, fue elegida presidente.*	By working so hard, she was elected president.
***Por** ganar el campeonato, recibió unos trofeos impresionantes.*	By winning the championship, he received some impressive trophies.

- ◆ **before an infinitive meaning some chore (goal) that is yet to be done (fulfilled)**

*La pizarra todavía está **por** borrar.*	The blackboard still needs to be erased.
*Todavía queda mucho **por** hacer.*	There is still a lot left to do.

2) THE USES OF "PARA"

◆ **destination**

*Caminamos **para** Whole Foods.*	We are walking to Whole Foods.
*Salgo **para** Clarksville.*	I'm leaving for Clarksville.

◆ **intended for (recipient)**

*Las tazas son **para** la cocina.*	The cups are for the kitchen.
*Adquirí la casa **para** mi madre.*	I acquired the house for my mother.

◆ **deadline**

*La tarea **para** mañana es terminar el libro.*	The homework for tomorrow is to finish the book.
***Para** las ocho, habrá anochecido.*	By eight o'clock, it will have grown dark.

◆ **purpose, use**

*Compré un estante **para** libros.*	I bought a bookshelf.
*Tengo doce tazas **para** té.*	I have twelve teacups.
*Los lápices son **para** escribir.*	Pencils are for writing.

◆ **exception to a generalization**

***Para** un chico de siete años, sabe muchísimo.*	For a boy of seven years, he knows a lot.
***Para** una niña de dos años, es muy alta.*	For a two-year old, she is very tall.

◆ **before an infinitive, meaning "in order to"**

***Para** hablar bien el español, hay que practicarlo todos los días.*	In order to speak Spanish well, one must practice it every day.
*Lucharon **para** sobrevivir.*	They fought in order to survive.
*Estudio **para** ser ingeniero.*	I'm studying to be an engineer.
*Estudio **para** ingeniero.*	I'm studying to be an engineer.

(In the last sentence, *"ser"* is understood.)

◆ **employment**

*Trabajo **para** la compañía telefónica.*	I work for the phone company.

Note: In a sentence about a paid employee, one would use *"para."* However, volunteer work would usually use *"por,"* with "motive" or "on behalf of" as the reason. e.g., *Trabajo por la Cruz Roja.* I work (volunteer) for the Red Cross.

◆ **viewpoint**

***Para** ti, mis problemas no son importantes.*	For you, my problems aren't important.

WITH PRACTICE, MANY OF THESE USES WILL COME NATURALLY. ——————

Here are a few more related things to learn about *"por"* and *"para"*:

1 The verbs *buscar, pedir,* and *esperar* don't need *"por"* or *"para."* The word "for" is built into the verb.

***Busqué** la moneda perdida.*	I looked for the lost coin.
***Pido** pan.*	I ask for bread.
*Te **esperábamos** en el parque.*	We were waiting for you in the park.

2 Here are some set expressions with *"por"* and *"para"* that you should memorize.

Por		Para	
estar por →	to be in favor of; to have yet to be completed	*estar para* →	expresses that something is about to happen
por ahora →	for now	*para entonces* →	by that time
por casualidad →	by chance	*No sirve para nada.* →	It is of no use.
por cierto →	certainly	*para que* →	in order that
por consiguiente →	consequently	*para siempre* →	forever
por ejemplo →	for example		
por eso →	therefore		
por favor →	please		
por fin/por último →	finally		
por lo menos →	at least		
por lo tanto →	therefore		
por lo visto →	apparently		
por supuesto →	of course		

 # PRACTICE EXERCISES

1. Use either *"por"* or *"para"* in the following sentences, if necessary:

a. La novela *Cien años de soledad* fue escrita _____ Gabriel García Márquez.

b. Tenemos mucho que hacer _____ mañana. No sé si podremos terminarlo todo.

c. _____ una alumna del tercer año, escribe muy bien las palabras en español.

d. Ese avión puede volar a una velocidad de mil kilómetros _____ hora.

e. _____ aprender toda la gramática, estudié tres horas cada día.

f. Tuve que ir a la tienda _____ Doritos y salsa.

g. Le vendí a Marcos la foto de mi héroe, Dale Earnhardt, _____ diez dólares.

h. Salimos _____ Alemania en dos horas; en seis horas llegaremos a Munich.

i. Estos vasos son _____ el jugo.

j. Javier Bardem y Penélope Cruz descansaron en la playa _____ dos horas.

k. Era necesario que buscáramos _____ el gato abandonado.

l. "Gané el campeonato _____ practicar muchísimas horas", dijo Rafael Nadal.

m. _____ profesor de español, juega muy bien a los deportes.

n. No salió bien en el examen _____ ser idiota.

o. Te voy a querer _____ siempre.

p. Roberto Clemente sacrificó mucho _____ su familia.

q. Me quedan dos tacos _____ calentar.

r. Preparamos una cena especial _____ mi madre.

s. ¡_____ fin han llegado mis amigos!

t. ¿Tienes tiempo _____ ver la película de Alejandro González Iñárritu, *The Revenant*?

u. Estamos _____ salir, así que no puedo hablar contigo ahora.

v. La mesa todavía está _____ limpiar.

w. Cuando trabajaba _____ Telemundo, ganaba catorce dólares la hora.

2. Fix the eight *"por/para"* errors in the following paragraph:

Para favor, no quiero ir contigo otra vez. Siempre conduces demasiado rápido, a más de ochenta millas por hora; por eso me pones muy nervioso. Por un chico tan inteligente, conduces como un idiota. Estuve contigo en tu coche para veinte minutos la semana pasada y me volviste loco. Aunque estudies por ingeniero, te falta sentido común. En el futuro tendré que conducir en tu lugar — sí, voy a conducir para ti. No te estoy dando estos consejos gratis; te los doy para veinte dólares. Algún día, cuando estés en la cárcel, vas a pensar en mí. He buscado para tus padres por decírselo todo. Hasta luego, amiguito.

D) La puntuación y el empleo de las letras mayúsculas

1) Spanish Punctuation

Here are the names for common symbols of punctuation:

Symbols of Punctuation
. *punto* → period
, *coma* → comma
: *dos puntos* → colon
" " *comillas* → quotation marks
; *punto y coma* → semi-colon
¿? *signos de interrogación* → question marks
¡! *signos de exclamación* → exclamation points
... *puntos suspensivos* → ellipsis
- *guión* → hyphen, dash
* *asterisco* → asterisk
( ) *paréntesis* → parentheses

Spanish **punctuation** is quite similar to English punctuation. There are a number of differences, however, that you have probably noticed during your years of Spanish study.

◆ Upside down question marks and exclamation points come before questions and exclamations. These marks are handy because they give you some clue of what is coming in the sentence. These inverted marks are found:

a) at the beginning of a sentence

✳ **EXAMPLES:** *¿Qué hora es?*
¡No grites tanto, chico!
¿Por qué tenemos que colgar la ropa?
¡Qué cuadro tan bonito!

b) or at the actual point in a sentence where a question or exclamation starts

✳ **EXAMPLES:** *Bailas el tango, ¿no?*
Si llueve mañana, ¿vas a la piscina?
Cuando Luisa me abrazó en el coche, le grité: "¡No!".

◆ In Spanish, you use a period with numerals where English uses a comma. In addition, Spanish uses a comma where English uses a period. Let's look at some figures:

Spanish notation		English notation
5.000 pájaros	→	5,000 birds
intereses a 5,5%	→	5.5% interest
$1.000.000,55 (un millón de dólares con 55 centavos)	→	$1,000,000.55 (a million dollars and 55¢)

◆ In a series of three or more items, the Spanish writing system does not use a comma between the final two items. In English, we may choose to place a comma there.

✳ **EXAMPLES:** *Venden fruta, bebidas y pan.*
They sell fruit, drinks, and bread.

El grupo Los Tigres del Norte tiene experiencia, tiempo y talento.
The group Los Tigres del Norte has experience, time, and talent.

◆ In a dialogue, a Spanish writer signals a new speaker with long dashes.

✳ **EXAMPLES:** *–Hola, Giancarlo. ¿Cómo estás?*
–Todo va bien, pero me duele la espalda.
–Habla con tu madre, porque ella sabe mucho.
–Gracias por tu consejo, Juan. Nos vemos.

◆ Be certain to write titles of books, plays, and films in italics, and put quotation marks around the titles of short stories, poems, works of art and songs.

✳ **EXAMPLES:** *La vida es sueño* de Calderón de la Barca
"La conciencia" de Ana María Matute
Yerma de Federico García Lorca
"Las medias rojas" de Emilia Pardo Bazán
"La muerte y la brújula" de Jorge Luis Borges
"The Road Not Taken" de Robert Frost
"Quién me iba a decir" de David Bisbal

◆ Periods and commas are found <u>outside</u> of quotation marks, rather than inside as in English.

✳ **EXAMPLES:** *"Acabo de ver el nuevo vídeo de Calle 13", le dije a mi amiga.*
Laura respondió: "Es genial".

◆ When writing a letter — either to a friend or to a business — you should use a colon, rather than a comma, after the salutation.

 EXAMPLES: *Querido Juan:*   *Estimada Dra. Sánchez:*
Dear John,   Dear Dr. Sánchez:

2) SPANISH CAPITALIZATION

Here are some important things to keep in mind about Spanish capitalization:

a) In Spanish you must capitalize the first word of a sentence and all proper nouns.

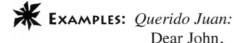 **EXAMPLE:** *Esta tarde voy a Managua.*

b) Unlike English, the names of months, days of the week, names of languages, and adjectives of nationality are not capitalized.

EXAMPLES: *El lunes, el martes y el viernes son mis días de la semana favoritos.*
"Mi cumpleaños es el veintidós de noviembre", dijo Hannah.
"Creo que el español es muy bonito", dijo la chica panameña.

c) Titles of respect *(señor, señorita, señora, doctor, doctora, profesor, profesora, don, doña)* are not capitalized unless they are abbreviated or begin a sentence.

EXAMPLES: *La señora Gómez y el señor Sánchez van a llegar pronto.*
"Hola, Sr. Ramírez y Dra. Martínez", dijo el profesor Smith.
"Voy a ver a don Silvestre Aguilar", dijo Jamie González.
Voy a ver al señor Reynolds, el hombre norteamericano que conoce
al embajador venezolano, D. Luis Carlos Villegas.

d) In titles of books, poems, songs, or works of art, only the first word is usually capitalized.

EXAMPLES: La dama del alba *es un drama muy conocido de Alejandro Casona.*
"Las meninas" es la obra más famosa de Velázquez en el Prado.

e) The subject pronoun *"yo"* is not capitalized as "I" would be in English unless it begins a sentence.

EXAMPLE: *Fernando y yo fuimos a un buen concierto de David Bisbal.*
Fernando and I went to a good concert of David Bisbal.

◆ Years ago, when you capitalized a word in a typed paper, the use of a written accent mark " ´ " or a tilde " ~ " was not obligatory, mainly because some typewriters and computers were unable to create them. Nowadays, however, the punctuation marks are considered necessary.

✳ **EXAMPLES:** *LOS MIÉRCOLES VAMOS AL CINE*
LA NI—A NO LLEGÓ A CASA
SE VIO EL RELÁMPAGO POR TODAS PARTES

PRACTICE EXERCISES

Fix all sixteen errors of capitalization and punctuation in this paragraph:

 !Caramba! El Jueves pasado Yo compré un diccionario nuevo. El diccionario es de españa, pero todos los autores son Italianos. En total, hay 100,545 entradas en el diccionario. Fue escrito por Don Román Palabra, un conocido Profesor de Zaragoza. Estoy seguro de que mi profesora, la Señora Carmen Santana, va a estar muy emocionada. El título del diccionario es Muchas Palabras. ¿Es un buen título, no? !Cómprate uno lo más pronto posible! La verdad es que me compré tres cosas: un diccionario, una computadora, y dos botellas de aspirina. Mi médico Japonés me recomendó que tomara aspirina, agua, y fruta. Bueno, esto es todo por hoy. Gasté más de 1,000 euros esta mañana. Es increíble, ¿no?

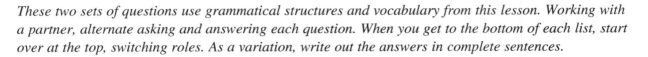
These two sets of questions use grammatical structures and vocabulary from this lesson. Working with a partner, alternate asking and answering each question. When you get to the bottom of each list, start over at the top, switching roles. As a variation, write out the answers in complete sentences.

A) ¿**Por** quién fue escrito *Don Quijote*?

¿**Para** qué compañía trabajan tus padres?

Por estudiar mucho, ¿has aprendido mucho español este año?

¿Cuánto dinero me das **por** mi copia de *Breaking the Spanish Barrier*?

¿Tienes que ir a la librería hoy **por** libros o lápices?

¿Tienes que ir a la librería hoy **para** comprar libros o lápices?

Para un hombre un poco viejo, el beisbolista Bartolo Colón es increíble, ¿no crees?

B) ¿Dónde **se sirve** buena comida en tu pueblo?

¿Conoces un restaurante donde **se sirvan** hamburguesas jugosas?

¿Dónde **se habla** italiano?

¿En qué país **se hablan** inglés y francés oficialmente?

¿**Sirven** buena comida en la cafetería de nuestra escuela?

¿**Hablan** italiano en Italia?

¿Qué lenguas **se hablan** en Estados Unidos?

A) LAS CONSTRUCCIONES CON "SE"

1. Complete these sentences with the appropriate form of the verb in parentheses:

a. Se _____ muchos anuncios interesantes durante los partidos de fútbol americano. (ver)

b. Se _____ los sueldos cuando el negocio no iba bien. (bajar)

c. En este aeropuerto se _____ el equipaje en el segundo piso. (recoger)

d. Se _____ a los alumnos que merecen una beca. (entrevistar)

e. El anuncio se _____ mañana en *USA Today*. (publicar)

f. Anoche se _____ dos botellas de agua mineral en el restaurante donde cenamos. (derramar)

g. No se _____ entradas aquí. (vender)

2. Underline and correct the six errors that appear in this description of the movie *Misión imposible*:

Desde el principio, se entiende que Tom Cruise es el héroe de la película, pero no se saben quién es el malo. Durante una misión muy peligrosa, se matan a casi todos los amigos de Tom. Sólo sobrevive una mujer guapísima y no se explican cómo se escapó de la muerte. En la película se buscan a los enemigos con la ayuda de la computadora y se mandan mucho correo electrónico. Todos los personajes son misteriosos y Tom no puede confiar en nadie. Pero se ven que Tom es más inteligente, más fuerte y, por supuesto, más guapo que todos sus enemigos.

3. Write the correct form of the verb provided:

a. Se _____ confundir fácilmente a Jorge con su hermano. (poder)

b. Se _____ que el alcohol no es bueno para la salud. (pensar)

c. No se _____ con seguridad si hay vida en otros planetas. (saber)

d. Anoche se le _____ al público de un incendio muy grave en el centro de la ciudad. (avisar)

e. Normalmente se _____ los impuestos antes del 15 de abril. (pagar)

f. En Alemania se _____ muy rápido por la autopista. (conducir)

g. Cuando yo era joven, se _____ mucho de política en mi familia. (hablar)

h. En nuestro colegio se _____ poco durante la temporada de baloncesto. (estudiar)

4. Translate the following sentences using an impersonal construction:

a. One goes out a lot at night in San José.

_____

b. One takes this exit in order to go to the center of town.

_____

c. In this school one needs to use e-mail a lot.

_____

B) El uso de las construcciones con la tercera persona plural indefinida para expresar la voz pasiva

1. Create a passive sentence by conjugating the verb in parentheses in the indefinite third person plural:

a. Me gusta este programa. Cada semana _____ entrevistas con gente muy interesante. (hacer)

b. La semana pasada _____ a tres estudiantes por haber fumado en la cafetería. (castigar)

c. Cuando vivía en Chicago, en mi barrio siempre _____ luces en los árboles en Navidad. (colgar)

d. Prefiero ir de compras a aquella tienda donde te _____ pagar con tarjeta de crédito. (permitir)

e. ¡Qué suerte! Aquí _____ coches por poco dinero. (alquilar)

2. Translate the following sentences, using a passive construction:

a. The children are given milk at eleven o'clock.

_____

b. They started the concert a little late.

_____

c. The business was developed by my grandfather.

_____

C) LOS USOS DE "POR" Y "PARA"

1. Complete the following sentences with *"por"* or *"para,"* if necessary:

a. Conseguí una beca el verano pasado para estudiar en California _____ dos meses.

b. La canción *"Chantaje"* fue interpretada _____ Shakira y Maluma.

c. ¿Cuál es el mejor método _____ ahorrar dinero?

d. _____ un chico de cinco años, sabe mucho.

e. Se pagó mucho dinero _____ los bienes personales de Jackie Kennedy Onassis.

f. _____ mí, la voz de Montserrat Caballé es fantástica.

g. Anoche, en Netflix, busqué _____ la nueva película de Diego Luna, pero no la encontré.

h. Me gustaban *Los juegos del hambre* y *Misión imposible* _____ su estilo dramático.

i. Ayer en el restaurante, pedí _____ una ensalada de zanahorias.

j. Cuando hace buen tiempo, nos gusta pasear _____ el barrio.

2. Underline and correct the eight errors in the following letter:

Querido Jorge:

Anoche busqué para tu número de teléfono para dos horas, pero no pude encontrarlo. Para eso te escribo esta carta. Estoy muy contento por qué tengo un nuevo trabajo: ya trabajo por "Other Music", una tienda de discos muy famosa en Nueva York. El gerente de la tienda es muy amable. ¡Me permite comprar discos compactos para sólo cinco dólares! Por eso, ya he comprado mucha música, y cada día vienen mis amigos a casa por escucharla. ¡Se dicen que soy el chico más popular de la escuela!

Un abrazo,

Ricardo

D) LA PUNTUACIÓN Y EL EMPLEO DE LAS LETRAS MAYÚSCULAS

Underline and correct the eight errors in the following advertisement. Look for problems with capitalization, punctuation, the impersonal *"se"* and *"por"* and *"para"*:

¿Tiene Ud. la piel seca e irritada? Se parece Ud. a un cocodrilo?

Pruebe la crema Jergen! Es la crema más suave, más aromática, y más

eficaz del mundo. Usa la crema Jergen para todo el cuerpo, y no es sólo

por mujeres. En europa, el 15.5% de los hombres utilizan esta avanzada

crema norteamericana. La crema Jergen está formulada con ingredientes

totalmente naturales y se pueden comprar ahora en Walgreens.

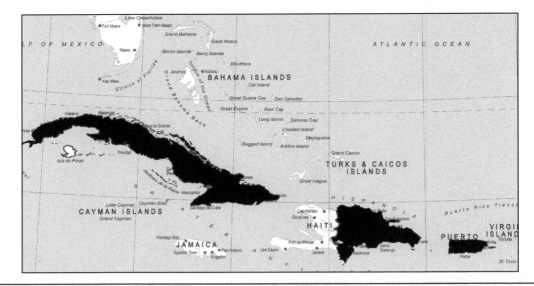

CUBA, REPÚBLICA DOMINICANA & PUERTO RICO

CUBA

CAPITAL:	La Habana
POBLACIÓN:	11.500.000
GOBIERNO:	república socialista
PRESIDENTE:	Miguel Díaz-Canel
DINERO ($):	peso cubano
PRODUCTOS:	azúcar, minerales, tabaco
MÚSICA, BAILE:	habanera, jazz, mambo, rumba, son
SITIOS DE INTERÉS:	Castillo del Morro
COMIDA TÍPICA:	congris, fruta, moros y cristianos, plátanos

REPÚBLICA DOMINICANA

CAPITAL:	Santo Domingo
POBLACIÓN:	10.800.000
GOBIERNO:	república democrática
PRESIDENTE:	Danilo Medina Sánchez
DINERO ($):	peso dominicano
PRODUCTOS:	azúcar, cacao, carne, fruta, minerales, tabaco
MÚSICA, BAILE:	bachata, marimba, merengue
SITIOS DE INTERÉS:	Lago Enriquillo, Pico Duarte
COMIDA TÍPICA:	chivo asado, comida criolla, mondongo, sancocho

PUERTO RICO

CAPITAL:	San Juan
POBLACIÓN:	3.700.000
GOBIERNO:	estado libre asociado (commonwealth)
GOBERNADOR:	Ricardo Rosselló
DINERO ($):	dólar americano
PRODUCTOS:	agricultura, azúcar, café, piña, ron, tabaco
MÚSICA, BAILE:	bomba, salsa
SITIOS DE INTERÉS:	Isla Mona, Ponce, El Yunque
COMIDA TÍPICA:	arroz con habichuelas, asopao, empanadillas, mofongo, pollo frito con tostones

CUBANOS FAMOSOS:

José Capablanca
(AJEDRECISTA)

Fidel Castro
(DICTADOR)

Celia Cruz
(CANTANTE)

Gloria Estefan
(CANTANTE)

José Martí
(POETA)

DOMINICANOS FAMOSOS:

Julia Álvarez
(ESCRITORA)

Francisco Casanova
(CANTANTE)

Alex Rodríguez
(BEISBOLISTA)

Óscar de la Renta
(DISEÑADOR)

PUERTORRIQUE—OS FAMOSOS:

Roberto Clemente
(BEISBOLISTA)

José Feliciano
(MÚSICO)

José Ferrer
(ACTOR)

Ricky Martin
(CANTANTE)

Concha Meléndez
(ESCRITORA)

Rita Moreno
(ACTRIZ)

Chichi Rodríguez
(GOLFISTA)

 # VOCABULARIO LECCIÓN DIEZ

VERBOS

desesperar	to despair, to lose hope	*exigir*	to demand, to require
despedirse (i) de	to say goodbye to	*fabricar*	to manufacture
dirigir	to direct, to manage	*fiarse de*	to trust
disfrutar (de)	to enjoy	*fijarse en*	to notice
disparar	to shoot	*fingir*	to pretend, to fake
divertirse (ie)	to enjoy oneself, to have a good time	*firmar*	to sign
doblar	to fold, to bend	*fregar (ie)*	to scour, to scrub
doler (ue)	to ache, to hurt	*fundar*	to found, to establish
durar	to last	*girar*	to revolve, to rotate, to turn
echar	to throw, to throw away	*gobernar (ie)*	to govern
enamorarse de	to fall in love with	*gozar (de)*	to enjoy
encender (ie)	to light (e.g., a fire), to turn on (e.g., a light)	*grabar*	to engrave, to record
		hallar	to find
		helar (ie)	to freeze
enfadarse	to become angry	*heredar*	to inherit
engañar	to deceive, to cheat	*herir (ie)*	to wound
		hervir (ie)	to boil
entregar	to deliver, to hand over, to turn in	*impedir (i)*	to prevent
		imprimir	to print
equivocarse	to make a mistake, to be mistaken	*intentar*	to try, to attempt
		invertir (ie)	to invest (money)
escoger	to choose, to select	*jurar*	to swear
esconder	to hide	*juzgar*	to judge
escupir	to spit	*ladrar*	to bark
espiar	to spy	*lanzar*	to throw, to hurl, to pitch
estornudar	to sneeze		

LECCIÓN DIEZ

KEY GRAMMAR CONCEPTS

A) LOS ADVERBIOS → *Adverbs*

B) LOS ARTÍCULOS DEFINIDOS E INDEFINIDOS → *Definite and indefinite articles*

C) LOS PRONOMBRES RELATIVOS → *Relative pronouns*

D) LOS USOS DE "SER" Y "ESTAR" → *The uses of "ser" and "estar"*

A) LOS ADVERBIOS

Adverbs are used to modify verbs, adjectives, or other adverbs. These words tell how, when, where, or with what intensity something is done. Although a speaker may take liberties with the placement of these adverbs, they are usually placed after verbs and before adjectives or other adverbs.

1) ADVERBS THAT END IN "-MENTE"

Many adverbs use the ending *"-mente."*

EXAMPLES: *Soribel comió la hamburguesa **rápidamente**.*
Soribel ate the hamburger quickly.

*Alejandro completó el examen **cuidadosamente**.*
Alejandro finished the test carefully.

*Miguel Cabrera golpeó la pelota **fuertemente**.*
Miguel Cabrera hit the ball hard.

*Victor hizo su trabajo **felizmente**.*
Victor did his work happily.

In the above sentences, adverbs were constructed by adding *"-mente"* to the feminine form of the adjective.

Masculine Adjective		Feminine Adjective		Adverb
cuidadoso	→	*cuidadosa*	→	*cuidadosa**mente***
feliz	→	*feliz*	→	*feliz**mente***
fuerte	→	*fuerte*	→	*fuerte**mente***
rápido	→	*rápida*	→	*rápida**mente***

Helpful Tips: **1)** Did you notice that if an adjective has an accent mark (e.g., *rápido*), the adverb will maintain the accent on the same vowel (e.g., *rápidamente*)?
2) If an adjective ends in a consonant or the letter "e" (e.g., *feliz, fuerte*), simply add the ending *"-mente."*

2) OTHER ADVERBS

There are many adverbs that do not have the "-mente" ending.

Here is a list of some very common adverbs:

Common Adverbs			
abajo → below		*mañana* → tomorrow	
afuera → outside		*medio* → half	
alguna vez → sometime		*mucho* → a lot	
allí → there		*muy* → very	
anteayer → day before yesterday		*nunca (jamás)* → never	
antes → before		*poco* → a little	
aquí → here		*pronto* → soon	
arriba → up		*recién* → recently	
ayer → yesterday		*siempre* → always	
bastante → enough, quite		*también* → also, too	
bien → fine, well		*tampoco* → neither	
demasiado → too much		*tan* → so	
después → afterwards		*tanto* → so much	
hoy → today		*tarde* → late	
mal → badly, poorly		*temprano* → early	

Helpful Tips: **1)** Some words in this list can also be adjectives (e.g., *demasiado, medio, mucho, poco, tanto*). As adjectives, these words will have singular, plural, feminine, and masculine forms (e.g., **demasiadas** *entrevistas,* **tantos** *testigos, etc.*).
2) Some of these words could be nouns, too *(Hoy es lunes; anteayer fue sábado).*
3) When these words are <u>adverbs</u>, however, they have only one form. Study the following sentences carefully!

EXAMPLES: ***Mañana** voy a leer otro libro del Dr. Seuss.*
Tomorrow I'm going to read another Dr. Seuss book.

*Llegamos **temprano** al estreno de* On Your Feet.
We arrived early to the première of *On Your Feet*.

*Me siento **mal** hoy por la contaminación del aire.*
I feel bad today because of the air pollution.

*No como **nunca** en KFC; el problema es que me gusta **tanto** la comida que acabo gastando mucha plata.*
I never eat at KFC; the problem is that I like the food so much that I end up spending a lot of money.

*Las chicas son **demasiado** altas para jugar conmigo.*
The girls are too tall to play with me.

*¿Has visto **jamás** una ciudad tan grande como México, D.F.? –¡Nunca!*
Have you ever seen a city as large as Mexico City? –Never!

Note: This negative adverb may be used in an affirmative question. When using *"jamás,"* the speaker suggests that the scenario is improbable.

*¿Has estado **alguna vez** en una discoteca atestada?*
> Have you ever been in a crowded dance club?

Note: *"Alguna vez"* is a little more neutral in tone than *"jamás."*

*¡Qué mala suerte! No hay más comida para los invitados **recién llegados**.*
> What bad luck! There is no more food for the guests who just arrived.

*Voy al concierto. –¡Qué suerte! Yo voy **también**.*
> I'm going to the concert. –What luck! I'm going, too.

*No escuché la canción de Enrique Iglesias y Juan Luis Guerra. –Y yo **tampoco**.*
> I didn't listen to the Enrique Iglesias and Juan Luis Guerra song. – I didn't, either.

3) MULTIPLE "-MENTE" ADVERBS IN ONE SENTENCE

When there are two or more *"-mente"* adverbs in one sentence, only the final adverb will use the *"-mente"* ending. The first adverb(s) just uses the feminine form of the adjective.

EXAMPLES: *Imprimí los ejercicios **rápida** y **cuidadosamente**.*
> I printed the exercises quickly and carefully.

*Nuestros amigos de Santo Domingo se visten **elegante, creativa** y **artísticamente**.*
> Our friends from Santo Domingo dress elegantly, creatively, and artistically.

*Vamos a investigar el crimen **paciente, curiosa** y **eficientemente**.*
> We're going to investigate the crime patiently, curiously, and efficiently.

4) ANOTHER WAY TO MAKE ADVERBS

Prepositional phrases based on *"a," "con," "en,"* and *"por"* are frequently used as adverbs.

EXAMPLES: *A veces entregamos la tarea muy tarde.*
> At times we turn in the homework very late.

*Engaño a mis padres **con frecuencia** (frecuentemente).*
> I deceive my parents frequently.

*Golpeo la pelota **con fuerza** (fuertemente).*
> I hit the ball strongly.

*La chica canta los tangos **con cariño** (cariñosamente).*
> The girl sings the tangos affectionately.

*Toco la pieza **en ritmo** de salsa.*
I play the piece in salsa tempo.

*Comprendo el misterio **por instinto** (instintivamente).*
I understand the mystery instinctively.

PRACTICE EXERCISES

1. Form adverbs from the following adjectives using the *"mente"* form:

a. lento → _____

d. sincero → _____

b. extraño → _____

e. profesional → _____

c. triste → _____

f. incompetente → _____

2. Form adverbs from the following adjectives using *"a," "con," "en,"* or *"por"* with a noun:

a. frecuente → _____

c. instintivo → _____

b. cariñoso → _____

d. fuerte → _____

3. Translate the following sentences into Spanish:

a. Today I scoured the bathroom silently.

_____

b. María José Martínez is too tired to sign her name.

_____

c. I offered him advice carefully, sincerely, and professionally.

_____

4. Identify and correct the seven errors:

 Alicia estudia tanta. Siempre va con sus amigas a la reciente construida biblioteca de su colegio donde todos trabajan enérgicomente. Un día Alicia leyó un libro entero en menos de una hora. A veces se comporta locamente y obsesivamente. Le dije que ella simplamente debiera relajarse un poco. Me contestó con fuertemente que yo no debiera meterme en su vida. ¡Nunca más voy a hablar francomente con ella!

B) LOS ARTÍCULOS DEFINIDOS E INDEFINIDOS

1) DEFINITE ARTICLES

The **definite articles** in Spanish are *"el," "la," "los,"* and *"las."* These words are primarily used to identify a specific noun.

EXAMPLES: *Voy a escoger el casco que está en el escaparate.*
I'm going to choose the helmet that is in the store window.

Los chicos que llegaron ayer disfrutaron de nuestros juguetes.
The kids who arrived yesterday enjoyed our toys.

Definite articles are used widely in Spanish and serve many functions. The following list highlights ten situations when a definite article is required.

1 **Before days of the week (except after *"ser"*), seasons, and modified periods of time**

EXAMPLES: *El martes vamos a celebrar el cumpleaños de Sarita.*
On Tuesday, we're going to celebrate Sarita's birthday.

Siempre tenemos exámenes los viernes.
We always have tests on Friday.

Note: Did you notice in these last two sentences that Spanish speakers use the definite article *"el" ("los")* where an English speaker would say "on"?

La primavera es mi estación preferida.
Spring is my favorite season.

No remé mucho el año pasado.
I didn't row much last year.

BUT: *Hoy es martes.* Today is Tuesday. (No definite article!)

2 **With titles of respect, except for *"don"* and *"doña,"* when talking about someone** (In direct address, however, definite articles are left out.)

✳ **EXAMPLES:** *El señor Ordóñez me enseñó mucho.*
Mr. Ordóñez taught me a lot.

Después de la clase voy a hablar con la profesora Cepeda; siempre me da buenos consejos.
After class I'm going to talk with Professor Cepeda; she always gives me good advice.

BUT: *Hola, señora Díaz. ¿Cómo está Ud.?* (No definite article)
En ese momento llegó don Luis Góngora. (No definite article)

¡CUIDADO! *"Don"* and *"doña"* never require a definite article.

3 **Before certain geographical locations**

✳ **EXAMPLES:** *Mi amigo Luis vive en (el) Perú.*
My friend Luis lives in Peru.

Me encantaría pasar el verano en (el) Canadá.
I would love to spend the summer in Canada.

Here are some countries, cities, and states that commonly use the definite article:

(la) Argentina	*(los) Estados Unidos*	*(el) Paraguay*
(el) Brasil	*(la) Florida*	*(el) Perú*
(el) Canadá	*la India*	*el Reino Unido*
(la) China	*(el) Japón*	*(el) Uruguay*
(el) Ecuador		

Note: Nowadays, Spanish speakers are omitting these articles more and more (except for *"la India," "el Reino Unido"* and locations where the article is an integral part of the name, e.g., *Las Bahamas, La Habana, La Paz, El Salvador, etc.*).

4 **When speaking in general terms or with abstract nouns**

✳ **EXAMPLES:** *El amor es algo maravilloso.*
    Love is a wonderful thing.

   El agua es necesaria para vivir.
    Water is necessary to live.

   Se sacrificaron por la justicia.
    They sacrificed themselves for justice.

5 **With a person's first name when modified**

✳ **EXAMPLES:** *La bella Lola acaba de hervir el agua.*
    Beautiful Lola has just boiled the water.

   El pobre Ramón había perdido su boleto de lotería.
    Poor Ramón had lost his lottery ticket.

6 **With the names of languages** (except when <u>directly</u> following *"hablar,"* *"enseñar,"* *"entender,"* *"escribir,"* *"estudiar,"* *"leer,"* *"saber"*)

✳ **EXAMPLES:** *El japonés es una lengua útil.*
    Japanese is a useful language.

   El portugués y el español son bastante similares.
    Portuguese and Spanish are quite similar.

   Lionel Messi habla frecuentemente el español con sus vecinos.
    Lionel Messi frequently speaks Spanish with his neighbors.
    BUT: *Hablo español. Entiendo y leo latín.*

7 **With body parts or articles of clothing** (especially with reflexive verbs)

✳ **EXAMPLES:** *Me lavo las manos con jabón.*
    I wash my hands with jabón.
    Note: The sentence *"Me lavo mis manos"* would likely sound redundant to a Spanish speaker because the pronoun *"me"* already identifies whose hands are being washed.

   Me pongo los guantes cuando hace frío.
    I put on (my) gloves when it is cold.

   Al acostarme, me quito las zapatillas y la bata.
    Upon going to bed, I take off my slippers and robe.

   Hoy Heather tiene el pelo rubio.
    Today Heather is blonde.

   Me rompí la pierna.
    I broke my leg.

8 **With words that indicate weight, rate, or measure** (an alternative to *"por"*)

🌟 **EXAMPLES:** *Las patatas cuestan dos dólares **el** (por) kilo.*
Potatoes cost two dollars per kilo.

*Tuve que pagar tres dólares **la** (por) docena cuando compré huevos en esa tienda.*
I had to pay three dollars a dozen when I bought eggs in that store.

9 **With the infinitive to form a noun**

🌟 **EXAMPLE:** *A veces **el** ladrar de mi perro me vuelve loco.*
At times my dog's barking drives me crazy.

10 **To tell time**

🌟 **EXAMPLES:** *Son **las** tres y media.*
It's three-thirty.

*Es **la** una.*
It is one o'clock.

*Para **las** cuatro habré entregado este dibujo.*
By four o'clock, I will have delivered this sketch.

Vamos a ver The Wizard of Oz *a **las** ocho esta noche.*
We're going to watch *The Wizard of Oz* at eight o'clock tonight.

WHEN ARE DEFINITE ARTICLES NORMALLY OMITTED?

The following list reviews six situations when the definite article is normally omitted:

1 **Before days of the week after the verb *"ser"***

🌟 **EXAMPLE:** *Hoy es martes.*
Today is Tuesday.

2 **With a title of respect when you are speaking directly to someone**

🌟 **EXAMPLE:** *Hola, señora Arámbula. ¿Cómo está Ud.?*
Hello, Mrs. Arámbula. How are you?

3 Before the names of languages when <u>directly</u> following *"enseñar," "entender," "escribir," "estudiar," "hablar," "leer," "saber"*

✳ **EXAMPLES:** *Hablamos alemán en la discoteca.*
We speak German in the discotheque.

Leemos francés, pero no lo hablamos.
We read French, but we don't speak it.

4 Usually after *"de"* and *"en"* with seasons or names of languages

✳ **EXAMPLES:** *Tengo una clase de italiano.*
I have an Italian class.

En (el) otoño se caen las hojas de los árboles.
In the fall, leaves fall from the trees.

Prefiero hablar en inglés.
I prefer to speak in English.

5 Before a number after the name of royalty or of a pope

✳ **EXAMPLES:** *Carlos V (Carlos quinto) es mi rey favorito.*
Charles the Fifth is my favorite king.

Juan Pablo II (Juan Pablo segundo) nunca visitó mi pueblo.
John Paul the Second never visited my town.

6 When used in apposition (i.e., a noun or noun phrase placed with another and usd as an explanatory equivalent)

✳ **EXAMPLES:** *La Habana, capital de Cuba, es mi ciudad favorita.*
Havana, the capital of Cuba, is my favorite city.

Ana Duato, actriz en Cuéntame, *tiene mucho talento.*
Ana Duato, an actress in *Cuéntame*, has a lot of talent.

2) INDEFINITE ARTICLES

The **indefinite articles** in Spanish are *"un," "una," "unos,"* and *"unas."* These words usually refer to nouns in a general way, without identifying a specific object or person. The following sentences illustrate the primary use of indefinite articles. The plural form has the sense of "a few" or "some" and is sometimes omitted.

✳ **EXAMPLES:** *Esta tarde me gustaría comer **una** pizza entera.*
This afternoon I'd like to eat an entire pizza.

*Busco **un** empleado que hable sueco y coreano.*
  I'm looking for an employee who speaks Swedish and Korean.

***Unos** amigos de Marcos se comunicaron anoche por Internet.*
  Some of Mark's friends got in touch with each other last night on
  the Internet.

WHEN ARE INDEFINITE ARTICLES OMITTED?

Here are four situations when the indefinite article is omitted:

1 **With an <u>unmodified</u> noun that identifies profession, nationality, political persuasion, or religion**

 EXAMPLES: *María es dentista y su marido, Lorenzo, es profesor.*
  Mary is a dentist, and her husband, Lorenzo, is a professor.

 Ella es cubana y él es puertorriqueño.
  She is (a) Cuban, and he is (a) Puerto Rican.

 BUT: *María es una dentista excelente.*
  Mary is an excellent dentist.

 Carlos es un mexicano orgulloso.
  Carlos is a proud Mexican.

2 **After the preposition *"con"* and *"sin,"* unless needed to emphasize a number**

 EXAMPLES: *Lisa salió sin sombrero hoy.*
  Lisa left without a hat today.

 Maruja escribe con pluma.
  Maruja writes with a pen.

 BUT: *José llegó con un guante.*
  Joe arrived with (only) one glove.

3 **When the speaker doesn't want to emphasize a particular number, or in a negative sentence**

 EXAMPLES: *Tengo pluma y lápiz; estoy preparado.*
  I have a pen and pencil; I'm prepared.

 Carolina Herrera lleva chaqueta y botas negras.
  Carolina Herrera is wearing a jacket and black boots.

 No tengo ni coche ni bicicleta.
  I don't have a car or a bicycle.

4 **With certain words in which the idea of "a" is "built into" the word**
(e.g., *ciento/cien, cierto, medio, mil, otro, qué, tal*)

✳ **EXAMPLES:** *Pero, ¡no tengo **cien** dólares!*
But I don't have a hundred dollars!

***Cierto** hombre alto va a llegar hoy.*
A certain tall man is going to arrive today.

*Dame **medio** kilo de queso, por favor.*
Give me a half-kilo of cheese, please.

***Mil** globos rojos se vieron en París.*
A thousand red balloons were seen in Paris.

*Voy a comenzar mi dieta **otro** día.*
I'm starting my diet another day.

*Me gusta "Tu recuerdo" de Ricky Martin. ¡**Qué** canción!*
I like *"Tu recuerdo"* by Ricky Martin. What a song!

*Nunca habíamos oído **tal** grito.*
We had never heard such a shout.

PRACTICE EXERCISES

1. Use the appropiate definite article, if necessary:

a. _____ Sra. Barnes me va a ayudar con el jardín.

b. Normalmente vamos a la ópera _____ miércoles.

c. Felipe _____ II fue un rey de mucha importancia.

d. Eran _____ cuatro y media cuando el tren salió para Santa Fe.

e. Hablamos bien _____ español.

f. _____ gritar en la biblioteca no es una buena idea, sobre todo si el bibliotecario está presente.

g. Miguel de Cervantes, _____ autor de *Don Quijote*, nació en 1547.

h. Los chocolates se venden a cuatro dólares _____ libra.

i. Nos lavamos _____ manos antes de comer.

j. Buenos días, _____ señor Ozete y _____ señora Garner. ¿Cómo están Uds.?

2. **Use the appropiate indefinite article, if necessary:**

   a. No tengo mucha hambre. Por eso, sólo voy a comer _____ hamburguesa.

   b. Tengo que buscar _____ otro cliente.

   c. _____ turistas se dirigieron al Centro de Turismo.

   d. Federico Reyes es _____ profesor guapo e inteligente.

   e. Todos los invitados son _____ australianos.

   f. Creo que más de _____ cien caballos van a correr el día del Kentucky Derby.

   g. Hoy no tenemos ni _____ libro ni _____ cuaderno.

   h. Esta mañana Marcos llegó con sólo _____ zapato sin dar niguna explicación.

   i. Me gustaría encender _____ mil velas ahorita.

   j. _____ mujer elegante y misteriosa, la que conduce el BMW blanco, acaba de llegar.

   k. El banquero me dijo que yo necesitaría _____ millón de dólares para montar una empresa.

3. **Identify and correct the eight errors in the following report:**

No lo vas a creer. El chico que llegó ayer se parecía al rey Juan Carlos el II de España. Les hablé en español a ese chico, Cristóbal, y a su padre, señor Gustavo Arteaga. Estaba contento de que Cristóbal se hubiera lavado sus manos antes de la entrevista. Normalmente un mil

estudiantes o más llegan a la entrevista con las manos sucias. Durante

juventud es necesario practicar la higiene básica diariamente. Un día,

chico alto llegó con chocolate en la cara y me dio una caja de chocolates

que había comprado a cinco dólares una libra. De todos modos, Cristóbal

y su padre salieron sin un paraguas a pesar de la lluvia.

C) LOS PRONOMBRES RELATIVOS

A **relative pronoun** connects two parts of a sentence. The relative pronoun connects the relative clause (usually the second part of a sentence) to the noun or pronoun for which it stands (the antecedent). Spanish has a number of words that serve as relative pronouns. By far, the most common is the word *"que."*

The following is a list of Spanish relative pronouns:

Relative Pronouns	

◆ *que*
 ◆ *quien, quienes*
 ◆ *el que, la que, los que, las que,*
   lo que, el cual, la cual, los cuales,
   las cuales, lo cual
	◆ *cuanto, cuanta, cuantos, cuantas*
	 ◆ *cuyo, cuya, cuyos, cuyas*

Helpful Tip: While we often choose not to use a relative pronoun in English, it is always required in Spanish (e.g., "The bread I ate was delicious" → *"El pan que comí estaba delicioso"*).

Let's look at examples of each type of relative pronoun.

1) QUE

"Que" can be be used to refer to a person, place, or thing. In English it could be translated as "who," "whom," "which," or "that."

EXAMPLES: *La escoba **que** compré es verde.*
The broom that I bought is green.

*Las cosas **que** más me molestan son la injusticia y el prejuicio.*
The things that bother me most are injustice and prejudice.

*El presidente **que** nació en Ecuador se llama Rafael Correa.*
The president who was born in Ecuador (and not in another country) is named Rafael Correa.

*La actriz **que** conocí anoche se llama Anne Hathaway.*
The actress whom I met last night is named Anne Hathaway.

"Que" follows most one-syllable prepositions when referring to a place or thing. The word *"CONDENA"* contains all prepositions that are commonly used with *"que"* (*"con que," "de que," "en que," "a que"*).

EXAMPLES: *La raqueta **con que** juego al tenis es fabricada por Head.*
The racquet with which I play tennis is made by Head.

*Los problemas **de que** hablo son bien graves.*
The problems of which I speak are quite serious.

*El apartamento **en que** vivimos tiene tres dormitorios.*
The apartment in which we live has three bedrooms.

*La ciudad **a que** me refiero es San Francisco.*
The city to which I refer is San Francisco.

2) QUIEN, QUIENES

The relative pronouns *"quien"* and *"quienes"* refer exclusively to people. They can mean either "who" or "whom." These words are used after prepositions and in non-restrictive clauses, offset by commas. A non-restrictive clause gives parenthetical, non-essential information.

EXAMPLES: *La mujer **a quien** quiero mucho es mi suegra.*
The woman whom I love a lot is my mother-in-law.

*Los estudiantes **de quienes** hablo son Margarita y Justin.*
The students of whom I speak are Margarita and Justin.

*El presidente, **quien** nació en Ecuador, se llama Rafael Correa.*
>The president, who by the way was born in Ecuador, is named
>Rafael Correa.

Note: This sentence contrasts with the one on the previous page because it gives non-essential information. Also, you may occasionally find the word *"que"* replacing *"quien"* in this type of sentence.

"Quien" and *"quienes"* also can begin a sentence — in that case they mean "One who," "He or she who," or "Those who."

✳ **EXAMPLES:** ***Quien** trabaja, avanza.*
>He (or she) who works, advances.

>***Quienes** practican, ganarán muchos partidos.*
>Those who practice will win many games.

3) EL QUE, LA QUE, LOS QUE, LAS QUE, LO QUE, EL CUAL, LA CUAL, LOS CUALES, LAS CUALES, LO CUAL

These longer forms have three main uses:

1 **When following all prepositions other than** *"con," "de," "en,"* **and** *"a"*
(e.g., *cerca de, delante de, detrás de, para, por, sin, sobre*)
Most prepositions on this list contain two syllables or more. *"Por"* is followed by these longer forms to avoid confusion with the word *"porque,"* while *"sin"* is followed by the longer forms to avoid confusion with *"sin que,"* one of the *ESCAPA* expressions (*Lección Ocho*).

✳ **EXAMPLES:** *Las playas **cerca de las cuales (las que)** se han construido hoteles de lujo son populares en verano.*
>The beaches near which they've built luxury hotels are popular in the summer.

>*El restaurante **delante del que (del cual)** está la biblioteca sirve comida italiana.*
>The restaurant in front of which is the library serves Italian food.

2 **When referring back to the first of two or more antecedents**

✳ **EXAMPLES:** *La tía de Ramón, **la cual (la que)** vive en San Francisco, se llama Amelia.*
>Ramón's aunt, who lives in San Francisco, is called Amelia.

*Los amigos de mis primos, **los que (los cuales)** nos visitan en verano, se llaman Gómez.*

> The friends of my cousins, who (i.e., the <u>friends</u> who) visit us in the summer, are named Gómez.

Note: If the sentence read: *"Los amigos de mis primos que nos visitan en verano se llaman Gómez,"* it would mean "The friends of my cousins who visit us in the summer are named Gómez" i.e., the <u>cousins</u> who visit us rather than the <u>friends</u> who visit us.

3 As an alternative to *"que," "quien,"* or *"quienes"* in a clause that is not restrictive (i.e., a clause that gives non-essential information)

EXAMPLES: *Ese jugador, **el cual (el que)** tiene talento, no jugó bien hoy.*
> That player, who (by the way) has talent, didn't play well today.

*La escritora, **la que (la cual)** nació en 1903, era mi abuela.*
> The writer, who (by the way) was born in 1903, was my grandmother.

The forms *"el que"* and *"el cual"* (and *"la que"* and *"la cual,"* etc.) are interchangeable in all of the examples above, although *"el cual,"* etc. is used more often. However, only *"El que"* (He who), *"La que"* (She who), and *"Los/Las que"* (Those who/The ones that) may <u>begin</u> a sentence as in the following two examples.

EXAMPLES: *El que habla mucho, escucha poco.*
> He who speaks a lot, listens a little.

Los que compraste eran baratos.
> The ones you bought were cheap.

The neuter forms *"lo que"* and *"lo cual"* can be used interchangeably when the antecedent is an idea or clause.

EXAMPLES: *Vamos a Santo Domingo ahora, **lo cual (lo que)** nos hace muy felices.*
> We are going to Santo Domingo now, which makes us very happy.

*El teléfono sonó a medianoche, **lo que (lo cual)** me asustó.*
> The phone rang at midnight, which scared me.

Only *"lo que"* can be used, however, if the meaning is "what" or "that which." As a consequence, a sentence can begin with *"Lo que,"* but not *"Lo cual."*

EXAMPLES: *Lo que me gusta es jugar al ajedrez con mi hermano Marcos.*
> What I like is playing chess with my brother Mark.

Lo que no comprendes es que te quiero.
> What you don't understand is that I love you.

*Puedes decirles **lo que** quieras.*
> You can tell them what you want.

4) CUANTO, CUANTA, CUANTOS, CUANTAS

These relative pronouns mean "all that" or "as much as" or "as many as."

✳ EXAMPLES: *Voy a hacer **cuanto** me pidas.*
> I'm going to do all that you ask of me.

*Hacemos tortas de chocolate aquí, y te podemos vender **cuantas** quieras.*
> We make chocolate cakes here, and we can sell you as many as you want.

Note: The subjunctive (*"pidas"* and *"quieras"*) is used because *"cuanto"* and *"cuantas"* in these sentences are indefinite antecedents — GHOSTS!

*Ronaldo siempre mete muchos goles y ayer metió **cuantos** necesitábamos para ganar.*
> Ronaldo always scores many goals, and yesterday he scored as many as we needed to win.

Note: No subjunctive here. *"Cuántos"* refers to the specific number of goals that we needed to win yesterday.

5) CUYO, CUYA, CUYOS, CUYAS

These words mean "whose" and agree in number and gender with the noun that directly <u>follows</u> them. *"Cuyo"* is considered a possessive relative pronoun and operates grammatically as an adjective. It agrees not with the possessor, but rather with what is possessed.

✳ EXAMPLES: *La niña, **cuyo** padre es el presidente de una empresa quesera, tiene mucho dinero.*
> The girl, whose father is the president of a company that makes cheese, has a lot of money.

*Los ladrones, **cuyas** máscaras se encontraron cerca del banco, están en la cárcel ahora.*
> The robbers, whose masks were found near the bank, are now in jail.

*Ramón es el chico **cuya** raqueta está en mi coche.*
> Ramón is the boy whose racquet is in my car.

¡CUIDADO! *"Cuyo"* cannot be used as an interrogative. Do not confuse *"cuyo"* with *"¿De quién?"*, even though both can mean "whose." *"Cuyo"* agrees in number and gender with the noun which follows (*El chico cuya mochila es verde es mi hermano.* The boy whose backpack is green is my brother), while *"¿De quién?"* asks a question: "Whose is it?" (*¿De quién es la mochila?* Whose backpack is it?).

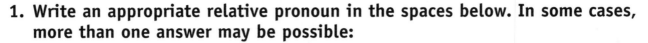

1. **Write an appropriate relative pronoun in the spaces below. In some cases, more than one answer may be possible:**

   a. El capitán del equipo, _____ es mi hermano, se llama Jim.

   b. Los amigos de Elena, _____ grabaron una canción nueva, nunca me hablan.

   c. _____ no me gusta es pasar mucho tiempo esperando el autobús.

   d. Vi al actor _____ pantalones eran de cuero.

   e. La casa _____ está cerca del semáforo es muy linda.

   f. Susana y Julia, _____ me llamaron anoche, estaban equivocadas.

   g. El hombre detrás de_____ me senté en la conferencia era calvo.

   h. _____ no duermen mucho se enfadan fácilmente.

   i. En este restaurante hacemos tacos; vamos a prepararte

   _____ necesites para tu fiesta.

   j. El apartamento en _____ vivo no tiene mucha agua caliente por la mañana.

   k. Los chicos a _____ conocimos anoche son dominicanos.

   l. No vamos a Puerto Rico esta primavera, _____ me molesta mucho.

   m. La persona _____ hermano era presidente se llama Jeb.

n. La razón por _____ no puedo ir al cine contigo es que tengo que lavarme el pelo y doblar la ropa.

o. Los ejercicios de este texto, _____ se ven aquí, fueron escritos en un MacBook.

2. Identify and correct the ten errors in the following paragraph:

Mi novia, María, a quien es de Los Ángeles, asistió a la Universidad de Georgia. Los tíos de ella, la cual viven en Georgia, estaban muy contentos de que María asista a su universidad favorita. Los señores McKee, cuyos casa fue construida en el año 1820, invitaban a María a cenar frecuentemente. Lo cual le gustaba mucho a María era la comida que servía la señora McKee. Siempre tenía cuanto platos deliciosos uno se pudiera imaginar. El señor McKee, con que María hablaba a menudo, dio un discurso un día en la Plaza Mayor, delante del que se encontraba el Banco Nacional. Al final del discurso, las personas cuyas coches estaban estacionados ilegalmente recibieron una multa del jefe de policía. Su tío estaba furioso y juró que nunca perdonaría a ese hombre. Los cuales trataban mal a su tío siempre lo sentían.

Learning to understand the differences between *"ser"* and *"estar"* often presents a special challenge for students. With practice, however, these differences become second nature.

1) The uses of "ser"

a) To express a defining characteristic

Examples: *Mis parientes **son** altos e inteligentes.*
My relatives are tall and intelligent.

*El español **es** muy bonito.*
Spanish is very beautiful.

b) With *"de,"* to tell where someone or something is from; origin

Examples: *Tito **es** de las Filipinas.*
Tito is from the Philippines.

*José Capablanca **era** de La Habana, Cuba.*
José Capablanca was from Havana, Cuba.

*Mi camiseta **es** de Zara.*
My T-shirt is from Zara.

c) To tell time or to give a date

Examples: ***Son** las diez y media.*
It's ten-thirty.

***Eran** las cuatro de la tarde cuando comenzaron las celebraciones para el presidente en Washington, D.C.*
It was four o'clock in the afternoon when the celebrations in Washington, D.C. began for the president.

*Hoy **es** sábado, 29 de agosto.*
Today is Saturday, the 29th of August.

d) With *"de,"* to indicate possession

Examples: *Las joyas **eran** de mi abuela.*
The jewelry was my grandmother's.

*Las guitarras **son** de Tuti Fernández.*
The guitars belong to Tuti Fernández.

*El capitán del barco **es** mi tío.*
The ship's captain is my uncle.

e) To indicate profession, nationality, religion, political affiliation

✳ EXAMPLES: *Los jóvenes de mi barrio son republicanos.*
The young people in my neighborhood are Republicans.

Mi madre es abogada y mi padre es cocinero.
My mother is a lawyer, and my father is a cook.

f) To form the passive voice

✳ EXAMPLES: *Una canción fue escrita por One Republic, la otra por One Direction.*
One song was written by One Republic, the other by One Direction.

Las puertas fueron cerradas a las seis anoche.
The doors were closed last night at six.

g) To tell where, or at what time, an event is taking place

✳ EXAMPLES: *El partido de fútbol será a las tres.*
The soccer game will take place at three o'clock.

La cena es en el comedor grande.
The dinner is in the big dining room.

El baile será aquí.
The dance will take place here.

≋¡CUIDADO!≋ Remember, *"estar"* is used for location of <u>objects</u>: *"La pelota de fútbol está en el garaje"; "La enchilada está en la cocina." "Ser"* is for <u>events</u>.

h) With *"de,"* to tell what something is made of

✳ EXAMPLES: *La puerta es de madera.*
The door is made of wood.

Todas las corbatas de mi profesor son de poliéster.
All my teacher's ties are polyester.

i) To use with impersonal expressions

✳ EXAMPLES: *Es bueno que estés aquí ahora para hablar con Belinda.*
It's good that you're here now to speak with Belinda.

Será necesario que todos me escuchen bien.
It will be necessary that everyone listen to me carefully.

j) For mathematical equations

✳ **EXAMPLES:** *Dos y dos **son** cuatro.* $2 + 2 = 4$

                          *Cuatro por siete **son** veintiocho.* $4 \times 7 = 28$

2) THE USES OF "ESTAR"

a) To express a condition (physical, mental, or emotional), as opposed to a defining characteristic

✳ **EXAMPLES:** ***Estoy** muy enferma porque comí demasiados perros calientes.*
I'm very sick because I ate too many hot dogs.

***Estamos** tristes porque perdimos el campeonato.*
We are sad because we lost the championship.

b) To identify location, whether temporary or permanent

✳ **EXAMPLES:** ***Estoy** en Honolulu y hace muy buen tiempo.*
I'm in Honolulu, and the weather is great.

***Estamos** en abril, el mes más lluvioso del año.*
It's April, the most rainy month of the year.

*Chicago **está** en Illinois.*
Chicago is in Illinois.

*¿A cuántos **estamos** hoy? –**Estamos** a diecinueve de mayo.*
What's the date? –It's May 19th.

Note: Treat the last example as a set expression, which uses the first person plural of *"estar."* It's almost as though we were walking on a giant calendar, and we look down to discover: "Oh — we're on May 19th!"

c) To form the progressive tense

✳ **EXAMPLES:** ***Estamos** estudiando los usos de "estar" ahora.*
We are studying the uses of *"estar"* now.

***Estábamos** durmiendo cuando sonó el despertador.*
We were sleeping when the alarm clock went off.

d) To indicate a change from the norm or to emphasize the special state or nature of something

✴ **EXAMPLES:** *¡Estás muy guapo hoy!*
    You look great today!

Note: The idea here is that you have gotten all dressed up, your hair looks great, etc. By using a form of *"estar,"* the speaker indicates that you look special today!

¡Caramba, Pepe! ¡Estás flaquísimo!
    My goodness, Pepe! You look so thin!

Note: The speaker comments that Pepe looks skinnier than normal — he must have lost weight, or his clothes make him look slimmer.

¡Qué buenas están estas tortillas!
    These tortillas are (taste) great!

e) To talk about certain weather conditions

✴ **EXAMPLES:** *Está nublado hoy en Seattle.*
    It's cloudy today in Seattle.

La tarde estaba clara y fría.
    The afternoon was clear and cold.

f) To form certain set expressions

✴ **EXAMPLES:** *Estoy de vacaciones en julio.*
    I'm on vacation in July.

Los tomates están a tres dólares la libra.
    Tomatoes are at three dollars a pound.

g) To emphasize a resultant state, not an action, when paired with past participles functioning as adjectives

✴ **EXAMPLES:** *Estamos sentados en la primera fila.*
    We are seated in the first row.

Mi vaca, Elsie, está muerta.
    My cow, Elsie, is dead.

¿La embajada? Está cerrada. La cerraron esta mañana.
    The embassy? It's closed. They closed it this morning.

3) DIFFERENCES BETWEEN "SER" AND "ESTAR"

It is interesting to see how adjectives used with *"ser"* and *"estar"* have quite different meanings. Most of the sentences in the column on the left, using the verb *"ser,"* describe defining characteristics. The sentences on the right, with the verb *"estar,"* describe conditions.

SER	ESTAR
*El hielo **es** frío.* Ice is cold. (defining characteristic)	*Esta sopa **está** fría.* This soup is cold. (condition)
*Las uvas **son** verdes.* The grapes are green. (their usual color)	*Las uvas **están** verdes.* The grapes are not ripe.
*Ramón **es** listo.* Ramón is smart.	*Ramón **está** listo.* Ramón is ready.
*Linda **es** pálida.* Linda is pale. (generally)	*Linda **está** pálida.* Linda looks pale. (condition)
*José **es** guapo.* José is good-looking.	*José **está** muy guapo esta noche.* José looks great (handsome) tonight.
*Muchos dicen que el señor Ramírez **es** muy aburrido.* Many say that Mr. Ramírez is very boring. (general characteristic)	*Todos los chicos en la clase del señor Ramírez **están** aburridos.* All the kids in Mr. Ramírez's class are bored. (right now)
*La casa **es** alquilada por el dueño.* The house is rented out by the owner. (passive construction)	*La casa ya **está** alquilada.* The house is already rented. (resultant state)

PRACTICE EXERCISES

1. **Write the appropriate form of *"ser"* or *"estar"*:**

a. Santo Domingo _____ la capital de República Dominicana.

b. Sentía mucho que ellos no _____ presentes durante la reunión.

c. _____ a fines de abril. ¡Qué suerte!

d. Esta pulsera _____ para mi tía.

e. Los chicos _____ bailando cerca del garaje anoche.

f. Las uvas _____ verdes; por eso no voy a probarlas.

g. Creo que no podremos ver las estrellas. _____ un poco nublado.

h. ¡Qué bonita _____ María hoy!

i. La reunión con los arquitectos _____ en la sala de conferencias.

j. Los pájaros _____ muertos porque comieron veneno.

k. Si yo _____ rey de España, viviría en Madrid.

l. Los libros _____ escritos por monjes hace muchos siglos.

m. Ahora nosotros _____ muy felices porque hemos jugado bien.

n. Estas canchas de tenis _____ de cemento.

o. María _____ muy lista; siempre sabe las respuestas en los exámenes de alemán.

p. ¿Dónde _____ el partido de baloncesto?

q. Raúl _____ de Cuba, pero hoy _____ en Caracas.

r. Antes, mi madre _____ una artista muy conocida.

s. ¿Cómo _____ vosotros? –Muy bien.

t. Yo _____ de vacaciones ahora en Mayagüez.

2. **Identify and correct the eight errors in the following account, written while on vacation in Florida:**

Fui muy alegre durante las vacaciones. El cielo siempre era claro y no había ninguna nube. Mi antiguo compañero de cuarto, Pedro, me acompañó y él está un hombre muy cómico. Un día fue leyendo un libro, cuando me dijo: "Mira, Juan. ¿Por qué eres tan serio hoy?". Le dije que yo, al contrario, estaba alegre. No me contestó. Luego abrí el armario y vi una caja grande que era allí. Estaba un regalo de Pedro con una carta: "Esta maleta nueva es para ti; tus maletas viejas son en el coche. Feliz cumpleaños".

These two sets of questions use grammatical structures and vocabulary from this lesson. Working with a partner, alternate asking and answering each question. When you get to the bottom of each list, start over at the top, switching roles. As a variation, write out the answers in complete sentences.

A) ¿Has **lanzado** alguna vez en un partido de béisbol?

¿Les has **jurado** a tus padres que vas a estudiar más en el futuro?

¿A qué temperatura **hierve** el agua?

¿Es divertido **fregar** el suelo cuando está sucio?

¿De qué personas **te fías**?

Si una persona **estornuda**, ¿qué le dices?

¿**Exigen** mucho los profesores en nuestra escuela?

B) ¿Cuál **es** la capital de Puerto Rico?

¿Dónde **está** Tegucigalpa?

¿Por quién **fue** escrita la novela *Cien años de soledad*? (García-Márquez)

¿**Estamos** hablando en inglés o en español ahora?

¿Dónde **fue** el Super Bowl este año?

¿Qué hora **era** cuando te despertaste hoy?

¿**Está** cerrada la puerta de la clase?

PRUEBA DE REPASO

A) LOS ADVERBIOS

1. Change the following adjectives to adverbs:

a. perezoso → _____

b. fácil → _____

c. nervioso → _____

d. melancólico → _____

e. verdadero → _____

f. fuerte → _____

2. Translate the following sentences:

a. The class is too boring for me.

_____

b. Yesterday I was happy because they delivered my new piano.

_____

c. He interrupted me abruptly. (abrupt = *brusco*)

_____

B) LOS ARTÍCULOS DEFINIDOS E INDEFINIDOS

1. Fill in the appropriate definite or indefinite article, if necessary:

a. Mis abuelos siempre van a _____ Florida durante el mes de febrero.

b. Me gustaría pasar un semestre estudiando en _____ México.

c. _____ señora Fiorina quería ser presidente de _____ Estados Unidos.

d. _____ señora melancólica apareció en la puerta.

e. Diego Luna es _____ actor.

f. Mañana es _____ sábado; ¿qué quieres hacer esta noche?

g. _____ música es muy importante en la vida.

h. Si tuviera _____ mil dólares en el bolsillo, iría de compras al Emporio Armani.

2. **Underline and correct the six errors that appear in this sad poem:**

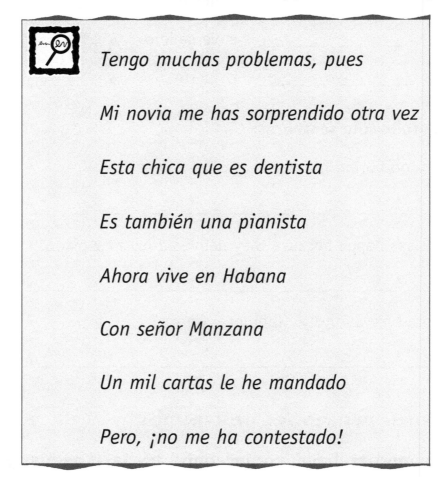

Tengo muchas problemas, pues

Mi novia me has sorprendido otra vez

Esta chica que es dentista

Es también una pianista

Ahora vive en Habana

Con señor Manzana

Un mil cartas le he mandado

Pero, ¡no me ha contestado!

C) LOS PRONOMBRES RELATIVOS

1. **Complete these sentences with the appropriate relative pronoun. More than one answer may be possible:**

a. La persona _____ me engañó era mi mejor amiga.

b. A mucha gente le gusta contar chismes, _____ me irrita.

c. _____ nos confundía era el acento extranjero del profesor.

d. El perro _____ ladraba tanto se llamaba Fido.

e. Esa señora, _____ negocio no va bien, está descontenta.

f. La razón por _____ te llamo es que quiero ir contigo a la nueva película de *Zoe Saldaña*.

g. _____ ahorran mucho dinero duermen mejor por la noche.

h. Mi maestra de español siempre hablaba muy rápido,

_____ me asustaba.

i. Las casas entre _____ vivimos son azules.

j. ¡_____ estoy intentando decirte es que no quiero salir contigo!

2. Translate the following sentences:

a. The light that appeared in the sky was a new star.

_____

b. Those who get angry easily do not have many friends.

_____

c. What bothers me is that I sometimes make mistakes on the tests.

_____

D) Los usos de "ser" y "estar"

1. Complete the following sentences with *"ser"* or *"estar"*:

a. José Ferrer y Rita Moreno _____ mis actores favoritos.

b. _____ las diez de la noche cuando por fin firmaron el contrato.

c. Las luces de la casa _____ encendidas, pero cuando llamé a la puerta, nadie contestó.

d. Vosotros _____ satisfechos porque habéis heredado mucho dinero.

e. ¿En qué edificio _____ la reunión esta noche?

f. ¿Dónde _____ la sala de reuniones?

g. Bob Marley _____ de Jamaica.

h. Lorena, ¡_____ guapísima con ese vestido!

i. Anoche mis padres _____ espiándome mientras hablaba con mi novio en el salón.

j. El libro _____ escrito por Sandra Cisneros el año pasado.

2. **Identify and correct the twelve errors of various kinds in this announcement from a local newspaper:**

¡Cantando es bueno para la salud!

El grupo musical quien se llama **Los sonidos** es buscando para un

cantante masculino. Las audiciones estarán en la iglesia próximo Lunes.

Si Ud. es un cantante y es interesado en nuestro grupo, ¡viene y cante

para nosotros! Los cuales lleguen temprano podrán tomar café y galletas.

Las audiciones empiezan a cuatro de la tarde: ¡No llegue tarde!

PARAGUAY & URUGUAY

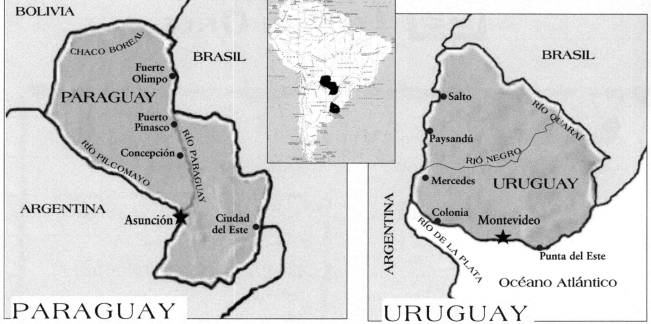

PARAGUAY

URUGUAY

PARAGUAY

CAPITAL:	Asunción
POBLACIÓN:	6.900.000
GOBIERNO:	república constitucional
PRESIDENTE:	Mario Abdo Benítez
DINERO ($):	guaraní
PRODUCTOS:	agricultura, algodón, ganadería, madera, maíz
MÚSICA, BAILE:	danza de la botella, polka
SITIOS DE INTERÉS:	Chaco, Ciudad del Este, El río Paraguay, Las Ruinas Jesuitas
COMIDA TÍPICA:	bori-bori, chipas, palmitos, so'o ku'i, sopa paraguaya, tereré

URUGUAY

CAPITAL:	Montevideo
POBLACIÓN:	3.500.000
GOBIERNO:	república constitucional
PRESIDENTE:	Tabaré Vázquez
DINERO ($):	peso uruguayo
PRODUCTOS:	carne, cemento, cuero, vino
MÚSICA, BAILE:	música gauchesca, tango, vals
SITIOS DE INTERÉS:	Colonia del Sacramento, Punta del Este
COMIDA TÍPICA:	asado, cazuela, chivitos, mate, parrillada, puchero

PARAGUAYOS FAMOSOS:

Agustín Barrios
(MÚSICO)

Augusto Roa Bastos
(ESCRITOR)

José Luis Chilavert
(FUTBOLISTA)

Luis Alberto
del Paraná
(CANTANTE)

URUGUAYOS FAMOSOS:

Juan Manuel Blanes
(PINTOR)

José Gervasio Artigas
(HÉROE NACIONAL)

Pedro Figari (PINTOR)

Juan Carlos Onetti
(ESCRITOR)

Horacio Quiroga
(ESCRITOR)

Enrique Rodó
(ESCRITOR)

VOCABULARIO LECCIÓN ONCE

VERBOS

lograr	to obtain, to succeed in	*pescar*	to fish
luchar	to fight, to struggle	*pretender*	to aspire to, to seek, to claim to be
lucir	to shine	*prometer*	to promise
llenar	to fill	*quejarse de*	to complain (about)
maullar	to meow (like a cat)	*reflejar*	to reflect
medir (i)	to measure	*regalar*	to give a gift
merecer	to deserve, to merit	*regresar*	to return
mezclar	to mix	*reinar*	to reign
mojar	to wet, to moisten	*renovar (ue)*	to renovate, to renew
morder (ue)	to bite	*resolver (ue)*	to resolve, to solve a problem
nombrar	to name		
ocultar	to hide	*rodear*	to surround
odiar	to hate	*sacar*	to take out
parar	to stop	*sobrar*	to remain, to be left over
parecer	to seem, to appear		
parecerse a	to resemble	*subrayar*	to underline
patinar	to skate	*suceder*	to happen
peinar	to comb	*suponer*	to suppose
pelear	to fight	*tapar*	to cover
perseguir (i)	to pursue, to go after to persecute	*toser*	to cough
		tragar	to swallow
pertenecer a	to belong to	*vencer*	to conquer, to defeat

LECCIÓN ONCE

KEY GRAMMAR CONCEPTS

A) LOS ADJETIVOS → *Adjectives*

B) LOS ADJETIVOS POSESIVOS → *Possessive adjectives*

C) LOS NÚMEROS CARDINALES Y ORDINALES → *Cardinal and ordinal numbers*

D) LOS ADJETIVOS Y LOS PRONOMBRES DEMOSTRATIVOS → *Demonstrative adjectives and pronouns*

E) LOS USOS DE LA PALABRA "LO" → *The uses of the word "lo"*

A) LOS ADJETIVOS

Adjectives are used to describe nouns. In Spanish, adjectives agree in number and gender with the nouns they describe.

1) AGREEMENT BETWEEN NOUNS AND ADJECTIVES

a) **Most masculine adjectives end in "o," while most feminine adjectives end in "a."**
The ending "-s" is added to make these adjectives plural.

> **EXAMPLES:**
> | | |
> |---|---|
> | *el chico **alto*** | the tall boy |
> | *la chica **alta*** | the tall girl |
> | *los teléfonos **viejos*** | the old telephones |
> | *las papas **deliciosas*** | the delicious potatoes |

b) **Some adjectives end with the letter "e" or with a consonant.**
These adjectives can describe both masculine and feminine nouns. Adjectives ending with the letter "e" become plural by adding "-s." Adjectives ending with a consonant become plural by adding "-es."

> **EXAMPLES:**
> | | |
> |---|---|
> | *el cuento **triste*** | the sad story |
> | *la monja **triste*** | the sad nun |
> | *el bombero **cortés*** | the polite firefighter |
> | *la profesora **cortés*** | the polite teacher |
> | *los edificios **grandes*** | the big buildings |
> | *las sillas **grandes*** | the big chairs |
> | *un chico **joven*** | a young boy |
> | *las chicas **jóvenes*** | the young girls |

*el coche **azul***	the blue car
*una taza **azul***	a blue cup
*los libros **fáciles***	the easy books
*las composiciones **fáciles***	the easy compositions
*una idea **común***	a common idea
*unos hábitos **comunes***	some common habits
*el paraguas **roto***	the broken umbrella
*los paraguas **rotos***	the broken umbrellas

Note: An accent is added to some adjectives in the plural form: *joven → jóvenes,* while an accent is removed in other plural forms: *común → comunes.* These changes are in accordance with the regular rules of accentuation (see *Lección Cinco*).

c) **With certain adjectives of nationality that end in a consonant,** the feminine form is made by adding an "-a." The feminine plural ending of these adjectives is "-as."

✳ **EXAMPLES:**

*un coche **japonés***	a Japanese car
*unos coches **japoneses***	some Japanese cars
*una receta **japonesa***	a Japanese recipe
*unas recetas **japonesas***	some Japanese recipes
*un vino **francés***	a French wine
*una criada **francesa***	a French maid
*un paciente **inglés***	an English patient
*una bufanda **inglesa***	an English scarf

Note: The accent marks drop off these feminine forms, following the regular rules of accentuation.

d) **There are some other adjectives that end in "or" and "ón"** that are also made feminine by adding an "-a."

✳ **EXAMPLES:**

*un amigo **hablador***	a talkative friend
*unos amigos **habladores***	some talkative friends
*una amiga **habladora***	a talkative friend
*unas amigas **habladoras***	some talkative friends
*un tono **burlón***	a mocking (playful) tone
*una canción **burlona***	a mocking (playful) song

Note: The accent mark drops off the feminine form of *"burlón,"* as in the example above.

e) *"El"* and *"un"* have come to be used directly before feminine nouns beginning with a stressed "a."

This development may have come about because the "a" sound of *"la"* and *"una"* was absorbed by the stressed "a" in a word that followed. Saying *"el agua"* instead of *"la agua,"* (which would sound like "lagua"), and *"un águila"* instead of *"una águila"* allows the pronunciation of each word to stay distinct.

EXAMPLES:

el agua fría	the cold water
un hacha afilada	a sharp axe
el hacha afilada	the sharp axe
un alma tranquila	a peaceful soul
el hada madrina feliz	the happy fairy godmother

Note: In the plural form, these nouns take the articles that you would expect: *las aguas frías, unas hachas afiladas, unas almas tranquilas, unas hadas madrinas felices.* Also: *la otra hacha, la feroz águila.*

f) **When there are two subjects of different gender, an adjective is masculine plural if it follows the noun.**

EXAMPLES: *Las plantas y los árboles son **bonitos**.*
The plants and trees are pretty.

*Algunos gobiernos y empresas son **corruptos**.*
Some governments and businesses are corrupt.

However, if an adjective precedes the noun, it will agree with the noun that follows.

EXAMPLES: *Hay **muchas** vacas y caballos en esta finca.*
There are many cows and horses on this farm.

*¿**Cuántos** lápices y plumas tienes aquí?*
How many pencils and pens do you have here?

g) **If a plural noun that indicates single units is modified** by more than one adjective, the adjectives will be singular.

EXAMPLES: *los coches **italiano** y **francés***
the Italian and French cars (one of each)

*las alumnas **japonesa** y **australiana***
the Japanese and Australian students (one of each)

h) Certain adjectives can precede a noun. In this case, they will lose the "o" before a masculine, singular noun.

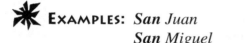 **EXAMPLES:**

un **buen** libro	a good book
el **tercer** día	the third day
algún coche	some car
el **primer** beso	the first kiss
un **mal** día	a bad day

i) *"Grande"* **becomes** *"gran"* **before any <u>singular</u> noun.**

EXAMPLES:

el **gran** filósofo	the great philosopher
la **gran** idea	the great idea

Note: The meaning of this adjective changes from "big" to "great" when it precedes the noun.

j) *"Santo"* **becomes** *"San"* **before masculine names,** with the exception of words beginning with the letters "To" and "Do." (The feminine form *"Santa"* is invariable.)

EXAMPLES:

San Juan	**Santo** Domingo	(**Santa** María)
San Miguel	**Santo** Tomás	(**Santa** Fe)

k) Adjectives (and many nouns) that end in "-ista" have the same form for both masculine and feminine.

EXAMPLES:

el chico **idealista**	the idealistic boy
la chica **idealista**	the idealistic girl
el jugador **optimista**	the optimistic player
la persona **optimista**	the optimistic person

l) *"Cualquiera"* **becomes** *"cualquier"* **before either masculine or feminine nouns.**

EXAMPLES:

cualquier libro	whichever (any) book
cualquier pluma	whichever (any) pen

Note: The plural form of this adjective, *"cualesquiera,"* is rarely used nowadays. Spanish speakers tend to use the singular form with the singular noun (*"cualquier libro"* instead of *"cualesquiera libros"*).

m) *"Ciento"* **becomes** *"cien"* **before any noun** or before any larger number
(e.g., *"mil," "millón,"* etc.)

⁕ **EXAMPLES:** *cien libros*
cien playas
cien mil mosquitos
cien millones de dólares
BUT: *ciento dos*

¡CUIDADO! The plural of *"cien"* is *"cientos"* not *cienes (e.g., *Había cientos de mosquitos por la playa.* There were hundreds of mosquitoes along the beach.)

2) PLACEMENT OF ADJECTIVES ——————————————

Usually adjectives follow the nouns they describe, although there are exceptions.

a) Adjectives that follow nouns

Most descriptive adjectives that distinguish one noun from another follow the noun. These adjectives help to make clear which noun the speaker is describing. They include adjectives of size, nationality, personality, color, type, etc.

⁕ **EXAMPLES:** *Los chicos **guapos** de Haverford llegaron tarde.*
The good-looking boys of Haverford arrived late.

*El conjunto **guatemalteco** tocó dos piezas.*
The Guatemalan group played two pieces.

*A mí no me gustan las papas **fritas** de Burger King.*
I don't like Burger King's french fries.

*"Las flores **rojas** siempre me atraen", dijo el toro Fernando.*
"Red flowers always attract me," said Ferdinand, the bull.

*La casa **violeta** me repugna.*
The purple house repulses me.

*Nunca invito a esos niños **malcriados** a mis fiestas.*
I never invite those spoiled kids to my parties.

*Las ventanas **rotas** era un símbolo de los problemas en ese barrio.*
Note: Although in theory *"era"* agrees with *"símbolo,"* the general tendency in today's Spanish is to put the verb in the plural if either the subject or the predicate is in the plural.
The broken windows were a symbol of the problems in that neighborhood.

b) Adjectives that precede nouns

1 Adjectives that are limiting

Adjectives that are limiting (definite and indefinite articles, demonstratives, possessives, ordinal and cardinal numbers, and indefinites) normally come before the noun they describe.

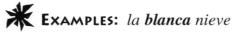 **EXAMPLES:**

el sueldo	the salary
unas mentiras	some lies
este cocodrilo	this crocodile
tu escoba	your broom
veintiuna trompetas	twenty-one trumpets
la primera cita	the first date
algún ladrón	some robber
poco dinero	a little money
mucha lluvia	a lot of rain

2 Adjectives that describe inherent characteristics or traits

Certain adjectives are placed before the noun because they describe an inherent characteristic or trait that is most often associated with that particular noun. Because these adjectives do not seek to set aside one group of nouns from another, they are not usually placed after the noun.

 EXAMPLES:

la blanca nieve	the white snow
el frío hielo	the cold ice
su precioso niño	your beautiful child
la famosa estrella de cine, Natalie Portman	the famous movie-star, Natlie Portman
la fabulosa esposa de Paco Marino	the fabulous wife of Paco Marino

Note: *"La esposa fabulosa de Paco Marino"* could imply that Paco has more than one wife!

c) Adjectives that either precede or follow the noun

1 Some adjectives can be used either before or after a noun without changing the meaning.

EXAMPLES:

un buen chico/un chico bueno	a good boy
una mala temporada/una temporada mala	a bad season
el primer ensayo/el ensayo primero	the first essay

Other adjectives can be used either before or after a noun, but there is considerable difference in meaning.

✳ EXAMPLES:

mi *vieja (**antigua**)* profesora	my former professor
mi profesora *vieja*	my old (in years) professor
el *gran* hombre, Einstein	the great man, Einstein
el hombre *grande,* Arnold Schwarzenegger	the big man, Arnold Schwarzenegger
mi *pobre* amigo	my poor (no luck) friend
mi amigo *pobre*	my poor (no money) friend
el *nuevo* libro	the new (just published) book
el libro *nuevo*	the new (not used) book
el *mismo* profesor	the same teacher
el profesor *mismo*	the teacher himself
mi *antiguo* apartamento	my former (not current) apartment
mi apartamento *antiguo*	my old (in years; not brand new!) apartment

 # PRACTICE EXERCISES

1. **Write the appropriate form of the words in parentheses to create phrases that agree in number and gender.**

a. _____ agua _____ (el/frío)

b. _____ aviones _____ (el/ruidosa)

c. _____ sacapuntas _____(mi/rota)

d. _____ actitud _____ (uno/burlón)

e. _____ alumnos _____ (el/española)

f. _____ problemas _____ (mucho/común)

g. _____ representante _____ (uno/francesa)

h. _____ águila _____ (uno/majestuoso)

i. _____ empleados _____ (el/idealista)

j. _____ Domingo y _____ Bernardino (Santo/Santo)

2. **Translate the following expressions:**

   a. our poor aunt Sally, who is very rich

   _____

   b. the former president of the United States, Bill Clinton

   _____

   c. the great, small party

   _____

   d. the calm soul

   _____

   e. the talkative man and the mocking (playful) presentation

   _____

3. **Write each adjective in the correct space, being certain that it agrees with the noun:**

   a. _____ blusa _____ (este)

   b. _____ hacha _____ (uno)

   c. unos _____ jugadores _____ (alto)

   d. _____ fincas _____ (veintiuno)

   e. la _____ cita _____ (tercero)

   f. _____ playas tropicales _____ (ciento)

   g. la _____ nieve _____ (blanco)

B) LOS ADJETIVOS POSESIVOS

Possessive adjectives are words that are used to tell to whom or to what something belongs. There are two kinds of possessives: the short forms and the long forms.

1) THE SHORT FORMS

The following possessive adjectives are placed before the noun that they modify. They agree in number and gender with that noun.

mi/mis	*nuestro/nuestra/nuestros/nuestras*
tu/tus	*vuestro/vuestra/vuestros/vuestras*
su/sus	*su/sus*

EXAMPLES:

mi amigo	my friend
nuestros enemigos	our enemies
tus planes	your plans
sus ideas	his/her/your/your (pl.)/their ideas
su castillo	his/her/your/your (pl.)/their castle
vuestras capillas	your (pl.) chapels

Helpful Tip: Did you notice that *"sus ideas"* and *"su castillo"* have many different translations? To avoid confusion, you may choose an alternate possessive construction that uses the preposition *"de"* and a pronoun that follows a preposition.

EXAMPLES:

sus ideas	=	las ideas **de él**	his ideas
		las ideas **de ella**	her ideas
		las ideas **de Ud.**	your ideas
		las ideas **de Uds.**	your (pl.) ideas
		las ideas **de ellos**	their ideas
		las ideas **de ellas**	their ideas
su castillo	=	el castillo **de él**	his castle
		el castillo **de ella**	her castle
		el castillo **de Ud.**	your castle
		el castillo **de Uds.**	your (pl.) castle
		el castillo **de ellos**	their castle
		el castillo **de ellas**	their castle

2) THE LONG FORMS

The longer possessive forms are normally placed directly after a noun. They also agree in number and gender with the noun that they describe. The long forms are used to place special emphasis on the <u>possessor</u>.

mío/mía/míos/mías	*nuestro/nuestra/nuestros/nuestras*
tuyo/tuya/tuyos/tuyas	*vuestro/vuestra/vuestros/vuestras*
suyo/suya/suyos/suyas	*suyo/suya/suyos/suyas*

EXAMPLES: *un libro **mío***
a book of mine (<u>my</u> book)

*unos libros **míos***
some books of mine (<u>my</u> books)

*una prima **suya***
a cousin of his/hers/yours/yours (pl.)/theirs (<u>his</u> cousin, etc.)

*unas amigas **suyas***
some friends of his/hers/yours/yours (pl.)/theirs (<u>his</u> friends, etc.)

*unos libros **suyos***
some books of his/hers/yours/yours (pl.)/theirs (<u>his</u> books, etc.)

Unlike the short forms, the long forms may stand on their own after *"ser,"* free and clear from the noun.

EXAMPLES: *Las botellas son **mías**.*
The bottles are mine.

*Esa opinión es **tuya**.*
That opinion is yours.

These long forms can also serve as pronouns along with a definite article.

EXAMPLES: *Mi coche y **el tuyo** son semejantes.*
My car and yours are similar.

*Su casa y **la nuestra** están en el mismo barrio*
Your house and ours are in the same neighborhood.

At times, 3rd person possessive adjectives, long and short, can be ambiguous. Simply use the alternate form of *"de"* and a pronoun *(él, ella, Ud., ellos, ellas, Uds.)* to avoid confusion.

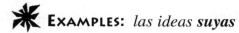 **EXAMPLES:** *las ideas suyas* = *las ideas de él*
                                     las ideas de ella
                                     las ideas de Ud.
                                     las ideas de ellos
                                     las ideas de ellas
                                     las ideas de Uds.

               el anuncio suyo = *el anuncio de él*
                                     el anuncio de ella
                                     el anuncio de Ud.
                                     el anuncio de ellos
                                     el anuncio de ellas
                                     el anuncio de Uds.

Helpful Tip: This construction makes it possible to avoid repeating the same noun twice in a sentence: "My book and yours are good" — *"Mi libro y **el tuyo** son buenos"* (rather than *"Mi libro y tu libro son buenos"*). Also: "Your plants and hers are beautiful" — *"Tus plantas y **las suyas** son bonitas"* or *"Tus plantas y **las de ella** son bonitas."*

 # PRACTICE EXERCISES

1. Translate the following sentences:

a. Your books and mine do not belong to the school.

_____

b. The forest is ours; the pile of firewood is theirs.

_____

c. his e-mail (express in three different ways)

_____

_____

_____

d. I hate her false pride and his.

_____

2. Write the correct form of a possessive adjective in the appropriate space:

a. _____ lugar _____ (my)

b. un _____ espacio _____ (of his — 2 ways)

c. _____ aniversario _____ (our)

d. su motocicleta y _____ (ours — 2 ways)

e. _____ cumpleaños y el tuyo (my)

f. nuestro problema y _____ (hers — 2 ways)

3. Find and correct the six errors in this letter:

20 de abril de 2019

Estimado Sr. Sánchez:

Mi hermano Santiago y yo tenemos problemas con nuestros coches,

las cuales compramos en la tienda su el fin de semana pasado. Por

desgracia, se nos han roto los motores. Mi hermano está furioso. Mi

coche y suyo nos costaron muchísimo dinero. ¿Hay garantía? Espero que

su palabra vale más que los coches suyo. De no ser así, mi abogado,

el señor Vaalacárcel, le va a llamar pronto. Estoy seguro de que nuestro

solución será agradable para todos.

Atentamente,

Juan Tomás

1) CARDINAL NUMBERS

0	*cero*	8	*ocho*	16	*dieciséis (diez y seis)*
1	*uno*	9	*nueve*	17	*diecisiete (diez y siete)*
2	*dos*	10	*diez*	18	*dieciocho (diez y ocho)*
3	*tres*	11	*once*	19	*diecinueve (diez y nueve)*
4	*cuatro*	12	*doce*	20	*veinte*
5	*cinco*	13	*trece*	21	*veintiuno*
6	*seis*	14	*catorce*		*(veintiún pájaros . . .*
7	*siete*	15	*quince*		*veintiuna entradas)*

The cardinal numbers 21–29 used to be written as either one word or as three. Today, however, the one-word form is standard. Note the accents on *veintidós, veintitrés* and *veintiséis.*

21	*veintiuno*	26	*veintiséis*
22	*veintidós*	27	*veintisiete*
23	*veintitrés*	28	*veintiocho*
24	*veinticuatro*	29	*veintinueve*
25	*veinticinco*		

The compound numbers from 31–99 have always been written as three words.

30	*treinta*	70	*setenta*
31-39	*treinta y uno, treinta y dos, etc.*	80	*ochenta*
40	*cuarenta*	90	*noventa*
50	*cincuenta*	100	*ciento/cien*
60	*sesenta*		

Helpful Tips: **1)** The word *"ciento"* is shortened to *"cien"* before any noun (*cien libros, cien tarjetas*) or before a larger number *(cien mil).*
2) The word *"y"* is only used in Spanish between groups of tens and ones (e.g., *sesenta y seis*).
3) "One hundred (and) one" is expressed in Spanish by *"ciento uno."*

101	ciento uno	400	cuatrocientos	700	setecientos
200	doscientos	500	quinientos	800	ochocientos
300	trescientos	600	seiscientos	900	novecientos

Helpful Tip: When describing a feminine noun, the numerals 200-900 change to agree with that noun (*doscientas, trescientas*, etc.). 321 potatoes = **trescientas** **veintiuna** *patatas*; **But:** 451 helmets = **cuatrocientos** *cincuenta y un cascos*

1000	mil	100.000	cien mil
1001	mil uno	1.000.000	un millón
2001	dos mil uno	3.000.000	tres millones
10.000	diez mil		

Helpful Tips: **1)** A million boats = *un millón* **de** *barcos*. You must place *"de"* between *"millón"* and a subsequent noun.
2) Don't forget that in Spanish, you use a period where in English you would use a comma!

2) ORDINAL NUMBERS

The most common ordinal numbers are the first ten. After that, a Spanish speaker will most often choose to use a cardinal number.

1ST	primero	8TH	octavo	15TH	decimoquinto
2ND	segundo	9TH	noveno	16TH	decimosexto
3RD	tercero	10TH	décimo	17TH	decimoséptimo
4TH	cuarto	11TH	undécimo	18TH	decimoctavo
5TH	quinto	12TH	duodécimo	19TH	decimonoveno
6TH	sexto	13TH	decimotercero	20TH	vigésimo
7TH	séptimo	14TH	decimocuarto		

Helpful Tips: **1)** The words *"primero"* and *"tercero"* lose their *"o"* **before** a masculine, singular noun (*el primer libro, el tercer capítulo*). All other ordinal numbers retain the *"o"* before a masculine, singular noun (*el octavo período, el décimo alumno*).
2) All ordinal numbers change the *"o"* to an *"a"* when describing a singular, feminine noun (*la primera clase, la decimonovena pregunta*).
3) Ordinal numbers can be abbreviated: *1º,1ª, 2º, 2ª, 3º, 3ª*, etc.

21ˢᵀ–29ᵀᴴ	*vigésimo primero, vigésimo segundo, etc.*	70ᵀᴴ	*septuagésimo*
30ᵀᴴ	*trigésimo*	80ᵀᴴ	*octogésimo*
40ᵀᴴ	*cuadragésimo*	90ᵀᴴ	*nonagésimo*
50ᵀᴴ	*quincuagésimo*	100ᵀᴴ	*centésimo*
60ᵀᴴ	*sexagésimo*		

Helpful Tip: The ordinal numbers 100th–199th are expressed: *centésimo primero, centésimo segundo,* etc.

You will rarely, if ever, run into any of the following words; they are here for reference only!

200ᵀᴴ	*ducentésimo*	800ᵀᴴ	*octingentésimo*
300ᵀᴴ	*tricentésimo*	900ᵀᴴ	*noningentésimo*
400ᵀᴴ	*cuadringentésimo*	1000ᵀᴴ	*milésimo*
500ᵀᴴ	*quingentésimo*	5000ᵀᴴ	*cinco milésimo*
600ᵀᴴ	*sexcentésimo*	1,000,000ᵀᴴ	*millonésimo*
700ᵀᴴ	*septingentésimo*		

3) THINGS TO REMEMBER ABOUT CARDINAL AND ORDINAL NUMBERS

a) Cardinal numbers are used for dates.

EXAMPLES: *el **veintinueve** de agosto*
August 29ᵀᴴ

*el **doce** de julio de mil novecientos sesenta y tres*
July 12ᵀᴴ, 1963

Note: On the first day of the month, you should also say: *Hoy es el **primero** (uno) de febrero, el cumpleaños de mi amigo.*

b) You can use either a cardinal or ordinal number to identify a chapter, lesson, problem, street, row, etc.

EXAMPLES:

*el **primer** ejercicio*	=	*el ejercicio **uno***
*la **tercera** parte*	=	*la parte **tres***
*el **séptimo** párrafo*	=	*el párrafo **siete***
*la **octava** estrofa*	=	*la estrofa **ocho***

Note: After "ten," a cardinal number is usually used, sometimes preceded by "*número*": *lección once, el episodio (número) veinte.*

c) In a title, ordinal numbers are used from one to ten (*primero → décimo*). After that, cardinal numbers are used.

EXAMPLES: *Felipe IV (**cuarto**) aparece en muchos retratos de Velázquez.*
Philip the Fourth appears in many of Velázquez's paintings.

*Un día Román Martínez XII (**doce**) asistirá a este colegio.*
One day Román Martínez the Twelfth will attend this high school.

d) Put the cardinal number first and the ordinal second.

If both a cardinal and ordinal number are used in the same sentence, a Spanish speaker will normally put the cardinal number first and the ordinal second. In English, we tend to do the opposite.

 EXAMPLES: *Las **seis primeras** palabras de* Don Quijote *son:"En un lugar de La Mancha . . ."*
The first six words of *Don Quijote* are: "In a place in La Mancha . . ."

*Las **dos primeras** canciones de Maná fueron éxitos.*
Mana's first two songs were hits.

 # PRACTICE EXERCISES ▶

1. Write out the following in Spanish:

a. 21 scissors _____

b. 32 hangers _____

c. 101 tickets _____

d. 2,000 drops of water _____

e. the fifth exit _____

f. the second press conference _____

g. the first ten students _____

h. the twentieth miracle (two ways) _____

_____

i. the first mystery _____

j. the third toenail _____

k. 2,571 suitcases _____

l. 1,000,000 legends _____

m. Fifth Avenue _____

n. 1999 _____

o. fourteen masses _____

p. the sixtieth manager _____
(two ways)

_____

q. 101 pizzas _____

r. February 10, 1931 _____

s. June 5, 1923 _____

t. 5 million brooms _____

u. 10,526 stars _____

2. **Find and correct the eight errors in the following list of ten items:**

> *Lo que encontré este verano en la playa:*
>
> *1. veintidos botellas vacías*
>
> *2. uno paraguas roto*
>
> *3. una carta con la fecha "23 de julio de 2016"*
>
> *4. las primeras tres páginas de* Vogue
>
> *5. veintiuno pedazos de cristal*
>
> *6. un millón piedras bonitas*

7. *un mil frascos vacíos de crema protectora*

8. *doscientas treinta y un toallas verdes del Hotel Palace*

9. *ochos salvavidas guapos*

10. *un frasco de* champú

🔑 D) LOS ADJETIVOS Y LOS PRONOMBRES DEMOSTRATIVOS

1) THE USES AND FORMS OF DEMONSTRATIVE ADJECTIVES

Demonstrative adjectives help to identify and distinguish a noun from other nouns of the same type. These adjectives generally precede the noun that they modify. The corresponding words in English are: "**this**," "**these**," "**that**," and "**those**."

Here are the Spanish equivalents:

Demonstrative Adjectives		
Masculine	**Feminine**	
este	*esta*	this (close to speaker)
estos	*estas*	these (close to speaker)
ese	*esa*	that
esos	*esas*	those
aquel	*aquella*	that (way over there)
aquellos	*aquellas*	those (way over there)

"Aquel" and its other forms help to identify something that is a great distance away, the farthest distance away of a number of objects, or something quite removed in time from the speaker's context.

✳ **EXAMPLES:**

este detalle	this detail
esa tela	that cloth
esos Packers de Green Bay	those Green Bay Packers
aquella montaña	that mountain (way over there)
estos problemas	these problems
aquel pájaro	that bird (over yonder)
esa constante interrupción	that constant interruption
estas primeras miradas	these first glances

ese hombre terco	that stubborn man	
este chico, ese chico y	this boy, that boy, and that boy	
aquel chico	(over there)	
aquellos días de juventud	those days of youth	

Helpful Tip: Some students have trouble remembering if *"este"* means "this" or "that" or if *"estos"* means "these" or "those." The following rhyme may help you keep these forms straight:

"This" *(este, esta)* and "these" *(estos, estas)* have "t's."

---

2) WHEN DEMONSTRATIVE ADJECTIVES FOLLOW A NOUN

At times, one chooses to have a demonstrative adjective <u>follow</u> a noun. The feeling created is one that is negative, sarcastic, or of contempt. The forms most commonly used in this construction are: *"ese, esa, esos, esas."*

✳ **EXAMPLES:** *No me gusta el gerente **ese**.*
I don't like that manager.

*No vamos a hablar con las chicas **esas**.*
We aren't going to talk to those girls.

3) TURNING A DEMONSTRATIVE ADJECTIVE INTO A PRONOUN

By adding an accent* to a demonstrative adjective, you turn it into a pronoun. The pronunciation is not affected. In addition, there are three neuter forms. These never have accent marks.

Masculine/Feminine Pronouns		Neuter Pronouns	
éste/ésta *éstos/éstas*	this (one) these (things, people, etc.)	*esto*	this (idea, concept, situation, or unidentified object)
ése/ésa *ésos/ésas*	that (one) those (things, people, etc.)	*eso*	that (idea, concept, situation, or unidentified object)
aquél/aquélla *aquéllos/aquéllas*	that (one) → far away those (things, people, etc.) → far away	*aquello*	that (idea, concept, situation, or unidentified object)

*These accent marks are beginning to disappear in modern Spanish.

✳ **EXAMPLES:** *¿Vas a comprarme esta corbata o **aquélla**?*
Are you going to buy me this tie or that one (over there)?

*Este empleado y **ése** son amigos míos.*
This employee and that one are friends of mine.

*Esta playa y **aquéllas** en Montevideo son preciosas.*
This beach and those in Montevideo are lovely.

*¿Qué es **esto**? –Es un regalo para ti.*
　　What's this? –It's a present for you.

*Vamos al cine y después a pescar. ¿Qué piensas de **eso**?*
　　We're going to the movies and afterwards to fish. What do you think
　　of that (idea)?

*¿Prefieres este libro o **ése**? –Me gusta **éste**.*
　　Do you prefer this book or that one? –I like this one.

Note: As you can see in the examples above, the neuter pronouns *(esto, eso, aquello)* are
used with ideas, or with objects that are unknown or that haven't been identified.

4) THE SPECIAL USE OF THE DEMONSTRATIVE PRONOUNS "ÉSTE/ÉSTA/ ÉSTOS/ÉSTAS" WITH "AQUÉL/AQUÉLLA/AQUÉLLOS/AQUÉLLAS"

In a sentence in which you wish to refer back to two antecedents, first mention the
<u>second</u> antecedent by using *"éste/ésta/éstos/éstas"* and then mention the <u>first</u> antecedent
by using *"aquél/aquélla/aquéllos/aquéllas."* These correspond to: "the latter" and "the
former."

EXAMPLES: *Ellen DeGeneres y Jimmy Fallon tienen programas de televisión; **éste**
trabaja durante la noche y **aquélla** trabaja durante el día.*
　　Ellen DeGeneres and Jimmy Fallon have TV programs; the former
　　(that one, way back there at the beginning of the sentence — Ellen
　　DeGeneres) works during the day, and the latter (this one — Jimmy
　　Fallon) works at night.

*Marcos y Sharon son novios; **ésta** vive en New Hampshire y **aquél** vive
en Illinois.*
　　Mark and Sharon are a couple; the former (Mark) lives in Illinois, and
　　the latter (Sharon) in New Hampshire.

¿ ◆ ? Did you notice that after each semi-colon in these sentences, Spanish and
English speakers refer back to the antecedents in reverse order?

5) AN ALTERNATE FORM OF THE DEMONSTRATIVE PRONOUN

There is another construction used to create a demonstrative pronoun: the definite articles *(el, la, los, las, lo)* are combined with the words *"de"* or *"que."*

 EXAMPLES: *Mi chaqueta y **la de** Juanes son idénticas.*
My jacket and Juanes's (that of Juanes) are identical.

*Mis maletas y **las que** tú tienes son caras.*
My suitcases and those that you have are expensive.

*Mi suéter es diferente **del de** mi primo.*
My sweater is different from my cousin's (that of my cousin).

***Los que** se quejan a menudo van a tener dificultades en esta clase.*
Those who complain frequently are going to have difficulties in this class.

PRACTICE EXERCISES

1. Write an appropriate form of a demonstrative adjective or pronoun in the following sentences:

a. _____ chica de aquí no quiere regresar a la clase.

b. _____ montañas en la distancia están cubiertas de nieve.

c. Bill Clinton y Ronald Reagan son presidentes famosos del siglo veinte;

_____ era de California y _____ es de Arkansas.

d. Mi bolsa y _____ Graciela son idénticas.

e. Nunca voy a resolver nada con los chicos _____ .

f. ¿Qué es _____ que tienes en la mano? ¿Es un regalo para mí?

g. Primero vamos en coche al Hard Rock Café y después vamos a pie a tu

casa. ¿Qué piensas de _____?

h. Mi tía y mi abuelo van a darme dinero cuando me gradúe de la universidad;

_____ va a darme mil dólares y _____

veinticinco.

i. ¿Prefieres este cuchillo, ése o _____?

j. _____ madrugan siempre tienen éxito.

2. Identify and correct the seven errors in this journal entry:

¡Qué día! El chico ése que vi en la lavandería era muy mal

educado. Primero, mi detergente y la de él eran idénticos; por eso me

pidió que le diera mi detergente, porque él no quería usar el suyo. La

hermana de él tampoco era muy amable; mientras éste me robaba el

detergente, aquél me sacó la ropa mojada de la secadora antes de que

estuviera seca. No me gustó ese. Prefiero eses días de hace muchos años

cuando no habían lavanderías. Todos lavaban la ropa en casa o en el río.

Nunca voy a volver a ese lavandería.

Adjectives or adverbs can function as abstract nouns in combination with the neuter article *"lo."*

✳ **EXAMPLES:** *"**Lo bueno**, si breve, dos veces bueno". (Baltasar Gracián)*
"That which is good, if it is brief, is twice as good."

*No nos gusta **lo despacio** que ella se peina.*
We don't like how slowly she combs her hair.

*Comprendo **lo peligrosos** que son esos ladrones.*
I understand how dangerous those robbers are.

*Mi amiga y yo siempre pensamos **lo mismo**.*
My friend and I always think the same.

*No sabes **lo rica** que es esa actriz de* Ingobernable.
You don't know how rich the actress is in *Ingobernable.*

Helpful Tips: **1)** When speaking in a general way, the adjective will stay masculine singular as in the first example above.
2) When describing specific nouns, the adjectives will agree with those nouns. Even when the adjective is plural or feminine, the neuter *"lo"* stays the same — e.g., *Comprendo **lo peligrosos** que son esos ladrones; No podía creer **lo buena** que era la película* Amores Perros.

"Lo" is often used with *"ser," "estar,"* and *"parecer"* to represent a previously stated idea or description.

✳ **EXAMPLES:** *Soy actriz, pero mi madre no **lo es**.*
I'm an actress, but my mom is not.

*Estamos muy cansados, pero nuestros perros no **lo están**.*
We are tired, but our dogs are not.

*¿Es Ud. dentista? –No, no **lo soy**.*
Are you a dentist? –No, I'm not.

*¿Son muy atléticos esos estudiantes? –No, no **lo parecen**.*
Are those students very athletic? –No, they don't seem to be.

The neuter article *"lo"* is also used in many idiomatic expressions:

a lo lejos → in the distance		*lo más pronto posible* → as soon as possible
a lo mejor → probably		*por lo consiguiente* → consequently, hence
de lo contrario → or else, otherwise		*por lo demás* → otherwise, apart from that
lo de siempre → the same as usual		
por lo general → generally		*por lo tanto* → therefore
por lo menos → at least		*por lo visto* → apparently

The neuter article *"lo"* can be used with the long form of the possessive adjective to mean "that which is mine, yours, etc."

✳ **EXAMPLES:** ***Lo nuestro*** *vale mucho.*
That which is ours (Ours) is worth a lot.

*Cuando vengas a mi casa, quiero que sepas que **lo mío** es tuyo.*
When you come to my house, I want you to know that what (that which) is mine is yours.

*No quiero meterme en **lo suyo**, Sr. López.*
I don't want to butt into your business, Mr. López.

PRACTICE EXERCISE

Translate the following, using the word *"lo"*:

a. That which is interesting fascinates me.

_____

b. They are carpenters, but we are not.

_____

c. We will solve the problem as soon as possible.

_____

d. I never knew how nice they were.

_____

e. You will never take away from me that which is mine.

_____

These two sets of questions use grammatical structures and vocabulary from this lesson. Working with a partner, alternate asking and answering each question. When you get to the bottom of each list, start over at the top, switching roles. As a variation, write out the answers in complete sentences.

A) ¿De qué está **rodeada** nuestra escuela?

¿Es difícil para ti **tragar** alguna medicina?

¿Te has **peleado** alguna vez con tu primo favorito?

Cuando viajas en coche con tu familia, ¿**paran** Uds. de vez en cuando?

¿Te gusta cuando los gatos **maúllan** por la noche?

¿Le **ocultas** algo a tu novio/a?

¿**Has medido** las ventanas de esta clase?

B) ¿Cuál es el **segundo** libro de *La Biblia*?

¿Tiene Ud. **mil** dólares o **millones de** dólares?

¿Cuáles son las **tres primeras** palabras de nuestro himno nacional?

¿En qué año estamos?

¿Cuántos son **40** por **40**?

¿Cuál es la **sexta** letra de la palabra "alfabeto"?

¿Cuántos son **101** y **212**?

LA TORTILLA PURA

At the end of the book (p.349), you will read the tale of a woman who is said to make the best "tortilla española" in all of Spain. Listen to the audio as you read along. Afterwards, you will find comprehension questions (p.352), which you can answer aloud or in written form.

PRUEBA DE REPASO

A) LOS ADJETIVOS

1. Write the appropriate form of the definite/indefinite article and adjective:

a. _____ persona _____ (un/nervioso)

b. _____ almacenes _____ (un/enorme)

c. _____ entrevistas _____ (el/largo)

d. _____ gusto _____ (un/vulgar)

e. _____ consejos _____ (el/inútil)

f. _____ autoridad _____ (un/francés)

g. _____ Tomás y _____ Miguel (Santo/Santo)

h. _____ mil pájaros _____ (ciento/rojo)

2. Translate the following:

a. my old (former), idealistic professor (masculine)

_____

b. the great music of the Beatles and the Rolling Stones

_____

c. the cold waters

_____

d. a sad woman

_____

e. some red shirts and (red) pants

_____

f. any day

_____

3. Write the correct form of the adjective in the appropriate place:

a. _____ bata _____ (un/largo)

b. _____ detalle _____ (un/pequeño)

c. _____ semana _____ (el/primero)

d. _____ amiga _____ (mi/malo)

e. _____ libro _____ (ninguno/rojo)

B) LOS ADJETIVOS POSESIVOS

1. Translate each phrase into Spanish. In each case, multiple answers will be requested.

a. my rights (2)   _____   _____

b. her salary (3)

_____   _____   _____

c. their (masc.) mail (3)

_____   _____   _____

d. her wedding (3)

_____   _____   _____

e. their (fem.) rings (3)

_____   _____   _____

2. Translate the following sentences:

a. The policeman stopped his car and mine.

_____

b. Their house and yours (informal) are in the same neighborhood.

_____

c. We paid a lot for her ticket and ours.

_____

C) LOS NÚMEROS CARDINALES Y ORDINALES

1. Write out the following numbers (in Spanish!):

a. 202 _____   **d.** 27 _____

b. 15 _____   **e.** 660 _____

c. 100 _____   **f.** 30,500 _____

2. Translate the following:

a. a million dollars   _____

b. the first of January,   _____
the second of January

c. the third example   _____

d. the first four suitcases   _____

e. July 4, 1776   _____

f. 100,321 scholarships   _____

D) LOS ADJETIVOS Y LOS PRONOMBRES DEMOSTRATIVOS

Complete the following sentences with a demonstrative pronoun or adjective. You may use *"el que, la que . . ."* in addition to *"éste, ésta . . ."*.

    a. Louisa May Alcott y Edith Wharton fueron autoras norteamericanas;

    _____ escribió *Ethan Frome* y _____

    Little Women.

    b. La chica _____ se pelea con todo el mundo.

    c. _____ manzana que estoy comiendo está muy buena.

    d. ¿Están renovando esta casa, ésa o _____?

    e. ¿Quieres fumarte un cigarrillo conmigo? –¡De ninguna manera!

    _____ no es bueno para la salud.

    f. Emmanuel, _____ sombrero ancho que llevas es bastante feo.

    g. Esta revista deportiva es _____ compré en Asunción.

    h. Scott Joplin y Louis Armstrong fueron músicos muy conocidos;

    _____ tocaba la trompeta y _____

    tocaba el piano.

    i. Vosotros habéis logrado mucho en la vida. Estamos muy orgullosos de

    _____.

    j. Esos periódicos japoneses son _____ lee mi madre.

E) Los usos de la palabra "lo"

1. Translate the following sentences, using the word *"lo"*:

a. Are you a salesclerk? –No, I am not.

_____

b. She is very tired, and her children are, too.

_____

c. You can't imagine how interesting these drawings are!

_____

2. Identify and correct the ten errors in the following dialogue:

—¿Aló?

—Hola, habla Darío. ¿Tienes unos minutos por hablar?

—Sí, sí, para supuesto. ¿Qué quieres me decir?

—Lo cual quiero decirte es la fácil que es la prueba. La he

tomado hoy por qué mañana no seré en clase.

—¿Qué prueba? ¿La que español?

—Sí, hombre, sí. Al principio parece ser difícil, pero

realmente no la es. Ya verás cuando la tomas mañana.

—No puede ser. Las pruebas de español siempre son difíciles.

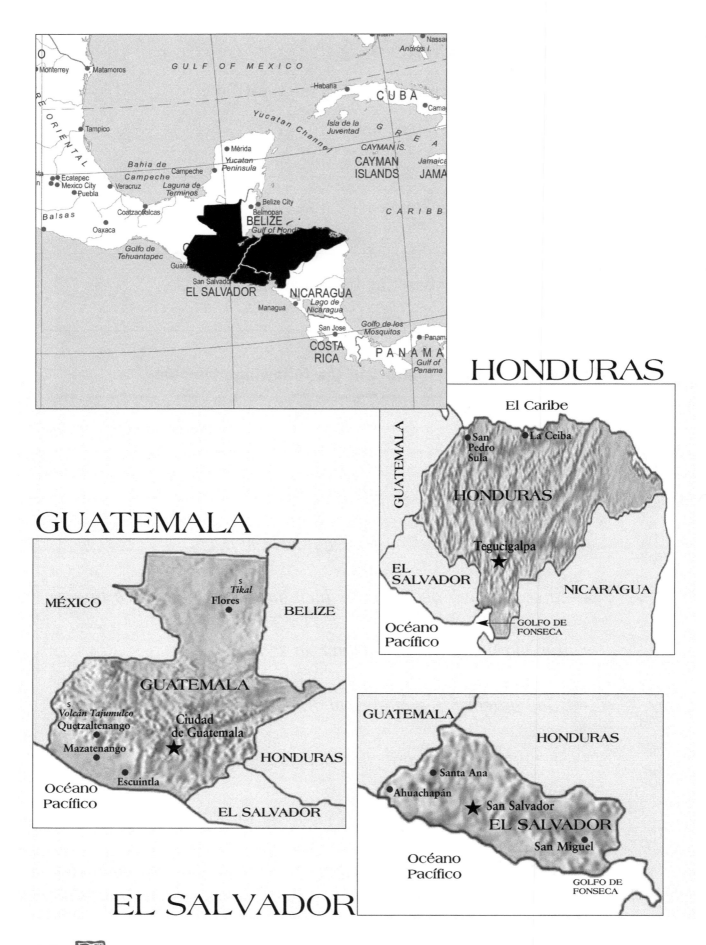

GULF OF MEXICO

Monterrey
Matamoros

Habana
CUBA
Cama

Isla de la
Juventad

Yucatan Channel
CAYMAN IS.
Mérida
Yucatan
Peninsula
CAYMAN
ISLANDS
Jamaica
JAMA

Bahía de
Campeche
Campeche

Ecatepec
Mexico City
Puebla
Veracruz
Laguna de
Términos

CARIBB

Coatzacoalcos
Belize City
Belmopan
BELIZE
Gulf of Hond

Balsas

Oaxaca

Golfo de
Tehuantepec

Guate

San Salvador
EL SALVADOR
NICARAGUA
Lago de
Nicaragua
Managua

Golfo de los
Mosquitos

San Jose
Panam

COSTA
RICA
PANAMA
Gulf of
Panama

HONDURAS

El Caribe

GUATEMALA
San
Pedro
Sula
La Ceiba

HONDURAS

Tegucigalpa

EL
SALVADOR
NICARAGUA

Océano
Pacífico
GOLFO DE
FONSECA

GUATEMALA

MÉXICO

s
Tikal
Flores
BELIZE

GUATEMALA

s
Volcán Tajumulco
Quetzaltenango
Ciudad
de Guatemala

Mazatenango
HONDURAS

Escuintla
Océano
Pacífico
EL SALVADOR

GUATEMALA

HONDURAS

Santa Ana
Ahuachapán
San Salvador
EL SALVADOR

San Miguel
Océano
Pacífico
GOLFO DE
FONSECA

EL SALVADOR

GUATEMALA, HONDURAS & EL SALVADOR

GUATEMALA

CAPITAL:	La Ciudad de Guatemala
POBLACIÓN:	17.000.000
GOBIERNO:	república democrática constitucional
PRESIDENTE:	Jimmy Morales
DINERO ($):	quetzal
PRODUCTOS:	azúcar, bananas, café, carne
MÚSICA, BAILE:	marimba, son
SITIOS DE INTERÉS:	Chichicastenango, Islas de la Bahía, Lago Atitlán, El Petén, Tikal, Volcán Pacaya
COMIDA TÍPICA:	chiles rellenos, guacamole, pepián, pescaditos, tamales, tapado, tortillas

HONDURAS

CAPITAL:	Tegucigalpa
POBLACIÓN:	9.100.000
GOBIERNO:	república constitucional democrática
PRESIDENTE:	Juan Orlando Hernández
DINERO ($):	lempira
PRODUCTOS:	azúcar, bananas, cacao, carne, fruta, minerales, tabaco
MÚSICA, BAILE:	punta, sique
SITIOS DE INTERÉS:	Copán (ruinas de los mayas), Santa Bárbara
COMIDA TÍPICA:	aguacate, carne asada, casabe, plátanos, sopa de camarones, tortillas

EL SALVADOR

CAPITAL:	San Salvador
POBLACIÓN:	6.300.000
GOBIERNO:	república
PRESIDENTE:	Salvador Sánchez Cerén
DINERO ($):	colón, dólar americano
PRODUCTOS:	agricultura, artesanía, azúcar, café
MÚSICA, BAILE:	danza de los historiantes, marimba
SITIOS DE INTERÉS:	Joya de Cerén, Izalco, La Palma, San Andrés, Santa Ana
COMIDA TÍPICA:	pan con pavo, pupusas, tamales

GUATEMALTECOS FAMOSOS:

Ricardo Arjona
(CANTANTE)

Miguel Asturias
(ESCRITOR)

Rigoberta Menchú
(ACTIVISTA)

Carlos Mérida
(ARTISTA)

Augusto Monteroso
(ESCRITOR)

HONDUREÑOS FAMOSOS:

Guillermo Anderson
(MÚSICO)

Julio Escoto
(ESCRITOR)

Lempira
(HÉROE NACIONAL)

Francisco Morazán
(POLÍTICO)

Gabriela Núñez
(POLÍTICA)

José Antonio Velázquez
(PINTOR)

SALVADOREÑOS FAMOSOS:

Raúl Díaz Arce
(FUTBOLISTA)

Jorge González
(FUTBOLISTA)

Claudia Lars
(ESCRITORA)

Alberto Masferrer
(ESCRITOR)

Óscar Romero
(ACTIVISTA, ARZOBISPO)

Practice this vocabulary with our mobile app! Visit tobreak.com/app for more details.

 # VOCABULARIO LECCIÓN DOCE

EXPRESIONES IDIOMÁTICAS

aprender de memoria	to learn by heart	*pasárselo bien/mal*	to have a great/ bad time
contar con	to count on	*poner la mesa*	to set the table
dar una vuelta	to take a walk/drive	*portarse bien/mal*	to behave well/ poorly
darle asco a	to be loathsome to, to be sickened by	*prestar atención*	to pay attention
darse cuenta de	to realize (i.e., come to awareness of)	*realizar*	to realize (e.g., a dream, a goal)
dejar de (+ infinitive)	to stop doing something	*sacar (prestado) un libro*	to check out a book
echar de menos	to miss someone, something	*salirse con la suya*	to have one's way
echar(le) la culpa	to blame (someone)	*tener en cuenta*	to take into consideration
estar de moda	to be in style		
guardar silencio	to keep silent	*tener éxito*	to be successful
hacer caso	to pay attention to	*tener lugar*	to take place
hacer cola	to wait in line	*tener prisa*	to be in a hurry
hacer la maleta	to pack	*tener que ver con*	to have to do with
hacer un viaje	to take a trip	*tener razón*	to be right
hacer una pregunta	to ask a question	*tener vergüenza*	to be ashamed
		tomar apuntes	to take notes
llevarse bien (mal) con	to get along well (badly) with	*tomar el pelo*	to tease, to pull one's leg
montar un negocio	to start a business	*tomar una decisión*	to make a decision
pasar la aspiradora	to vacuum	*(no) valer la pena*	to (not) be worth the trouble
		volverse loco/a	to go crazy

LECCIÓN DOCE

<table>
<tr><td rowspan="5">KEY GRAMMAR CONCEPTS</td><td>**A)** **EL USO DE "PERO," "SINO" Y "SINO QUE"** → *The use of "pero," "sino," and "sino que"*</td></tr>
<tr><td>**B)** **LAS CONSTRUCCIONES REFLEXIVAS Y RECÍPROCAS** → *Reflexive and reciprocal constructions*</td></tr>
<tr><td>**C)** **LOS INDEFINIDOS AFIRMATIVOS Y NEGATIVOS** → *Affirmative and negative indefinites*</td></tr>
<tr><td>**D)** **EXPRESIONES TEMPORALES CON "HACER" Y "LLEVAR"** → *Expressions of time using "hacer" and "llevar"*</td></tr>
<tr><td>**E)** **UNA SECCIÓN DE PRÁCTICA . . . ¡ROMPIENDO LA BARRERA!** → *A practice section . . . breaking the barrier!*</td></tr>
</table>

A) EL USO DE "PERO," "SINO" Y "SINO QUE"

In addition to the simple conjunctions presented in *Lección Uno,* Spanish uses other words that help to connect clauses within sentences: *"pero," "sino,"* and *"sino que,"* which can mean "but," "nevertheless," or "but rather."

1) PERO

"Pero" is the most common way to say "but." It is found after affirmative clauses or after negative clauses when there are no direct contrasts of equivalent parts of speech (i.e., of nouns, adjectives, adverbs, or verbs).

EXAMPLES: *Soy de Wisconsin, **pero** no me gusta comer queso.*
I'm from Wisconsin, but I don't like to eat cheese.

*No soy de Wisconsin, **pero** me gusta comer queso.*
I'm not from Wisconsin, but I like to eat cheese.

*Todavía no han llegado los demás, **pero** tú puedes comenzar a poner la mesa si quieres.*
The others haven't arrived yet, but you can start to set the table if you want.

2) SINO

"Sino" means "but rather" and is used after a negative clause when there is a direct contradiction in the second clause.

✳ **EXAMPLES:** *Nunca como hamburguesas con queso, **sino** sin queso.*
  I never eat cheeseburgers, but rather plain hamburgers.

*No soy alto, **sino** bajo.*
  I'm not tall, but (rather) short.

*Este día no está pasando rápida, **sino** lentamente.*
  This day is not going by quickly, but (rather) slowly.

*No deseamos acostarnos, **sino** dar una vuelta por el pueblo.*
  We don't want to go to bed, but rather to take a walk through town.

¿ ◆ ❓ Did you notice that the contradictions in all of the above sentences were of <u>identical</u> parts of speech? (e.g., nouns — *hamburguesas con queso/hamburguesas sin queso*; adjectives — *alto/bajo*; adverbs — *rápidamente/lentamente*; infinitives — *acostarnos/dar una vuelta*)

3) SINO QUE

"Sino que" also means "but rather" and is found after a negative clause when there is a contradicting idea expressed with a <u>conjugated</u> verb in the second clause.

✳ **EXAMPLES:** *No preparamos enchiladas en esta cocina, **sino que** las comemos.*
  We don't <u>prepare</u> enchiladas in this kitchen, but rather we <u>eat</u> them.

*No perdimos el campeonato, **sino que** lo ganamos.*
  We didn't <u>lose</u> the championship, but rather we <u>won</u> it.

*No abrí mi libro, **sino que** lo cerré.*
  I didn't <u>open</u> my book, but rather I <u>closed</u> it.

Helpful Tips: To decide among *"pero," "sino,"* and *"sino que,"* remember:

◆ When following an <u>affirmative</u> clause, <u>always</u> use *"pero."*

◆ When following a <u>negative</u> clause, but there is no direct contrast of an equivalent part of speech, use *"pero."*

◆ When following a <u>negative</u> clause, and there is a direct contrast of a noun, adjective, adverb, or infinitive, use *"sino."*

◆ When following a <u>negative</u> clause, and there is a direct contrast of a conjugated verb, use *"sino que."*

◆ Only *"sino"* and *"sino que"* can mean "but rather." *"Pero"* means "but."

PRACTICE EXERCISE

Choose among *"pero," "sino,"* or *"sino que"* to complete the following sentences:

a. A Javier Bardem le gustaría tener más tiempo libre, _____ tiene muchas cosas que hacer cada día.

b. Durante el viaje no vi ningún oso, _____ muchos leones.

c. No como Corn Flakes, _____ Special K.

d. No estoy muy nervioso, _____ es cierto que no me siento bien.

e. Mariah Carey no escribió la canción, _____ la cantó.

f. Vamos a Tucson este verano, _____ no vamos a visitar a mi abuelita.

g. No pensamos ahorrar dinero durante el festival de la Calle Ocho,

_____ gastarlo.

h. Me di cuenta de que *Volver,* la película de Almodóvar, no es cómica, _____ seria.

i. Mi nombre no es Jack, _____ John.

j. En mi colegio, el equipo de fútbol no tiene mucho talento, _____ todos se divierten.

k. No voy a estudiar matemáticas esta primavera, _____ física.

l. No hará sol por la mañana en Miami, _____ va a llover.

B) LAS CONSTRUCCIONES REFLEXIVAS Y RECÍPROCAS

The constructions for **reflexive and reciprocal actions** share many of the same pronouns. As a consequence, a sentence such as *"Siempre nos decimos la verdad"* can be interpreted two different ways: "We always tell ourselves the truth" or "We always tell each other the truth." This section will look at each construction, offering methods to avoid ambiguity.

1) REFLEXIVE CONSTRUCTIONS

In *Lección Cuatro* we reviewed the pronouns that are used for reflexive verbs: *me, te, se, nos, os, se.* In a reflexive construction, the subject and the direct object refer to the same person or object. To emphasize the reflexive nature of a sentence, and to distinguish the sentence from a reciprocal construction, a speaker may choose to add: *a mí, a ti, a sí, a nosotros, a nosotras, a vosotros, a vosotras, a sí* plus the word *mismo, misma, mismos, or mismas.*

EXAMPLES: *Se dieron los mejores asientos a sí mismos.*
They gave the best seats to themselves.

Me considero a mí mismo un gran experto en ajedrez.
I consider myself an expert in chess.

Nos miramos a nosotras mismas en el espejo antes de comenzar el baile.
We looked at ourselves in the mirror before beginning the dance.

El jefe se llama a sí mismo "El Grandote".
The boss calls himself "The Big Guy."

Note: If it is clear from context, or if there is no need to give special emphasis to the reflexive nature of the sentence, the phrase *"a sí mismo, a sí misma, etc."* may be left out of a sentence.

2) RECIPROCAL CONSTRUCTIONS

Spanish speakers make use of the following pronouns for a reciprocal action: *nos, os, se.* Reciprocal actions include: I do something to you that you do to me, he does something to her that she does to him, one group of people does something to another group that the other group does to the first group, etc.

For emphasis, or to distinguish a reciprocal sentence from a reflexive sentence, a Spanish speaker will add one of the following:

(el) uno a(l) otro	*(los) unos a (los) otros*
(la) una a (la) otra	*(las) unas a (las) otras*

Notice that it is not possible to "mix" genders: *"una a otro" is incorrect. In a mixed group, you must use the masculine "o" ending: "(el) uno a (al) otro" or "(los) unos a (los) otros."

 EXAMPLES: *Nos hablamos **unos a otros** cada fin de semana.*
We speak to each other (we speak to another group of people; they speak to us) each weekend.

*Micheline y Catherine **se comunican** por correo electrónico.*
Micheline and Catherine communicate with each other by e-mail.

***Os besáis** frecuentemente enfrente de los profesores.*
You all kiss each other frequently in front of the teachers.

*Siempre **se echan** la culpa el **uno al otro**.*
They always blame each other.

Helpful Tip: If it is clear from the context, it is not necessary to add *"el uno al otro, la una a la otra,* etc."

PRACTICE EXERCISES

1. Translate the following sentences, making certain that there is no ambiguity in your interpretation:

a. We call each other every night to talk about my boyfriend.

_____

_____

b. She considers herself one of the fastest athletes in Virginia.

_____

_____

c. They told themselves that the weather was not important.

_____

_____

d. They embrace each other upon waking each morning.

_____

_____

2. **Insert the missing word to complete the following reflexive or reciprocal sentences:**

a. Se dicen a _____ mismos que hoy en día es difícil montar un negocio sin un buen portal cibernético.

b. Como te expliqué ayer, no _____ llamo Luisa Sánchez, sino Luis Sánchez.

c. Carlos y Rosaura se miran _____ a _____ durante la clase de química.

d. No nos alabamos a nosotras _____ tanto como debiéramos.

e. _____ cepillas los dientes sólo una vez al año. ¿Por qué entonces nunca tienes caries?

f. Se regalaron a _____ mismas el nuevo álbum del estadounidense Romeo Santos.

3. Find and fix the five errors in the following paragraph:

Nunca me admito a yo mismo la verdad. Por ejemplo, me digo: "No tengo buena suerte, sino tengo mala suerte". Un día, cuando estaba hablando con mi hermano, nos dijimos el una al otro que nunca habíamos ido a Disneyland como nuestros amigos. Pero la verdad es que habíamos ido allí muchísimas veces. ¿Por qué no nos confesamos la verdad? A veces es difícil para una persona admitirse a si mismo lo que es verdad y lo que es mentira.

C) LOS INDEFINIDOS AFIRMATIVOS Y NEGATIVOS

Here are the most common **indefinite words**. Affirmative words are listed on the left and their corresponding negative words are on the right.

Affirmative		Corresponding Negative
algo (something)	→	*nada* (nothing)
lo demás (the rest [neuter])	→	*nada* (nothing)
alguien (someone)	→	*nadie* (no one)
los (las) demás (the others/the rest)	→	*nadie* (no one)
alguno/a(s) (some)	→	*ninguno/a* (none/any)
ambos/(as) (both)	→	*ninguno/a* (no one/none)
cada (each)	→	*ninguno/a* (none/no)
cualquier (any)	→	*ninguno/a* (none/no)
otro/a(s) (another)	→	*ninguno/a* (none/no)
todo/a(s) (all)	→	*ninguno/a* (none/no one)
uno/a(s) (a)	→	*ninguno/a* (none/no)
mucho/a(s) (much, many)	→	*poco/a(s)* (a few)
tanto/a(s) (so much, so many)	→	*(tan) poco/a(s)* (a little, so little)

The following sentences use many of these indefinite words.

EXAMPLE: *Veo a **alguien** en el coche. ¿Quién será? –Pues, yo no veo a **nadie**.*
I see someone in the car. I wonder who it is? –Well, I don't see anyone.

Note: The personal *"a"* is used before *"alguien"* and *"nadie"* (and all other pronouns which stand for a person) when they are direct objects of a verb. The personal *"a"* is used whenever the direct object refers to a specific person (e.g., *Quiero **a** Lucy.*)

EXAMPLES: *¿Viene a ayudarme **alguna** enfermera esta tarde? –Lo siento, no viene **nadie**.*
Is any (some) nurse coming this afternoon to help me? –I'm sorry, no one is coming.

> **Note:** The word *"alguna"* agrees with *"enfermera."*

*¿Tienes **algunos** secretos para mantener la belleza? –No, por desgracia no tengo **ninguno**.*
Do you have any (some) secrets for staying beautiful? –Unfortunately, I don't have any (I have none).

Note: The words *"ninguno"* and *"ninguna"* are used only in the singular; if there is "none" of something, it is illogical to have a plural form of "nothingness." An exception, however, would be with a word like *"tijeras"* that doesn't really have a singular form. I have no scissors = *No tengo ningunas tijeras.*

EXAMPLE: *No tengo amigo **alguno**.*   I have no friend at all.

Note: At times, an affirmative, indefinite adjective in the singular may follow a noun in a negative sentence. The effect is stylistic, emphasizing the idea of "none at all."

EXAMPLE: *El alcalde se **lo** dice **todo** a la prensa.*
The mayor tells everything to the press.

Note: When *"todo"* is the direct object of a verb, the word *"lo"* usually precedes the verb.

EXAMPLES: ***Cualquier** cuaderno y **cualquier** pluma me parecen aceptables para esta clase.*
Any notebook and any pen seem acceptable for this class.

***Cualquier** revista que compres en aquel quiosco será cara.*
Any magazine that you buy at that stand will be expensive.

 Remember that *"cualquiera"* is shortened to *"cualquier"* before **any** singular noun, masculine or feminine. The plural form *"cualesquiera"* is rarely used anymore; Spanish speakers prefer to use the singular form with a singular noun. In the sentence above, *"compres"* is in the subjunctive because *"cualquier revista"* is indefinite.

EXAMPLE: ***Algún** libro es mejor que **ningún** libro.*
Some book is better than no book.

 "Alguno" and *"ninguno"* are shortened to *"algún"* and *"ningún"* before a singular, masculine noun.

✳ **EXAMPLE:** *Busco **algo** que sea interesante, pero no encuentro **nada**.*
I'm looking for something that is interesting, but I can't find anything.

▨▨▨▨ **¡CUIDADO!** Remember that if the main clause is indefinite or negative (FANTASMA), the verb in the
▨▨▨▨ dependent clause must be in the subjunctive.

✳ **EXAMPLES:** *No vino **nadie nunca**.*   No one ever came.
***Nunca** vino **nadie**.*   No one ever came.
*¡**Nunca jamás** vino **nadie**!*   No one EVER, EVER came!

Note: You always need to have at least one negative word before the verb in a negative statement. *"Habla nadie"*
is not a correct sentence is Spanish. It should be: *"No habla nadie"* or *"Nadie habla."* The adverbial combination
"nunca jamás" can be used to make a statement especially emphatic, as in the last example.

✳ **EXAMPLES:** *Juan Soler y Maki tienen prisa y por eso vienen conmigo en el coche;*
***los demás** tendrán que ir a pie.*
Juan Soler and Maki are in a hurry, so they are coming with me
in the car; the rest will have to go by foot.
Note: *"Los demás"* refers to a group of people in this first example.

Primero vamos a lavar los platos; después pasaremos la aspiradora por
*la alfombra. **Lo demás** lo haremos mañana.*
First we'll wash the dishes; afterwards, we'll vacuum the rug. The rest
we'll do tomorrow.

Note: In the sentence: *"Lo demás lo haremos mañana,"* the direct object pronoun *"lo"* (in *"lo haremos"*) seems
redundant (the rest we will do [it] tomorrow). When a direct object *(lo demás)* <u>precedes</u> a verb, a direct object
pronoun *(lo)* is also required. The neuter *"lo demás"* is used in this sentence to refer to a number of activities.

PRACTICE EXERCISE

1. Fill in the blank with an indefinite pronoun or adjective:

a. _____ personas en mi familia tienen mucho éxito en el
trabajo; otras no lo tienen.

b. ¿Hay alguien en esta clase que conociera a Octavio Paz? –No, no hay

_____ que lo conociera.

c. ¿Tienes muchas horas libres en una semana típica? –No, no tengo

_____.

d. Sólo María y yo vamos a ver *Top Chef* esta noche; _____van a
la cantina.

e. No tengo dinero _____.

f. Voy a hacer la tarea y lavarme el pelo esta noche; _____ lo haré mañana.

g. _____ persona que llegue tarde tendrá problemas con el presidente Mauricio Funes.

h. Estoy seguro de que _____ ladrón entró en mi casa anoche y robó el anillo de mi esposa.

i. "Se lo confesé _____ a la policía", explicó el ladrón que había robado el anillo la noche anterior.

j. _____ vino a la puerta y dijo: "¿Qué pasa, tío?".

2. Find the seven errors in the following postscript, written at the end of a letter by the author of a Spanish grammar book:

P.D. Y algo más. No hay alguien que merezca más las gracias que mis estudiantes. Cada persona en mis clases me han ayudado tantas con ideas excelentes y creativas. Cualquiera estudiante que me haya ayudado recibirá más que palabras de gracias. No hay algo que yo pueda hacer hoy, pero pronto vamos a tener una fiesta grande para celebrar el fin de este trabajo mutuo. Es verdad, no les tomo el pelo. Sólo voy a invitar a los estudiantes de español, y lo demás no podrán venir. Aunque Uds. son muy listos y la saben todo, espero que hayan aprendido un poco este año. Bueno pues, amigos. Mil gracias y nos vemos.

The word *"hace"* is used in a construction that describes something that began in the past and is still going on in the present:

> *"Hace"* + **X** + *que* + **Verb** = **I have been doing something for X.**
> (period of time)   (in present tense)   (period of time)

✳ EXAMPLES: *Hace diez años que **toco** el piano.*
I have been playing the piano for ten years.

*¿**Hace** mucho tiempo que **vives** en esa casa de Miami Beach?*
Have you been living in that house in Miami Beach for a long time?

***Hace** muchos meses que no **tenemos** noticias de ellos.*
We haven't had news from them in many months.

As you can see, this concept is expressed a little differently in English and Spanish. The first Spanish sentence translates literally: "It makes ten years that I play the piano." In English we would normally say: "I have been playing the piano for ten years."

You can also talk about the length of time an action has been taking place by using *"desde hace."*

✳ EXAMPLES: *No **hablo** con ella **desde hace** mucho tiempo.*
I have not spoken with her for quite a while.

*No **tenemos** noticias de ellos **desde hace** mucho tiempo.*
We have not heard from them in a long time.

A similar *"hace"* construction describes events that took place a certain amount of time ago. The formula is the same with the exception that the verb is now in the preterite.

> *"Hace"* + **X** + *que* + **Verb** = **I did something a certain amount of time AGO.**
> (period of time)   (in preterite)

✳ EXAMPLES: *Hace dos horas que Ud. **tomó** la nueva medicina.*
You took the new medicine two hours ago.

***Hace** media hora que **recibí** la llamada.*
I received the call a half hour ago.

In the following construction, the *"que"* is omitted if the preterite verb comes first in the sentence.

✳ **EXAMPLES:** *Ud. **tomó** la medicina hace dos horas.*
  You took the medicine two hours ago.

  ***Recibí** la llamada hace media hora.*
  I received the call a half hour ago.

The word *"hacía"* is used in the construction below with a verb in the imperfect tense to denote an action that occurred in the past and that was still in progress.

> *"Hacía"* + <u>X</u> + *que* + <u>Verb</u> = **I had been doing something for <u>X</u>.**
> (period   (in   (period
> of time)   imperfect)   of time)

✳ **EXAMPLES:** ***Hacía** tiempo que Ignacio **arreglaba** su cuarto.*
  Ignacio had been tidying up his room for quite some time.

  ***Hacía** muchos años que **ahorrábamos** dinero.*
  We had been saving money for many years.

You can also talk about the length of time an action had been taking place by using *"desde hacía."*

✳ **EXAMPLES:** *Ignacio **arreglaba** su cuarto **desde hacía** tiempo.*
  Ignacio had been tidying up his room for quite some time.

  ***Ahorrábamos** dinero **desde hacía** mucho tiempo.*
  We had been saving money for some time.

Here are the five variations of the *"hacer"* expressions presented in this section:

> **1** *Hace dos horas que como enchiladas.*
>   I have been eating enchiladas for two hours.
>
> **2** *Como enchiladas desde hace dos horas.*
>   I have been eating enchiladas for two hours.
>
> **3** *Hace dos horas que comí enchiladas (Comí enchiladas hace dos horas).*
>   I ate enchiladas two hours ago.
>
> **4** *Hacía dos horas que comía enchiladas.*
>   I had been eating enchiladas for two hours.
>
> **5** *Comía enchiladas desde hacía dos horas.*
>   I had been eating enchiladas for two hours.

Finally, another very common way to express ongoing action uses a form of *"llevar"* followed by a length of time and then a present participle.

> **Form of *"llevar"* + Length of time + Present participle**

 EXAMPLES: *Llevo tres meses viviendo en San Francisco.*
I've been living in San Franciso for three months.

Ricardo Arjona lleva muchos años cantando.
Ricardo Arjona has been singing many years.

Llevaba tres años jugando al tenis cuando gané mi primer trofeo.
I had been playing tennis for three years when I won my first trophy.

PRACTICE EXERCISE

Fill in the blank with the appropriate form of the verb:

a. _____ muchos años que vivimos en San Salvador. (Hacer)

b. Hacía mucho tiempo que yo _____ el autobús cuando, por fin, llegó. (esperar)

c. Hablo español bien desde _____ muchos años. (hacer)

d. Tú _____ en San Miguel hace muchos años, aproximadamente 20. (vivir)

e. Uds. _____ estampillas desde hacía treinta años. (coleccionar)

f. Hace mucho tiempo que no nos _____ francamente. (hablar)

g. Hace unos años que Ricky Martin _____ su casa con una magnífica vista de la Bahía de Biscayne. (vender)

h. Llevamos tres horas _____ en la cola. (esperar)

This final section contains forty sentences that test material you have learned throughout this book. All sentences will be followed by some words of advice. For best practice, cover up the hints as you first attempt an answer.

1. El año que viene yo _____ con Scott Gómez. (patinar)

> **Hint:** Don't forget the future endings: "*é, ás, á, emos, éis, án.*"

2. Si lo aprendieras todo de memoria, yo no lo _____. (creer)

> **Hint:** "If clauses" should be your specialty. Remember that the imperfect subjunctive goes with a conditional.

3. Cuando éramos niños, siempre _____ tortilla española. (comer)

> **Hint:** This sentence describes past, habitual action.

4. Cada día yo _____ mi camisa favorita antes de bajar a desayunar. (escoger)

> **Hint:** You probably want to use the present indicative or the imperfect. Remember the spelling-changers in the present tense; you need to preserve the sound of the infinitive.

5. No me voy a casar hasta que _____ este año escolar. (terminar)

> **Hint:** Does "CHAD-ATE" ring a bell? The subjunctive is used after certain adverbial expressions when referring to events that haven't happened yet.

6. No creo que tú _____ tomado muchos apuntes hoy. (haber)

> **Hint:** You are not affirming the statement in the dependent clause. Do you remember the subjunctive of "*haber*"? What does that karate expert yell?

7. Paco me dijo que él no _____ a la fiesta esta noche. (ir)

> **Hint:** First, realize that a command is <u>not</u> being given here. Paco told me that <u>he</u> wouldn't be going to the party tonight. Either the conditional could be used here as "the future of the past," or the imperfect tense or the pluperfect.

8. Estábamos _____ cuando sonó la alarma de incendios. (charlar)

> **Hint:** The progressive tense is formed with *"estar," "seguir,"* or *"continuar"* followed by the present participle.

9. Así que yo _____ en la actriz, ella se fue. (fijarse)

> **Hint:** Here's another "CHAD-ATE." This time, however, the time frame is in the past. The action already took place. Use the preterite.

10. ¡Deja ya de preocuparte! ¿No estás cansada de _____ tanto? (llorar)

> **Hint:** If you remember one thing from this year of study, know that the infinitive is used after a preposition!

11. Ayer Julia y Roberto _____ el libro del inglés al español. (traducir)

> **Hint:** Here you must use an irregular preterite form. Remember, there is no "i" after the "j" in this conjugation.

12. ¡Ojalá que los actores _____ pronto! (enamorarse)

> **Hint:** After verbs or expressions of emotion, the subjunctive is the mood of choice.

13. No lo habíamos _____ todo antes de las once. (hacer)

> **Hint:** You have undoubtedly mastered the perfect tenses by now. Don't forget the irregular past participles, REVV MAC PHDD.

14. No dudábamos que _____ las cinco y media cuando Penélope Cruz y su hermana Mónica llegaron. (ser)

> **Hint:** If you do not call something into doubt, you affirm it. Therefore, use the indicative. Do not forget that the imperfect tense is used to tell time in the past. Also, remember that *"las cinco y media"* is plural.

15. Negabas que _____ mucho sol el verano pasado. (hacer)

> **Hint:** A denial from the past. Past subjunctive, right?

16. Por favor, señores. ¡_____ inmediatamente! (Sentarse)

> **Hint:** An affirmative *"Uds."* command uses the subjunctive. Remember to attach all object pronouns to the end of an affirmative command; in a negative command, those pronouns will precede the verb. Don't forget that a written accent mark must be added to this reflexive command to keep the stress in the right place.

17. Si _____ ahora, no podríamos nadar en la piscina. (llover)

> **Hint:** Another "if clause." You will want the imperfect subjunctive here, the "partner" of the conditional.

18. Si hubiéramos tenido más suerte, _____ el partido. (ganar)

> **Hint:** This "if clause" begins with the pluperfect subjunctive. Remember that you will need the conditional perfect. Compound tenses usually go with other compound tenses in these sentences.

19. Hay que _____ muchas preguntas en esa clase. (hacer)

> **Hint:** After *"tener que"* and *"hay que"* you need to use an infinitive.

20. No había ningún chico en mi dormitorio que _____ el piano. (tocar)

> **Hint:** A classic "FANTASMA" sentence. It's written in the past, so use a past subjunctive.

21. ¿Se _____ marchado Uds. ayer antes del mediodía? (haber)

> **Hint:** By writing the imperfect of *"haber,"* you will be correctly forming the pluperfect tense. Don't forget that there are accents on every form of **-ER** and **-IR** verbs in the imperfect.

22. Yo cantaré con tal que Uds. _____ silencio. (guardar)

> **Hint:** *"Con tal que"* is part of *ESCAPA*. These adverbial expressions will <u>always</u> require a subjunctive form. Your only question in this sentence is whether to use present or past subjunctive.

23. Tienes razón. Estoy _____ con agua fría ahora. (ducharse)

> **Hint:** Another progressive sentence. Remember to write an accent when you add a pronoun to a present participle.

24. Antes de que nosotros _____, mi abuelo llegará con el helado. (dormirse)

> **Hint:** Another *ESCAPA*.

25. Si ellas _____ dinero, comprarán unos discos de Jessy y Joy. (tener)

> **Hint:** This "if clause" is one of "scientific analysis." The present tense will go with the future.

26. En el futuro mi familia _____ un viaje a Fort Worth, en Texas, para visitar a Jim y Lori. (hacer)

> **Hint:** This sentence has an irregular future form. In addition, remember that there is only <u>one</u> family. Therefore, the verb will be in the third person singular.

27. Busco una persona que me _____. (comprender)

> **Hint:** An indefinite antecedent leads to thoughts of "FANTASMA." Use the subjunctive.

28. Cuando Elena _____, yo siempre la echo de menos. (viajar)

> **Hint:** A CHAD-ATE adverbial expression, referring to <u>habitual</u> action. Use the present tense.

29. Mis amigos se comportan como si _____ vergüenza. (tener)

> **Hint:** Always use the imperfect subjunctive (or pluperfect subjunctive) after *"como si."*

30. ¡Callaos ahora mismo! ¡No me _____ vuestros secretos! ¡Me da asco escucharos! (decir)

> **Hint:** You want a *"vosotros/vosotras"* negative command. Use the subjunctive!

In nine of the following ten sentences, you will find one error. Identify and correct each error. There will be one correct sentence.

31. Se me cayó los pantalones anoche; me deprimió mucho que todos me vieran.

> **Hint:** What is the <u>subject</u> of the first part of the sentence? Think of the construction used for accidental, unintentional events.

32. ¿Ya me has comprado algunas tarjetas? –No, no te he comprado ningunas.

> **Hint:** Is *"ningunas"* commonly used?

33. Ni Roberto ni Joaquín va mucho a la biblioteca; es triste que no les guste leer.

> **Hint:** What form does Spanish use after *"ni . . . ni"*?

34. Mañana compraremos trescientas veintiún enchiladas para la fiesta; seguro que nadie se morirá de hambre.

> **Hint:** There is some agreement problem here.

35. No había nadie que pudiera traducirme aquel manuscrito tan misterioso.

> **Hint:** This sentence is correct. Could you tell?

36. Manolo e Isabel llegan esta noche; ésta quiere hablar conmigo y aquel quiere matarme.

> **Hint:** A demonstrative adjective needs a written accent mark to become a pronoun.

37. La princesa cuya marido murió ha sufrido mucho; espero que todo le vaya bien en el futuro.

> **Hint:** The possessive relative pronoun *"cuyo"* always agrees with the noun that <u>follows</u>.

38. Se hirieron a los niños inocentes en el tiroteo. ¿Cuándo va a terminar esta locura?

> **Hint:** This impersonal sentence needs a <u>singular</u> verb.

39. Esta noche voy a hablar con el Señor Esaí Morales. Me gustaría que me prestara atención.

> **Hint:** Titles are not capitalized unless they are abbreviated or found at the beginning of a sentence.

40. Estoy ocupadísima ahora. No quiero salir, sino que quedarme en casa.

> **Hint:** *"Sino que"* is only used when a <u>conjugated</u> verb follows.

These two sets of questions use grammatical structures and vocabulary from this lesson. Working with a partner, alternate asking and answering each question. When you get to the bottom of each list, start over at the top, switching roles. As a variation, write out the answers in complete sentences.

A) ¿**Vale la pena** estudiar mucho cada día?

¿**Te portas bien** en todas tus clases?

¿**Pasas la aspiradora** en la alfombra de la sala?

¿En qué situación es bueno **guardar silencio**?

¿En qué clase **lo pasas** bien?

¿**Aprendes de memoria** fácilmente el vocabulario nuevo?

¿Dónde **tuvo lugar** la Serie Mundial de béisbol el año pasado?

B) ¿Cuántos minutos **hace** que hablas conmigo?

¿Cuántos años **hace** que eres estudiante en esta escuela?

¿**Llevas** muchos años estudiando español?

¿**Llevabas** muchos años estudiando español cuando llegaste a esta escuela?

¿Cuántos años **hacía** que estudiabas español cuando llegaste a esta escuela?

¿Cuántos años **hace** que naciste?

¿**Llevas** muchos años practicando un instrumento musical?

PRUEBA DE REPASO

A) EL USO DE "PERO," "SINO" Y "SINO QUE"

1. Complete the following sentences with either *"pero," "sino"* or *"sino que"*:

a. Los guerrilleros no lucharon contra los campesinos, _____ contra el gobierno.

b. Me gustaría dar un paseo, _____ está lloviendo.

c. No pudimos entrar directamente a la discoteca, _____ tuvimos que hacer cola por media hora.

d. Me lo estoy pasando muy bien en Tegucigalpa, _____ echo de menos a mi familia en los Estados Unidos.

e. Mi hermano mayor no compró un coche nuevo, _____ una moto.

f. Julia Roberts no tiene el pelo liso, _____ rizado.

g. Pensábamos que el perro había desaparecido, _____ la verdad era que se había escondido en el garaje.

h. No me gustan las zanahorias, _____ me repugnan.

i. Tomás no tiene amigos, _____ es muy simpático.

2. Translate the following:

a. I don't want to prepare the dinner, but I will set the table.

_____

_____

b. These tickets are not expensive, but cheap.

_____

_____

c. My mother said nothing to me, but rather she kept silent until my father came home.

_____

_____

B) LAS CONSTRUCCIONES REFLEXIVAS Y RECÍPROCAS

1. Complete the following sentences appropriately:

a. Esas chicas hablan de _____ mismas como si fueran mejores que los demás.

b. Ayer _____ di cuenta de que se me habían perdido los apuntes para la clase de historia.

c. Marta y su amiga Luz se escriben _____ a _____ dos veces al año.

d. Ramón se echa la culpa a _____ mismo de la separación de sus padres.

e. Es verdad que _____ llevo mal con mi madrastra.

f. Los señores García se regalaron a sí _____ la nueva canción de David Bisbal, _Tú eres la magia._

g. Tú me fastidias porque siempre _____ sales con la tuya.

h. Os engañáis a vosotras _____ al pensar de esa manera.

2. Translate the following sentences:

a. My aunt and uncle miss each other when they are not together.

_____

_____

b. The managers ask each other questions at the beginning of each meeting.

_____

_____

c. She confuses herself when she tries to do too many things.

_____

_____

3. Identify and correct the eight errors in the following paragraph:

Estoy muy contenta porque hoy es el primera de mayo y la escuela terminará pronto. Me pregunto a me misma: ¿Es posible que el año académico haya pasado tanto rápidamente? No pienso en todo la tarea que tengo, sino que en las vacaciones de verano. Me gustaría pasar todos los días en la playa, sino tengo que trabajar para mis padres, las cuales han montado un negocio esto año.

C) Los indefinidos afirmativos y negativos

1. Complete each sentence with an indefinite pronoun or adjective:

a. _____ película que haga Meryl Streep será fabulosa.

b. De toda esta comida, sólo me gusta el pollo; ¡_____ no me apetece!

c. _____ de Uds. tendrán que hacer cola por unos minutos. No hay mesas para todos en este momento.

d. Ahorita Julio y Paco están dando un paseo; _____ se quedaron en casa.

e. La maestra está descontenta porque _____ alumno aprendió de memoria el poema de Federico García Lorca.

f. ¿Te llevas bien con todos? –Pues, por desgracia, no me llevo bien con

_____.

g. Mi abuela siempre tiene razón. Parece que ella lo sabe _____.

h. ¿Hay _____ que quiera dar una vuelta conmigo?

i. No recibimos correo _____.

j. Uds. nunca tienen vergüenza de _____.

2. Translate the following:

a. No one ever paid attention to me.

_____

b. Any house that you rent will be expensive.

_____

c. He is looking for a book that interests him.

_____

D) Expresiones temporales con "hacer" y "llevar"

1. Complete the following sentences with the appropriate verb form:

a. _____ mucho tiempo que Roselyn Sánchez es actriz. (Hacer)

b. Tú _____ portugués desde hacía muchos años. (hablar)

c. _____ tres años que Teresa llegó a Quetzaltenango. (Hacer)

d. Hacía muchos años que nuestro equipo no _____ bien en la Copa Mundial. (jugar)

e. Tú _____ muchos años viviendo en Santa Ana, ¿verdad? (llevar)

2. Translate the following:

a. I've been a Spanish student for three years.

_____

b. We went to San Salvador three months ago.

_____

E) Una sección de práctica

Complete the following sentences:

a. –Paco, ¿cabes en esa silla tan estrecha? –Pues no. No _____ en esta maldita silla. (caber)

b. Cuando sonó el teléfono, yo estaba durmiendo y mi esposo estaba

_____ el periódico. (leer)

c. Cuando me gradúe de esta escuela, _____ a mi profesora de español. (echar de menos)

d. La empresa fabricó más computadoras _____ pudo vender. (than)

e. Voy a fregar este suelo hasta que _____. (brillar)

f. Me molestó mucho que mi hermana _____ más dinero que yo. (heredar)

g. Soñamos con _____ a pescar este fin de semana. (ir)

h. A mi madre le preocupa que yo no _____ muchos apuntes en mis clases. (tomar)

i. ¿En qué sala _____ la reunión esta noche? (ser/estar)

j. ¡Pobre Carlos! _____ perdieron las gafas de sol en la playa. (add object pronouns)

k. ¡Qué desastre! Mi horario y _____ mi novia son totalmente diferentes. (my girlfriend's)

l. No quiero quedarme callado en este momento, _____ prefiero gritar. (pero/sino/sino que)

m. _____ mucho tiempo que no veía a mi cuñado. (hacer)

n. Si yo fuera profesora, _____ español. (enseñar)

o. Si ellos _____ pronto, podríamos ver juntos el nuevo episodio de *Big Little Lies*. (llegar)

¡Felicidades!
YOU'VE BROKEN THE SPANISH BARRIER!

CULTURA

cuento: short story, tale
palabras: words
célebre: famous
autora: author
chilena-estadounidense: Chilean-American
crea/crear: creates/to create
personaje: character
mujer: woman
vende/vender: sells/to sell
unos centavos: a few cents
escribe/escribir: (she) writes/to write
cartas de enamorados: love letters
enemigos: enemies
incluso: even
discursos: speeches
país: country
sentado: sitting
sobre la acera: on the sidewalk
principales avenidas: main avenues
se encuentra/encontrarse: is/to be
hombre: man
hace/hacer: does/to do
mundo: world
lo que hace…: what … does
comenzó a/comenzar a: began to/to begin to,
  to start to
poesía: poetry
en serio: seriously, in earnest
año: year
1995: mil novecientos noventa y cinco
se sienta/sentarse: (he) sits (down)/to sit (down)
contra la pared: against the wall
apenas: barely
entre: among
multitud: crowd
transita por/transitar por: walks along/
  to walk along
espera/esperar: (he) waits/to wait
hasta que alguien: until someone
se le acerca/acercarse: approaches him/
  to approach
cartelito: little sign
anuncia/anunciar: reads/to read, to announce
te regalo mi poesía: I give you my poetry
por la voluntad: for whatever you think is worth
le ofrece/ofrecer: (he) offers/to offer
a cualquier persona: to anyone
gratis: free
acaba de escribir: (he) has just written
claro: sure, of course
propinas: tips
así: that way
dice/decir: (he) says/to say
puede/poder: (he) can/to be able to
ganarse la vida: earn a living
ir tirando nada más: just get by
día típico: typical day
para pedirle: to request

El Poeta de la Gran Vía
por Marco Espinosa y Hugo Martínez

En su **cuento** "Dos **Palabras**", Isabel Allende, **célebre autora chilena-estadounidense, crea** un **personaje** – Belisa Crepusculario – una **mujer** que **vende** palabras. Por **unos centavos, escribe** versos originales, **cartas de enamorados**, insultos para **enemigos, incluso discursos** para el futuro presidente del **país**.

Sentado sobre la acera de la Gran Vía, una de las **principales avenidas** de Madrid, **se encuentra** un **hombre** que **hace** en este **mundo lo que hace** Belisa Crepusculario en el mundo de ficción. Enrique Bayano, poeta de La Gran Vía, **comenzó a** escribir **poesía en serio** en el **año 1995**.

Se sienta en la acera **contra la pared** – **apenas** visible **entre** la **multitud** que **transita por** la avenida – y **espera hasta que alguien se le acerca.**

Con un **cartelito** que **anuncia**: "**TE REGALO MI POESÍA POR LA VOLUNTAD**", le **ofrece a cualquier persona** un poema **gratis**, uno que **acaba de escribir**. **Claro**, acepta con gratitud **propinas** y **así dice** que **puede ganarse la vida** – o como dice él – "**ir tirando nada más**". En un **día típico**, de 30 a 50 personas se acercan **para pedirle** un poema.

Entre los temas **más destacados** del señor Bayano están "**el amor**" y "**la vida**", **escritos siempre** con un aire muy positivo. Sus poetas y **escritores preferidos** son Federico García Lorca, José Ángel Valente, Pablo Neruda y Gabriel García Márquez. **Nos dio** este **consejo** para los **nuevos** poetas: "**Que cada uno siga** su **propio criterio**".

Su **mente** está **abierta a** crear con **papel** y **tinta** cualquier petición del público. **Por ejemplo**, el día que **charlábamos** con él, un **chico de apenas cinco años** **le pidió** un **dibujito** de un animal. **Se lo hizo en un dos por tres al gusto del niño**. **Aunque** el señor Bayano **admite abiertamente** que lo que hace él **a veces** "es difícil" y que **tiene que trabajar largas horas** "por necesidad", está **muy orgulloso** de su trabajo. "Siempre **intento hacer** con mi papel y tinta **algo que le dé alegría** a una persona" **nos dijo**. "Eso **me hace feliz**".

"De este **sueño no quiero despertar**"

Yo soñé que **soñaba**
Dentro de un sueño **otro** sueño
Dentro del sueño **estabas**
Estabas en este sueño **bella** y **tan lozana**
¡Tu **cara**, tu **pelo**, tu **sonrisa**!
Tus **ojos** de **misterio que me atraen una locura**
Cuando sueño contigo
Me llena de orgullo la vida
Porque eres tú niña y mujer
Esa mujer **de verdad**.

Que **robas** mis **pensamientos**
En mis horas de soledad
Los días **van pasando**
Yo **me sigo enamorando**
Mucho más que el **primer** día
Sí, mucho más niña mía
Esperando que llegue el día
Que te sienta solo mía

De este sueño
No quiero despertar.

- Enrique Bayano, 2008

más destacados: most prominent, outstanding
el amor: love
la vida: life
escritos: written
siempre: always
escritores: writers
preferidos: favorite
nos dio/dar: (he) gave us/to give
consejo: (piece of) advice
nuevos: new
que cada uno siga: let everyone follow
propio: own
criterio: taste, judgment
mente: mind
abierta a: open to
papel: paper
tinta: ink
por ejemplo: for example
charlábamos/charlar: we were talking/to talk, chat
chico: little kid
de apenas cinco años: hardly 5 years old
le pidió/pedir: ask him for/to ask for
dibujito: little drawing
se lo hizo: (he) made it (for him)
en un dos por tres: in no time at all
al gusto del niño: to the child's liking
aunque: even though
admite abiertamente: admits openly
a veces: sometimes
tiene que/tener que: (he) has to/to have to, must
trabajar: to work
largas horas: long hours
muy orgulloso: very proud
intento/intentar: I try/to try, to attempt
hacer: to do, to make
algo que: something that
le dé alegría/dar: gives joy/to give
nos dijo/decir: he told us/to tell
me hace feliz: makes me happy
sueño: dream
no quiero: I don't want
despertar: to wake up
yo soñé/soñar: I dreamed/to dream
soñaba: I was dreaming
dentro de: within
otro: another
estabas/estar: were you/to be
bella: beautiful
tan lozana: so fresh, so full of life
cara: face
pelo: hair
sonrisa: smile
ojos: eyes
misterio: mystery
que me atraen: I'm attracted to
una locura: madly
cuando sueño contigo: when I dream about you
me llena/llenar: (it) fills me/to fill
de orgullo: with pride
porque eres tú: because you are
de verdad: real
robas/robar: (you) steal/to steal
pensamientos: thoughts
van pasando: go by
yo me sigo enamorando: I keep on falling in love
primer: first
esperando que llegue el día: waiting for the day
que te sienta: when I feel you are
solo mía: only mine

Think Spanish!

1. ¿Quién es Isabel Allende y de dónde es?

_____

2. ¿Cómo se llama la protagonista de "Dos palabras" y qué clase de versos escribe?

_____

_____

3. ¿Qué es la Gran Vía y dónde está?

_____

4. ¿Quién es Enrique Bayano y qué les ofrece a las personas que se le acercan?

_____

_____

5. ¿Cuántas personas se le acercan a Enrique Bayano para pedirle poemas en un día normal?

_____

6. ¿Cuáles son los temas más destacados de Enrique Bayano?

_____

_____

7. ¿Qué hace Enrique Bayano para el chico de apenas cinco años?

_____

8. ¿Pide algo Enrique Bayano a cambio de sus poemas?

_____

9. ¿Quiénes son los poetas y escritores preferidos de Enrique Bayano?

_____

_____

10. ¿Qué intenta lograr Enrique Bayano con su obra?

_____

TRADICIONES

El Día de las Velitas
COLOMBIA

por Yanini Ibarra

día: day
casas: houses
se llenan/llenar: are filled/to fill
resplandor: glow, brightness
miles: thousands
pequeñas: small
velas: candles
se encienden/encender: are lighted/to light
para darle la bienvenida: to welcome
se celebra/celebrar: is celebrated/to celebrate
velitas: little candles
alumbrado: lighting, illumination
a través de: through
se recuerda a/recordar a: people remember/
  to remember (someone)
se da inicio a: begin
festejos: celebrations
preparativos: preparations
muy temprano: very early
se reúnen/reunirse: get together/to get together
pensar: to think
van a organizar: they are going to organize
mayoría: majority
las ponen/poner: put them/to put
entrada: entrance
las encienden/encender: light them/to light
jardín: garden
terraza: terrace
balcones: balconies
algunos: some
pueblos: villages
cobran/cobrar: take on/to take on
tal magnitud: such a scale, such magnitude
hasta se corta el tránsito: even the traffic is cut
lector: reader
se preguntará: might ask himself or herself
¿por qué tantas velas?: why so many candles?
según: according to
pasará por: will come to
bendecirlas/bendecir: to bless them/to bless
motivo: reason
intentan/intentar: attempt/to attempt, to try
formar: to form, to make
sendero: path
vereda: sidewalk
guiarán/guiar: will guide/to guide
hacia: towards
cada hogar: each home
lo colme/colmar: (she) fills it/to fill
bendiciones: blessings
luz: light
pero no sólo: but not only
se prenden/prender: are lighted/to light
compran/comprar: buy/to buy
faroles: lanterns
lucecitas: little lights
se lanzan/lanzar: are lit/to light *(literally: to throw)*
fuegos artificiales: fireworks
se vuelva/volverse: becomes/to become
inolvidable: unforgettable
chicos: children
salen/salir: go out/to go out
jugar: to play
calle: street
vecinos: neighbors
se encuentran/encontrarse: meet/to meet
conversar acerca de: to talk about
han preparado/preparado: have prepared/to prepare
recibir: to receive
no son creyentes: are non-believers
no practican/practicar: do not practice/to practice
se unen/unirse: (they) join/to join
interpretan/interpetar: interpret/to interpret
se comienza/comenzar: one starts/to start
llegada: arrival
fin de año: end of the year
alegría: joy, happiness
estar juntos: to be together

12 diciembre de 2007

El **día** 7 de diciembre las **casas** de los colombianos **se llenan** de un **resplandor** mágico: **miles** y miles de **pequeñas velas** se encienden para darle **la bienvenida** a la Virgen. Ese día **se celebra** el Día de las **Velitas** o el Día del **Alumbrado**, una celebración **a través de** la cual **se recuerda a** la Inmaculada Concepción y **se da inicio a** los **festejos y preparativos** para la Navidad. Desde **muy temprano**, las familias **se reúnen** para **pensar** cómo **van a organizar** sus velitas. La **mayoría las ponen** en la **entrada** de sus casas, pero muchos **las encienden** en el **jardín**, la **terraza**, los **balcones** y los patios. En **algunos pueblos**, los festejos **cobran tal magnitud** que **hasta se corta el tránsito**.

El **lector se preguntará**: **¿por qué tantas velas**?, ¿para qué? **Según** la tradición, el 8 de diciembre es el día de la Virgen. Ese día, ella **pasará por** cada una de las casas para **bendecirlas**. Por este **motivo**, las velitas **intentan formar** un **sendero** desde la **vereda** hasta la entrada de la casa. Ellas **guiarán** a la Virgen **hacia** el interior de **cada hogar** para que **lo colme** de **bendiciones** y de **luz**.

Pero no sólo se prenden velas. Muchos **compran** pequeños **faroles** o **lucecitas**, y hasta **se lanzan fuegos artificiales** que hacen que esa noche **se vuelva inolvidable**. Los **chicos salen** a **jugar** a la **calle** y los **vecinos se encuentran** para **conversar acerca de** cómo **han preparado** su casa para **recibir** a la Virgen. Aquellos que **no son creyentes** o **no practican** la religión católica, también **se unen** al festejo. Ellos **interpretan** la fiesta como un momento familiar en el que **se comienza** a celebrar la **llegada** del **fin de año** y la **alegría** de **estar juntos**.

1. ¿En que país se celebra el Día de las Velitas?

_____

2. ¿En qué fecha *"se llenan las casas de un resplandor mágico"*?

_____

3. ¿Cuántas velitas se encuentran ese día?

_____

4. ¿Qué otro nombre tiene esta celebración?

_____

5. ¿Dónde colocan estas velitas normalmente?

_____

_____

6. Según la gente creyente, ¿quién pasará por cada casa?

_____

7. ¿Quiere la gente que la Virgen entre en su casa?

_____

8. En esta fiesta, ¿sólo se prenden velitas?

_____

9. ¿Qué cosa se puede ver en el cielo por la noche?

_____

10. ¿Es esta fiesta exclusivamente para los creyentes?

_____

_____

a escena: on stage
tablao: stage, dance floor
comienza/comenzar: begins/to begin, to start
mezcla: mixture
ritmos: rhythms, beats
sonidos: sounds
joven español: Spanish young man
nació/nacer: was born/to be born
corazón: heart
estremeciendo con: bursting with, brimming with
promete ir: promises to go
más allá: beyond
fronteras: borders, frontiers
paredes: walls
pocos: few (people)
conocen/conocer: know/to know
verdadero: real
nombre: name
no lo utilizan: don't use it
lo olvidan fácilmente: forget it easily
lo apodaron: (they) nicknamed him
ha pasado a ser/pasar a ser: has become/to become
sello personal: personal stamp, personal imprint
mundo: world
tocando/tocar: playing (music)/to play
trabaja/trabajar: he works/to work
conjunto: group
componiendo/componer: composing/to compose
lograr: achieve
lenguaje: language

polivalente: multi-skilled, versatile
ha trabajado/trabajar: has worked/to work
casi todos: almost all
campos: fields
abarca/abarcar: cover/to cover, to span
vamos a hablar: we are going to talk
carrera: career
ciudad: city
sur: south

lo que hago/hacer: what I do/to do, to make
ambos: both
estilos: styles

tocaste/tocar: (you) played/to play (an instrument)
sabes/saber: do you know how/to know
comencé/comenzar: I started/to start
estudiando/estudiar: studying/to study
de mayor: as an older boy
empecé/empezar: I began/to begin, to start
como a los diez años: (when I was) about 10 years old
luego: then
necesidades: needs
tuve que intentar: I had to try to
aprender: to learn
bajo: bass

más ricos: richest
existen/existir: exist/to exist
por desgracia: unfortunately
sigue siendo: continues to be
minorías: a small number of people

"All That Jazz – Una Entrevista con Tuti Fernández"

Iván Calderón

Prólogo: Cuatro, tres, dos… ¡A escena en el tablao! **Comienza** una auténtica presentación musical, en especial por la **mezcla** de **ritmos** y **sonidos**. Nuestro artista es un **joven español** que **nació** en el **corazón** de Albacete. **Estremeciendo con** talento el territorio nacional, **promete ir más allá** porque sus **fronteras** no son **paredes**. **Pocos conocen** su **verdadero nombre** y los que lo saben **no lo utilizan** y **lo olvidan fácilmente**. Desde que era un niño **lo apodaron** *Tuti* y ahora **ha pasado a ser** su **sello personal** en las composiciones de su autoría. En el **mundo** de la música *Tuti* empieza **tocando** guitarra flamenca pero luego evoluciona en la guitarra eléctrica. Incontables horas **trabaja** con su **conjunto**, el Tuti Fernández Quintet, **componiendo** hasta **lograr** resultados magníficos, una fusión de sonidos que mezcla el jazz con el flamenco en el **lenguaje** de la improvisación.

Iván Calderón: Tuti Fernández es un **polivalente** guitarrista y productor musical de España que **ha trabajado** en **casi todos** los **campos** que **abarca** el mundo de la música. **Vamos a hablar** con él sobre su **carrera** y su gran interés en la música. Hola, Tuti. ¿De dónde eres tú?

Tuti Fernández: Yo soy de Albacete, una **ciudad** española que está en el **sur** de La Mancha, la tierra del Quijote.

I: Qué bien. ¿Cuál es tu estilo de música favorito?

T: Mis estilos de música favoritos son el flamenco y el jazz. **Lo que hago** es una mezcla de **ambos estilos**.

I: Muy interesante. ¿Cuál era el primer instrumento que **tocaste** y cuántos instrumentos **sabes** tocar?

T: Comencé de pequeñito **estudiando** percusión. **De mayor empecé** a interesarme por la guitarra, **como a los diez años**, y **luego**, por mis **necesidades** como músico, **tuve que intentar aprender** un poquito de otros instrumentos, como el **bajo** y el piano.

I: Fantástico. ¿Qué significa el jazz para ti y es popular el jazz en España?

T: El jazz para mí es uno de los lenguajes musicales **más ricos** que **existen**. **Por desgracia**, el jazz en España **sigue siendo** una música para **minorías**.

I: ¿Cuándo **decidiste hacerte** artista profesional?

T: Fue la **primera vez** que **me subí** a un **escenario**. Tenía diecinueve años. Estaba tocando **delante de** mucha **gente** y **sentí cosas** que **nunca había sentido**. Por eso, decidí hacerme músico profesional.

I: ¿Quiénes han sido las influencias más importantes en tu carrera?

T: Dentro de los artistas españoles, los músicos que más **me han influenciado han sido** Paco de Lucía, Camarón y Chano Domínguez. Y dentro de los artistas internacionales, quizá Chick Corea y Pat Metheny.

I: ¿Estás nervioso cuando tocas en un concierto?

T: Sí. Normalmente **me pongo nervioso** cuando tengo que subirme a un escenario, pero ya he aprendido a **templar** los nervios **pensando que cuando toco sólo tengo que decir** la **verdad**.

I: Tengo un dato de **última hora. Hemos oído** que **has colaborado** recientemente en una **película** española nominada para un Óscar titulada *La dama y la muerte*. **Cuéntanos un poquitín** de este **proyecto**.

T: Es un proyecto precioso en el que **yo he grabado** las guitarras de la **banda sonora**. Es un **corto** de animación en tres dimensiones que **ya ha conseguido** un Premio Goya, **algo parecido** a los Óscar españoles.

I: Tal vez cuando la gente **escuche** esto, tú ya tienes un Óscar en l**a mano**. ¿Cómo **influye** en tu música la cultura española?

T: La cultura española influye mucho en mi música, sobre todo la cultura del flamenco.

I: ¿Sería posible escuchar una selección de tu música?

T: Por supuesto. Me encantaría que escucharais un extracto de una pieza que **se llama** *"Me siento bien"*. En ella colaboran en la **voz** mi **hermana** Ester Fernández y el **cantaor** JJ Chaleco. **Espero que os guste**.

I: ¡Qué bien, Tuti! Muchas gracias por estar con nosotros.

T: Gracias a vosotros. Hasta pronto.

decidiste hacerte: did you decide to become
primera vez: first time
me subí a/subirse a: I got on/to get on (something)
escenario: stage
delante de: in front of
gente: people
sentí cosas: I felt things
nunca había sentido/sentir: I had never felt/ to feel

dentro de: among
me han influenciado/influenciar: have influenced me/to influence
han sido/ser: have been/to be

me pongo nervioso: I get nervous
templar: calm
pensando que/pensar: thinking that/to think
cuando toco: when I play
sólo tengo que decir: I just have to tell
verdad: truth

tengo un dato: I have a piece of information
última hora: last minute
hemos oído/oír: we have heard/to hear
has colaborado/colaborar: you have collaborated/ to collaborate
película: movie, film
cuéntanos/contar: tell us/to tell
un poquitín: a little bit
proyecto: project

yo he grabado/grabar: I (have) recorded/to record
banda sonora: soundtrack
corto: short (film)
ya ha conseguido: it already has won
algo parecido: something like

tal vez: perhaps
escuche/escuchar: listen/to listen
mano: hand
influye/influir: does it influence/to influence

por supuesto: of course
me encantaría/encantar: I would love/to love
se llama/llamarse: is called/to be called
voz: voice
hermana: sister
cantaor: flamenco singer
espero que: I hope that
os guste/gustar: you like it/to like

Para escuchar más música de Tuti Fernández visiten:

www.flamencojazz.es
www.myspace.com/tutifernandez

1. ¿De dónde es Tuti Fernández?

_____

_____

2. ¿Cuáles son los estilos preferidos de Tuti?

_____

3. Nombre tres instrumentos que toca Tuti.

_____

4. ¿Qué significa el jazz para Tuti?

_____

5. ¿A qué edad decidió hacerse músico profesional Tuti?

_____

6. ¿Qué artistas le han influenciado más a Tuti?

_____

_____

7. ¿Está nervioso Tuti cuando toca en un concierto?

_____

_____

8. ¿Cómo se llama la película nominada para un Óscar y ganadora de un Premio Goya en la cual tocó Tuti Fernández la guitarra?

_____

9. ¿Cómo se llama la pieza que presentó Tuti al final de la entrevista?

_____

10. ¿Con quién colaboró Tuti en la canción que nos presentó?

_____

TORTILLA PURA
por Iván Calderón

TRACK 10 DISC 3

puerta: door
se abre/abrirse: opens/to open
halada: pulled
manos suaves: soft hands
abuela: grandmother
primero: first
nos hace entrar: (she) lets us in
luego: then
nos muestra/mostrar: (she) shows us/
   to show
cada rincón de la casa: all around the house
   (literally: every corner of the house)
finalmente: finally
nos lleva/llevar: (she) takes us/to take
escondite: hiding place
cocina: kitchen
equipada con: equipped with
para hacer: to make, to create
cocinera: (female) cook
sótano: basement
linda casa: lovely house
ubicada: located
estrecha calle: narrow street
llamada/llamar: called/to call
pintó/pintar: painted/to paint
lienzo: canvas
sartén: frying pan
añade/añadir: adds/to add
para realizar: to make
propia: own
obra maestra: masterpiece
sentada: sitting
banquito: little stool
prepara/preparar: (she) prepares/to prepare
cada uno: each one
mientras: while
nos relata/relatar: (she) tells us/to tell, to relate
historias: stories
sobre: about
receta: recipe
aprendió/aprender: (she) learned/to learn
de su madre: from her mother
conquista corazones: (it) conquers hearts
pueblo: town
fiestas de toros: bull festivities
aun: even
más antiguas: older
allí: there
tan ricas: so tasty
fama: fame
se extiende/extenderse: extends/to extend
más allá de las calles: beyond the streets
dicen que: they say that
no sólo ... sino de: not only ... but also in
... más ricas de: tastiest ... in

La **puerta se abre, halada** por las **manos suaves** de una **abuela. Primero, nos hace entrar;** **luego nos muestra cada rincón de la casa** y, **finalmente, nos lleva** a su **escondite** secreto: una **cocina equipada con** todos los utensilios **para hacer** su arte. El santuario de esta **cocinera** está en el

sótano de su **linda casa**, **ubicada** en una **estrecha calle llamada** Diego Velázquez, en honor al famosísimo artista que **pintó** *Las Meninas*. El **lienzo** de esta abuela es una **sartén** a la cual ella **añade** sus ingredientes **para realizar** su **propia obra maestra.**

Sentada en su **banquito, prepara cada uno** de los ingredientes **mientras nos relata historias sobre** la **receta** que a**prendió de su madre.** Esta receta **conquista corazones** en Cuéllar, un **pueblo** de la provincia de Segovia, famoso por sus **fiestas de toros** que son **aún más antiguas** que las de Pamplona. **Allí,** Doña Pura Medina Quevedo prepara unas tortillas **tan ricas** que su **fama se extiende más allá de las calles** de su pueblo. **Dicen que** ella hace **no sólo** las tortillas **más ricas de** Cuéllar, **sino de** toda España.

En algunos **países de habla hispana**, cuando **alguien anuncia** que **va a comer** una tortilla, **quiere decir** que va a **consumir** esa **cosa delgada** y **redonda, hecha de harina de maíz** o **trigo, sobre** la cual **se ponen** ingredientes como **queso**, tomate, **pollo,** etc.

Pero en España la cosa es muy **distinta**: allí el ingrediente **principal** de la tortilla es el **huevo**. Y de todas las tortillas de España, dicen que **la mejor** es la que **se conoce como** "tortilla española", hecha con huevos y **patatas**.

Aún no hemos terminado la primera y ya viene otra sobre la marcha; pero ésta no es **para nosotros**. La **cantidad** de tortillas que doña Pura prepara es **casi** increíble: en un **año típico** ella hace unas **800** tortillas, que **se sirven** de tapa en un bar **al lado de su casa. No es ninguna casualidad** que esas tortillas **lleguen al público** en un bar, especialmente **si se tiene en cuenta** que ese bar es de su **hijo** Tomás. Allí, con la **ayuda** de Froilán, hijo de Tomás y **nieto** de Pura, él **ofrece** una **amplia** variedad de tapas y **bebidas** que **atrae** a una clientela de todos los **rincones** de la provincia.

La **gente** visita el bar **para tomar una copa, escuchar** música o **compartir** con los amigos; pero, sobre todo, para **degustar** las delicias que prepara la **reina** de las tortillas. Purita, **gran mujer** en un pueblo pequeño: los **hispanoparlantes te enviamos un beso, o mejor dos**: uno en **cada mejilla, como se acostumbra en tu tierra.**

países de habla hispana: Spanish-speaking countries
alquien: someone
anuncia/anunciar: announces/ to announce
va a comer: (s/he) is going to eat
quiere decir: (s/he) means
consumir: to consume, to eat
cosa: thing
delgada: thin
redonda: round
hecha de: made of
harina de maíz: corn flour
trigo: wheat
sobre: on (top of)
se ponen/poner: are put/to put
queso: cheese
pollo: chicken
distinta: different
principal: main
huevo: egg
la mejor: the best
se conoce como: is known as
patatas: potatoes *(in Spain)*
aún no hemos terminado: we haven't finished yet
la primera: the first one
y ya viene otra: and here comes another one
sobre la marcha: right away, on the double
para nosotros: for us
cantidad: number, amount
casi: almost
año típico: typical year
800: ochocientas
se sirven/servir: are served/to serve
al lado de su casa: next door (to her)
no es ninguna casualidad: it's not a coincidence
lleguen al público: reach the public
si se tiene en cuenta: if one takes into account
hijo: son
ayuda: help
nieto: grandson
ofrece/ofrecer: offers/to offer
amplia: wide
bebidas: drinks
atrae/atraer: attracts/to attract
rincones: places, corners
gente: people
para tomar una copa: to have a drink
escuchar: to listen to
compartir: to share
degustar: to taste, to sample
reina: queen
gran mujer: great woman
hispanoparlantes: Spanish speakers
te enviamos/enviar: (we) send you/to send
beso: kiss
o mejor dos: or, even better, two
cada mejilla: each cheek
como se acostumbra: as is customary
en tu tierra: in your homeland, where you come from

huevos: eggs
calabacín: zucchini
patatas: potatoes *(in Spain)*
aceite de oliva: olive oil
media cebolla: half an onion
sal: salt
pelar: peel
echar: put, pour
sartén: frying pan, skillet
hasta que: until
cubra bien: (it) covers … well
fondo: bottom
taza: cup
más o menos: more or less
cortar: cut
trocitos pequeños: small pieces
añadir: add
una cucharadita: a teaspoonful
mezclarlo todo bien: mix everything well
recipiente: container
poner: put
mezcla: mixture
a fuego lento: (to cook) over a low heat
remover: stir
frecuentemente: frequently, often
blando: soft
doradito: golden
batir: beat
escurrir: drain
cocinada: cooked
agregarla: add it
misma: same
un poco de: a little bit of
calentarlo bien: heat it well
después de: after
tapar: cover
tapa: lid
cazuela: casserole, saucepan
plato grande: big plate
voltear: turn over
rápidamente: quickly
devolver: return
no cocinada: uncooked
hacia abajo: facedown
todo estará listo: everything will be ready
preparar: prepare
donde: where
se va a servir: (it) will be served
darle la vuelta: turn it over
una vez más: one more time
¡ya está!: that's it!

Receta secreta de Tortilla a la Pura

Ingredientes:

5 **huevos**
1 **calabacín**
5 ó 6 **patatas**
aceite de oliva
media cebolla
sal

Pelar el calabacín y las patatas.

Echar el aceite en una **sartén hasta que cubra bien** el **fondo** (una **taza más o menos**).

Cortar en **trocitos pequeños** la patata, el calabacín y la cebolla.

Añadir una cucharadita de sal y **mezclarlo todo bien** en un **recipiente.**

Poner la **mezcla** en la sartén **a fuego lento** y **remover frecuentemente** hasta que todo esté **blando** y **doradito.**

Batir los huevos bien en un recipiente.

Escurrir la mezcla **cocinada** y **agregarla** a los huevos, mezclando bien.

En la **misma** sartén, añadir **un poco de** aceite, **calentarlo bien** y poner la mezcla de huevos, patatas, calabacín y cebolla.

Después de unos minutos, **tapar** la sartén con la **tapa** de una **cazuela** o un **plato grande** y **voltear rápidamente.**

Devolver la tortilla a la sartén con la parte **no cocinada hacia abajo.**

En unos minutos **todo estará listo … Preparar** el plato **donde se va a servir, darle la vuelta una vez más** y **¡ya está!**

351

1. ¿Qué hace esta abuela en su "escondite" secreto?

_____

2. ¿Quién es Diego Velázquez y cómo se llama una de sus obras maestras?

_____

_____

3. ¿En qué pueblo vive esta abuela y en qué provincia está ese pueblo?

_____

4. ¿De quién aprendió Pura su receta de tortilla?

_____

5. ¿Qué tipo de fiesta tiene lugar en Cuéllar, una fiesta aún más antigua que la de Pamplona?

_____

6. ¿Cuáles son las diferencias principales entre las tortillas españolas y las tortillas que hacen en otros países de habla hispana?

_____

_____

_____

7. ¿Cuántas tortillas hace doña Pura Medina Quevedo en un año?

_____

8. ¿Cómo se llama el bar donde se sirven las tortillas de Pura y quién es el dueño?

_____

9. ¿Cómo se llama el nieto de Pura?

_____

10. En la conclusión del artículo dicen que la gente visita el bar para hacer muchas cosas. ¿Qué cosas?

_____

CONJUGACIONES DE HABLAR, COMER, VIVIR

CONJUGATIONS OF HABLAR, COMER AND VIVIR

	PRESENTE (present) (I speak, etc.)		
	hablar	**comer**	**vivir**
(yo)	hablo	como	vivo
(tú)	hablas	comes	vives
(Ud., él, ella)	habla	come	vive
(nosotros/nosotras)	hablamos	comemos	vivimos
(vosotros/vosotras)	habláis	coméis	vivís
(Uds., ellos, ellas)	hablan	comen	viven

	PRETÉRITO (preterite) (I spoke, etc.)		
	hablé	comí	viví
	hablaste	comiste	viviste
	habló	comió	vivió
	hablamos	comimos	vivimos
	hablasteis	comisteis	vivisteis
	hablaron	comieron	vivieron

	IMPERFECTO (imperfect) (I used to speak, I was speaking, etc.)		
	hablaba	comía	vivía
	hablabas	comías	vivías
	hablaba	comía	vivía
	hablábamos	comíamos	vivíamos
	hablabais	comíais	vivíais
	hablaban	comían	vivían

	PARTICIPIO PASADO (past participle) (spoken)		
	hablado	comido	vivido

	PRESENTE PERFECTO (present perfect) (I have spoken, etc.)		
	he hablado	he comido	he vivido
	has hablado	has comido	has vivido
	ha hablado	ha comido	ha vivido
	hemos hablado	hemos comido	hemos vivido
	habéis hablado	habéis comido	habéis vivido
	han hablado	han comido	han vivido

	PLUSCUAMPERFECTO (past perfect or pluperfect) (I had spoken, etc.)		
	había hablado	había comido	había vivido
	habías hablado	habías comido	habías vivido
	había hablado	había comido	había vivido
	habíamos hablado	habíamos comido	habíamos vivido
	habíais hablado	habíais comido	habíais vivido
	habían hablado	habían comido	habían vivido

	FUTURO (future) (I will speak, etc.)		
	hablaré	comeré	viviré
	hablarás	comerás	vivirás
	hablará	comerá	vivirá
	hablaremos	comeremos	viviremos
	hablaréis	comeréis	viviréis
	hablarán	comerán	vivirán

	FUTURO PERFECTO (future perfect) (I will have spoken, etc.)		
	habré hablado	habré comido	habré vivido
	habrás hablado	habrás comido	habrás vivido
	habrá hablado	habrá comido	habrá vivido
	habremos hablado	habremos comido	habremos vivido
	habréis hablado	habréis comido	habréis vivido
	habrán hablado	habrán comido	habrán vivido

CONDICIONAL (conditional) (I would speak, etc.)

hablaría	comería	viviría
hablarías	comerías	vivirías
hablaría	comería	viviría
hablaríamos	comeríamos	viviríamos
hablaríais	comeríais	viviríais
hablarían	comerían	vivirían

CONDICIONAL PERFECTO (conditional perfect) (I would have spoken, etc.)

habría hablado	habría comido	habría vivido
habrías hablado	habrías comido	habrías vivido
habría hablado	habría comido	habría vivido
habríamos hablado	habríamos comido	habríamos vivido
habríais hablado	habríais comido	habríais vivido
habrían hablado	habrían comido	habrían vivido

PRESENTE DEL SUBJUNTIVO (present subjunctive)

hable	coma	viva
hables	comas	vivas
hable	coma	viva
hablemos	comamos	vivamos
habléis	comáis	viváis
hablen	coman	vivan

PRESENTE PERFECTO DEL SUBJUNTIVO (present perfect subjunctive)

haya hablado	haya comido	haya vivido
hayas hablado	hayas comido	hayas vivido
haya hablado	haya comido	haya vivido
hayamos hablado	hayamos comido	hayamos vivido
hayáis hablado	hayáis comido	hayáis vivido
hayan hablado	hayan comido	hayan vivido

IMPERFECTO DEL SUBJUNTIVO (past subjunctive)

hablara	comiera	viviera
hablaras	comieras	vivieras
hablara	comiera	viviera
habláramos	comiéramos	viviéramos
hablarais	comierais	vivierais
hablaran	comieran	vivieran

PLUSCUAMPERFECTO DEL SUBJUNTIVO (past perfect subjunctive)

hubiera hablado	hubiera comido	hubiera vivido
hubieras hablado	hubieras comido	hubieras vivido
hubiera hablado	hubiera comido	hubiera vivido
hubiéramos hablado	hubiéramos comido	hubiéramos vivido
hubierais hablado	hubierais comido	hubierais vivido
hubieran hablado	hubieran comido	hubieran vivido

PARTICIPIO PRESENTE (present participle) (speaking)

hablando	comiendo	viviendo

IMPERATIVOS (commands) (Speak!)

(tú +)	habla	come	vive
(tú -)	no hables	no comas	no vivas
(Ud. +/-)	hable	coma	viva
(nosotros/nosotras +/-)	hablemos	comamos	vivamos
(vosotros/vosotras +)	hablad	comed	vivid
(vosotros/vosotras -)	no habléis	no comáis	no viváis
(Uds. +/-)	hablen	coman	vivan

TABLA DE VERBOS

TO FORM THE COMPOUND TENSES OF THE
FOLLOWING VERBS, SIMPLY FOLLOW
THE MODELS PRESENTED FOR
"HABLAR, COMER, VIVIR."

INDICATIVO

SUBJUNTIVO

ANDAR

participios	presente	pretérito	imperfecto	futuro	condicional	presente	imperfecto
andando	ando	anduve	andaba	andaré	andaría	ande	anduviera
andado	andas	anduviste	andabas	andarás	andarías	andes	anduvieras
	anda	anduvo	andaba	andará	andaría	ande	anduviera
	andamos	anduvimos	andábamos	andaremos	andaríamos	andemos	anduviéramos
	andáis	anduvisteis	andabais	andaréis	andaríais	andéis	anduvierais
	andan	anduvieron	andaban	andarán	andarían	anden	anduvieran

CABER

participios	presente	pretérito	imperfecto	futuro	condicional	presente	imperfecto
cabiendo	quepo	cupe	cabía	cabré	cabría	quepa	cupiera
cabido	cabes	cupiste	cabías	cabrás	cabrías	quepas	cupieras
	cabe	cupo	cabía	cabrá	cabría	quepa	cupiera
	cabemos	cupimos	cabíamos	cabremos	cabríamos	quepamos	cupiéramos
	cabéis	cupisteis	cabíais	cabréis	cabríais	quepáis	cupierais
	caben	cupieron	cabían	cabrán	cabrían	quepan	cupieran

CAER

participios	presente	pretérito	imperfecto	futuro	condicional	presente	imperfecto
cayendo	caigo	caí	caía	caeré	caería	caiga	cayera
caído	caes	caíste	caías	caerás	caerías	caigas	cayeras
	cae	cayó	caía	caerá	caería	caiga	cayera
	caemos	caímos	caíamos	caeremos	caeríamos	caigamos	cayéramos
	caéis	caísteis	caíais	caeréis	caeríais	caigáis	cayerais
	caen	cayeron	caían	caerán	caerían	caigan	cayeran

COMENZAR

participios	presente	pretérito	imperfecto	futuro	condicional	presente	imperfecto
comenzando	comienzo	comencé	comenzaba	comenzaré	comenzaría	comience	comenzara
comenzado	comienzas	comenzaste	comenzabas	comenzarás	comenzarías	comiences	comenzaras
	comienza	comenzó	comenzaba	comenzará	comenzaría	comience	comenzara
	comenzamos	comenzamos	comenzábamos	comenzaremos	comenzaríamos	comencemos	comenzáramos
	comenzáis	comenzasteis	comenzabais	comenzaréis	comenzaríais	comencéis	comenzarais
	comienzan	comenzaron	comenzaban	comenzarán	comenzarían	comiencen	comenzaran

CONDUCIR

participios	presente	pretérito	imperfecto	futuro	condicional	presente	imperfecto
conduciendo	conduzco	conduje	conducía	conduciré	conduciría	conduzca	condujera
conducido	conduces	condujiste	conducías	conducirás	conducirías	conduzcas	condujeras
	conduce	condujo	conducía	conducirá	conduciría	conduzca	condujera
	conducimos	condujimos	conducíamos	conduciremos	conduciríamos	conduzcamos	condujéramos
	conducís	condujisteis	conducíais	conduciréis	conducirías	conduzcáis	condujerais
	conducen	condujeron	conducían	conducirán	conducirían	conduzcan	condujeran

CONOCER

participios	presente	pretérito	imperfecto	futuro	condicional	presente	imperfecto
conociendo	conozco	conocí	conocía	conoceré	conocería	conozca	conociera
conocido	conoces	conociste	conocías	conocerás	conocerías	conozcas	conocieras
	conoce	conoció	conocía	conocerá	conocería	conozca	conociera
	conocemos	conocimos	conocíamos	conoceremos	conoceríamos	conozcamos	conociéramos
	conocéis	conocisteis	conocíais	conoceréis	conocerías	conozcáis	conocierais
	conocen	conocieron	conocían	conocerán	conocerían	conozcan	conocieran

INDICATIVO | SUBJUNTIVO

CONSTRUIR

participios	presente	pretérito	imperfecto	futuro	condicional	presente	imperfecto
construyendo	construyo	construí	construía	construiré	construiría	construya	construyera
construido	construyes	construiste	construías	construirás	construirías	construyas	construyeras
	construye	construyó	construía	construirá	construiría	construya	construyera
	construimos	construimos	construíamos	construiremos	construiríamos	construyamos	construyéramos
	construís	construisteis	construíais	construiréis	construiríais	construyáis	construyerais
	construyen	construyeron	construían	construirán	construirían	construyan	construyeran

DAR

participios	presente	pretérito	imperfecto	futuro	condicional	presente	imperfecto
dando	doy	di	daba	daré	daría	dé	diera
dado	das	diste	dabas	darás	darías	des	dieras
	da	dio	daba	dará	daría	dé	diera
	damos	dimos	dábamos	daremos	daríamos	demos	diéramos
	dais	disteis	dabais	daréis	daríais	deis	dierais
	dan	dieron	daban	darán	darían	den	dieran

DECIR

participios	presente	pretérito	imperfecto	futuro	condicional	presente	imperfecto
diciendo	digo	dije	decía	diré	diría	diga	dijera
dicho	dices	dijiste	decías	dirás	dirías	digas	dijeras
	dice	dijo	decía	dirá	diría	diga	dijera
	decimos	dijimos	decíamos	diremos	diríamos	digamos	dijéramos
	decís	dijisteis	decíais	diréis	diríais	digáis	dijerais
	dicen	dijeron	decían	dirán	dirían	digan	dijeran

DORMIR

participios	presente	pretérito	imperfecto	futuro	condicional	presente	imperfecto
durmiendo	duermo	dormí	dormía	dormiré	dormiría	duerma	durmiera
dormido	duermes	dormiste	dormías	dormirás	dormirías	duermas	durmieras
	duerme	durmió	dormía	dormirá	dormiría	duerma	durmiera
	dormimos	dormimos	dormíamos	dormiremos	dormiríamos	durmamos	durmiéramos
	dormís	dormisteis	dormíais	dormiréis	dormiríais	durmáis	durmierais
	duermen	durmieron	dormían	dormirán	dormirían	duerman	durmieran

ESTAR

participios	presente	pretérito	imperfecto	futuro	condicional	presente	imperfecto
estando	estoy	estuve	estaba	estaré	estaría	esté	estuviera
estado	estás	estuviste	estabas	estarás	estarías	estés	estuvieras
	está	estuvo	estaba	estará	estaría	esté	estuviera
	estamos	estuvimos	estábamos	estaremos	estaríamos	estemos	estuviéramos
	estáis	estuvisteis	estabais	estaréis	estaríais	estéis	estuvierais
	están	estuvieron	estaban	estarán	estarían	estén	estuvieran

HABER

participios	presente	pretérito	imperfecto	futuro	condicional	presente	imperfecto
habiendo	he	hube	había	habré	habría	haya	hubiera
habido	has	hubiste	habías	habrás	habrías	hayas	hubieras
	ha	hubo	había	habrá	habría	haya	hubiera
	hemos	hubimos	habíamos	habremos	habríamos	hayamos	hubiéramos
	habéis	hubisteis	habíais	habréis	habríais	hayáis	hubierais
	han	hubieron	habían	habrán	habrían	hayan	hubieran

INDICATIVO						SUBJUNTIVO	

HACER

participios	presente	pretérito	imperfecto	futuro	condicional	presente	imperfecto
haciendo	hago	hice	hacía	haré	haría	haga	hiciera
hecho	haces	hiciste	hacías	harás	harías	hagas	hicieras
	hace	hizo	hacía	hará	haría	haga	hiciera
	hacemos	hicimos	hacíamos	haremos	haríamos	hagamos	hiciéramos
	hacéis	hicisteis	hacíais	haréis	haríais	hagáis	hicierais
	hacen	hicieron	hacían	harán	harían	hagan	hicieran

IR

participios	presente	pretérito	imperfecto	futuro	condicional	presente	imperfecto
yendo	voy	fui	iba	iré	iría	vaya	fuera
ido	vas	fuiste	ibas	irás	irías	vayas	fueras
	va	fue	iba	irá	iría	vaya	fuera
	vamos	fuimos	íbamos	iremos	iríamos	vayamos	fuéramos
	vais	fuisteis	ibais	iréis	iríais	vayáis	fuerais
	van	fueron	iban	irán	irían	vayan	fueran

JUGAR

participios	presente	pretérito	imperfecto	futuro	condicional	presente	imperfecto
jugando	juego	jugué	jugaba	jugaré	jugaría	juegue	jugara
jugado	juegas	jugaste	jugabas	jugarás	jugarías	juegues	jugaras
	juega	jugó	jugaba	jugará	jugaría	juegue	jugara
	jugamos	jugamos	jugábamos	jugaremos	jugaríamos	juguemos	jugáramos
	jugáis	jugasteis	jugabais	jugaréis	jugaríais	juguéis	jugarais
	juegan	jugaron	jugaban	jugarán	jugarían	jueguen	jugaran

NEGAR

participios	presente	pretérito	imperfecto	futuro	condicional	presente	imperfecto
negando	niego	negué	negaba	negaré	negaría	niegue	negara
negado	niegas	negaste	negabas	negarás	negarías	niegues	negaras
	niega	negó	negaba	negará	negaría	niegue	negara
	negamos	negamos	negábamos	negaremos	negaríamos	neguemos	negáramos
	negáis	negasteis	negabais	negaréis	negaríais	neguéis	negarais
	niegan	negaron	negaban	negarán	negarían	nieguen	negaran

OÍR

participios	presente	pretérito	imperfecto	futuro	condicional	presente	imperfecto
oyendo	oigo	oí	oía	oiré	oiría	oiga	oyera
oído	oyes	oíste	oías	oirás	oirías	oigas	oyeras
	oye	oyó	oía	oirá	oiría	oiga	oyera
	oímos	oímos	oíamos	oiremos	oiríamos	oigamos	oyéramos
	oís	oísteis	oíais	oiréis	oiríais	oigáis	oyerais
	oyen	oyeron	oían	oirán	oirían	oigan	oyeran

OLER

participios	presente	pretérito	imperfecto	futuro	condicional	presente	imperfecto
oliendo	huelo	olí	olía	oleré	olería	huela	oliera
olido	hueles	oliste	olías	olerás	olerías	huelas	olieras
	huele	olió	olía	olerá	olería	huela	oliera
	olemos	olimos	olíamos	oleremos	oleríamos	olamos	oliéramos
	oléis	olisteis	olíais	oleréis	oleríais	oláis	olierais
	huelen	olieron	olían	olerán	olerían	huelan	olieran

PEDIR

participios	presente	pretérito	imperfecto	futuro	condicional	presente	imperfecto
pidiendo	pido	pedí	pedía	pediré	pediría	pida	pidiera
pedido	pides	pediste	pedías	pedirás	pedirías	pidas	pidieras
	pide	pidió	pedía	pedirá	pediría	pida	pidiera
	pedimos	pedimos	pedíamos	pediremos	pediríamos	pidamos	pidiéramos
	pedís	pedisteis	pedíais	pediréis	pediríais	pidáis	pidierais
	piden	pidieron	pedían	pedirán	pedirían	pidan	pidieran

PODER

participios	presente	pretérito	imperfecto	futuro	condicional	presente	imperfecto
pudiendo	puedo	pude	podía	podré	podría	pueda	pudiera
podido	puedes	pudiste	podías	podrás	podrías	puedas	pudieras
	puede	pudo	podía	podrá	podría	pueda	pudiera
	podemos	pudimos	podíamos	podremos	podríamos	podamos	pudiéramos
	podéis	pudisteis	podíais	podréis	podríais	podáis	pudierais
	pueden	pudieron	podían	podrán	podrían	puedan	pudieran

PONER

participios	presente	pretérito	imperfecto	futuro	condicional	presente	imperfecto
poniendo	pongo	puse	ponía	pondré	pondría	ponga	pusiera
puesto	pones	pusiste	ponías	pondrás	pondrías	pongas	pusieras
	pone	puso	ponía	pondrá	pondría	ponga	pusiera
	ponemos	pusimos	poníamos	pondremos	pondríamos	pongamos	pusiéramos
	ponéis	pusisteis	poníais	pondréis	pondríais	pongáis	pusierais
	ponen	pusieron	ponían	pondrán	pondrían	pongan	pusieran

QUERER

participios	presente	pretérito	imperfecto	futuro	condicional	presente	imperfecto
queriendo	quiero	quise	quería	querré	querría	quiera	quisiera
querido	quieres	quisiste	querías	querrás	querrías	quieras	quisieras
	quiere	quiso	quería	querrá	querría	quiera	quisiera
	queremos	quisimos	queríamos	querremos	querríamos	queramos	quisiéramos
	queréis	quisisteis	queríais	querréis	querríais	queráis	quisierais
	quieren	quisieron	querían	querrán	querrían	quieran	quisieran

REÍR

participios	presente	pretérito	imperfecto	futuro	condicional	presente	imperfecto
riendo	río	reí	reía	reiré	reiría	ría	riera
reído	ríes	reíste	reías	reirás	reirías	rías	rieras
	ríe	rió	reía	reirá	reiría	ría	riera
	reímos	reímos	reíamos	reiremos	reiríamos	riamos	riéramos
	reís	reísteis	reíais	reiréis	reiríais	riáis	rierais
	ríen	rieron	reían	reirán	reirían	rían	rieran

SABER

participios	presente	pretérito	imperfecto	futuro	condicional	presente	imperfecto
sabiendo	sé	supe	sabía	sabré	sabría	sepa	supiera
sabido	sabes	supiste	sabías	sabrás	sabrías	sepas	supieras
	sabe	supo	sabía	sabrá	sabría	sepa	supiera
	sabemos	supimos	sabíamos	sabremos	sabríamos	sepamos	supiéramos
	sabéis	supisteis	sabíais	sabréis	sabríais	sepáis	supierais
	saben	supieron	sabían	sabrán	sabrían	sepan	supieran

INDICATIVO						SUBJUNTIVO	

SEGUIR

participios	presente	pretérito	imperfecto	futuro	condicional	presente	imperfecto
siguiendo	sigo	seguí	seguía	seguiré	seguiría	siga	siguiera
seguido	sigues	seguiste	seguías	seguirás	seguirías	sigas	siguieras
	sigue	siguió	seguía	seguirá	seguiría	siga	siguiera
	seguimos	seguimos	seguíamos	seguiremos	seguiríamos	sigamos	siguiéramos
	seguís	seguisteis	seguíais	seguiréis	seguiríais	sigáis	siguierais
	siguen	siguieron	seguían	seguirán	seguirían	sigan	siguieran

SER

participios	presente	pretérito	imperfecto	futuro	condicional	presente	imperfecto
siendo	soy	fui	era	seré	sería	sea	fuera
sido	eres	fuiste	eras	serás	serías	seas	fueras
	es	fue	era	será	sería	sea	fuera
	somos	fuimos	éramos	seremos	seríamos	seamos	fuéramos
	sois	fuisteis	erais	seréis	seríais	seáis	fuerais
	son	fueron	eran	serán	serían	sean	fueran

TENER

participios	presente	pretérito	imperfecto	futuro	condicional	presente	imperfecto
teniendo	tengo	tuve	tenía	tendré	tendría	tenga	tuviera
tenido	tienes	tuviste	tenías	tendrás	tendrías	tengas	tuvieras
	tiene	tuvo	tenía	tendrá	tendría	tenga	tuviera
	tenemos	tuvimos	teníamos	tendremos	tendríamos	tengamos	tuviéramos
	tenéis	tuvisteis	teníais	tendréis	tendríais	tengáis	tuvierais
	tienen	tuvieron	tenían	tendrán	tendrían	tengan	tuvieran

TRAER

participios	presente	pretérito	imperfecto	futuro	condicional	presente	imperfecto
trayendo	traigo	traje	traía	traeré	traería	traiga	trajera
traído	traes	trajiste	traías	traerás	traerías	traigas	trajeras
	trae	trajo	traía	traerá	traería	traiga	trajera
	traemos	trajimos	traíamos	traeremos	traeríamos	traigamos	trajéramos
	traéis	trajisteis	traíais	traeréis	traeríais	traigáis	trajerais
	traen	trajeron	traían	traerán	traerían	traigan	trajeran

VENIR

participios	presente	pretérito	imperfecto	futuro	condicional	presente	imperfecto
viniendo	vengo	vine	venía	vendré	vendría	venga	viniera
venido	vienes	viniste	venías	vendrás	vendrías	vengas	vinieras
	viene	vino	venía	vendrá	vendría	venga	viniera
	venimos	vinimos	veníamos	vendremos	vendríamos	vengamos	viniéramos
	venís	vinisteis	veníais	vendréis	vendríais	vengáis	vinierais
	vienen	vinieron	venían	vendrán	vendrían	vengan	vinieran

VER

participios	presente	pretérito	imperfecto	futuro	condicional	presente	imperfecto
viendo	veo	vi	veía	veré	vería	vea	viera
visto	ves	viste	veías	verás	verías	veas	vieras
	ve	vio	veía	verá	vería	vea	viera
	vemos	vimos	veíamos	veremos	veríamos	veamos	viéramos
	veis	visteis	veíais	veréis	veríais	veáis	vierais
	ven	vieron	veían	verán	verían	vean	vieran

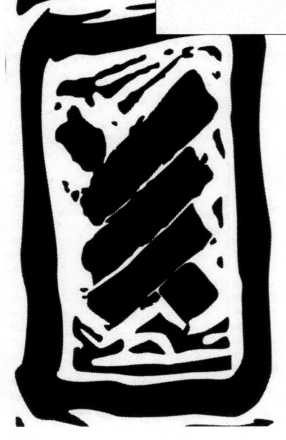

DICCIONARIO
ESPAÑOL-INGLÉS

A

a. . . . . at, to
a eso de . . . . at approximately
a la derecha . . . . to the right
a la izquierda . . . . .to the left
a lo largo. . . . . along
a menudo. . . . . often
a pesar de . . . . in spite of
a veces. . . . . at times, sometimes
abajo . . . . below
abandonar. . . . . to abandon
abeja (la) . . . . .bee
abierto/a . . . . open
abogado/a (el/la). . . . . lawyer
abordar . . . . .to board
abrazar . . . . to embrace, to hug
abrazo (el). . . . . .embrace
abrelatas (el). . . . . .can opener
abrigo (el). . . . . coat, overcoat
abril. . . . . April
abrir . . . . to open
abuela (la). . . . . grandmother
abuelo (el). . . . . grandfather
aburrido/a . . . . .bored, boring
aburrirse . . . . . . .to become (get) bored
acabar de. . to have just (done something)
accidente (el). . . . . .accident
acción (la). . . . . action
aceite (el) . . . . oil
acera (la). . . . . sidewalk
acero (el). . . . . .steel
acompañar . . . . to accompany
acondicionador de aire (el)
. . . . .air conditioner
aconsejar. . . . . to advise
acordeón (el). . . . . accordion
acostarse (ue) . . . . .to go to bed
acostumbrarse a . . . . to get used to
actitud (la). . . . . attitude
actor (el) . . . . actor
actriz (la). . . . . .actress
actual. . . . . current, present day
acusar . . . . to accuse
adelante. . . . . forward, ahead
adicional . . . . additional
admitir. . . . . .to admit
adquirir (ie). . . . . to acquire
adversario/a (el/la). . . . . opponent
aeropuerto (el) . . . . airport
afeitar(se) . . . . to shave (oneself)
aficionado/a (el/la). . . . . fan
afilado/a . . . . sharp (e.g., knife)
afuera . . . . .outside
afueras (las) . . . . suburbs
agencia de viajes (la) . . . . .travel agency
agosto . . . . .August
agotado/a . . . . exhausted

agradecer . . . . . to thank, be grateful for
agradecido/a. . . . . grateful
agrio/a (amargo/a). . . . . .bitter, sour
agua (el) (f.) . . . . water
agudo/a. . . . . sharp, astute
águila (el) (f.) . . . . eagle
ahora. .now
ahora mismo . . . . .right now
ahorrar . . . . .to save
ajedrez (el) . . . . chess
ajo (el). . . . . garlic
ala (el) (f.). . . . . wing
alabar . . . . to praise
alarma (la) . . . . .alarm
alba (el) (f.). . . . . dawn
albóndiga (la) . . . . meatball
alcalde (el). . . . . mayor
alcanzar. . . . . .to reach
alcoba (la). . . . . bedroom
alegrarse de . . . . to be happy about
alegre . . . . happy
alegría (la) . . . . .joy, happiness
alemán (el). . . . . German
alfabeto (el). . . . . .alphabet
alfombra (la). . . . . carpet, rug
algo . . . . something
algodón (el). . . . . cotton
alguien. . . . . someone
alguno/a . . . . some
allí. . . . . there
almacén (el) . . . . department store
almohada (la) . . . . pillow
almorzar (ue) . . . . to have lunch
alquilado/a . . . . rented
alquilar . . . . to rent
alrededor. . . . . around
alto/a .tall
alumno/a (el/la). . . . . .student
alzar . . . . .to raise (up)
amable. . . . . friendly, kindly, nice
amante (el/la) . . . . lover
amar . . . . .to love
amarillo/a . . . . yellow
ambos/as . . . . both
amenazar. . . . . .to threaten
amigo/a (el/la). . . . . .friend
amor (el) . . . . .love
amoroso/a . . . . loving
análisis (el) . . . . analysis
anaranjado/a. . . . . orange
ancho/a . . . . wide
anchoa (la) . . . . .anchovy
andar . . . . to walk
andén (el) . . . . platform
anillo (el). . . . . ring
anillo de compromiso (el)
. . . . engagement ring
anoche. . . . . last night

anochecer . . . . to become night
anormal. . . . . .abnormal
ansioso/a. . . . . .anxious, eager
anteayer. . . . . . .the day before yesterday
anteojos (los). . . . . .glasses
antes (de). . . . . before
anuncio (el). . . . . .advertisement,
announcement
añadir . . . . to add
año (el) . . . . year
apagar. . . . . to turn off
aparecer . . . . to appear
apasionadamente . . . . passionately
apetecer. . . . . to appeal to
aplaudir. . . . . to applaud
aplazar . . . . to postpone
aplicado/a . . . . applied, dedicated,
industrious
apostar (ue). . . . . .to bet
apoyar. . . . . .to support, to aid
aprender . . . . to learn
aprender de memoria
. . . . to learn by heart
apretar (ie) . . . . . . to tighten, to squeeze
apunte (el). . . . . note
apurado/a . . . . rushed, in a hurry
aquel, aquella . . . . . . that (over yonder)
aquí. . . . . here
árabe (el) . . . . Arabic
arándano (el) . . . . cranberry, blueberry
araña (la) . . . . spider
árbitro (el). . . . . .referee
árbol (el) . . . . tree
arbusto (el) . . . . .bush
ardiente . . . . burning, passionate
arena (la) . . . . .sand
arete (el) . . . . .earring
aretes (los) . . . . earrings
armario (el). . . . . .closet
armonía (la) . . . . harmony
arquitecto/a (el/la) . . . . architect
arreglar . . . . to arrange, to fix
arrepentirse (ie) (de). . . . . .to regret
arriba . . . . up
arrojar . . . . .to throw
arroyo (el) . . . . stream
arroz (el) . . . . rice
arte (el) (f.) . . . . art
asado/a . . . . .roasted
asar . . . . to roast
ascensor (el) . . . . elevator
así . . . . in this way
asiento (el) . . . . seat
asistente de vuelo (el/la). . flight attendant
asistir. . . . . to attend
aspiradora (la) . . . . .vacuum cleaner
astuto/a . . . . .astute
asunto (el) . . . . .matter, subject

asustar . . . . to frighten, to scare
atacar . . . . to attack
atado/a . . . . tied
ataque (el) . . . . .attack
atento/a . . . . attentive
aterrizar . . . . .to land
atestado/a . . . . crowded
atlético/a . . . . athletic
atraer . . . . to attract
atrás . . . . behind
atreverse a . . . . .to dare to
atrevido/a . . . . .bold, daring
aumentar . . . . .to increase
aunque . . . . although
autobús (el) . . . . .bus
autógrafo (el) . . . . autograph
autopista (la) (autovía)
. . . . highway, freeway
autoridad (la) . . . . authority
avanzado/a . . . . .advanced
avaricioso/a . . . . greedy
averiguar . . . . to find out
avión (el) . . . . airplane
avisar . . . . to notify, to let know
ayer . . . . .yesterday
ayuda (la) . . . . help
ayudar . . . . .to help
ayunar . . . . to fast
ayuntamiento (el) . . . . .city hall
azúcar (el, la) . . . . sugar
azul . . . . blue

B

bailar .to dance
bailarín (el), bailarina (la) . . . . . . dancer
bajar . . . . .to go down, to get off
(a train, etc.)
bajo . . . . under
bajo/a . . . . short
baloncesto (el) . . . . basketball
balcón (el) . . . . balcony
ballena (la) . . . . whale
banco (el) . . . . bench, pew, bank
banda (la) . . . . band
bandeja (la) . . . . tray
bandera (la) . . . . flag
banquero/a (el/la) . . . . banker
bañador (el) . . . . bathing suit
bañarse . . . . to take a bath
bañera (la) . . . . .tub
baño (el) . . . . .bathroom
banquete (el) . . . . banquet
barato/a . . . . .cheap
barba (la) . . . . beard
barco (el) . . . . boat
barrio (el) . . . . neighborhood,
section, quarter
barrote (el) . . . . bar (of a window
or a prison cell)
bastante . . . . enough, quite

basura (la) . . . . garbage
basurero/a (el/la) . . . . garbage collector
bata (la) . . . . bathrobe
batalla (la) . . . . battle
batidor/a (el/la) . . . . beater
batir . . . . to beat
bebé (el) . . . . baby
beber . . . . to drink
bebida (la) . . . . drink
beca (la) . . . . scholarship
béisbol (el) . . . . .baseball
belleza (la) . . . . beauty
bello/a . . . . beautiful
bendecir . . . . to bless
besar . . . . to kiss
beso (el) . . . . kiss
biblioteca (la) . . . . library
bibliotecario/a (el/la) . . . . .librarian
bicicleta (la) . . . . .bicycle
bien . . . . .fine, well
bienes . . . . possessions, property
bigote (el) . . . . mustache
bilingüe . . . . bilingual
billete (el) . . . . ticket (for bus, train, etc.)
billetera (la) . . . . wallet
biología (la) . . . . biology
bisabuela (la) . . . . . . great-grandmother
bisabuelo (el) . . . . great-grandfather
bistec (el) . . . . steak
blanco/a . . . . white
blando/a . . . . soft
blusa (la) . . . . blouse
boca (la) . . . . mouth
bocadillo (el) . . . . sandwich
boda (la) . . . . wedding
boleto (el) . . . . ticket
bolígrafo (el) . . . . pen
bolsa (la) . . . . bag, purse
bombero/a (el/la) . . . . firefighter
bombones (los) . . . . chocolates
bonito/a . . . . .pretty
borracho/a . . . . .drunk
borrar . . . . to erase
bosque (el) . . . . .forest, woods
bosque de lluvia (el) . . . . rain forest
bota (la) . . . . boot
botas (las) . . . . boots
botella (la) . . . . bottle
boleto (el) . . . . ticket
bravo/a . . . . brave, fierce, angry
brazo (el) . . . . arm
brillar . . . . to shine
brindar . . . . to toast (drink)
brújula (la) . . . . compass
brusco/a . . . . .abrupt, sudden
buenas noches . . . . good evening,
. . . . .good night
buenas tardes . . . . good afternoon
bueno/a . . . . good
buenos días . . . . good morning
buey (el) . . . . ox

bufanda (la) . . . . scarf
buitre (el) . . . . .vulture
bullicioso/a . . . .noisy, rowdy, boisterous
buscar . . . . .to look for
buzón (el) . . . . mailbox

C

caballo (el) . . . . horse
cabello (el) . . . . hair
caber . . . . to fit
cabeza (la) . . . . .head
cada . . . . each, every
caer .to fall
caerle bien (mal) . . . . to get along
well (poorly)
café (el) . . . . coffee
cafetera (la) . . . . coffee maker
caja (la) . . . . box
cajón (el) . . . . .drawer
calcetines (los) . . . . socks
calendario (el) . . . . .calendar
calentamiento global (el) global warming
calentar (ie) . . . . to heat
caliente . . . . warm, hot
callarse . . . . to be quiet
calle (la) . . . . street
caluroso/a . . . . hot
calvo/a . . . . bald
calzoncillos (los) . . . . . men's underwear
cama (la) . . . . bed
cámara (la) . . . . .camera
camarero/a (el/la) (mesero/a) . . . . waiter
cambiar . . . . .to change
cambio (el) . . . . .change
caminar . . . . to walk
caminata (la) . . . . stroll, walk
camión (el) . . . . truck
camisa (la) . . . . shirt
camiseta (la) . . . . .T-shirt
campamento (el) . . . . camp
campana (la) . . . . bell
campaña (la) . . . . .campaign
campeón (el), campeona (la)
. . . . champion
campeonato (el) . . . . championship
campista (el/la) . . . . camper
campo (el) . . . . field, country(side)
cancelado/a . . . . .cancelled
cancha (la) . . . . court
canción (la) . . . . .song
candidato/a (el/la) . . . . .candidate
canela (la) . . . . cinnamon
cansado/a . . . . .tired
cansancio (el) . . . . . . .tiredness, fatigue
cantante (el/la) . . . . singer
cantar . . . . to sing
cañón (el) . . . . canyon, cannon
caoba (la) . . . . mahogany
capaz . . . . capable
capitán . . . . .captain

cara (la) . . . . face
caracola (la) . . . . seashell
carbón (el). . . . . coal
caries (la) . . . . cavity
cárcel (la) . . . . jail
cariño (el) . . . . affection
cariñoso/a . . . . affectionate
carnaval (el) . . . . carnival
carne (la). . . . . meat
carnicero/a (el/la). . . . . butcher
caro/a . . . . expensive
carpintero/a (el/la) . . . . carpenter
carrera (la) . . . . race, career
carretera (la). . . . . road, highway
carta (la). . . . . letter
cartel (el). . . . . poster
cartero/a (el/la). . . . . mail carrier
casa (la) . . . . house
casarse . . . . to get married
casarse con . . . . to get married to
casco (el). . . . . helmet
casi . . . . almost
castaño/a. . . . . chesnut
castigar . . . . to punish
castigo (el) . . . . punishment
castillo (el) . . . . castle
catarata (la) . . . . waterfall
catedral (la) . . . . cathedral
causar . . . . to cause
cauteloso/a . . . . . cautious, careful, wary
caza (la) . . . . hunting
celda (la). . . . . cell
célebre. . . . . celebrated, famous
celoso/a. . . . . .jealous
cementerio (el) . . . . cemetery
cenar . . . . .to have supper
centro (el) . . . . center, downtown
centro comercial (el). . . . . mall
cepillarse. . . . to brush one's (hair, teeth)
cerca . . . . .near(by)
cerca (de) . . . . near
cercano/a. . . . . nearby, neighboring
ceremonia (la). . . . . ceremony
cero . . . . zero
cerrado/a . . . . closed
cerradura (la) . . . . lock
cerrar (ie) . . . . to close
césped (el). . . . . lawn
chaleco (el) . . . . vest
champaña (la), (el champán). champagne
chaqueta (la). . . . . .jacket
charlar. . . . . to chat
chica (la) . . . . .girl
chicle (el) . . . . gum
chico (el) . . . . boy
chico/a. . . . . little, small
chimenea (la) . . . . . chimney, fireplace
chiste (el). . . . . .joke
chófer (el). . . . . chauffeur
ciclismo (el). . . . . cycling
ciego/a. . . . . blind

cielo (el) . . . . sky, heaven
ciencia (la) . . . . science
científico/a (el/la) . . . . scientist
cierto/a . . . . certain
cigarrillo (el). . . . . cigarette
cine (el) . . . . cinema, movie theater
cinturón (el) . . . . belt
cinturón de seguridad (el) . . . . . seatbelt
circo (el) . . . . .circus
circular . . . . .round, circular
cita (la) . . . . date
ciudad (la). . . . . city
ciudadano/a (el/la) . . . . citizen
clarinete (el) . . . . clarinet
claro/a. . . . . clear
clase (la) . . . . class
cliente/clienta (el/la). . . .client, customer
clima (el) . . . . climate
clínica (la). . . . . .clinic, hospital
cloro (el) . . . . chlorine
coche (el). . . . . car
cochinillo (el) . . . . baby pig
cocina (la). . . . . kitchen
cocinar . . . . to cook
cocinero/a (el/la). . . . . cook
coco (el) . . . . coconut
código postal (el) . . . . .zip code
coger . . . . .to take, to catch
cola (la). . . . . line, tail
colección (la) . . . . collection
coleccionar . . . . to collect
colega (el/la). . . . . colleague
colegio (el) . . . . high school
colgar (ue). . . . . to hang (up)
collar (el) . . . . necklace
colocar . . . . to place, to arrange
combinar. . . . . to combine
comedor (el) . . . . dining room
comenzar (ie) . . . . .to begin
comer. . . . . to eat
comida (la) . . . . .food
comisaría (la) . . . . .police station
como . . . . as, since, like
¿cómo? . . . . how?
cómodo/a. . . . . .comfortable
compañero/a de cuarto (el/la)
. . . . roommate
compasión (la) . . . . compassion
competición (la) . . . . .competition
competir (i). . . . . to compete
competitivo/a. . . . . competitive
comportarse . . . . .to behave
comprar. . . . . to buy
comprender. . . . . to understand
computadora (la) . . . . computer
común . . . . common
con. .with
concierto (el) . . . . concert
concurso (el) . . . . .contest
conducir . . . . to drive
conferencia de prensa (la)

. . . . press conference
confesar (ie) . . . . to confess
confianza (la) . . . . .confidence, trust (in)
confiar en . . . . .to trust
confundido/a . . . . confused
confundir. . . . . to confuse
confuso/a. . . . . confused, confusing
congelador (el) . . . . .freezer
conocer . . . . to know (a person)
conocido/a. . . . . well-known
consecutivo/a. . . . . consecutive
conseguir (i) . . . . .to get, to obtain
consejo (el) . . . . advice
conservar. . . . . to conserve
constante . . . . .constant
constelación (la) . . . . constellation
construir . . . . .to build, to construct
contaminado/a. . . . . .contaminated
contar (ue). . . . . to count, to tell
contar (ue) chismes. . . . . to gossip
contar con . . . . to count on
contento/a . . . . .content, happy
contestador automático (el)
. . . . answering machine
contestar . . . . .to answer
continente (el). . . . . continent
contra . . . . .against
contraseña (la) . . . . .password
contrato (el) . . . . contract
convencer . . . . to convince
convertir (ie) . . . . to convert
corazón (el). . . . . heart
corbata (la). . . . . tie
cordero (el) . . . . lamb
cordial. . . . . cordial, polite
cordialidad (la). . . . . .cordiality
cordones (los) . . . . .shoelaces
corpulento/a . . . . stout, heavy-set, burly
corregir (i). . . . . .to correct
correo (el). . . . . .mail
correo electrónico (el) . . . . e-mail
correr . . . . .to run
corriente . . . . current, present
corrupto/a . . . . .corrupt
cortacésped (el). . . . . lawn mower
cortar. . . . . .to cut
corte (la) . . . . court
cortés. . . . . courteous, polite
cortesía (la). . . . . .courtesy
cortinas (las) . . . . curtains
corto/a. . . . . short
cosa (la) . . . . thing
cosecha (la). . . . . .crop
costa (la). . . . . coast
costar (ue). . . . . to cost
costurera (la) . . .seamstress, dressmaker
crema (la). . . . . cream
crimen (el). . . . . .crime
cotidiano/a . . . . daily, everyday
crear . . . . to create, to make
crecer . . . . to grow, to increase

creer . . . . to believe
cremallera (la) . . . . zipper
criada (la) . . . . maid
cristal (el) . . . . glass (the material)
cristiano/a . . . . Christian
crucero (el) . . . . cruise (ship)
cruel . . . . cruel, mean
cuaderno (el) . . . . notebook
cuadrado/a . . . . square
cuadro (el) . . . . painting
¿cuál? . . . . which?, what?
¿cuál(es)? . . . . which one(s)?
cualquier . . . . any
cualquiera . . . . anybody
¿cuándo? . . . . when?
¿cuánto/a(s)? . . . . . . how much?/many?
cuarto (el) . . . . . . room, quarter, fourth
(cuarto de) baño (el) . . . . bathroom
cubiertos (los) . . . . silverware
cubrir . . . . to cover
cuchara (la) . . . . spoon
cuchillo (el) . . . . knife
cuenta (la) . . . . bill
cuento (el) . . . . story, tale
cuero (el) . . . . leather
cuidadoso/a . . . . careful, cautious
cuidar . . . . to care for
culpa (la) . . . . fault, guilt
culpable . . . . guilty
cumbre (la) . . . . summit, peak
cumplir . . . . to complete, fulfill
cumpleaños (el) . . . . birthday
cuñada (la) . . . . sister-in-law
cuñado (el) . . . . brother-in-law
cura (el) . . . . priest
curso (el) . . . . course

D

dama (la) . . . . lady
dama de honor (la) . . . . . . maid of honor
dar . . . . to give
dar una vuelta . . . . . to take a walk/drive
darle asco a . . . . to be loathsome to,
to be sickened by
darse cuenta de . . . . to realize
(i.e., come to awareness of)
de . . . . of, from
de flores . . . . flowered
de la mañana . . . . . A.M. (in the morning)
de la noche . . . . P.M. (in the evening)
de la tarde . . . . P.M. (in the afternoon)
de lunares . . . . polka-dot
de nuevo, otra vez . . . . again
de rayas . . . . striped
de repente . . . . suddenly
debajo . . . . underneath
debajo de . . . . below, under
deber . . . . to owe, ought to
débil . . . . weak
década (la) . . . . decade

decidir . . . . to decide
décimo/a . . . . tenth
declarar . . . . to declare
defecto (el) . . . . defect
dejar . . . . to leave (behind), to allow
dejar de (+ infinitive)
. . . . to stop doing something
delante de . . . . in front of
deletrear . . . . to spell
demás (los/las) . . . . (the) others
demasiado/a (adv.) . . . . too much
demasiado/a (adj.) . . . . too much,
(pl. too many)
dentista (el/la) . . . . dentist
dentro de . . . . inside of
dependienta (la) . . . . salesclerk
dependiente (el) . . . . salesclerk
deporte (el) . . . . sport
deportes (los) . . . . sports
deportivos (los) . . . . tennis shoes
deprimido/a . . . . depressed
deprimir . . . . to depress
derecha (la) . . . . right
derecho (el) . . . . right, privilege
derecho/a (adj.) . . . . right
derramar . . . . to spill
derrota (la) . . . . defeat
desafortunadamente . . . . . unfortunately
desaparecer . . . . to disappear
desarrollar . . . . to develop
desastre (el) . . . . disaster
desayunar . . . . to have breakfast
descansar . . . . to rest, to relax
descubrir . . . . to discover
desde . . . . since, from
desear . . . . to desire
desesperar . . . . . . to despair, to lose hope
desfile (el) . . . . parade
desgraciadamente . . . . unfortunately
desierto (el) . . . . desert
desordenado/a . . . . messy, not neat
despacho (el) . . . . office
despacio . . . . slowly
despedida (la) . . . . farewell, parting
despedirse (i) (de) . . . . to say goodbye to
despertador (el) . . . . alarm clock
despertarse (ie) . . . . to wake up
después (de) . . . . after
destino (el) . . . . destiny, fate, destination
destruir . . . . to destroy
detrás . . . . behind
desván (el) . . . . attic
desvestirse (i) . . . . to undress
detalle (el) . . . . detail
detener . . . . to detain, to stop
detrás, detrás de . . . . behind
deuda (la) . . . . debt
devolver (ue) . . . . . to return (an object)
día (el) . . . . day
diadema (la) . . . . headband
diamante (el) . . . . diamond

dibujo (el) . . . . sketch, painting, drawing
dichoso/a . . . . . . lucky, happy, fortunate
diciembre . . . . December
diente (el) . . . . tooth
diestro/a . . . . right-handed
dieta (la) . . . . diet
difícil . . . . difficult
difunto/a . . . . dead
dinero (el) . . . . money
dios (el) . . . . god
diosa (la) . . . . goddess
dirigir . . . . to direct
disciplina (la) . . . . discipline
disco (el) . . . . record
disco compacto (el) . . compact disc (CD)
discoteca (la) . . . . discotheque, nightclub
discreto/a . . . . discreet
discurso (el) . . . . speech
diseñar . . . . to design
disfraz (el) . . . . disguise, costume
disfrutar de . . . . to enjoy
disparar . . . . to shoot
distinto/a . . . . different, distinct
divertirse (ie) . . . . to enjoy oneself,
to have a good time
divino/a . . . . divine
divorcio (el) . . . . divorce
doblar . . . . to fold
doble . . . . double
doler (ue) . . . . to hurt
docena (la) . . . . dozen
doler (ue) . . . . to ache, to hurt
dolor (el) . . . . pain, grief
dominar . . . . to dominate
domingo . . . . Sunday
¿dónde? . . . . where?
dorado/a . . . . golden
dormir (ue) . . . . to sleep
dos veces . . . . twice
droga (la) . . . . drug
ducha (la) . . . . shower
ducharse . . . . to take a shower
duda (la) . . . . doubt
dudoso/a . . . . doubtful
dueño/a (el/la) . . . . owner
dulce . . . . sweet
durante . . . . during
durar . . . . to last
durazno (el) . . . . peach
duro/a . . . . hard

E

echar . . . . to throw, to throw away
echar de menos . . . . . . to miss someone,
something
echar(le) la culpa a . . to blame(someone)
economía (la) . . . . economy
edad (la) . . . . age
edificio (el) . . . . building
ejercicio (el) . . . . exercise

él . . . . he, him
electricista (el/la) . . . . electrician
eléctrico/a . . . . electric
elegancia (la) . . . . elegance
elegir (i) . . . . to choose, to elect
ella . . . . she, her
ellas/os . . . . they, them
embajador (el) . . . . ambassador
embarazoso/a . . . . embarrassing
emocionado/a, ilusionado/a . . . . . excited
empatado/a . . . . tied
empezar (ie) . . . . to begin
empleado/a (el/la) . . . . employee
empleo (el) . . . . job
empresa (la) . . . . company
en . . . . in, on
en absoluto . . . . in no way
en casa . . . . at home
en seguida (enseguida) . . . . .at once
en vez de . . . . instead of
en voz alta . . . . aloud
enamorarse de . . . . . to fall in love with
encender (ie) . . . . . . to light (e.g., a fire),
                       to turn on (e.g., a light)
enchufar . . . . .to plug in
encima de . . . . on top of
encontrar (ue) . . . . to find, to meet
enemigo (el) . . . . enemy
energía nuclear (la) . . . . nuclear energy
enero . . . . January
enfadar(se) . . . . to become angry
enfermero/a (el/la) . . . . nurse
enfermo/a . . . . sick
enfrente de . . . . in front of
engañado/a . . . . tricked
engañar . . . . to deceive, to cheat
engordar . . . . to get fat
enojarse . . . . to become angry
enojo (el) . . . . anger
enorme . . . . enormous
ensalada (la) . . . . salad
ensayo (el) . . . . essay
enseñanza (la) . . . . .teaching
enseñar . . . . to teach
entender (ie) . . . . to understand
entero/a . . . . whole, entire
enterrar (ie) . . . . .to bury
entrada (la) . . . . admission, ticket,
                                        entrance
entrar . . . . to enter
entre . . . . between, among
entregar . . . . . . to deliver, to hand over,
                                      to turn in
entrenador (el), entrenadora (la)
. . . . .coach
entrenamiento (el) . . . . training
entrevista (la) . . . . interview
entrevistar . . . . .to interview
enviar . . . . .to send
envidioso/a . . . . envious, jealous
episodio (el) . . . . episode

época (la) . . . . era
equipaje (el) . . . . luggage
equipo (el) . . . . team
equivocado/a . . . . mistaken
equivocarse . . . . .to make a mistake
escalar una montaña . to scale a mountain
escalera (la) . . . . ladder, stair
escaleras (las) . . . . stairs
escapar . . . . to escape
escena (la) . . . . scene
escoba (la) . . . . broom
escoger . . . . to choose, to select
esconder . . . . to hide
escribir . . . . to write
escritor (el), escritora (la) . . . . . . .writer
escritorio (el) . . . . .desk
escuchar . . . . to listen to
escudo (el) . . . . .shield, coat of arms
escuela (la) . . . . school
escupir . . . . to spit
escurrir . . . . to strain (e.g., pasta)
ese/a . . . . that
esencial . . . . essential
esfuerzo (el) . . . . effort
esmalte de uñas (el) . . . . nail polish
espacio (el) . . . . space
espaguetis (los) . . . . spaghetti
espárrago (el) . . . . asparagus
especial . . . . special
espectáculo (el) . . . . . show, performance
espejo (el) . . . . mirror
esperar . . . . .to hope, to wait
espeso/a . . . . .thick, dense
espiar . . . . to spy
esposa (la) . . . . wife
esposo (el) . . . . .husband
esquí (el) . . . . skiing
esquina (la) . . . . corner (of a street)
esta mañana . . . . this morning
esta noche . . . . .tonight
esta tarde . . . . this afternoon
estación de tren (la) . . . . . . train station
estacionamiento (el) . . . . . . .parking lot
                                        (garage)
estacionar . . . . .to park
estadio (el) . . . . stadium
estampilla (la) . . . . .stamp
estante (el) . . . . shelf
estar . . . . to be
estar de acuerdo . . . . .to agree
estar de moda . . . . to be in style
estatua (la) . . . . .statue
este . . . . east
este/a . . . . this
estilo (el) . . . . .style
estómago (el) . . . . .stomach
estornudar . . . . to sneeze
estrecho/a . . . . .narrow
estrella (la) . . . . star
estreno (el) . . . . .debut, premiere
estudiante (el/la) . . . . .student

estudiar . . . . to study
estúpido/a, tonto/a . . . . stupid
eterno/a . . . . eternal
evitar . . . . .to avoid
examen (el) . . . . .test
excursión (la) . . . . . . excursion, trip
exigir . . . . to demand, to require
éxito (el) . . . . success
exitoso/a . . . . successful
exótico/a . . . . exotic
explicar . . . . to explain
explorador(a) (el/la) . . . . .explorer
exposición (la) . . . . art show, fair,
                                        exhibition
extranjero/a . . . . .foreign
extraño/a (raro/rara) . . . . .strange
extraordinario/a . . . . extraordinary
extraterrestre . . . . .extraterrestrial

F

fábrica (la) . . . . .factory
fabricar . . . . to manufacture
fácil .easy
falda (la) . . . . .skirt
falsificado/a . . . . fake
falta (la) . . . . .lack, absence
fama (la) . . . . fame
fantástico/a . . . . .fantastic
fascinar . . . . to fascinate
fastidiar . . . . to annoy
fe (la) . . . . .faith
febrero . . . . February
fecha (la) . . . . date
felicidad (la) . . . . happiness
felicidades (las) . . . . congratulations
felicitar . . . . to congratulate
feliz . . . . happy
fenomenal . . . . .phenomenal
feo/a .ugly
feroz . . . . fierce, ferocious
fiarse de . . . . .to trust
fideo (el) . . . . noodle
fiel . . . . faithful
fiesta (la) . . . . party
fijarse en . . . . to notice
fijo/a . . . . .fixed, firm
fila (la) . . . . row
filosofía (la) . . . . philosophy
fin de semana (el) . . . . weekend
final (el) . . . . .final, end
finca (la) . . . . .farm
fingir . . . . .to pretend, to fake
fino/a . . . . fine, delicate
firmar . . . . .to sign
firmeza (la) . . . . firmness
física (la) . . . . physics
flaco/a . . . . thin, skinny
flauta (la) . . . . .flute
flecha (la) . . . . arrow
flor (la) . . . . flower

folleto (el) . . . . brochure	
formidable . . . . wonderful, terrific	
fortuna (la) . . . . fortune	
foto (la) . . . . photo	
foto(grafía) (la) . . . . photo(graph)	
francés (el) . . . . French (language)	
franco/a . . . . frank	
frasco (el) . . . . bottle	
frase (la) . . . . sentence	
frecuentemente . . . . frequently	
fregadero (el) . . . . sink (in kitchen)	
fregar (ie) . . . . to scour, to scrub	
freír (i) . . . . to fry	
frente (la) . . . . forehead	
fresco/a . . . . fresh, cool	
frío/a . . . . cold	
frontera (la) . . . . border, frontier	
frustrado/a . . . . frustrated	
fuego (el) . . . . fire	
fuente (la) . . . . fountain	
fuerte . . . . strong	
fumar . . . . to smoke	
funcionar . . . . to work, to function	
fundar . . . . to found, to establish	
furioso/a . . . . furious, very mad	
fútbol (el) . . . . soccer	
fútbol americano (el) . . . . football	

G

gafas (las) . . . . glasses	
galería de arte (la) . . . . art gallery	
galleta (la) . . . . cookie	
gallina (la) . . . . hen	
ganar . . . . to win, to earn	
ganso (el) . . . . goose	
garaje (el) . . . . garage	
garganta (la) . . . . throat	
gasolinera (la) . . . . gas station	
gastar . . . . to spend, to waste	
gato (el) . . . . cat	
generoso/a . . . . generous	
genial . . . . . smart, original, exceptional	
gente (la) . . . . people	
geranio (el) . . . . geranium	
gerente (el) . . . . manager	
gesto (el) . . . . gesture	
gira (la) . . . . tour	
girar . . . . . . to revolve, to rotate, to turn	
globo (el) . . . . balloon	
gobernador/a (el/la) . . . . governor	
gobernar (ie) . . . . to govern	
gobierno (el) . . . . government	
gol (el) . . . . . goal (e.g., soccer, hockey)	
golpear . . . . to beat, to hit, to punch	
gordo/a . . . . fat	
gorra (la) . . . . hat, cap	
gota (la) . . . . drop (of liquid)	
gozar de . . . . to enjoy	
gracias . . . . thanks	
grabadora (la) . . . . tape recorder	

grabar . . . . to engrave, to record	
graduarse . . . . to graduate	
gran . . . . great	
grande . . . . big	
graniza . . . . it is hailing	
granizar . . . . to hail	
granja (la) . . . . farm	
gratis . . . . free	
grave . . . . serious	
grifo (el) . . . . faucet	
gris . . . . grey	
gritar . . . . to shout	
grosero/a . . . . rude, crude	
guante (el) . . . . glove	
guantes (los) . . . . gloves	
guapo/a . . . . good-looking	
guardar . . . . to guard, to keep	
guardar silencio . . . . to keep silent	
guerra (la) . . . . war	
guerrero/a (el/la) . . . . warrior	
guerrillero/a (el/la) . . . . guerrilla	
guía (el/la) . . . . tour guide	
guitarra (la) . . . . guitar	
gusto (el) . . . . taste	

H

había . . . . there was, there were	
hábil . . . . clever, intelligent	
habitación doble (la) . . . . . double room	
hablar . . . . to talk, to speak	
hacer . . . . to do, to make	
hacer caso . . . . to pay attention to	
hacer cola . . . . to wait in line	
hacer la maleta . . . . to pack	
hacer un viaje . . . . to take a trip	
hacer una pregunta . . . . to ask a question	
hacia . . . . towards	
hallar . . . . to find	
hamburguesa (la) . . . . hamburger	
harina (la) . . . . flour	
harto/a . . . . fed up, enough	
hasta . . . . until	
hasta luego . . . . see you later	
hay . . . . there is, there are	
hecho (el) . . . . fact	
hecho/a a mano . . . . handmade	
heladería (la) . . . . ice cream store	
helado (el) . . . . ice cream	
helar (ie) . . . . to freeze	
helicóptero (el) . . . . helicopter	
hemisferio (el) . . . . hemisphere	
heredar . . . . to inherit	
herida (la) . . . . wound, injury	
herido/a . . . . wounded	
herir (ie) . . . . to wound	
hermana (la) . . . . sister	
hermano (el) . . . . brother	
héroe (el) . . . . hero	
heroína (la) . . . . heroine	
herramienta (la) . . . . tool	

hervir (ie) . . . . to boil	
hielo (el) . . . . ice	
hierba (la) . . . . grass	
higiene (la) . . . . hygiene	
hija (la) . . . . daughter	
hijo (el) . . . . son	
himno (el) . . . . hymn	
historia (la) . . . . history, story	
hockey sobre hielo (el) . . . . . . ice hockey	
hogar (el) . . . . home, hearth	
hoja (la) . . . . leaf	
hombre (el) . . . . man	
hondo/a . . . . deep	
hora (la) . . . . hour	
horario (el) . . . . schedule	
(horno de) microondas (el)	
. . . . microwave (oven)	
hotel (el) . . . . hotel	
hoy . . . . today	
huelga (la) . . . . strike	
huevo (el) . . . . egg	
humilde . . . . humble	
huracán (el) . . . . hurricane	

I

idéntico/a . . . . identical	
idioma (el) . . . . language	
iglesia (la) . . . . church	
ilegal . . . . illegal	
ilustre . . . . illustrious	
imagen (la) . . . . image	
imbécil . . . . imbecile	
impedir (i) . . . . to prevent	
impermeable (el) . . . . raincoat	
impresionante . . . . impressive	
impreso/a . . . . printed	
imprimir . . . . to print	
impuesto (el) . . . . tax	
incendio (el) . . . . fire	
incluso . . . . including, even (adv.)	
incómodo/a . . . . uncomfortable	
increíble . . . . incredible	
infancia (la) . . . . childhood	
infeliz . . . . unhappy	
inferior . . . . inferior, lower	
informe (el) . . . . report	
ingeniero/a (el/la) . . . . engineer	
ingenuo/a . . . . naive	
inglés (el) . . . . English	
ingrediente (el) . . . . ingredient	
inmortal . . . . immortal	
insistir en . . . . to insist on	
insoportable . . . . unbearable, intolerable	
inspiración (la) . . . . inspiration	
instalar . . . . to install	
instinto (el) . . . . instinct	
instrucciones (las) . . . . instructions	
insultar . . . . to insult	
integridad (la) . . . . integrity	
intenso/a . . . . intense	

intentar . . . . to try, to attempt
interés (el) . . . . interest
interesante . . . . interesting
internacional . . . . international
interrumpir . . . . to interrupt
íntimo/a . . . . intimate, close
inútil . . . . useless
invertir (ie) . . . . to invest (money)
invierno (el) . . . . winter
invitado/a (el/la) . . . . guest
invitar . . . . to invite
ir . . . . to go
ir de camping . . . . to go camping
ir de compras . . . . to go shopping
ir de viaje . . . . to travel
irritar . . . . to irritate
isla (la) . . . . island
izquierdo/a . . . . left

J

jabón (el) . . . . soap
jamón (el) . . . . ham
japonés (el) . . . . Japanese
jardín (el) . . . . garden
jardín botánico (el) . . . . botanical garden
jardín (parque) zoológico (el) . . . . zoo
jardinero/a (el/la) . . . . gardener
jaula (la) . . . . cage
jefa (la) . . . . boss
jefe (el) . . . . boss
jirafa (la) . . . . giraffe
jonrón (el) . . . . homerun
jóvenes (los) . . . . youth, youngsters
joyería (la) . . . . jewelry
jubilado/a . . . . retired
judío/a . . . . Jewish
jueves . . . . Thursday
juez/jueza (el/la) . . . . judge
jugador/a (el/la) . . . . player
jugar (ue) . . . . to play
jugo (el) . . . . juice
juicio (el) . . . . judgement, trial
julio . . . . July
junio . . . . June
juntos/as . . . . together
jurar . . . . to swear
justo/a . . . . just, fair, appropriate
juventud (la) . . . . youth
juzgar . . . . to judge

L

lacio/a . . . . straight (e.g., hair)
lado (el) . . . . side
ladrar . . . . to bark
ladrón (el) . . . . robber
ladrona (la) . . . . robber
lago (el) . . . . lake
lágrima (la) . . . . tear
lamentar . . . . to regret

lámpara (la) . . . . lamp, light
langosta (la) . . . . lobster
lanzador (el) . . . . pitcher
lanzar . . . . . . to throw, to hurl, to pitch
lápiz (el) . . . . pencil
lápiz de labios (el pintalabios) . . lipstick
largo/a . . . . long
lata (la) . . . . can
lavabo (el) . . . . sink (in bathroom)
lavadora (la) . . . . washer
lavaplatos (el) . . . . dishwasher
lavar . . . . to wash
lavarse . . . . to wash oneself
leal . . . . loyal
lección (la) . . . . lesson
leche (la) . . . . milk
lector/a (el/la) . . . . reader
leer . . . . to read
lejano/a . . . . distant
lejos . . . . far (away)
lejos de . . . . far from
lengua (la) . . . . tongue, language
lentes de contacto (los, las)
. . . . contact lenses
lentilla (la) . . . . contact lens
lentillas (las) . . . . contact lenses
lento/a . . . . slow
leña (la) . . . . firewood
león (el) . . . . lion
lesión (la) . . . . injury
lesionado/a . . . . injured
letra (la) . . . . lyrics, letter
levantarse . . . . to get up
leve . . . . slight, light
leyenda (la) . . . . legend
libertad (la) . . . . liberty
libra (la) . . . . pound
libre . . . . free, available
libro (el) . . . . book
licencia (la) . . . . license
líder (el) . . . . leader
ligero/a . . . . light
limón (el) . . . . lemon
limonada (la) . . . . lemonade
limpiar . . . . to clean
limpio/a . . . . clean
lindo/a . . . . pretty
liso/a . . . . smooth, flat
listo/a . . . . ready, clever, smart
loco/a . . . . crazy
locura (la) . . . . madness, insanity, folly
lograr . . . . to obtain, to succeed in
loro (el) . . . . parrot
lotería (la) . . . . lottery
luchador (el) . . . . wrestler
luchar . . . . . . to fight, to struggle
lucir . . . . to shine
luego . . . . later
luminoso/a . . . . bright, brilliant
luna (la) . . . . moon
luna de miel (la) . . . . honeymoon

lunes . . . . Monday
lupa (la) . . . . magnifying glass
luz (la) . . . . light

LL

llama (la) . . . . llama
llamar . . . . to call
llave (la) . . . . key
llegada (la) . . . . arrival
llegar . . . . to arrive
llenar . . . . to fill
lleno/a . . . . full
llevar . . . . to take, to carry
llevarse bien (mal) con
. . . . to get along well (badly) with
llorar . . . . to cry
llover (ue) . . . . to rain
lluvia (la) . . . . rain

M

madera (la) . . . . wood
madrastra (la) . . . . stepmother
madre (la) . . . . mother
madrina (la) . . . . godmother
madrugada (la) . . . . dawn
maduro/a . . . . mature, ripe
maestría (la) . . . . master's degree
maestro/a (el/la) . . . . teacher
mal . . . . bad, poorly
malcriado/a . . . . . ill-bred, bad-mannered
maldito/a . . . . accursed, damned
maleducado/a . . . . rude
maleta (la) . . . . suitcase
malo/a . . . . bad
mancha (la) . . . . stain
manchado/a . . . . stained
mandar . . . . to order, to send
mandón (m.) . . . . bossy
mandona (f.) . . . . bossy
mano (la) . . . . hand
manta (la) . . . . blanket
mantel (el) . . . . tablecloth
mantener . . . . to maintain, to keep
mantequilla (la) . . . . butter
manzana (la) . . . . apple
mañana . . . . tomorrow
mapa (el) . . . . map
máquina (la) . . . . machine
mar (el) . . . . sea
maravilla (la) . . . . marvel
maravilloso/a . . . wonderful, marvelous
marcharse . . . . to go away
marciano (el) . . . . Martian
marido (el) . . . . husband
marinero/a (el/la) . . . . sailor
marisco (el) . . . . seafood, shellfish
martillo (el) . . . . hammer
marrón . . . . brown
martes . . . . Tuesday

marzo . . . . March
más . . . . more
masticar . . . . to chew
matar . . . . .to kill
matemáticas (las) . . . . math
matrícula (la) . . . . tuition
maullar . . . . to meow (like a cat)
mayo . . . . .May
mayor . . . . older
medalla (la) . . . . medal
mediano/a . . . . .medium, average
medianoche (la) . . . . midnight
médico/a (el/la) . . . . doctor
mediodía (el) . . . . noon
medir (i) . . . . .to measure
mejor . . . . .better, best
melancólico/a . . . . . gloomy, melancholy
melocotón (el) . . . . peach
melodía (la) . . . . melody
mencionar . . . . to mention
menor . . . . younger
menos . . . . less
mensaje (el) . . . . message
mentir (ie) . . . . to lie, to fib
mentira (la) . . . . lie
mentiroso/a . . . . lying, untruthful
mercado (el) . . . . market
merecer . . . . to deserve, to merit
mes (el) . . . . month
mesa (la) . . . . table
meta (la) . . . . goal (objective)
meteorólogo (el) . . . . meteorologist
meter . . . . to put into
método (el) . . . . method
metro (el) . . . . .metro, subway
mezclado/a . . . . mixed
mezclar . . . . to mix
mezquita (la) . . . . mosque
mientras . . . . while
miércoles . . . . Wednesday
miga (la) . . . . crumb
mil . . . . thousand
milagro (el) . . . . miracle
milla (la) . . . . .mile
millón . . . . .million
mimado/a . . . . .spoiled
ministro (el) . . . . minister
mirar . . . . .to look at
misa (la) . . . . mass (church)
mismo/a . . . . same
misterio (el) . . . . mystery
misterioso/a . . . . .mysterious
mochila (la) . . . . .backpack
moda (la) . . . . .style, fashion
modesto/a . . . . .modest
mofeta (la) (el zorrillo) . . . . .skunk
mojado/a . . . . wet
mojar . . . . to wet, to moisten
molestar . . . . to bother
monasterio (el) . . . . monastery
moneda (la) . . . . coin

monja (la) . . . . nun
monje (el) . . . . .monk
montaña (la) . . . . .mountain
montar en bicicleta . . . . .to ride a bicycle
montar un negocio . . . to start a business
montón (el) . . . . .heap, pile
morado/a . . . . purple
morder (ue) . . . . to bite
moreno/a . . . . .brunette, brown
morir (ue) . . . . .to die
mosca (la) . . . . fly
mostrar (ue) . . . . to show
moto(cicleta) (la) . . . . motorcycle
mover (ue) . . . . .to move
móvil (el) . . . . .cellphone
mucho .a lot
muchos/as . . . . many
mudarse . . . . .to move (relocate)
mudo/a . . . . .mute, dumb
mujer (la) . . . . woman
mula (la) . . . . mule
multa (la) . . . . fine
mundo (el) . . . . .world
muñeca (la) . . . . doll, wrist
museo (el) . . . . .museum
música (la) . . . . .music
músico/a (el/la) . . . . musician
musulmán . . . . Muslim
mutuo/a . . . . .mutual
muy . . . . .very

N

nacer . . . . to be born
nada . . . . nothing
nadar . . . . to swim
nadie . . . . no one
naranja (la) . . . . orange
nariz (la) . . . . .nose
nata (batida) (la) . . . . . (whipped) cream
natación (la) . . . . swimming
naturaleza (la) . . . . nature
nave (la) . . . . ship
navegar . . . . to sail
necesitar . . . . to need
necio/a . . . . stupid, foolish
negar (ie) . . . . to deny
negocio (el) . . . . .business
negro/a . . . . black
nevar (ie) . . . . to snow
nevera (la) . . . . refrigerator
ni . . . . neither, nor
niebla (la) . . . . .fog
nieta (la) . . . . granddaughter
nieto (el) . . . . grandson
nieve (la) . . . . snow
ninguno/a . . . . none
nivel (el) . . . . level
niña (la) .girl
niñero/a (el, la) . . . . babysitter

niñez (la) . . . . childhood
niño (el) . . . . boy
no . . . . no
noche (la) . . . . night
nombrar . . . . .to name
noreste (el) . . . . northeast
noroeste (el) . . . . northwest
norte . . . . north
nosotros/as . . . . we
noticias (las) . . . . news
novela (la) . . . . novel
novia (la) . . . . . . bride, fiancée, girlfriend
noviazgo (el) . . . . .engagement
noviembre . . . . November
novio (el) . . . . . groom, fiancé, boyfriend
nublado/a . . . . cloudy
nuevo/a . . . . new
nunca . . . . never

O

obra (la) . . . . work
obrero/a (el/la) . . . . .worker
o(b)scuro/a . . . . .dark, obscure
obstinado/a (terco) . . stubborn, obstinate
occidental . . . . western
océano (el) . . . . .ocean
octubre . . . . October
ocultar . . . . to hide
ocupado/a . . . . .busy
ocurrir . . . . to occur, to happen
odiar . . . . to hate
oeste . . . . .west
ofender . . . . to offend
oficina (la) . . . . .office
ofrecer . . . . to offer
oír . . . . .to hear
ojalá . . . . if only
ojo (el) . . . . .eye
ola (la) . . . . wave
oler (ue) . . . . to smell
olla (la) . . . . .pot
optimista (el/la) . . . . optimist
opuesto (el) (n.) . . . . .opposite
opuesto/a (adj.) . . . . .opposite
ordenador (el) . . . . computer (Spain)
ordinario/a . . . . .ordinary
organizar . . . . to organize
órgano (el) . . . . .organ
orgullo (el) . . . . pride
orgulloso/a . . . . .proud
oriental . . . . .eastern
original . . . . original
orilla (la) . . bank, shore (of river, ocean)
oro (el) . . . . gold
orquesta (la) . . . . orchestra
oscuridad (la) . . . . darkness
oscuro/a . . . . dark
oso (el) . . . . bear
ostra (la) . . . . oyster

otoñal . . . . autumnal
otoño (el) . . . . fall
otra vez, de nuevo . . . . again
otro/a . . . . another, other
oveja (la) . . . . sheep

P

padre (el) . . . . father
padrino (el) . . . . godfather
padrino de boda (el) . . . . best man
pagar . . . . to pay
país (el) . . . . country
paisaje (el) . . . . landscape, scenery
pájaro (el) . . . . bird
pala (la) . . . . shovel
palabra (la) . . . . word
palacio (el) . . . . palace
pálido/a . . . . pale
palomitas (las) . . . . popcorn
pampas (las) . . . . plains
pan (el) . . . . bread
panadero/a (el/la) . . . . baker
pantalla (la) . . . . screen
pantalones (los) . . . . pants
pantalones cortos (los) . . . . shorts
pañuelo (el) . . . . handkerchief, scarf
papa (la) . . . . potato
papel (el) . . . . paper
paquete (el) . . . . package
par . . . . pair
para . . . . by, for, in order to
para que . . . . in order that
para siempre . . . . forever
parabrisas (el) . . . . windshield
paraguas (el) . . . . umbrella
parar . . . . to stop
parecer . . . . to seem, to appear
parecerse a . . . . to resemble
pared (la) . . . . wall
pareja (la) . . . . pair, couple
pariente (el) . . . . relative
parrilla (la) . . . . grill
parque (el) . . . . park
parque de atracciones (el)
. . . . amusement park
partido (el) . . . . game
pasado/a . . . . past, last
pasajero/a (e/la) . . . . passenger
pasaporte (el) . . . . passport
pasar . . . . to pass
pasar (tiempo) . . . . to spend (time)
pasar la aspiradora . . . . to vacuum
pasárselo bien/mal . . . . . to have a great/
bad time
pasear . . . . to take a stroll
paseo (el) . . . . stroll, trip
pasillo (el) . . . . hallway
pastel (el) . . . . cake
pastilla (la) . . . . pill
patata (la) . . . . potato

patinador (el) . . . . skater
patinaje (el) . . . . skating
patinar . . . . to skate
patines (los) . . . . skates
patria (la) . . . . country, homeland
payaso (el) . . . . clown
pecado (el) . . . . sin
pedazo (el) . . . . piece
pedir (i) . . . . . . to ask for, to order (food)
pedir (i) prestado . . . . to borrow
pegar . . . . to hit
peinado (el) . . . . hairdo, hairstyle
peinado/a . . . . combed
peinar . . . . to comb
peinarse . . . . to comb one's hair
pelea (la) . . . . fight
pelear . . . . to fight
película (la) . . . . film (used in a
camera), movie
peligro (el) . . . . danger
pelirrojo/a . . . . red-headed
pelo (el) . . . . hair
pelota (la) . . . . ball
pelotero (el) . . . . ballplayer
peluquero/a (el/la) . . barber, hairdresser
pena (la) . . . . pain
pendiente (el) . . . . earring
pendientes (los) . . . . earrings
penoso/a . . . . painful
pensar (ie) . . . . to think
pensar en . . . . to think about
peor . . . . worse, worst
pequeño/a . . . . small
pera (la) . . . . pear
percha (la) . . . . hanger
perder (ie) . . . . to lose
perder (tiempo) . . . . to waste (time)
perdonar . . . . to pardon
perezoso/a . . . . lazy
periódico (el) . . . . newspaper
permiso (el) . . . . permission
permitir . . . . to permit, to allow
perro (el) . . . . dog
perrito caliente (el) . . . . hot dog
perseguir (i) . . . . to pursue, to persecute
pertenecer a . . . . to belong to
pesado/a . . . . heavy, annoying
pescado (el) . . . . fish
pesas (las) . . . . weights
pescar . . . . to fish
pesimista (el/la) . . . . pessimist
peso (el) . . . . weight
petróleo (el) . . . . oil, petroleum
pez (el) . . . . fish
piano (el) . . . . piano
picadura (la) (de mosquito)
. . . . (mosquito) bite
pícaro/a . . . . roguish, rascally
pie (el) . . . . foot
piedra (la) . . . . stone, rock
piel (la) . . . . skin

pierna (la) . . . . leg
pimienta (la) . . . . pepper
pino (el) . . . . pine tree
(el) pintalabios (lápiz de labios) . lipstick
pintar . . . . to paint
pintor/a (el/la) . . . . painter
pintoresco/a . . . . picturesque
pintura (la) . . . . painting
piscina (la) . . . . swimming pool
piso (el) . . . . floor
pizarra (la) . . . . blackboard
placer . . . . to please
planchar . . . . to iron
planeta (el) . . . . planet
plástico (el) . . . . plastic
plátano (el) . . . . plantain, banana
plato (el) . . . . plate, dish
playa (la) . . . . beach
plazo (el) . . . . period of time
pluma (la) . . . . pen
pobre . . . . poor
poco . . . . a little
poder (ue) . . . . to be able to
poderoso/a . . . . powerful
poesía (la) . . . . poetry
poetisa (la) . . . . poet
poliéster (el) . . . . polyester
política (la) . . . . politics
político/a . . . . political
pollo (el) . . . . chicken
poner . . . . to put
poner la mesa . . . . to set the table
ponerse . . . . to put on
por . . . . by, for, through
por consiguiente . . . . consequently
por desgracia . . . . unfortunately
por ejemplo . . . . for example
por eso . . . . therefore, so
por fin . . . . finally
por qué . . . . why?
por supuesto . . . . of course
porcentaje . . . . percentage
porque . . . . because
portada (la) . . . . cover
portal cibernético (el) . . . . website
portarse bien/mal . . . . to behave
well/poorly
portero/a (el/la) . . . . goalie
porvenir (el) . . . . future
postal . . . . postcard
postizo/a . . . . false, fake
postre (el) . . . . dessert
precio (el) . . . . price
precioso/a . . . . precious, cute
preciso/a . . . . . necessary, precise, clear
preferir (ie) . . . . to prefer
premiar . . . . to reward
premio (el) . . . . prize
prender . . . . to turn on (lights, etc.)
prensa (la) . . . . press (media)
preocupado/a . . . . worried, upset

preocuparse. . . . . to worry
preparar . . . . to prepare
presentación (la). . . . . .presentation
prestar. to lend
prestar atención . . . . . . to pay attention
pretender. . . . . to aspire to, to seek,
to claim to be
primavera (la). . . . . spring
primero/a. . . . . first
primo/a (el/la). . . . . cousin
principio (el). . . . . beginning
prisa . . . . hurry
probar (ue) . . . . to try, to taste
problema (el). . . . . .problem
producir. . . . . to produce
profesor (el) . . . . .teacher
profesora (la) . . . . .teacher
profundo/a. . . . . .deep
prohibir . . . . to prohibit
prometer . . . . to promise
pronto . . . . .soon
propina (la). . tip (e.g., given to a waiter)
propio/a. . . . . .own, proper
proteger. . . . . .to protect
protegido/a . . . . protected
próximo/a . . . . next
proyecto (el) . . . . .project
prueba (la) . . . . .proof, quiz, test
pueblo (el). . . . . town, village
puerta (la). . . . . .door
pues. well, so
puesta del sol (la) . . . . sunset
pulido/a. . . . . .polished
pulir. . . . . to polish
pulmón (el) . . . . lung
pulsera (la) . . . . bracelet
punto (el). . . . . point
puntualmente. . . . . punctually
pupitre (el) . . . . student desk

Q

que. . . . . that, which
¿qué?. . . . . .what?, which?
qué. . . . . what
quebrado/a . . . . .broken
quebrarse . . . . to break
quedar. . . . . .to remain
queja (la). . . . . complaint
quejarse de . . . . . . to complain (about)
quemado/a. . . . . burnt
quemar . . . . .to burn
querer (ie) . . . . . to wish, to want, to like
querido/a. . . . . dear
queso (el). . . . . cheese
¿quién? . . . . who?
química (la). . . . . chemistry
quiosco (el) . . . . newspaper stand
quitarse . . . . to take off

R

rabino (el). . . . . rabbi
radio (el/la). . . . . radio
raíz (la) . . . . root
rana (la) . . . . frog
rápidamente . . . . quickly
raqueta (la). . . . . racquet
raro/a . . . . rare, strange
rascacielos (el) . . . . skyscraper
rastrillo (el). . . . . rake
ratón (el) . . . . mouse
rayas (las) . . . . stripes
real . . . . real, royal
realidad (la) . . . . reality
realizar . . . . to realize
(e.g., a dream, a goal)
receta (la) . . . . recipe, prescription
recibir . . . . to receive
recibo (el) . . . . receipt
recién. . . . . recent, recently
reciente . . . . recent
recoger . . . . to collect
recomendar (ie) . . . . to recommend
recordar (ue). . . . . to remember
recuperar. . . . . to recover
red (la) . . . . net, network
redondo/a . . . . .round
referir (ie) . . . . to refer
reflejar. . . . . to reflect
reflexionar. . . . . . to think over, to reflect
refrigerador (el) . . . . refrigerator
regalar. . . . . to give a present, gift
regalo (el) . . . . .present
regar (ie). . . . . to water
regresar. . . . . to return
reina (la) . . . . .queen
reinar. . . . . to reign
reír (i) . . . . .to laugh
relación (la) . . . . relationship
relámpago (el). . . . . lightning
relajarse . . . . to relax
reloj (el) . . . . clock, watch
remo (el) . . . . .rowing
remoto/a . . . . .remote
reñir (i) . . . . to scold
renovar (ue) . . . . to renovate
renunciar. . . . . to resign, to quit
repaso (el). . . . . review
repetir (i). . . . . to repeat
reportero/a (el/la). . . . . reporter
representante (el) . . . . . . representative
requesón . . . . .cottage cheese
resbaladizo/a. . . . . slippery
reservación (la). . . . . reservation
residencia (la). . . . residence, dormitory
resolver (ue) . . . . to resolve, to solve
a problem
respetar. . . . . .to respect
respirar. . . . . to breathe
respuesta (la) . . . . .answer, reply

restaurante (el) . . . . restaurant
restaurar . . . . .to restore
resultado (el). . . . . result
resumen (el) . . . . summary
retrato (el). . . . . picture, portrait
reunión (la) . . . . meeting, reunion
revelar. . . . . to reveal
revista (la). . . . . .magazine
rey (el). . . . . king
rezar . . . . .to pray
rincón (el) . . . . corner
rico/a. rich
riesgo (el) . . . . risk
rígido/a . . . . .rigid
río (el) . . . . .river
risa (la) . . . . laugh, laughter
risueño/a . . . . smiling, cheerful
ritmo (el) . . . . .rhythm
rizado/a . . . . curly
roble (el) . . . . oak
rodear . . . . to surround
rogar (ue) . . . . to beg
rojo/a. . . . . .red
romper. . . . . .to break
roncar . . . . to snore
ropa (la) . . . . .clothes
ropa interior (la). . . . . underwear
rosa (la). . . . . rose
rosado/a . . . . pink
roto/a. . . . . broken
rubio/a. . . . . .blond(e)
ruido (el) . . . . noise
ruidoso/a . . . . noisy
ruinas (las) . . . . ruins
rumbo (el) . . . . .direction, road
ruta (la). . . . . route

S

sábado (el) . . . . Saturday
saber . . . . to know (a fact)
saber de memoria . . . . . to know by heart
sabiduría (la) . . . . .knowledge
sabio/a. . . . . wise, learned
sabroso/a. . . . . tasty, delicious
sacacorchos (el) . . . . corkscrew
sacapuntas (el) . . . . pencil sharpener
sacar . . . . .to take out
sacar (fotos) . . . . .to take (pictures)
sacar (prestado) un libro
. . . . to check out a book
saco de dormir . . . . sleeping bag
sacrificio (el). . . . . .sacrifice
sagrado/a . . . . sacred
sal (la) .salt
sala (de estar) (la) . . . . living room
salado/a. . . . . .salty
salchicha (la) . . . . sausage
salida (la) . . . . exit
salida del sol (la) . . . . sunrise
salir. . . . . to leave

salirse con la suya . . . to have one's way
saludo (el) . . . . greeting
salvo/a . . . . safe
sano/a . . . . healthy
santo (el) . . . . saint
sargento (el) . . . . sargent
sartén (el/la) . . . . frying pan
satisfacer . . . . to satisfy
satisfecho/a . . . . satisfied
saxofón (el) . . . . saxophone
secadora (la) . . . . dryer
secadora de pelo (la) . . . . . . hair dryer
seco/a . . . . dry
secretario/a (el/la) . . . . secretary
secreto (el) . . . . secret
seda (la) . . . . silk
seguir (i) . . . . to follow
según . . . . according to
segundo/a . . . . second
seguridad (la) . . . . . . security, certainty
seguro/a . . . . sure, secure
selva (la) . . . . jungle
semáforo(el) . . . . traffic light
semana (la) . . . . week
semanal . . . . weekly
semejante . . . . similar
senador/a (el/la) . . . . senator
sencillo/a . . . . simple
sentar (ie) . . . . to seat (someone)
sentarse (ie) . . . . to sit down
sentimiento (el) . . . . . feeling, sentiment
sentir (ie) . . . . to feel, to regret
separado/a . . . . separate
separar . . . . to separate
septiembre . . . . September
ser . . . . to be
ser humano (el) . . . . human being
serie (la) . . . . series
serio/a . . . . serious
serpiente (la) . . . . serpent, snake
servilleta (la) . . . . napkin
servir (i) . . . . to serve
si . . . . if
sí . . . . yes
siempre . . . . always
siglo (el) . . . . century
siguiente . . . . following, next
silbar . . . . to whistle
silla (la) . . . . seat, chair
sillón (el) . . . . armchair
símbolo (el) . . . . symbol
simpático/a . . . . likeable, nice
sin . . . . without
sinfonía (la) . . . . symphony
sinagoga (la) . . . . synagogue
sistema (el) . . . . system
sitio (el) . . . . site, place
soberbio/a . . . . proud, haughty
sobrar . . . . to remain, to be left over
sobre . . . . about, over, on top of
sobrevivir . . . . to survive

sobrina (la) . . . . niece
sobrino (el) . . . . nephew
sofá (el) . . . . sofa
soldado (el) . . . . soldier
soledad (la) . . . . solitude, loneliness
sólo . . . . only
solo/a . . . . alone
sombrero (el) . . . . hat
sonar (ue) . . . . to ring
soñar (ue) con . . . . . to dream about
sonido (el) . . . . sound
sonreír (i) . . . . to smile
sopa (la) . . . . soup
soplar . . . . to blow
sordo/a . . . . deaf
sorprendido/a . . . . surprised
sorpresa (la) . . . . surprise
soso/a . . . . lacking salt, bland
sospechar . . . . to suspect
sótano (el) . . . . basement
suave . . . . soft, smooth
suavemente . . . . suavely, smoothly
subir . . . . to go up, to get on (a bus, etc.)
subrayar . . . . to underline
suceder . . . . to happen
sucio/a . . . . dirty
sucursal (la) . . . . branch (office)
sudar . . . . to sweat
suegra (la) . . . . mother-in-law
suegro (el) . . . . father-in-law
sueldo (el) . . . . salary
suelo (el) . . . . floor
suelto/a . . . . loose
suerte (la) . . . . luck
suéter (el) . . . . sweater
sugerir (ie) . . . . to suggest
superior . . . . superior, upper
supermercado (el) . . . . supermarket
suponer . . . . to suppose
sur . . . . south
sureste (el) . . . . southeast
suroeste (el) . . . . southwest
susurrar . . . . to whisper
susurro (el) . . . . whisper

T

tacaño/a . . . . stingy
tailandés/a . . . . Thai
tal vez . . . . perhaps
talento (el) . . . . talent
tamaño (el) . . . . size
también . . . . also
tambores (los) . . . . drums
tan . . . . so
tanto (adv.) . . . . so much
tantos/as . . . . so many
tapar . . . . to cover
tarde . . . . late
tarea (la) . . . . task, assignment,
                                      homework

tarjeta (la) . . . . card, postcard
tarjeta postal (la) . . . . postcard
tatuaje (el) . . . . tattoo
taxi (el) . . . . taxi
taza (la) . . . . cup
té (el) . . . . tea
teatro (el) . . . . theater
tejado (el) . . . . roof
tejer . . . . to knit
tela (la) . . . . cloth, material
telaraña (la) . . . . spider web
teléfono (el) . . . . telephone
teléfono celular (el) . . . . cellphone
telenovela (la) . . . . soap opera
telescopio (el) . . . . telescope
televisión (la) . . . . television
televisor (el) . . . . television set
tema (el) . . . . theme
temer . . . . to fear
tempestad (la) . . . . storm
templo (el) . . . . temple
temporada (la)
. . . . season (e.g., sports season)
temprano . . . . early
tenedor (el) . . . . fork
tener . . . . to have
tener en cuenta . . . . to take into
                                      consideration
tener éxito . . . . to be successful
tener lugar . . . . to take place
tener prisa . . . . to be in a hurry
tener que ver con . . . . to have to do with
tener razón . . . . to be right
tener vergüenza . . . . to be ashamed
teñir (i) . . . . to dye
tenis (el) . . . . tennis
tercero/a . . . . third
terco/a . . . . stubborn
terminar . . . . to finish
terremoto (el) . . . . earthquake
tesorero/a (el/la) . . . . treasurer
tesoro (el) . . . . treasure
testigo (el) . . . . witness
texto (el) . . . . text
tía (la) . . . . aunt
tiburón (el) . . . . shark
tiempo (el) . . . . time
tienda (la) . . . . store
tienda de campaña (la) . . . . tent
tierra (la) . . . . soil, earth
tigre (el) . . . . tiger
tijeras (las) . . . . scissors
timbre (el) . . . . bell
tío (el) . . . . uncle
tipo (el) . . . . type
típico/a . . . . typical
tirano (el) . . . . tyrant
tiroteo (el) . . . . shooting
título (el) . . . . title
tiza (la) . . . . chalk
toalla (la) . . . . towel

tocadiscos (el) . . . . record player
tocador (el) . . . . dresser
tocar . . to play (an instrument), to touch
tocino (el) . . . . bacon
todavía . . . . still
todavía no . . . . not yet
todo . . . . all
tomar apuntes . . . . to take notes
tomar el pelo . . to tease, to pull one's leg
tomar una decisión . . . to make a decision
tomate (el) . . . . tomato
tonto/a . . . . foolish
torcer (ue) . . . . to twist, to bend
torero/a (el/la) . . . . bullfighter
tormenta (la) . . . . storm
torneo (el) . . . . tournament
torre (la) . . . . tower
torta (la) . . . . cake
tortuga (la) . . . . turtle
toser . . . . to cough
tostador (el) . . . . toaster
trabajar . . . . to work
traducir . . . . to translate
traer . . . . to bring
tragar . . . . to swallow
traje (el) . . . . suit
traje de baño (el) . . . . swimsuit
trama (la) . . . . plot (of a story)
tranquilamente . . . . calmly
tranquilo/a . . . . calm
tras . . . . behind, after
trasero/a . . . . back, rear (adj)
tratar (de) . . . . to try
tren (el) . . . . train
trigo (el) . . . . wheat
trineo (el) . . . . sled, sleigh
triste . . . . sad
triunfar . . . . to triumph
trofeo (el) . . . . trophy
trombón (el) . . . . trombone
trompeta (la) . . . . trumpet
tropezar (ie) . . . . to trip
tropical . . . . tropical
trozo (el) . . . . bit, piece, selection
trueno (el) . . . . thunder
tú . . . . you (familiar)
tulipán (el) . . . . tulip
tumba (la) . . . . tomb
túnel (el) . . . . tunnel

U

último/a . . . . last (of a group)
una vez . . . . once
único/a . . . . only, unique
universidad (la) . . . . university
universo (el) . . . . universe
uno/a . . . . a, an
unos/as . . . . some
uña (la) . . . . fingernail, toenail
urgente . . . . urgent

usted (Ud.) . . . . you (formal)
ustedes (Uds.) . . . . you all (formal)
uva (la) . . . . grape

V

vaca (la) . . . . cow
vacaciones (las) . . . . vacation
vacío/a . . . . empty
vagón (el) . . . . car (of train)
valer . . . . to be worth
valer (no) la pena . . . . to (not) be
worth the trouble
valle (el) . . . . valley
vaqueros (los) . . . . jeans
varios/as . . . . several, various
vaso (el) . . . . glass
vecino/a (el/la) . . . . neighbor
vegetal (el) . . . . vegetable
vela (la) . . . . candle, sailing
velocidad (la) . . . . speed
vejez (la) . . . . old age
vencer . . . . to defeat, to expire
vencimiento (el) . . . . expiration
vender . . . . to sell
veneno (el) . . . . poison
venganza (la) . . . . . . revenge, vengeance
venir . . . . to come
ventaja (la) . . . . advantage
ventana (la) . . . . window
ventilador (el) . . . . fan
ver . . . . to see
verano (el) . . . . summer
verdad (la) . . . . truth
¿verdad? . . . . isn't that so?
verdadero/a . . . . true, real
verde . . . . green
verdura (la) . . . . vegetable
vergüenza (la) . . . . embarrassment,
shame
vestido (el) . . . . dress
veterinario/a (el/la) . . . . veterinarian
viajar . . . . to travel
viaje (el) . . . . trip
víctima (la) . . . . victim
vídeo (el), video (el) . . . . VCR, video
viejo/a . . . . old
viento (el) . . . . wind
viernes (el) . . . . Friday
vino (el) . . . . wine
violencia (la) . . . . violence
violín (el) . . . . violin
virtud (la) . . . . virtue
viudo/a (el/la) . . . . widower, widow
vivir . . . . to live
volar (ue) . . . . to fly
volcán (el) . . . . volcano
volver (ue) . . . . to return
volverse loco/a . . . . to go crazy
vosotros/as . . . . you all (familiar)
voto (el) . . . . vote

vuelo (el) . . . . flight
vulgar . . . . common, ordinary

Y

y . . . . and
ya . . . . already
ya no . . . . no longer, anymore
yo I

Z

zanahoria (la) . . . . carrot
zapatero/a (el/la) . . . . cobbler, shoemaker
zapato (el) . . . . shoe
zoológico (el) . . . . zoo
zorrillo (el) (la mofeta) . . . . skunk
zorro (el) . . . . fox
zurdo/a . . . . left-handed

DICCIONARIO INGLÉS-ESPAÑOL

A

a, an . . . . *uno/a*
abandon (to) . . . . *abandonar*
able (to be) (to) . . . . *poder (ue)*
abnormal . . . . *anormal*
about, over, on top of . . . . *sobre*
abrupt, sudden . . . . *brusco/a*
absence, lack . . . . *(la) falta*
accident . . . . *(el) accidente*
accompany (to) . . . . *acompañar*
according to . . . . *según*
accordion . . . . *(el) acordeón*
accursed, damned . . . . *maldito/a*
accuse (to) . . . . *acusar*
ache (to), to hurt . . . . *doler (ue)*
acquire (to) . . . . *adquirir (ie)*
action . . . . *(la) acción*
actor . . . . *(el) actor*
actress . . . . *(la) actriz*
add (to) . . . . *añadir*
additional . . . . *adicional*
admission, entrance, ticket
. . . . *(la) entrada*
admit (to) . . . . *admitir*
adorable, beautiful . . . . *precioso/a*
advanced . . . . *avanzado/a*
advantage . . . . *(la) ventaja*
advice . . . . *(el) consejo*
advise (to) . . . . *aconsejar*
advertisement, announcement
. . . . *(el) anuncio*
affection . . . . *(el) cariño*
affectionate . . . . *cariñoso/a*
after . . . . *después (de)*
after, behind . . . . *tras*
afternoon (this) . . . . *esta tarde*
again . . . . *de nuevo, otra vez*
against . . . . *contra*
age . . . . *(la) edad*
agree (to) . . . . *estar de acuerdo*
ahead, forward . . . . *adelante*
aid (to), to support . . . . *apoyar*
air conditioner
. . . . *(el) acondicionador de aire*
airplane . . . . *(el) avión*
airport . . . . *(el) aeropuerto*
alarm . . . . *(la) alarma*
alarm clock . . . . *(el) despertador*
all . . . . *todo*
allow (to), to leave behind . . . . . . *dejar*
allow (to), to permit . . . . *permitir*
almost . . . . *casi*
alone . . . . *solo/a*
along . . . . *a lo largo*
aloud . . . . *en voz alta*
alphabet . . . . *(el) alfabeto*

already . . . . *ya*
also . . . . *también*
although . . . . *aunque*
always . . . . *siempre*
A.M. (in the morning) . . . . *de la mañana*
ambassador . . . . *(el) embajador*
among, between . . . . *entre*
amusement park
. . . . *(el) parque de atracciones*
an, a . . . . *uno/a*
analysis . . . . *(el) análisis*
anchovy . . . . *(la) anchoa*
and . . . . *y*
anger . . . . *(el) enojo*
angry, brave, fierce . . . . *bravo/a*
angry (to become) . . . . *enfadar(se),*
enojarse
announcement, advertisement
. . . . *(el) anuncio*
annoy (to) . . . . *fastidiar*
annoying, heavy . . . . *pesado/a*
another, other . . . . *otro/a*
answer (to) . . . . *contestar*
answering machine
. . . . *(el) contestador automático*
anxious, eager . . . . *ansioso/a*
any . . . . *cualquier*
anybody . . . . *cualquiera*
appeal to (to) . . . . *apetecer*
appear (to) . . . . *aparecer*
appear (to), to seem . . . . *parecer*
applaud (to) . . . . *aplaudir*
apple . . . . *(la) manzana*
applied, dedicated, industrious
. . . . *aplicado/a*
appropriate, just, fair . . . . *justo/a*
April . . . . *abril*
Arabic . . . . *(el) árabe*
architect . . . . *(el/la) arquitecto/a*
arm . . . . *(el) brazo*
armchair . . . . *(el) sillón*
around . . . . *alrededor*
arrange (to), to fix . . . . *arreglar*
arrange (to), to place . . . . *colocar*
arrival . . . . *(la) llegada*
arrive (to) . . . . *llegar*
arrow . . . . *(la) flecha*
art . . . . *(el) arte (f.)*
art gallery . . . . *(la) galería de arte*
art show, exhibition,
fair . . . . *(la) exposición*
as, since, like . . . . *como*
ashamed (to be) . . . . . . *tener vergüenza*
ask (a question) (to)
. . . . *hacer una pregunta*
ask (for) (to), to order (food) . . . *pedir (i)*
asparagus . . . . *(el) espárrago*

aspire to (to), to seek,
to claim to be . . . . *pretender*
assignment, task, homework
. . . . *(la) tarea*
astute . . . . *astuto/a*
astute, sharp . . . . *agudo/a*
at, to . . . . *a*
at approximately . . . . *a eso de*
at once . . . . *en seguida (enseguida)*
at times, sometimes . . . . *a veces*
athletic . . . . *atlético/a*
attack . . . . *(el) ataque*
attack (to) . . . . *atacar*
attempt (to), to try . . . . *intentar*
attend (to) . . . . *asistir*
attention (to pay) . . . . . *prestar atención*
attention (to pay) to . . . . . . *hacer caso a*
attentive . . . . *atento/a*
attic . . . . *(el) desván*
attitude . . . . *(la) actitud*
attract (to) . . . . *atraer*
August . . . . *agosto*
aunt . . . . *(la) tía*
authority . . . . *(la) autoridad*
autograph . . . . *(el) autógrafo*
autumnal . . . . *otoñal*
available, free . . . . *libre*
average, medium . . . . *mediano/a*
avoid (to) . . . . *evitar*

B

baby . . . . *(el) bebé*
baby pig . . . . *(el) cochinillo*
babysitter . . . . *(el, la) niñero/a*
backpack . . . . *(la) mochila*
bacon . . . . *(el) tocino*
bad . . . . *malo/a*
bad, poorly . . . . *mal*
bad-mannered, ill-bred . . . . *malcriado/a*
bag, purse . . . . *(la) bolsa*
baker . . . . *(el/la) panadero/a*
balcony . . . . *(el) balcón*
bald . . . . *calvo/a*
ball . . . . *(la) pelota*
balloon . . . . *(el) globo*
ballplayer . . . . *(el) pelotero*
banana . . . . *(la) banana, (el) plátano*
band . . . . *(la) banda*
bank, bench, pew . . . . *(el) banco*
bank, shore (of river, ocean)
. . . . *(la) orilla*
banker . . . . *(el/la) banquero/a*
banquet . . . . *(el) banquete*
bar (of a window or a prison cell)
. . . . *(el) barrote*
barber, hairdresser . . . *(el/la) peluquero/a*
bark (to) . . . . *ladrar*

baseball . . . . (el) béisbol
basement . . . .(el) sótano
basketball . . . . (el) baloncesto
bath (to take a) . . . . bañarse
bathing suit . . . . (el) bañador
bathrobe. . . . . (la) bata
bathroom . . . . (el) (cuarto de) baño
battle . . . . (la) batalla
be (to) . . . . .estar, ser
be able to (to) . . . . .poder (ue)
be born (to) . . . . .nacer
be happy about (to) . . . . alegrarse de
be worth (to) . . . . valer
beach . . . . (la) playa
bear . . . . (el) oso
beard . . . . (la) barba
beat (to). . . . . batir
beat (to), to hit . . . . golpear
beater. . . . . (el/la) batidor/a
beautiful . . . . bello/a
beautiful, adorable . . . . precioso/a
beauty . . . . (la) belleza
because . . . . .porque
become night (to) . . . . anochecer
bed. . . . .(la) cama
bed (to go to). . . . . acostarse (ue)
bedroom . . . (el) dormitorio, (la) alcoba
bee . . . . (la) abeja
before . . . . antes (de)
beg (to) . . . . suplicar, rogar (ue)
begin (to). . . comenzar (ie), empezar (ie)
beginning. . .(el) comienzo, (el) principio
behave (to) . . . . comportarse
behave well/poorly (to)
. . . . portarse bien/mal
behind . . . . .atrás, detrás, detrás de
behind, after . . . . tras
believe (to) . . . . creer
bell. . . . . (la) campana, (el) timbre
belong to (to). . . . . pertenecer a
below. . . . . .abajo
below, under . . . . debajo de
belt. . . . . (el) cinturón
bench, pew, bank . . . . (el) banco
bend (to), to twist . . . . .torcer (ue)
best man . . . . (el) padrino de boda
bet (to). . . . . apostar (ue)
better, best. . . . . .mejor
between, among . . . . entre
bicycle. . . . . (la) bicicleta
bicycle (to ride a) . . montar en bicicleta
big. .grande
bilingual . . . . bilingüe
bill. . . . . (la) factura, (la) cuenta
biology . . . . (la) biología
bird . . . .(el) pájaro
birthday. . . . . (el) cumpleaños
bit, piece, selection . . . . (el) trozo
bite (to) . . . . .morder (ue)
bite (mosquito)
. . . . (la) picadura (de mosquito)

bitter, sour . . . . agrio/a, (amargo/a)
black . . . . negro/a
blackboard. . . . . (la) pizarra
blame (to) . . . . .echarle la culpa a
blame (someone) (to)
. . . . culpar a, echar(le) la culpa
blanket. . . . . (la) manta
bland, lacking salt . . . . soso/a
bless (to) . . . . bendecir
blind . . . . ciego/a
blond(e). . . . . rubio/a
blouse . . . .(la) blusa
blow (to) . . . . soplar
blue . . . . azul
board (to). . . . . .abordar
boat . . . . (el) barco
boil (to) . . . . hervir (ie)
boisterous, rowdy, noisy . . . . bullicioso/a
bold, daring. . . . . atrevido/a
book. . . . . (el) libro
boot . . . . (la) bota
border, frontier . . . . (la) frontera
bored, boring. . . . . .aburrido/a
bored (to become [get]) . . . . . aburrirse
borrow (to) . . . . pedir (i) prestado
boss . . . .(la) jefa, (el) jefe
bossy . . . . . . .mandón (m.), mandona (f.)
botanical garden . . . .(el) jardín botánico
both . . . . .ambos/as
bother (to) . . . . molestar
bottle . . . . (la) botella, (el) frasco
box. . . . . (la) caja
boy. . . . .(el) chico, (el) niño
boyfriend, fiancé, groom. . . . . (el) novio
bracelet . . . . (la) pulsera
branch (office). . . . . (la) sucursal
brave, fierce, angry . . . . bravo/a
bread . . . . (el) pan
break (to). . . . . quebrar(se), romper(se)
breakfast (to have) . . . . desayunar
breathe (to) . . . . respirar
bride, fiancée, girlfriend . . . . . (la) novia
bright, brilliant . . . . luminoso/a
bring (to). . . . . traer
brochure . . . .(el) folleto
broken . . . . quebrado/a, roto/a
broom . . . . (la) escoba
brother . . . .(el) hermano
brother-in-law . . . . (el) cuñado
brown . . . . marrón
brunette, brown . . . . .moreno/a
brush one's (hair, teeth) (to). . cepillarse
build (to), to construct . . . . construir
building . . . . (el) edificio
bullfighter . . . . (el/la) torero/a
burly, stout, heavy-set. . . . . corpulento/a
burn (to) . . . . quemar
burning, passionate . . . . .ardiente
burnt . . . . quemado/a
bury (to) . . . . enterrar (ie)
bus. . . . .(el) autobús

bush. . . . . (el) arbusto
business. . . . . (el) negocio
busy. . . . . ocupado/a
butcher. . . . .(el/la) carnicero/a
butter. . . . . (la) mantequilla
buy (to) . . . . comprar
by, for, in order to. . . . . .para
by, for, through . . . . .por

C

cage. . . . . (la) jaula
cake. . . . .(la) torta, (el) pastel
calendar. . . . . (el) calendario
call (to) . . . . llamar
calm. . . . . tranquilo/a
calmly . . . . tranquilamente
camera. . . . . (la) cámara
camp . . . .(el) campamento
campaign. . . . .(la) campaña
camper. . . . .(el/la) campista
can. . . . . (la) lata
can opener. . . . . (el) abrelatas
cancelled . . . . .cancelado/a
candidate. . . . . (el/la) candidato/a
candle, sailing . . . .(la) vela
canyon. . . . . (el) cañón
capable . . . . .capaz
captain. . . . . capitán
car . . . .(el) carro, (el) coche
car (of train) . . . . (el) vagón
care for (to) . . . . cuidar (de)
career, race . . . .(la) carrera
careful, cautious . . . . .cuidadoso/a
careful, cautious, wary . . . . . cauteloso/a
carnival . . . . (el) carnaval
carpenter . . . . (el/la) carpintero/a
carpet, rug . . . .(la) alfombra
carrot. . . . .(la) zanahoria
carry (to), to take . . . . .llevar
castle . . . . (el) castillo
cat . . . . (el) gato
catch (to), to take . . . . .coger
cathedral . . . . (la) catedral
cause (to). . . . . causar
cautious, careful . . . . cuidadoso/a
cautious, careful, wary . . . . . cauteloso/a
cavity. . . . . (la) caries
celebrated, famous . . . . célebre
cell. . . . .(la) celda
cellphone. . (el) teléfono celular, (el) móvil
cemetery . . . . (el) cementerio
center, downtown . . . .(el) centro
century. . . . . (el) siglo
ceremony. . . . . (la) ceremonia
certain . . . . cierto/a
certainty, security . . . . (la) seguridad
chair, seat . . . . (la) silla
chalk . . . . (la) tiza
champagne . . . . (el) champán,
(el) champaña

champion . . .(el) campeón, (la) campeona
championship . . . . (el) campeonato
change . . . . (el) cambio
change (to) . . . . .cambiar
chat (to). . . . . charlar
chauffeur. . . . . (el) chófer
cheap. . . . . barato/a
cheat (to), to deceive. . . . . .engañar
check out a book (to)
. . . . sacar (prestado) un libro
cheerful, smiling. . . . . .risueño/a
cheese . . . . (el) queso
chemistry. . . . . (la) química
chess . . . . (el) ajedrez
chestnut. . . . . .castaño/a
chew (to). . . . . masticar
chicken . . . . (el) pollo
childhood. . . . . . .(la) niñez, (la) infancia
chimney, fireplace. . . . . . . (la) chimenea
chlorine. . . . .(el) cloro
chocolates . . . .(los) bombones,
. . . .(los) chocolates
choose (to), to elect. . . . . elegir (i)
choose (to), to select. . . . . escoger
Christian . . . . .cristiano/a
church . . . .(la) iglesia
church service, mass. . . . . (la) misa
cigarette. . . . . (el) cigarrillo
cinnamon. . . . .(la) canela
circular, round. . . . . circular
circus. . . . .(el) circo
citizen . . . . (el/la) ciudadano/a
city. . . . . (la) ciudad
city hall . . . . (el) ayuntamiento
claim to be (to), to aspire to,
to seek . . . . .pretender
clarinet. . . . . (el) clarinete
class. . . . .(la) clase
clean . . . . limpio/a
clean (to). . . . . limpiar
clear. . . . . .claro/a
clear, necessary, precise . . . . . .preciso/a
clever, skillful. . . . . hábil
clever, ready, smart. . . . . listo/a
client . . . .(el) cliente, (la) clienta
climate. . . . .(el) clima
clinic, hospital. . . . . (la) clínica
clock, watch . . . . (el) reloj
close (to) . . . . cerrar (ie)
close, intimate. . . . . .íntimo/a
closed . . . . cerrado/a
closet. . . . . (el) armario
cloth, material . . . . (la) tela
clothes. . . . . (la) ropa
cloudy . . . . nublado/a
clown. . . . . (el) payaso
coach . . (el) entrenador, (la) entrenadora
coal . . . . (el) carbón
coast . . . .(la) costa
coat, overcoat . . . .(el) abrigo
cobbler, shoemaker . . (el/la) zapatero/a

coconut . . . . (el) coco
corkscrew . . . . (el) sacacorchos
coffee. . . . .(el) café
coffee maker . . . . (la) cafetera
coin . . . .(la) moneda
cold . . . . frío/a
colleague . . . .(el/la) colega
collect (to) . . . . . . .coleccionar, recoger
collection. . . . . (la) colección
comb (to). . . . . peinar
comb one's hair (to) . . . . peinarse
combed . . . . peinado/a
combine (to) . . . . .combinar
come (to) . . . . venir
comfortable. . . . . cómodo/a
common. . . . . .común
common, ordinary. . . . . vulgar
compact disc (CD). . . (el) disco compacto
company . . . . (la) empresa
compartment (of train) . . . . . (el) vagón
compass. . . . . (la) brújula
compassion . . . . (la) compasión
compete (to) . . . . .competir (i)
competition . . . . (la) competición
competitive . . . . competitivo/a
complain (about) (to). . . . . . quejarse de
complaint. . . . . (la) queja
complete (to), to finish . . . . cumplir
computer . . . . (la) computadora
computer (Spain). . . . . . .(el) ordenador
concert. . . . . (el) concierto
confess (to) . . . . confesar (ie)
confidence, trust (in). . . . . (la) confianza
confuse (to). . . . . .confundir
confused . . . . .confundido/a
confused, confusing . . . . .confuso/a
congratulate (to) . . . . .felicitar
congratulations . . . . (las) felicidades
conquer (to), to defeat. . . . . vencer
consecutive . . . . consecutivo/a
consequently . . . . .por consiguiente
conserve (to) . . . . conservar
constellation . . . .(la) constelación
construct (to), to build . . . . . . construir
contact lens . . . . (la) lentilla
contact lenses . . . . (las) lentillas,
. . . .(los) lentes de contacto
contaminated. . . . . contaminado/a
content, happy . . . . .contento/a
contest . . . .(el) concurso
continent . . . .(el) continente
contract . . . . (el) contrato
convert (to) . . . . .convertir (ie)
convince (to) . . . . convencer
cook. . . . . (el/la) cocinero/a
cook (to) . . . . cocinar
cookie . . . . (la) galleta
cool, fresh . . . . .fresco/a
cordial, polite . . . . .cordial
cordiality . . . .(la) cordialidad
corkscrew . . . . (el) sacacorchos

corner . . . .(el) rincón
corner (of a street). . . . . . . (la) esquina
correct (to). . . . . corregir (i)
cost (to) . . . . .costar (ue)
costume, disguise . . . .(el) disfraz
cottage cheese . . . . requesón
cotton. . . . . (el) algodón
cough (to) . . . . toser
count (to), to tell . . . . contar (ue)
count on (to) . . . . .contar con
country . . . .(el) país
country, homeland . . . . (la) patria
couple, pair . . . . (la) pareja
course . . . .(el) curso
course, direction . . . .(el) rumbo
court . . . . (la) cancha
court . . . .(la) corte
courteous, polite . . . . cortés
courtesy . . . . (la) cortesía
cousin . . . .(el/la) primo/a
cover . . . .(la) portada
cover (to). . . . . cubrir, tapar
cow . . . . (la) vaca
cranberry. . . . . (el) arándano (rojo)
crazy . . . . loco/a
crazy (to go) . . . . volverse loco/a
cream . . . .(la) crema
cream (whipped) . . . . (la) nata
create (to), to make. . . . . crear
crime . . . . (el) crimen
crop . . . . (la) cosecha
crowded. . . . . atestado/a
crude, rude . . . . .grosero/a
cruel, mean . . . . cruel
cruise ship. . . . .(el) crucero
crumb . . . . (la) miga
cry (to). . . . . .llorar
cup. . . . .(la) taza
curly . . . . .rizado/a
current, present . . . . corriente
current, present day. . . . . actual
curtain(s) . . . . (la) cortina, (las) cortinas
cut (to). . . . . cortar
cute, precious . . . . .precioso/a
cycling. . . . . (el) ciclismo

D

daily, everyday . . . . cotidiano/a
damned, accursed . . . . .maldito/a
dance (to) . . . . bailar
dancer . . . . . .(el) bailarín, (la) bailarina
danger . . . . (el) peligro
dare to (to). . . . . atreverse a
daring, bold. . . . . atrevido/a
dark . . . . oscuro/a
dark, brunette . . . . .moreno/a
dark, obscure. . . . . o(b)scuro/a
darkness. . . . . (la) oscuridad
date . . . . (la) fecha, (la) cita
daughter. . . . .(la) hija

dawn . . . . . (el) alba (f.), (la) madrugada
day. . . . . (el) día
day before yesterday (the). . . . . anteayer
dead. . . . . muerto/a, difunto/a
deaf . . . . sordo/a
dear . . . . querido/a
debt . . . . (la) deuda
debut, premiére . . . . (el) estreno
decade . . . . (la) década
deceive (to), to cheat. . . . . .engañar
December . . . . diciembre
decide (to) . . . . .decidir
declare (to) . . . . declarar
dedicated, applied, industrious
. . . . .aplicado/a
deep. . . . . .hondo/a, profundo/a
defeat. . . . .(la) derrota
defeat (to), to conquer. . . . . vencer
defect. . . . . (el) defecto
delicate, fine . . . . .fino/a
delicious, tasty . . . . sabroso/a
deliver (to), to hand over,
    to turn in . . . . entregar
demand (to), to require . . . . .exigir
dense, thick. . . . . espeso/a
dentist . . . .(el/la) dentista
deny (to) . . . . negar (ie)
department store . . . . (el) almacén
depress (to) . . . . deprimir
depressed. . . . . .deprimido/a
desert . . . .(el) desierto
deserve (to), to merit. . . . . merecer
design (to) . . . . diseñar
desire (to) . . . . desear
desk. . . . . (el) escritorio
despair (to), to lose hope . . . .desesperar
dessert . . . . (el) postre
destiny, fate, destination . . . . (el) destino
destroy (to) . . . . destruir
detail . . . .(el) detalle
detain (to), to stop. . . . . detener
develop (to). . . . . desarrollar
die (to). . . . . morir (ue)
diet. . . . .(la) dieta
different, distinct. . . . . .distinto/a
difficult . . . . .difícil
dining room. . . . . (el) comedor
direct (to). . . . . dirigir
direction, course . . . . (el) rumbo
dirty. .sucio/a
disappear (to) . . . . desaparecer
disaster . . . . (el) desastre
discipline. . . . .(la) disciplina
discotheque, nightclub . . . (la) discoteca
discover (to) . . . . .descubrir
discreet . . . . discreto/a
disguise, costume . . . .(el) disfraz
dish, plate . . . .(el) plato
dishwasher. . . . .(el) lavaplatos
distant . . . . lejano/a
distinct, different. . . . . .distinto/a

divine. . . . . .divino/a
divorce. . . . . (el) divorcio
do (to), to make. . . . . .hacer
doctor . . . .(el/la) médico/a
dog. . . . .(el) perro
doll, wrist . . . .(la) muñeca
dominate (to). . . . . .dominar
door . . . .(la) puerta
dormitory, residence . . . . (la) residencia
double .doble
double room . . . . . (la) habitación doble
doubt . . . .(la) duda
doubtful . . . . .dudoso/a
down (to go), to get off
    (a train, etc.). . . . . bajar
downtown, center . . . .(el) centro
dozen. . . . . (la) docena
drain (to) (e.g., pasta) . . . . escurrir
drawer . . . .(el) cajón
drawing, sketch, painting
. . . . (el) dibujo
dream about (to) . . . . . . .soñar (ue) con
dress . . . . (el) vestido
dresser . . . .(el) tocador
dressmaker, seamstress . . . (la) costurera
drink . . . . (la) bebida
drink (to) . . . . .beber
drive (to) . . . . conducir
drop (of liquid) . . . . (la) gota
drug. . . . . (la) droga
drums. . . . .(los) tambores
drunk . . . . borracho/a
dry . . . . seco/a
dryer . . . .(la) secadora
dumb, mute . . . . mudo/a
during . . . . durante
dye (to) . . . . teñir (i)

E

each, every . . . . cada
eager, anxious . . . . .ansioso/a
eagle . . . . (el) águila (f.)
early. . . . . .temprano
earn (to), to win . . . . .ganar
earring. . . . .(el) arete, (el) pendiente
earthquake. . . . . (el) terremoto
east . . . . este
eastern. . . . . oriental
easy . . . . .fácil
eat (to). . . . . comer
eat lunch (to). . . . . almorzar (ue)
economy . . . . (la) economía
effort . . . . (el) esfuerzo
egg. . . . . (el) huevo
elect (to), to choose. . . . . elegir (i)
electric. . . . . eléctrico/a
electrician . . . . (el/la) electricista
elegance. . . . . (la) elegancia
elevator . . . . (el) ascensor
e-mail . . . . (el) correo electrónico

embarrassing. . . . . embarazoso/a
embarrassment, shame. . . . (la) vergüenza
embrace. . . . . (el) abrazo
embrace (to), to hug . . . . abrazar
employee. . . . .(el/la) empleado/a
empty. . . . . vacío/a
end, final . . . . (el) final
enemy . . . .(el/la) enemigo/a
engagement. . . . .(el) noviazgo
engagement ring
. . . . (el) anillo de compromiso
engineer. . . . .(el/la) ingeniero/a
English . . . . (el) inglés
engrave (to), to record . . . . .grabar
enjoy (to). . . . . . . .disfrutar de, gozar de
enjoy (to) oneself, to have
    a good time . . . . divertirse (ie)
end. . . . . (el) final
enormous. . . . . enorme
enough. . . . . .suficiente, bastante
enter (to) . . . . entrar
entire, whole . . . . .entero/a
entrance, admission, ticket
. . . .(la) entrada
envious, jealous. . . . . envidioso/a
episode . . . . (el) episodio
era . . . . (la) época
erase (to) . . . . borrar
escape (to) . . . . escapar
essay . . . . (el) ensayo
essential . . . . .esencial
establish (to), to found . . . . .fundar
eternal . . . . .eterno/a
every, each . . . . cada
everyday, daily . . . . cotidiano/a
exceptional, original, smart. . . . . . genial
excited. . . . . emocionado/a
excursion, trip. . . . . (la) excursión
exercise . . . . (el) ejercicio
exhausted. . . . . agotado/a
exhibition, show, fair . . . (la) exposición
exit. . . . . (la) salida
exotic. . . . . exótico/a
expensive. . . . . caro/a
expiration . . . . vencimiento (el)
explain (to) . . . . .explicar
explorer. . . . . (el/la) explorador/a
extraordinary . . . . extraordinario/a
extraterrestrial. . . . . extraterrestre
eye. . . . . (el) ojo

F

face . . . . (la) cara
fact. . . . . (el) hecho
factory . . . . (la) fábrica
fair, exhibition, show . . . (la) exposición
fair, appropriate, just. . . . . .justo/a
faithful. . . . . .fiel
fake . . . . falsificado/a
fake, false . . . . postizo/a

fake (to), to pretend, to feign
. . . .*fingir*
fall . . . . *(el) otoño*
fall (to) . . . . *caer*
fall in love with (to) . . . . *enamorarse de*
fame. . . . .*(la) fama*
famous, celebrated . . . . *célebre*
fan. . . . . *(el/la) aficionado/a*
fan. . . . .*(el) ventilador*
fantastic. . . . .*fantástico/a*
far (away) . . . .*lejos*
far from. . . . . *lejos de*
farewell, parting . . . . *(la) despedida*
farm . . . . *(la) finca, (la) granja*
fascinate (to) . . . .*fascinar*
fashion, style, ... *(la) moda*
fast (to) . . . .*ayunar*
fat . . . . *gordo/a*
fate, destiny, destination
. . . . *(el) destino*
father . . . . *(el) padre*
father-in-law . . . .*(el) suegro*
fatigue, tiredness. . . . . . . *(el) cansancio*
faucet. . . . .*(la) llave, (el) grifo*
fault, guilt . . . . *(la) culpa*
fear (to) . . . .*temer*
February . . . . *febrero*
fed up . . . . *harto/a*
feel (to), to regret . . . . *sentir (ie)*
feeling, sentiment . . . . . .*(el) sentimiento*
feign (to), to fake . . . .*fingir*
ferocious, fierce . . . . *feroz*
fiancé, boyfriend, groom. . . . .*(el) novio*
fiancée, girlfriend, bride . . . . . *(la) novia*
fib (to), to lie . . . .*mentir (ie)*
field. . . . .*(el) campo*
fierce, ferocious . . . . *feroz*
fierce, angry, brave . . . . *bravo/a*
fight. . . . .*(la) pelea*
fight (to) . . . .*pelear*
fight (to), to struggle. . . . . *luchar*
fill (to) . . . .*llenar*
film (used in a camera), movie
. . . . *(la) película*
final, end . . . . *(el) final*
finally . . . . *por fin*
find (to) . . . . *hallar*
find out (to) . . . . *averiguar*
find (to), to meet . . . .*encontrar (ue)*
fine . . . . *(la) multa*
fine, delicate . . . . *fino/a*
fine, well . . . . *bien*
finger. . . . . *(el) dedo*
fingernail, toenail . . . . *(la) uña*
finish (to) . . . . *terminar*
finish (to), to complete . . . . *cumplir*
fire. . . . . *(el) incendio, (el) fuego*
firefighter . . . .*(el/la) bombero/a*
fireplace, chimney. . . . . . *(la) chimenea*
firewood . . . . *(la) leña*
firmness . . . . *(la) firmeza*

first . . . . *primero/a*
fish. . . . . *(el) pescado, (el) pez*
fish (to) . . . . *pescar*
fit (to) . . . .*caber*
fix (to), to arrange. . . . .*arreglar*
fixed, firm . . . . *fijo/a*
flag . . . . *(la) bandera*
flat, smooth . . . . *liso/a*
flight . . . .*(el) vuelo*
flight attendant
. . . . . *(el/la) auxiliar (asistente) de vuelo*
floor. . . . . *(el) suelo, (el) piso*
flour. . . . .*(la) harina*
flower . . . . *(la) flor*
flute . . . . *(la) flauta*
fly . . . .*(la) mosca*
fly (to) . . . . *volar (ue)*
fog . . . .*(la) niebla*
fold (to). . . . . *doblar*
follow (to). . . . . *seguir (i)*
following, next . . . . *siguiente*
folly, madness, insanity . . . . . .*(la) locura*
food . . . . *(la) comida*
foolish, silly, stupid. . . . . *tonto/a*
foolish, stupid . . . . *necio/a*
foot . . . .*(el) pie*
football . . . . *(el) fútbol americano*
for, by, in order to . . . .*para*
for, by, through . . . .*por*
for example . . . .*por ejemplo*
forehead. . . . . *(la) frente*
foreign. . . . . *extranjero/a*
forest, woods. . . . . *(el) bosque*
forever. . . . . *para siempre*
fork . . . . *(el) tenedor*
fortunate, happy, lucky . . . . . .*dichoso/a*
fortune. . . . . *(la) fortuna*
forward, ahead . . . . *adelante*
found (to), to establish . . . .*fundar*
fountain. . . . . *(la) fuente*
fourth, quarter, room. . . . . . .*(el) cuarto*
fox . . . .*(el) zorro*
frank . . . . *franco/a*
free . . . . *libre, gratis*
freeway, highway
. . . . *autopista (la), (autovía)*
freeze (to) . . . . *helar (ie)*
freezer. . . . .*(el) congelador*
French (language) . . . .*(el) francés*
frequently . . . .*frecuentemente*
fresh, cool . . . . *fresco/a*
Friday . . . . *(el) viernes*
friend. . . . .*(la) amiga, (el) amigo*
friendly, kind. . . . . *amable*
frighten (to), to scare . . . . *asustar*
frog . . . . *(la) rana*
from, of . . . . *de*
from, since . . . . *desde*
frontier, border . . . . *(la) frontera*
frustrated. . . . . *frustrado/a*
fry (to) . . . . *freír (i)*

frying pan . . . . *(el/la) sartén*
full. . . . . *lleno/a*
function (to), to work . . . .*funcionar*
furious, very mad . . . .*furioso/a*
future. . . . . *(el) porvenir*

G

game . . . . *(el) juego, (el) partido*
garage . . . . *(el) garaje*
garbage collector. . . . . *(el/la) basurero/a*
garden . . . . *(el) jardín*
gardener. . . . . *(el/la) jardinero/a*
garlic . . . . *(el) ajo*
gas station . . . . *(la) gasolinera*
generous . . . . *generoso/a*
geranium . . . .*(el) geranio*
German . . . . *(el) alemán*
gesture. . . . . *(el) gesto*
get (to), to obtain . . . .*conseguir (i)*
get along well (badly) with (to)
. . . .*llevarse bien (mal) con*
get along well (poorly) (to)
. . . . *caerle bien (mal)*
get angry (to). . . . . . *enojarse, enfadarse*
get fat (to) . . . . *engordar*
get mad (to). . . . . *enfadarse*
get married to (to). . . . .*casarse con*
get off (a train, etc.) (to),
to go down. . . . . *bajar*
get on (a bus, etc.) (to),
to go up. . . . . *subir*
get up (to) . . . . *levantarse*
get used to (to) . . . . *acostumbrarse a*
get wet (to) . . . .*mojar*
giraffe . . . . *(la) jirafa*
girl. . . . .*(la) chica, (la) niña*
girlfriend, fiancée, bride . . . . . *(la) novia*
give (to). . . . .*dar*
give a present (to),
to give a gift. . . . . *regalar*
glass. . . . . *(el) vaso*
glass (the material)
. . . .*(el) vidrio, (el) cristal*
glasses . . . .*(las) gafas, (los) anteojos*
global warming
. . . . *(la) calentamiento global*
gloomy, melancholy. . . . . . *melancólico/a*
glove . . . .*(el) guante*
go (to) . . . . *ir*
go away (to) . . . . *irse, marcharse*
go camping (to). . . . . *ir de camping*
go down (to) . . . . *bajar*
go to bed (to). . . . . *acostarse (ue)*
goal (objective). . . . . *(la) meta*
goal (e.g., soccer, hockey) . . . . . *(el) gol*
goalie
. . . . . .*(el/la) arquero/a, (el/la) portero/a*
god. *(el) dios*
goddess . . . .*(la) diosa*
godfather. . . . .*(el) padrino*

godmother . . . . (la) madrina
gold . . . . (el) oro
golden . . . . dorado/a
good. bueno/a
good afternoon . . . . buenas tardes
good evening. . . . . buenas noches
good morning . . . . buenos días
good time (to have a),
    to enjoy oneself . . . . divertirse (ie)
good-looking. . . . . guapo/a
goodbye to (to say)
    . . . . .despedirse (i) (de)
goose. . . . . (el) ganso
gossip (to) . . . . contar (ue) chismes
govern (to). . . . . .gobernar (ie)
governor . . . . (el/la) gobernador/a
government . . . . (el) gobierno
graduate (to) . . . . graduarse
granddaughter . . . .(la) nieta
grandmother . . . . (la) abuela
grandfather . . . .(el) abuelo
grandson . . . . (el) nieto
grape . . . . (la) uva
grass . . . . (la) hierba
grateful . . . . .agradecido/a
grateful for (to be), to thank
    . . . . agradecer
great. . . . . .gran
great-grandfather. . . . . . . (el) bisabuelo
great-grandmother. . . . . . . (la) bisabuela
greedy . . . . avaricioso/a
green . . . . verde
greeting . . . .(el) saludo
grey . . . . gris
grief, pain . . . .(el) dolor
grill . . . .(la) parrilla
groom, fiancé, boyfriend. . . . .(el) novio
grow dark (to) . . . . anochecer
grow (to), to increase . . . . crecer
guard (to), to keep. . . . . .guardar
guerrilla . . . .(el/la) guerrillero/a
guest . . . .(el/la) invitado/a
guitar. . . . . (la) guitarra
guilt, fault . . . . (la) culpa
guilty . . . . culpable
gum (chewing) . . . . (el) chicle

H

hail (to) . . . . granizar
hair . . . . (el) cabello, (el) pelo
hair dryer. . . . . . . (la) secadora de pelo
hairdresser, barber
    . . . . (el/la) peluquero/a
hallway . . . .(el) pasillo
ham . . . .(el) jamón
hamburger. . . . . (la) hamburguesa
hammer . . . .(el) martillo
hand. . . . . (la) mano
hand over (to), to deliver,
    to turn in . . . . entregar

handmade . . . . hecho/a a mano
hang (up) (to) . . . . colgar (ue)
hanger . . . . (el) gancho, (la) percha
happen (to) . . . . suceder
happen (to), to occur . . . . .ocurrir
happiness. . . . . (la) felicidad
happiness, joy . . . . (la) alegría
happy. . . . . .alegre, feliz
happy, content . . . . .contento/a
happy, fortunate, lucky . . . . . .dichoso/a
hard . . . . duro/a
harmony . . . . (la) armonía
hat . . . . (el) sombrero
hate (to) . . . . odiar
haughty, proud . . . . .soberbio/a
have (to) . . . . tener
have breakfast (to) . . . . desayunar
have a great/bad time (to)
    . . . . pasárselo bien/mal
have just (to) (done
    something) . . . . acabar de
have lunch (to) . . . . almorzar (ue)
have one's way (to)
    . . . . salirse con la suya
have supper (to) . . . . cenar
he, him . . . . él
head. . . . . (la) cabeza
healthy. . . . . sano/a
heap, pile . . . . (el) montón
hear (to). . . . . oír
heart. . . . .(el) corazón
hearth, home . . . . (el) hogar
heat (to). . . . . calentar (ie)
heavy, annoying . . . . pesado/a
heavy-set, stout, burly . . . . . corpulento/a
helicopter. . . . . (el) helicóptero
helmet . . . . (el) casco
help . . . . (la) ayuda
help (to). . . . . .ayudar
hemisphere . . . .(el) hemisferio
hen. . . . . (la) gallina
her, she . . . . ella
here .aquí
hero . . . . (el) héroe
heroine. . . . .(la) heroína
hide (to). . . . . esconder, ocultar
high school
    . . . . (el) colegio, (la) escuela secundaria
highway. . . . . (la) carretera
highway, freeway
    . . . . (la) autopista (autovía)
him, he . . . . .él
history . . . .(la) historia
hit (to) . . . . .pegar
hit (to), to beat, to punch . . . . . golpear
home, hearth . . . . (el) hogar
home (at). . . . . en casa
homeland, country . . . . (la) patria
homerun . . . .(el) jonrón
homework, task. assignment
    . . . .(la) tarea

honeymoon . . . . (la) luna de miel
hope (to), to wait. . . . . esperar
horse . . . . (el) caballo
hospital, clinic. . . . . (la) clínica
hot . . . . .caluroso/a
hot, warm . . . . caliente
hot dog . . . .(el) perrito caliente
hotel. . . . . (el) hotel
hour . . . . (la) hora
house . . . . (la) casa
how? . . . .¿cómo?
how much? . . . .¿cuánto?
how many? . . . .¿cuánto/a(s)?
hug (to), to embrace . . . . abrazar
human being . . . .(el) ser humano
humble. . . . . humilde
hunting . . . . (la) caza
hurricane . . . . (el) huracán
hurl (to), to throw, to pitch . . . . . lanzar
hurt (to), to ache . . . . doler (ue)
hurry . . . . prisa
hurry (in a), rushed . . . . apurado/a
hurry (to be in a)
    . . . . .tener prisa, estar apurado/a
husband . . . . (el) marido, (el) esposo
hygiene . . . .(la) higiene
hymn . . . . (el) himno

I

I . . . . yo
ice . . . . (el) hielo
ice cream. . . . .(el) helado
ice cream store . . . . (la) heladería
ice hockey . . . . . . (el) hockey sobre hielo
identical . . . . idéntico/a
if . . . . .si
if only . . . . ojalá
ill-bred, bad-mannered . . . . . .malcriado/a
illegal. . . . . .ilegal
illustrious. . . . . ilustre
image. . . . . (la) imagen
imbecile. . . . . imbécil
immortal . . . . inmortal
impressive . . . . impresionante
in, on . . . . en
in front of . . . . . . delante de, enfrente de
in no way. . . . . en absoluto
in order that . . . . para que
in order to, by, for . . . . .para
in spite of . . . . a pesar de
in style (to be) . . . . estar de moda
in this way . . . . .así
including . . . . .incluso
increase (to) . . . . .aumentar
increase (to), to grow . . . . crecer
incredible. . . . . increíble
industrious, applied, dedicated
    . . . . .aplicado/a
inferior, lower . . . . inferior
ingredient . . . .(el) ingrediente

inherit (to) . . . . *heredar*
injured (sports) . . . . *lesionado/a*
injury . . . . *(la) lesión*
injury, wound . . . . *la herida*
insanity, folly, madness . . . . . .*(la) locura*
inside of . . . .*dentro de*
insist on (to) . . . . *insistir en*
inspiration . . . .*(la) inspiración*
install (to) . . . . *instalar*
instead of . . . .*en vez de*
instinct . . . .*(el) instinto*
instructions . . . . *(las) instrucciones*
insult (to) . . . . *insultar*
integrity . . . .*(la) integridad*
intense . . . .*intenso/a*
interest . . . .*(el) interés*
interesting . . . . *interesante*
international . . . .*internacional*
interrupt (to) . . . . *interrumpir*
interview . . . . *(la) entrevista*
interview (to) . . . .*entrevistar*
intimate, close . . . .*íntimo/a*
intolerable, unbearable . . . . *insoportable*
invest (to) (money) . . . . *invertir (ie)*
invite (to) . . . . *invitar*
iron (to) . . . . *planchar*
irritate (to) . . . . *irritar*
island . . . . *(la) isla*
isn't that so? . . . .*¿verdad?*
it is hailing . . . . *graniza*

J

jacket . . . .*(la) chaqueta*
jail . . . . *(la) cárcel*
January . . . .*enero*
Japanese . . . .*(el) japonés*
jealous . . . .*celoso/a*
jealous, envious . . . . *envidioso/a*
jewelry . . . . *(la) joyería*
Jewish . . . . *judío/a*
job . . . . *(el) trabajo, (el) empleo*
joke . . . . *(el) chiste*
joy, happiness . . . . *(la) alegría*
judge . . . . *(el/la) juez/jueza*
judge (to) . . . . *juzgar*
judgement, trial . . . . *(el) juicio*
juice . . . . *(el) jugo*
July . . . .*julio*
June . . . .*junio*
jungle . . . . *(la) selva, (la) jungla*
just, fair, appropriate . . . . *justo/a*

K

keep (to), to guard . . . .*guardar*
keep silent (to) . . . . *guardar silencio*
key . . . . *(la) llave*
kill (to) . . . .*matar*
kindly, friendly, nice . . . . *amable*
king . . . . *(el) rey*
kiss . . . . *(el) beso*

kiss (to) . . . . *besar*
kitchen . . . .*(la) cocina*
knife . . . .*(el) cuchillo*
knit (to) . . . .*tejer*
know (a fact) (to) . . . . *saber*
know (a person) (to) . . . . *conocer*
know (by heart) (to) . . *saber de memoria*
knowledge
. . . . . . *(el) conocimiento, (la) sabiduría*

L

lack, absence . . . . *(la) falta*
lacking salt, bland . . . . *soso/a*
ladder, stair . . . . *(la) escalera*
lady . . . .*(lal) dama*
lake . . . . *(el) lago*
lamb . . . .*(el) cordero*
lamp, light . . . . *(la) lámpara*
land (to) . . . . *aterrizar*
landscape, scenery . . . . *(el) paisaje*
language . . . . *(el) idioma*
language, tongue . . . . *(la) lengua*
last (of a group) . . . .*último/a*
last, past . . . . *pasado/a*
last (to) . . . . *durar*
last night . . . .*anoche*
late . . . . *tarde*
later . . . . *luego*
laugh, laughter . . . . *(la) risa*
laugh (to) . . . . *reír (i)*
lawn . . . .*(el) césped*
lawn mower . . . . *(el) cortacésped*
lawyer . . . . *(el/la) abogado/a*
lazy . . . .*perezoso/a*
leader . . . . *(el/la) líder*
leaf . . . . *(la) hoja*
learn (to) . . . . *aprender*
learn by heart (to)
. . . . *aprender de memoria*
learned, wise . . . . *sabio/a*
leather . . . . *(el) cuero*
leave (to) . . . .*irse, salir*
leave behind (to), to allow . . . .*dejar*
left . . . . *izquierdo/a*
left (to the) . . . .*a la izquierda*
left over (to be), to remain . . . . . *sobrar*
left-handed . . . . *zurdo/a*
leg . . . .*(la) pierna*
legend . . . . *(la) leyenda*
lemon . . . . *(el) limón*
lemonade . . . . *(la) limonada*
lend (to) . . . .*prestar*
less . . . . *menos*
lesson . . . . *(la) lección*
let know (to), to notify . . . . *avisar*
letter . . . .*(la) carta*
letter, lyrics . . . . *(la) letra*
level . . . .*(el) nivel*
liberty . . . .*(la) libertad*
librarian . . . . *(el/la) bibliotecario/a*
library . . . . *(la) biblioteca*

license . . . .*(la) licencia*
lie . . . .*(la) mentira*
lie (to), to fib . . . .*mentir (ie)*
light (adj.) . . . . *ligero/a*
light, lamp . . . . . . *(la) lámpara, (la) luz*
light, slight . . . . *leve*
light (to) (e.g., a fire), to turn
  on (e.g., a light)
. . . . *encender (ie), prender*
lightning . . . . *(el) relámpago*
like, as, since . . . . *como*
like (to), to wish, to want . . . .*querer (ie)*
line, tail . . . . *(la) cola*
lion . . . .*(el) león*
lipstick
. . . . . *(el) lápiz de labios (el) pintalabios*
listen to (to) . . . . *escuchar*
little, small . . . . *pequeño/a, chico/a*
little (a) . . . . *poco*
live (to) . . . .*vivir*
living room . . . . *(la) sala (de estar)*
llama . . . . *(la) llama*
loathsome to (to be),
  to be sickened by . . . . . . *darle asco a*
lobster . . . . *(la) langosta*
lock . . . . *(la) cerradura*
loneliness, solitude . . . .*(la) soledad*
long . . . . *largo/a*
look at (to) . . . . *mirar*
look for (to) . . . . *buscar*
lose (to) . . . .*perder (ie)*
lose hope (to), to despair . . . .*desesperar*
loose . . . . *suelto/a*
lot (a) . . . . *mucho*
lottery . . . .*(la) lotería*
love . . . . *(el) amor*
love (to) . . . . *amar*
lover . . . . *(el/la) amante*
loving . . . . *amoroso/a*
lower, inferior . . . . *inferior*
loyal . . . . *leal*
luck . . . . *(la) suerte*
lucky, happy, fortunate . . . .*dichoso/a*
luggage . . . . *(el) equipaje*
lung . . . . *(el) pulmón*
lying, untruthful . . . . *mentiroso/a*
lyrics, letter . . . . *(la) letra*

M

machine . . . . *(la) máquina*
mad (very), furious . . . . *furioso/a*
madness, insanity, folly . . . . . *(la) locura*
magazine . . . . *(la) revista*
magnifying glass . . . . *(la) lupa*
maid . . . .*(la) criada*
maid of honor . . . . *(la) dama de honor*
mail . . . . *(el) correo*
mail carrier . . . . *(el/la) cartero/a*
mailbox . . . . *(el) buzón*
maintain (to) . . . . *mantener*
make (to), to do . . . .*hacer*

make (to), to create . . . . *crear*
make a decision (to)
. . . . *tomar una decisión*
make a mistake (to) . . . . *equivocarse*
mall . . . . *(el) centro comercial*
man . . . . *(el) hombre*
manager . . . . *(el) gerente*
manufacture (to) . . . . *fabricar*
many . . . . *muchos/as*
map . . . .*(el) mapa*
March . . . . *marzo*
market . . . . *(el) mercado*
married (to get) . . . . *casarse*
Martian . . . . *(el) marciano*
marvel . . . . *(la) maravilla*
marvelous, wonderful . . . . *maravilloso/a*
mass (church) . . . . *(la) misa*
master's degree . . . .*(la) maestría*
material, cloth . . . .*(la) tela*
math . . . . *(las) matemáticas*
matter, subject . . . .*(el) asunto*
mature, ripe . . . .*maduro/a*
May . . . . *mayo*
mayor . . . . *(el) alcalde*
mean, cruel . . . . *cruel*
measure (to) . . . . *medir (i)*
meat . . . . *(la) carne*
meatball . . . .*(la) albóndiga*
medal . . . . *(la) medalla*
medium, average . . . . *mediano/a*
meet (to), to find . . . .*encontrar (ue)*
meeting, reunion . . . .*(la) reunión*
melancholy, gloomy . . . . . *melancólico/a*
melody . . . .*(la) melodía*
mention (to) . . . .*mencionar*
merit (to), to deserve . . . . *merecer*
meteorologist . . . . *(el) meteorólogo*
meow (like a cat) (to) . . . . *maullar*
message . . . . *(el) mensaje*
messy, not neat . . . . *desordenado/a*
method . . . . *(el) método*
metro, subway . . . . *(el) metro*
microwave oven
. . . . *(el) horno de microondas*
midnight . . . . *(la) medianoche*
mile . . . . *(la) milla*
milk . . . .*(la) leche*
million . . . . *(el) millón*
minister . . . . *(el) ministro*
miracle . . . .*(el) milagro*
mirror . . . . *(el) espejo*
miss someone (to),
something . . . .*echar de menos*
mistaken . . . .*equivocado/a*
mix (to) . . . . *mezclar*
mixed . . . . *mezclado/a*
modest . . . . *modesto/a*
moisten (to), to wet . . . .*mojar*
monastery . . . . *(el) monasterio*
Monday . . . . *lunes*
money . . . . *(el) dinero*

monk . . . . *(el) monje*
month . . . .*(el) mes*
moon . . . . *(la) luna*
more . . . . *más*
mosque . . . .*(la) mezquita*
mother . . . .*(la) madre*
mother-in-law . . . . *(la) suegra*
motorcycle . . . . *(la) moto(cicleta)*
mountain . . . .*(la) montaña*
mouse . . . .*(el) ratón*
mouth . . . . *(la) boca*
move (to) . . . .*mover (ue)*
move (to) (location) . . . . *mudarse*
movie . . . . *(la) película*
movie, film (used in
a camera) . . . . *(la) película*
movie theater . . . .*(el) cine*
much (too), (pl. too many)
. . . . *demasiado/a (adj.)*
mule . . . .*(la) mula*
museum . . . . *(el) museo*
music . . . . *(la) música*
musician . . . .*(el/la) músico/a*
Muslim . . . . *musulmán*
mustache . . . . *(el) bigote*
mute, dumb . . . . *mudo/a*
mutual . . . . *mutuo/a*
mysterious . . . . *misterioso/a*
mystery . . . . *(el) misterio*

N

nail polish . . . . *(el) esmalte de uñas*
naive . . . . *ingenuo/a*
name (to) . . . . *nombrar*
napkin . . . .*(la) servilleta*
narrow . . . . *angosto/a, estrecho/a*
nature . . . . *(la) naturaleza*
near . . . . *cerca (de)*
near(by) . . . .*cerca*
nearby, neighboring . . . . *cercano/a*
necessary, precise, clear . . . . . *preciso/a*
need (to) . . . . *necesitar*
neighbor . . . . *(el/la) vecino/a*
neighborhood, section,
quarter . . . . *(el) barrio*
neighboring, nearby . . . . *cercano/a*
neither, nor . . . .*ni*
nephew . . . . *(el) sobrino*
net, network . . . . *(la)*
red . . . .
never . . . . *nunca*
new . . . . *nuevo/a*
news . . . . *(las) noticias*
newspaper . . . . *(el) periódico*
newspaper stand . . . .*(el) quiosco*
next . . . . *próximo/a*
next, following . . . . *siguiente*
nice . . . . *amable, simpático/a*
niece . . . .*(la) sobrina*
night . . . . *(la) noche*

nightclub, discotheque . . . *(la) discoteca*
no . . . .*no*
no longer . . . . *ya no*
no one . . . . *nadie*
noise . . . . *(el) ruido*
noisy . . . . *ruidoso/a*
noisy, rowdy, boisterous . . . . *bullicioso/a*
none . . . . *ninguno/a*
noodle . . . . *(el) fideo*
noon . . . .*(el) mediodía*
nor, neither . . . .*ni*
north . . . . *norte*
northeast . . . . *(el) noreste*
northwest . . . . *(el) noroeste*
not neat, messy . . . . *desordenado/a*
not yet . . . . *todavía no*
note . . . .*(el) apunte*
notebook . . . . *(el) cuaderno*
nothing . . . . *nada*
notice (to) . . . . *fijarse en*
notify (to), to let know . . . . *avisar*
nose . . . . *(la) nariz*
novel . . . . *(la) novela*
November . . . . *noviembre*
now . . . .*ahora*
nuclear energy . . . . . *(la) energía nuclear*
nun . . . . *(la) monja*
nurse . . . . *(el/la) enfermero/a*

O

oak . . . .*(el) roble*
obscure, dark . . . . *o(b)scuro/a*
obstinate, stubborn . . . . *obstinado/a*
obtain (to), to get . . . . *conseguir (i)*
obtain (to), to succeed in . . . . *lograr*
occur (to), to happen . . . .*ocurrir*
ocean . . . . *(el) océano*
October . . . . *octubre*
of, from . . . . *de*
of course . . . . *por supuesto*
offend (to) . . . . *ofender*
offer (to) . . . .*ofrecer*
office . . . . *(el) despacho, (la) oficina*
often . . . . *a menudo*
oil . . . . *(el) aceite*
oil, petroleum . . . . *(el) petróleo*
old . . . . *viejo/a*
old age . . . . *(la) vejez*
older . . . . *mayor*
on, in . . . . *en*
on top of . . . . *encima de*
on top of, about, over . . . . *sobre*
once . . . . *una vez*
only, unique . . . . *único/a*
only . . . . *sólo*
open . . . . *abierto/a*
open (to) . . . . *abrir*
opponent . . . .*(el/la) adversario/a*
opposite (n.) . . . .*(el) opuesto*
opposite (adj.) . . . .*opuesto/a*

optimist . . . . (el/la) optimista
orange . . . . anaranjado/a
orange . . . .(la) naranja
orchestra . . . . (la) orquesta
order (to), to send . . . . mandar
order (to) (food), to ask for. . . . pedir (i)
ordinary. . . . . ordinario/a
ordinary, common. . . . . vulgar
organ . . . . (el) órgano
organize (to) . . . . organizar
original . . . . original
original, exceptional, smart. . . . . genial
other, another . . . . otro/a
others (the) . . . . (los/las) demás
ought to . . . . deber
outside. . . . . afuera
oven. . . . . (el) horno
over, about, on top of . . . . sobre
overcoat, coat . . . .(el) abrigo
owe (to). . . . . deber
own, proper. . . . . propio/a
owner. . . . . (el/la) dueño/a
ox. . . . . (el) buey
oyster. . . . .(la) ostra

P

pack (to) . . . . .hacer la maleta
package . . . .(el) paquete
pain . . . .(la) pena
pain, grief . . . .(el) dolor
painful. . . . . penoso/a
paint (to) . . . . pintar
painter . . . . (el/la) pintor/a
painting . . . . (la) pintura, (el) cuadro
painting, sketch, drawing . . . .(el) dibujo
pair .par
pair, couple . . . . (la) pareja
palace . . . . (el) palacio
pale . . . . .pálido/a
pants . . . . (los) pantalones
paper . . . .(el) papel
parade . . . .(el) desfile
pardon (to). . . . . .perdonar
park . . . . (el) parque
park (to). . . . . .estacionar
parking lot (garage)
 . . . .(el) estacionamiento
parrot. . . . .(el) loro
parting, farewell . . . .(la) despedida
party . . . .(la) fiesta
pass (to). . . . . .pasar
passenger. . . . . (el/la) pasajero/a
passionate, burning. . . . . .ardiente
passionately. . . . . apasionadamente
passport. . . . . (el) pasaporte
password . . . . (la) contraseña
past, last . . . . pasado/a
pay (to) . . . . .pagar
peach. . . . . (el) durazno
peach . . . .(el) melocotón

peak, summit. . . . .(la) cumbre
pear . . . . (la) pera
pen. . . . . (el) bolígrafo, (la) pluma
pencil. . . . . (el) lápiz
pencil sharpener . . . . (el) sacapuntas
people . . . .(la) gente
pepper . . . . (la) pimienta
percentage . . . . .porcentaje
performance, show . . . . .(el) espectáculo
perhaps . . . . tal vez
period of time . . . .(el) plazo
permission . . . .(el) permiso
permit (to), to allow . . . . .permitir
persecute (to), to pursue
 . . . . perseguir (i)
pessimist . . . . (el/la) pesimista
petroleum, oil . . . . (el) petróleo
pew, bench, bank . . . . (el) banco
phenomenal . . . . .fenomenal
philosophy. . . . . (la) filosofía
photo . . . .(la) foto
photo(graph) . . . .(la) foto(grafía)
physics. . . . .(la) física
piano . . . . (el) piano
picture, portrait . . . . (el) retrato
picturesque . . . . pintoresco/a
piece . . . . (el) pedazo
piece, bit, selection, portion . . . (el) trozo
pile, heap. . . . . (el) montón
pill. . . . . (la) pastilla
pillow . . . . (la) almohada
pine tree. . . . . (el) pino
pink . . . . rosado/a
pitch (to), to throw, to hurl . . . . . lanzar
pitcher . . . .(el) lanzador
place, site . . . .(el) sitio
place (to), to arrange. . . . . colocar
plains. . . . .(las) pampas
planet. . . . . (el) planeta
plant. . . . .(la) planta
plastic . . . . (el) plástico
plate, dish . . . . (el) plato
platform. . . . . (el) andén
play (to). . . . . jugar (ue)
play (to) (an instrument),
 to touch . . . . tocar
player. . . . . (el/la) jugador/a
please (to) . . . . placer
plot (of a story). . . . . (la) trama
plug in (to) . . . . enchufar
P.M. (in the afternoon). . . . . . .de la tarde
P.M. (in the evening) . . . . de la noche
poet . . . . (el) poeta, (la) poetisa
poetry . . . .(la) poesía
point . . . . (el) punto
poison . . . . (el) veneno
police station . . . .(la) comisaría
polish (to) . . . . pulir
polished. . . . . .pulido/a
polite, cordial . . . . .cordial
polite, courteous . . . . cortés

political . . . . .político/a
politics. . . . .(la) política
polka-dot . . . . de lunares
polyester . . . .(el) poliéster
poor. . . . . .pobre
poorly, bad . . . . mal
popcorn . . . . (las) palomitas
portion, piece, bit, selection . . . (el) trozo
possessions, property . . . . bienes
postcard. . . . .(la) (tarjeta) postal
poster. . . . . (el) cartel
postpone (to). . . . . aplazar
pot . . . .(la) olla
potato. . . . . (la) papa, (la) patata
pound. . . . . (la) libra
powerful . . . . poderoso/a
praise (to) . . . . alabar
pray (to). . . . . rezar
precious, cute . . . . precioso/a
precise, necessary, clear . . . . . preciso/a
prefer (to) . . . . .preferir (ie)
premiere, debut . . . . (el) estreno
prepare (to) . . . . preparar
prescription, recipe . . . . (la) receta
present . . . .(el) regalo
present, current . . . . corriente
present day . . . . actual
presentation . . . .(la) presentación
press conference
 . . . . (la) conferencia de prensa
press (media). . . . . (la) prensa
pretend (to), to fake . . . . .fingir
pretty. . . . . bonito/a, lindo/a
prevent (to) . . . . evitar, impedir (i)
price. . . . . (el) precio
pride . . . . (el) orgullo
priest . . . . (el) cura
print (to) . . . . imprimir
printed. . . . . impreso/a
privilege, right. . . . .(el) derecho
prize. . . . . (el) premio
problem. . . . . (el) problema
produce (to). . . . . producir
prohibit (to) . . . . .prohibir
project . . . . (el) proyecto
promise (to). . . . . prometer
proof, quiz, test . . . . (la) prueba
proper, own . . . . propio/a
property, possessions . . . . bienes
protect (to). . . . . proteger
protected . . . . protegido/a
proud. . . . . orgulloso/a
proud, haughty . . . . .soberbio/a
pull one's leg (to), to tease
 . . . . .tomar el pelo
punch (to), to hit . . . . golpear
punctually . . . . puntualmente
punish (to) . . . . castigar
punishment . . . . (el) castigo
purple . . . . .morado/a
purse, bag . . . .(la) bolsa

pursue (to), to persecute. . . . *perseguir (i)*
put (to). . . . . *poner*
put into (to) . . . .*meter*
put on (to) . . . . *ponerse*

Q

quarter, fourth, room. . . . .*(el) cuarto*
quarter, neighborhood,
   section . . . . *(el) barrio*
queen. . . . .*(la) reina*
quickly. . . . . *rápidamente*
quit (to), to resign . . . .*demitir, renunciar*
quiz, proof, test. . . . . *(la) prueba*

R

rabbi . . . .*(el) rabino*
race, career . . . .*(la) carrera*
racquet. . . . .*(la) raqueta*
radio . . . .*(el/la) radio*
rain . . . . *(la) lluvia*
rain (to) . . . .*llover (ue)*
rain forest . . . . *(el) bosque de lluvia*
raincoat . . . .*(el) impermeable*
raise (to) (up) . . . .*levantar, alzar*
rake . . . .*(el) rastrillo*
rare, strange. . . . . *raro/a*
rascally, roguish . . . .*pícaro/a*
read (to). *leer*
reader. . . . .*(el/la) lector/a*
ready, clever, smart. . . . . *listo/a*
real, royal . . . . *real*
real, true . . . . *verdadero/a*
reality . . . . *(la) realidad*
realize (to) (i.e., come to
   awareness of). . . . . . .*darse cuenta de*
realize (to) (e.g., a dream,
   a goal) . . . . *realizar*
receipt . . . .*(el) recibo*
receive (to) . . . . *recibir*
recent. . . . . *reciente*
recent/recently. . . . . *recién*
recipe, prescription . . . .*(la) receta*
record (to), to engrave . . . . *grabar*
recommend (to). . . . . . .*recomendar (ie)*
record . . . . *(el) disco*
record (to), to engrave . . . .*grabar*
record player. . . . .*(el) tocadiscos*
recover (to) . . . . *recuperar*
red . . . . *rojo/a*
red-headed. . . . . *pelirrojo/a*
refer (to) . . . .*referir (ie)*
referee . . . .*(el) árbitro*
reflect (to) . . . . *reflejar*
reflect (to), to think over. . . . *reflexionar*
refrigerator *(el) refrigerador, (la) nevera*
regret (to) . . . .*lamentar, sentir (ie),*
                      arrepentirse (ie) de
reign (to) . . . . *reinar*
relationship . . . . *(la) relación*
relative. . . . . *(el) pariente*

relax (to) . . . . *relajarse*
relax (to), to rest . . . . *descansar*
remain (to). . . . . *quedar*
remain (to), to be left over . . . . . *sobrar*
remember (to) . . . . *recordar (ue)*
remote. . . . . *remoto/a*
renovate (to) . . . . *renovar (ue)*
rent (to) . . . . *alquilar*
rented. . . . . *alquilado/a*
repeat (to) . . . . *repetir (i)*
reply . . . . *(la) respuesta*
report. . . . . *(el) informe*
reporter . . . .*(el/la) reportero/a*
representative . . . .*(el) representante*
require (to), to demand. . . . .*exigir*
resemble (to). . . . . *parecerse a*
reservation. . . . .*(la) reservación*
residence, dormitory . . . . .*(la) residencia*
resign (to), to quit . . . .*dimitir, renunciar*
resolve (to), to solve
   a problem. . . . . *resolver (ue)*
respect (to) . . . .*respetar*
rest (to), to relax . . . . *descansar*
restaurant. . . . .*(el) restaurante*
restore (to). . . . . *restaurar*
result . . . . *(el) resultado*
retired . . . . *jubilado/a*
return (to) . . . .*regresar, volver (ue)*
return (to) (an object). . . . . *devolver (ue)*
reunion, meeting. . . . .*(la) reunión*
reveal (to) . . . .*revelar*
revenge, vengeance. . . . . . *(la) venganza*
review . . . .*(el) repaso*
revolve (to), to rotate, to turn . . . . . *girar*
reward (to). . . . . *premiar*
rhythm. . . . .*(el) ritmo*
rice. . . . .*(el) arroz*
rich. . . . . *rico/a*
right. . . . . *(la) derecha*
right. . . . . *derecho/a*
right, privilege. . . . .*(el) derecho*
right (to be) . . . . *tener razón*
right (to the) . . . . *a la derecha*
right-handed . . . . *diestro/a*
right now. . . . . *ahora mismo*
rigid. . . . . *rígido/a*
ring . . . . *(el) anillo*
ring (to). . . . . *sonar (ue)*
ripe, mature. . . . .*maduro/a*
risk. . . . . *(el) riesgo*
river. . . . .*(el) río*
roast (to) . . . . *asar*
roasted. . . . . *asado/a*
robber . . . . *(el) ladrón, (la) ladrona*
rock, stone. . . . .*(la) piedra*
roguish, rascally . . . .*pícaro/a*
roof . . . .*(el) tejado*
room, quarter, fourth. . . . . . .*(el) cuarto*
roommate . . . . *(el/la) compañero/a*
                          de cuarto
root . . . .*(la) raíz*
rose . . . . *(la) rosa*

round. . . . .*redondo/a*
round, circular. . . . .*circular*
route . . . .*(la) ruta*
row . . . . *(la) fila*
rowdy, noisy, boisterous . . .*bullicioso/a*
rowing. . . . . *(el) remo*
royal, real . . . . *real*
rude . . . .*maleducado/a*
rude, crude . . . .*grosero/a*
rug, carpet. . . . .*(la) alfombra*
ruins. . . . . *(las) ruinas*
run (to) . . . . *correr*
rushed, in a hurry . . . .*apurado/a*

S

sacred . . . . *sagrado/a*
sacrifice. . . . .*(el) sacrificio*
sad . . . . *triste*
safe . . . .*seguro/a, salvo/a*
sail (to) . . . . *navegar*
sailing, candle . . . . *(la) vela*
sailor . . . .*(el/la) marinero/a*
saint . . . . *(el) santo*
salad . . . .*(la) ensalada*
salary. . . . . *(el) sueldo*
salesclerk. . . . .*el dependiente*
                       la dependienta
salt. . . . .*(la) sal*
salty. . . . . *salado/a*
same . . . .*mismo/a*
sand. . . . . *(la) arena*
sandwich . . . . *(el) bocadillo*
sargent . . . .*(el) sargento*
satisfied. . . . .*satisfecho/a*
satisfy (to) . . . . *satisfacer*
Saturday . . . .*(el) sábado*
sausage . . . .*(la) salchicha*
save (to). . . . . *ahorrar*
saxophone . . . .*(el) saxofón*
say (to), to tell. . . . . *decir*
say goodbye to (to) . . .*despedirse (i) (de)*
scale a mountain (to)
            escalar una montaña
scare (to), to frighten . . . . *asustar*
scarf. . . . .*(la) bufanda*
scene . . . . *(la) escena*
scenery, landscape . . . .*(el) paisaje*
schedule. . . . . *(el) horario*
scholarship . . . . *(la) beca*
school . . . .*(el) colegio, (la) escuela*
science. . . . . *(la) ciencia*
scientist . . . .*(el/la) científico/a*
scissors . . . . *(las) tijeras*
scold (to). . . . . *reñir (i)*
scour (to), to scrub . . . .*fregar (ie)*
screen . . . .*(la) pantalla*
sea. . . . . *(el/la) mar*
seafood, shellfish . . . .*(el) marisco*
seamstress, dressmaker . . .*(la) costurera*
seashell . . . .*(la) caracola*

season (e.g., sports season)
. . . . *(la) temporada*
seat . . . . *(el) asiento*
seat, chair . . . . *(la) silla*
seat (someone) (to) . . . . *sentar (ie)*
seatbelt . . . . . *(el) cinturón de seguridad*
second . . . . *segundo/a*
secret . . . . *(el) secreto*
secretary . . . . *(el/la) secretario/a*
section, neighborhood,
. . . . quarter . . . . *(el) barrio*
secure, sure . . . . *seguro/a*
security, certainty . . . . *(la) seguridad*
see (to) . . . . *ver*
see you later . . . . *hasta luego*
seek (to), to aspire to,
. . . . to claim to be . . . .*pretender*
seem (to), to appear . . . . *parecer*
select (to), to choose . . . . *escoger*
selection, bit, piece . . . . *(el) trozo*
sell (to) . . . . *vender*
senator . . . . *(el/la) senador/a*
send (to) . . . . *enviar, mandar*
sentence . . . .*(la) frase*
sentiment, feeling . . . . . .*(el) sentimiento*
separate . . . . *separado/a*
separate (to) . . . . *separar*
September . . . .*septiembre*
series . . . . *(la) serie*
serious . . . . *grave,*
serio/a . . . .
serpent, snake . . . .*(la) serpiente*
serve (to) . . . . *servir (i)*
set the table (to) . . . . *poner la mesa*
shame, embarrassment . . .*(la) vergüenza*
share (to) . . . . *compartir*
shark . . . . *(el) tiburón*
sharp (e.g., knife) . . . . *afilado/a*
sharp, astute . . . . *agudo/a*
shave (to) (oneself) . . . . *afeitar(se)*
she, her . . . . *ella*
sheep . . . .*(la) oveja*
shelf . . . . *(el) estante*
shellfish, seafood . . . .*(el) marisco*
shield, coat of arms . . . . *(el) escudo*
shine (to) . . . . *brillar, lucir*
ship . . . . *(la) nave*
shirt . . . . *(la) camisa*
shoe . . . . *(el) zapato*
shoelaces . . . .*(los) cordones*
shoemaker, cobbler . . . *(el/la) zapatero/a*
shoot (to) . . . . *disparar*
shooting . . . .*(el) tiroteo*
shopping (to go) . . . . *ir de compras*
shore, bank (of river, ocean) . . *(la) orilla*
short . . . . *bajo/a, corto/a*
shorts . . . .*(los) pantalones cortos*
shout (to) . . . .*gritar*
shovel . . . . *(la) pala*
show, performance . . . . .*(el) espectáculo*
show (to) . . . . *mostrar (ue)*

shower . . . . *(la) ducha*
shower (to take a) . . . . *ducharse*
sick . . . . *enfermo/a*
sickened by (to be),
. . . . to be loathsome to . . . . . *darle asco a*
side . . . . *(el) lado*
sidewalk . . . . *(la) acera*
sign (to) . . . . *firmar*
silk . . . . *(la) seda*
silly, stupid, foolish . . . .*tonto/a*
silverware . . . .*(los) cubiertos*
similar . . . . *semejante*
simple . . . .*sencillo/a*
sin . . . . *(el) pecado*
since, like, as . . . . *como*
since, from . . . .*desde*
sing (to) . . . . *cantar*
singer . . . .*(el/la) cantante*
sink (in bathroom) . . . .*(el) lavabo*
sink (in kitchen) . . . . . . *(el) fregadero*
sister . . . .*(la) hermana*
sister-in-law . . . . *(la) cuñada*
sit (to) (down) . . . . *sentarse (ie)*
site, place . . . .*(el) sitio*
size . . . . *(el) tamaño*
skate (to) . . . . *patinar*
skates . . . . *(los) patines*
skating . . . . *(el) patinaje*
sketch, drawing, painting . . . . *(el) dibujo*
skiing . . . .*(el) esquí*
skillful, clever . . . . *hábil*
skin . . . .*(la) piel*
skinny, thin . . . .*flaco/a*
skirt . . . .*(la) falda*
skunk . . . .*(el) zorrillo (la) mofeta)*
sky . . . . *(el) cielo*
skyscraper . . . . *(el) rascacielos*
sled, sleigh . . . . *(el) trineo*
sleep (to) . . . . *dormir (ue)*
sleeping bag . . . . *saco de dormir*
slight, light . . . . *leve*
slippery . . . . . *resbaloso/a, resbaladizo/a*
slow . . . . *lento/a*
slowly . . . . *despacio*
small . . . . *pequeño/a*
small, little . . . . *chico/a*
smart, original, exceptional . . . . . *genial*
smart, ready, clever . . . . *listo/a*
smell (to) . . . . *oler (ue)*
smile (to) . . . . *sonreír (i)*
smiling, cheerful . . . .*risueño/a*
smoke (to) . . . .*fumar*
smooth, flat . . . .*liso/a*
smooth, soft . . . . *suave*
smoothly, suavely . . . . *suavemente*
snake, serpent . . . .*(la) serpiente*
sneeze (to) . . . .*estornudar*
snore (to) . . . . *roncar*
snow . . . .*(la) nieve*
snow (to) . . . . *nevar (ie)*
so . . . .*tan*

so, therefore . . . . *por eso*
so, well . . . .*pues*
so many . . . . *tantos/as*
so much (adv.) . . . .*tanto*
soap . . . . *(el) jabón*
soap opera . . . .*(la) telenovela*
soccer . . . . *(el) fútbol*
socks . . . . *(los) calcetines*
sofa . . . .*(el) sofá*
soft . . . . *blando/a*
soft, smooth . . . . *suave*
soil, earth . . . . *(la) tierra*
soldier . . . .*(el) soldado*
solitude, loneliness . . . .*(la) soledad*
solve a problem (to),
. . . . to resolve . . . . *resolver (ue)*
some . . . . *alguno/a, unos/as*
someone . . . . *alguien*
something . . . .*algo*
sometimes, at times . . . . *a veces*
son . . . .*(el) hijo*
song . . . .*(la) canción*
soon . . . .*pronto*
sound . . . .*(el) sonido*
soup . . . . *(la) sopa*
sour, bitter . . . . *agrio/a, (amargo/a)*
south . . . .*sur*
southeast . . . . *(el) sureste*
southwest . . . . *(el) suroeste*
space . . . .*(el) espacio*
spaghetti . . . . *(el) espagueti*
speak (to), to talk . . . . *hablar*
special . . . . *especial*
speech . . . . *(el) discurso*
speed . . . . *(la) velocidad*
spell (to) . . . . *deletrear*
spend (time) (to) . . . . *pasar (tiempo)*
spend (to), to waste . . . . *gastar*
spider . . . . *(la) araña*
spider web . . . . *(la) telaraña*
spill (to) . . . .*derramar*
spit (to) . . . . *escupir*
spoiled . . . . *mimado/a*
spoon . . . . *(la) cuchara*
sport(s) . . . . .*(el) deporte, (los) deportes*
spring . . . .*(la) primavera*
spy (to) . . . . *espiar*
square . . . . *cuadrado/a*
squeeze (to), to tighten . . . . . *apretar (ie)*
stadium . . . . *(el) estadio*
stain . . . .*(la) mancha*
stained . . . . *manchado/a*
stair, ladder . . . . *(la) escalera*
stairs . . . .*(las) escaleras*
stamp . . . .*(la) estampilla*
star . . . .*(la) estrella*
start a business (to)
. . . . *montar un negocio*
statue . . . . *(la) estatua*
steak . . . . *(el) bistec*
steel . . . . *(el) acero*

still. . . . . *todavía*
stingy. *tacaño/a*
stomach. . . . . *(el) estómago*
stone, rock. . . . .*(la) piedra*
stop (to), to detain. . . . . *detener*
stop (to). *parar*
stop doing something (to)
. . . . *dejar de* (+ infinitive)
store. *(la) tienda*
storm . . . . . *(la) tempestad, (la) tormenta*
story, tale. . . . .*(el) cuento*
stout, heavy-set, burly. . . . . *corpulento/a*
straight (e.g., hair). . . . .*lacio/a*
strain (to) (e.g., pasta). . . . .*escurrir*
strange. . . . .*extraño/a*
strange, rare. . . . . *raro/a*
stream . . . . *(el) arroyo*
street . . . . *(la) calle*
strike . . . . *(la) huelga*
stripes . . . .*(las) rayas*
stroll, trip. . . . . *(el) paseo*
stroll, walk . . . . *(la) caminata*
strong. . . . .*fuerte*
struggle (to), to fight. . . . .*luchar*
stubborn. . . . . *obstinado/a (terco/a)*
stubborn, obstinate . . . .*obstinado/a*
student. . . . .*(el/la) alumno/a,*
(el/la) estudiante
student desk. . . . . *(el) pupitre*
study (to). . . . .*estudiar*
stupid. . . . .*estúpido/a*
stupid, foolish. . . . . *necio/a*
stupid, silly, foolish. . . . .*tonto/a*
style . . . .*(el) estilo*
style, fashion. . . . . *(la) moda*
suavely, smoothly. . . . . *suavemente*
subject, matter. . . . .*(el) asunto*
suburbs . . . . *(las) afueras*
subway, metro. . . . . *(el) metro*
succeed in (to), to obtain . . . . *lograr*
success. . . . . *(el) éxito*
successful . . . .*exitoso/a*
successful (to be) . . . .*tener éxito*
sudden, abrupt. . . . .*brusco/a*
suddenly . . . .*de repente*
sugar . . . .*(el/la) azúcar*
suggest (to) . . . . *sugerir (ie)*
suit. . . . .*(el) traje*
suitcase . . . .*(la) maleta*
summary . . . . *(el) resumen*
summer . . . .*(el) verano*
summit, peak. . . . .*(la) cumbre*
Sunday. . . . . *domingo*
sunrise. . . . . *(la) salida del sol*
sunset. . . . . *(la) puesta del sol*
superior, upper . . . .*superior*
supermarket. . . . .*(el) supermercado*
support (to), to aid . . . .*apoyar*
suppose (to). . . . . *suponer*
supposed . . . .*supuesto/a*
sure, secure . . . .*seguro/a*
surprise . . . . *(la) sorpresa*

surprised . . . . *sorprendido/a*
surround (to) . . . . *rodear*
survive (to) . . . . *sobrevivir*
suspect (to) . . . . *sospechar*
swallow (to) . . . . *tragar*
swear (to) . . . . *jurar*
sweat (to). . . . . *sudar*
sweater . . . . *(el) suéter*
sweet . . . . *dulce*
swim (to). . . . .*nadar*
swimming . . . . *(la) natación*
swimming pool . . . .*(la) piscina*
swimsuit . . . . *(el) traje de baño*
symbol. . . . .*(el) símbolo*
symphony . . . . *(la) sinfonía*
synagogue. . . . .*(la) sinagoga*
system . . . . *(el) sistema*

T

table. . . . .*(la) mesa*
tablecloth. . . . .*(el) mantel*
tail, line . . . . *(la) cola*
take (to), to catch . . . .*coger*
take a shower (to) . . . . *ducharse*
take a stroll (to). . . . .*pasear*
take a trip (to) . . . . *hacer un viaje*
take a walk/drive (to) . . . .*dar una vuelta*
take into consideration (to)
. . . . *tener en cuenta*
take notes (to) . . . . *tomar apuntes*
take off (to) . . . .*quitarse*
take out (to). . . . . *sacar*
take place (to) . . . . *tener lugar*
tale, story. . . . . *(el) cuento*
talent . . . . *(el) talento*
talk (to), to speak . . . .*hablar*
tall . . . .*alto/a*
tape recorder . . . . *(la) grabadora*
task, homework, assignment
. . . .*(la) tarea*
taste. . . . .*(el) gusto*
taste (to) . . . . *probar (ue)*
tasty, delicious . . . . *sabroso/a*
tax . . . .*(el) impuesto*
taxi. . . . . *(el) taxi*
tea . . . .*(el) té*
teach (to) . . . . *enseñar*
teacher. . . . .*(el/la) maestro/a*
teacher. . . . .*(el) profesor, (la) profesora*
teaching. . . . .*(la) enseñanza*
team. . . . . *(el) equipo*
tear. . . . .*(la) lágrima*
tease (to), to pull one's leg
. . . .*tomar el pelo*
telephone. . . . .*(el) teléfono*
telescope . . . . *(el) telescopio*
television. . . . . *(la) televisión*
television set . . . . *(el) televisor*
tell (to), to count . . . . *contar (ue)*
tell (to), to say. . . . . *decir*
temple . . . .*(el) templo*

tennis. . . . . *(el) tenis*
tent. . . . .*(la) tienda de campaña*
tenth. . . . .*décimo/a*
terrific, wonderful. . . . .*formidable*
test. . . . .*(el) examen*
test, proof, quiz. . . . .*(la) prueba*
text. *(el) texto*
thank (to), to be grateful for
. . . . *agradecer*
thanks . . . . *gracias*
that. . . . . *ese/a*
that (over yonder) . . . .*aquel, aquella*
that, which. . . . . *que*
theater . . . . *(el) teatro*
them, they . . . . *ellas/os*
theme . . . . *(el) tema*
there. . . . . *allí*
there are, there is. . . . . *hay*
there was, there were . . . .*había*
therefore, so . . . . *por eso*
they, them . . . . *ellas/os*
thick, dense. . . . . *espeso/a*
thin, skinny . . . .*flaco/a*
thing . . . . *(la) cosa*
think (to) . . . .*pensar (ie)*
think over (to), to reflect. . . . *reflexionar*
third . . . . *tercero/a*
this. . . . . *este/a*
this morning . . . . *esta mañana*
thousand . . . .*mil*
threaten (to). . . . . *amenazar*
throat . . . .*(la) garganta*
through, by, for . . . .*por*
throw (to) . . . .*arrojar*
throw (to), to throw away. . . . .*echar*
throw (to), to hurl, to pitch . . . . . .*lanzar*
thunder . . . . *(el) trueno*
Thursday . . . . *jueves*
ticket, entrance, admission
. . . .*(la) entrada*
ticket . . . .*(el) billete, (el) boleto*
tie. . . . .*(la) corbata*
tied. . . . .*atado/a, empatado/a*
tiger . . . .*(el) tigre*
tighten (to), to squeeze. . . . . .*apretar (ie)*
time . . . .*(el) tiempo*
tip (e.g., given to a waiter). . .*(la) propina*
tired. . . . . *cansado/a*
tiredness, fatigue. . . . .*(el) cansancio*
title . . . .*(el) título*
to, at . . . . *a*
toast (to) (drink) . . . . *brindar*
today . . . . *hoy*
toenail, fingernail . . . . *(la) uña*
together . . . . *juntos/as*
tomato . . . .*(el) tomate*
tomb . . . . *(la) tumba*
tomorrow. . . . . *mañana*
tongue, language . . . . *(la) lengua*
tonight. . . . . *esta noche*
too much. . . . . . . *demasiado/a(s) (adv.)*

too much, (pl. too many)
. . . . demasiado/a (adj.)
tool . . . . (la) herramienta
tooth . . . . (el) diente
touch (to), to play (an instrument)
. . . . tocar
tour . . . .(la) gira
tour guide . . . . (el/la) guía
tournament . . . . (el) torneo
towards . . . . hacia
towel . . . . (la) toalla
tower . . . . (la) torre
town, village . . . .(el) pueblo
traffic light . . . .(el) semáforo
train. . . . .(el) tren
train station . . . . (la) estación de tren
training . . . . (el) entrenamiento
translate (to) . . . . .traducir
travel (to). . . . . viajar, ir de viaje
travel agency. . . . . . .(la) agencia de viajes
tray . . . . (la) bandeja
treasure . . . . (el) tesoro
treasurer. . . . .(el/la) tesorero/a
tree. . . . .(el) árbol
trial, judgement . .(el) proceso, (el) juicio
tricked . . . . engañado/a
trip. . . . . (el) viaje
trip, excursion . . . . (la) excursión
trip, stroll. . . . . (el) paseo
trip (to) . . . . tropezar (ie)
triumph (to). . . . . triunfar
trombone. . . . . (el) trombón
trophy . . . . (el) trofeo
tropical . . . . tropical
truck . . . . (el) camión
true, real . . . . .verdadero/a
trumpet . . . .(la) trompeta
trust (in), confidence. . . . . (la) confianza
trust (to). . . . . confiar en, fiarse de
truth. . . . . (la) verdad
try (to) . . . . .tratar (de)
try (to), to attempt. . . . . intentar
T-shirt . . . .(la) camiseta
tub . . . . (la) bañera
Tuesday. . . . . martes
tuition . . . . (la) matrícula
tulip. . . . . (el) tulipán
tunnel. . . . . (el) túnel
turn (to), to revolve, to rotate
. . . . girar
turn in (to), to deliver,
to hand over. . . . . entregar
turn off (to) . . . . .apagar
turn on (to) . . . . prender
turn on (to) (e.g., a light)
to light (e.g., a fire). . . . . .encender (ie)
turtle . . . . (la) tortuga
twice . . . . .dos veces
twist (to), to bend . . . . .torcer (ue)
type . . . . (el) tipo
typical . . . . típico/a

tyrant. . . . . (el) tirano

U

ugly. . . . . feo/a
umbrella . . . . (el) paraguas
unbearable, intolerable . . . . insoportable
uncle . . . .(el) tío
uncomfortable. . . . . incómodo/a
under. . . . . bajo
under, below . . . . debajo de
underline (to). . . . . subrayar
underneath. . . . . debajo
understand (to) . . . . comprender,
entender (ie)
underwear . . . . (los) calzoncillos,
(la) ropa interior
undress (to) . . . . desvestirse (i)
unfortunately. . . . . .desafortunadamente,
por desgracia
unhappy. . . . . .desdichado/a, infeliz
unique, only . . . . único/a
universe. . . . . (el) universo
university. . . . . (la) universidad
until. . . . . hasta
untruthful, lying . . . . . . .mentiroso/a
up. . . . . arriba
up (to go). . . . . subir
upper, superior . . . . .superior
upset . . . . preocupado/a
urgent . . . . urgente
useless. . . . . inútil

V

vacation. . . . . (las) vacaciones
vacuum cleaner. . . . . (la) aspiradora
vacuum (to). . . . . . . pasar la aspiradora
valley. . . . . (el) valle
various. . . . . varios/as
VCR, video. . . . . . (el) video, (el) vídeo
vegetable. . . . . . (la) verdura, (el) vegetal
vengeance, revenge. . . . . . (la) venganza
very . . . . muy
vest . . . . (el) chaleco
veterinarian. . . . . . . (el/la) veterinario/a
victim . . . . (la) víctima
video, VCR. . . . . . . (el) video, (el) vídeo
violence. . . . .(la) violencia
violin. . . . . (el) violín
virtue . . . . (la) virtud
volcano . . . .(el) volcán
vote . . . .(el) voto
vulture. . . . . (el) buitre

W

wait (to), to hope. . . . . esperar
wait in line (to) . . . . .hacer cola
waiter. . . . (el/la) camarero/a (mesero/a)
wake (to) (up) . . . . .despertarse (ie)

walk, stroll . . . . (la) caminata
walk (to) . . . . .andar, caminar
wall . . . . (la) pared
wallet. . . . . (la) billetera
want (to), to wish, to like . . . .querer (ie)
war. . . . . (la) guerra
warm, hot . . . . caliente
warrior. . . . . (el/la) guerrero/a
wary, careful, cautious . . . . . cauteloso/a
wash (to) . . . . lavar
wash (oneself) (to) . . . . lavarse
washer. . . . .(la) lavadora
waste (to), to spend. . . . . gastar
waste (time) (to) . . . . . .perder (tiempo)
watch, clock . . . . (el) reloj
water . . . . (el) agua (f.)
water (to). . . . . .regar (ie)
waterfall . . . . (la) catarata
wave . . . . (la) ola
we . . . . nosotros/as
weak . . . . débil
website . . . .(el) portal cibernético
wedding. . . . . (la) boda
Wednesday . . . . .miércoles
week . . . .(la) semana
weekend . . . .(el) fin de semana
weekly. . . . . .semanal
weight . . . . (el) peso
weights . . . .(las) pesas
well, fine . . . . .bien
well, so . . . . .pues
well-known . . . . conocido/a
west. . . . . oeste
western . . . . occidental
wet. . . . . mojado/a
wet (to), to moisten. . . . . .mojar
whale. . . . . (la) ballena
what?. . . . . ¿qué?
what?, which? . . . .¿qué?, ¿cuál?
wheat. . . . . (el) trigo
when? . . . . ¿cuándo?
where?. . . . . ¿dónde?
which?, what? . . . .¿cuál?, ¿qué?
which one(s)? . . . .¿cuál(es)?
which, that. . . . . que
while . . . . mientras
whisper . . . . (el) susurro
whisper (to). . . . . susurrar
whistle. . . . . .silbar
white . . . . blanco/a
who? . . . .¿quién?
whole, entire . . . . .entero/a
why? . . . . ¿por qué?
wide. . . . . ancho/a
widower/widow. . . . . . .(el/la) viudo/a
wife . . . . (la) esposa
win (to), to earn . . . . .ganar
wind. . . . . (el) viento
window . . . .(la) ventana
windshield. . . . . . . (el) parabrisas
wine. . . . .(el) vino

wing. . . . .*(el) ala (f.)*
winter . . . . *(el) invierno*
wise, learned. . . . . *sabio/a*
wish (to), to want, to like

. . . .*querer (ie)*
with. . . . . *con*
with *(to have to do)* . . . .*tener que ver con*
without . . . . *sin*
witness. . . . .*(el/la) testigo*
wonderful, marvelous. . . . *maravilloso/a*
wonderful, terrific. . . . .*formidable*
woman. . . . . *(la) mujer*
wood . . . . *(la) madera*
woods, forest. . . . . *(el) bosque*
word . . . .*(la) palabra*
work . . . .*(el) trabajo, (la) obra*
work (to). . . . .*trabajar*
work (to), to function . . . .*funcionar*
worker. . . . . *(el/la) obrero/a*
world . . . .*(el) mundo*
worry (to) . . . . *preocuparse*
worse, worst . . . .*peor*
worth the trouble (to [not] be)

. . . . *(no) valer la pena*
wound, injury . . . . *la herida*
wound (to). . . . . *herir (ie)*
wounded . . . .*herido/a*
wrestler . . . . *(el) luchador*
wrist, doll . . . .*(la) muñeca*
write (to) . . . . *escribir*
writer. . . . . *(el/la) escritor/a*

Y

year . . . . *(el) año*
yellow . . . .*amarillo/a*
yes. . . . . *sí*
yesterday. . . . . *ayer*
you (familiar) . . . .*tú*
you (formal) . . . . *usted (Ud.)*
you all (familiar). . . . . *vosotros/as*
you all (formal). . . . .*ustedes (Uds.)*
younger. . . . . *menor*
youngsters, youth . . . . *(los) jóvenes*
youth. . . . . *(la) juventud*
youth, youngsters . . . . *(los) jóvenes*

Z

zero . . . .*cero*
zip code. . . . . *(el) código postal*
zipper. . . . . *(la) cremallera*
zoo. . . . . .*(el) jardín (parque) zoológico,*
                                    (el) zoológico

ÍNDICE